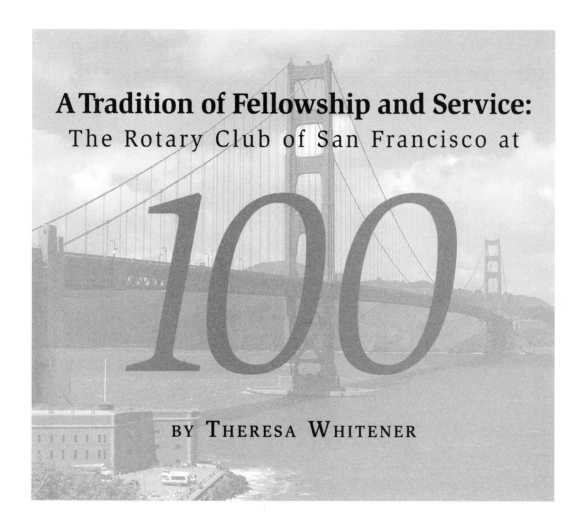

A Tradition of Fellowship and Service:
The Rotary Club of San Francisco at

100

BY THERESA WHITENER

THE ROTARY CLUB OF SAN FRANCISCO

ISBN 978-0-615-19202-4

Cover design: Maura Zimmer
Interior design: Laura Lind Design

Cover photos
Top (left-right):
—Homer Wood, Founder of the Rotary Club of San Francisco
—San Francisco Rotary and the Boys & Girls Club celebrate the ground-breaking of the new Mission Branch clubhouse
—Boys & Girls Club members use computers donated by San Francisco Rotary
—The Golden Gate Bridge. Photo by Jon Sullivan

Bottom (left-right):
—San Francisco Rotarians lead a parade celebrating the Panama-Pacific International Exposition, 1911
—Children from the Salvation Army Harbor House helped by San Francisco Rotary
—San Francisco Rotarians participate in San Francisco's annual AIDS Walk
—A Rotavision surgery team provides eye correction for indigent children in developing countries

Rotary is an opportunity to do good beyond yourself.

—Marshall Rotary Blum, 2000

CONTENTS

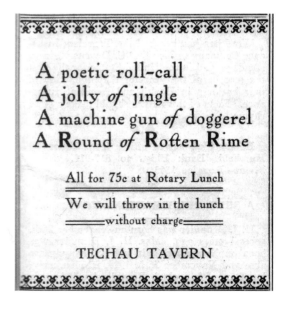

A poetic roll-call
A jolly *of* jingle
A machine gun *of* doggerel
A Round *of* Rotten Rime

All for 75c at Rotary Lunch

We will throw in the lunch
═══without charge═══

TECHAU TAVERN

FOREWORD

In 1908, Theodore Roosevelt was President; the Wright Brothers tested a contraption that would become the airplane; Henry Ford began production of the Model T; and the Chicago Cubs won their last World Series. In that same year, a young lawyer named Homer Wood led a few good-minded men to form a second Rotary club in San Francisco. A few months later, the new club extended the Rotary idea to the world. The Rotary Club of San Francisco story has been one of inspiration since the club first met on November 12, 1908.

Who knew what the Rotary Club of San Francisco would mean for a Chicago club started three years before? It was the first step in becoming the international organization that now has over 32,000 clubs and 1.2 million members in more than 200 countries and territories.

Through world wars, depression, natural disasters, and health epidemics, Rotary has touched countless lives with projects of dignity and compassion. In the following pages, you will learn how the Rotary Club of San Francisco has served our community since the era of the great San Francisco earthquake.

The achievements of the first hundred years of the Rotary Club of San Francisco provide a foundation for our next one hundred years. Theresa Whitener has written an extensively researched document of our rich and colorful history of Rotary service. Within this book are the major milestones and triumphs we have experienced along the way.

Rotary brings talented and idealistic people together in fellowship and service. The endless opportunities to serve our global community include enrichment programs for local youth, care for needy families, support for education, providing clean drinking water, microcredit, training for pediatric physicians, and hundreds of other humanitarian projects.

Enjoy this book as it takes you on a journey through the history of the Rotary Club of San Francisco, the Club that literally extended Rotary to the world.

—Eric Schmautz, President, The Rotary Club of San Francisco, 2008–2009

PREFACE

This is a changing world; we must be prepared to change with it. The story of Rotary will have to be written again and again.

—Rotary founder Paul Harris, 1955

The rich history of the Rotary Club of San Francisco has been chronicled before this book. In 1940, historian William Mountin wrote the fine *History of the Rotary Club of San Francisco*, and on the occasion of its seventy-fifth anniversary in 1983, the club commissioned *Seventy-Five Years in San Francisco: A History of Rotary Club Number 2*, by Mitchell Postel. Rotary International's historian David Forward narrated the story of the San Francisco club's founding and its rapid extension to other cities in *A Century of Service: The Story of Rotary International*, published in 2003.

The present book was conceived in 2000 by club President Bill Ecker and Past District Governor Bill Sturgeon, to commemorate San Francisco Rotary's 100th anniversary in 2008. Club member Roger Steiner headed the task of bringing the book about under the oversight of the San Francisco Rotary Foundation. He contacted Professor Richard Abrams of the History Department at the University of California at Berkeley. As a history graduate student, I accepted the job and undertook the research phase. Along the way, I researched thousands of documents and conducted dozens of interviews.

This book is the result of that effort. It sets forth an account that begins in post-earthquake San Francisco, when a young man formed a club for fellowship and mutual benefit among businessmen in the city. Over time, the club transformed itself through several stages of purpose: self-benefit, cooperation, ethical improvement, humanitarianism, and international goodwill. Through the course of a century, the Rotary Club of San Francisco evolved into the extraordinary organization we see today— an association of business professionals dedicated to serving their community and the world.

Chapter One ("A New Club for San Francisco") tells the story of Homer Wood's chance meeting with Manuel Muñoz in a San Francisco hotel lobby in 1908. Manuel told Homer of a new business club in Chicago, called "Rotary". The Chicago club had been started by a lawyer named Paul Harris, who sought the acquaintance and fellowship of other businessmen like himself. Homer Wood, also a lawyer, was intrigued with the idea. He brought a group of San Francisco businessmen and professionals together, and they formed the Rotary Club of San Francisco—the second Rotary club in the world. The new club flourished, and in short order, Homer and his fellow San Francisco Rotarians extended the idea to businessmen in Oakland, Seattle, Los Angeles, and New York, who in turn formed new Rotary clubs in their cities. The idea spread, and by 1910, the sixteen Rotary clubs in the United States formed the National Association of Rotary Clubs. Two years later, with clubs in Canada, Great Britain, and Ireland, the association renamed itself the International Association of Rotary Clubs—the forerunner of Rotary International.

Chapter Two ("From Back-Scratching to Service") describes the new club's search for a purpose—was it to be a business club or a service club? Very early, the new Rotarians turned to business promotion, "boosting," and reciprocal trading as their club's reason for being. After several years passed and public opinion soured against Rotary's boosting idea, the Rotarians redirected their efforts to civic and community service. As the 1920s opened, the club adopted service for San Francisco's young people as its longstanding community-service interest.

Chapter Three ("Three Men of Rotary") narrates the life stories of three important men in San Francisco Rotary's history. Paul Harris, the young lawyer who yearned for fellowship and founded the Rotary Club of Chicago, envisioned Rotary as the powerful force for international friendship and goodwill that it is today. Homer Wood, the San Franciscan who founded the Rotary Club of San Francisco, has been called "the missionary" of Rotary, and was responsible for the explosive extension of the Rotary idea on the West Coast and elsewhere. "Bru" Brunnier, a young engineer, joined San Francisco Rotary shortly after it was formed, and went on to become the club's most illustrious member. He served as president of Rotary International in 1952–53. When he died in 1971, he had been a Rotarian for sixty-three years—the longest-serving Rotarian in the world.

In Chapter Four ("Difficult Decades") we learn of three challenges that confronted the club. World War I brought about San Francisco Rotary's first experience with international service, as Rotarians provided wartime relief for the suffering in Europe. The Great Depression of the 1930s tested the club's capacity for humanitarian service to the people of San Francisco. During World War II, San Francisco Rotary again stepped up, providing assistance for servicemen abroad and on the home front, as well as postwar relief to Europe. At war's end, club members hosted delegates and consultants who convened the San Francisco conference for the charter-signing that established the United Nations.

Chapters Five ("The Service Club Matures") and Six ("Service Throughout the World") address San Francisco Rotary's second fifty years. At the beginning of this period, the club established the San Francisco Rotary Foundation to provide a permanent, growing fund for Rotary's good works. The second half-century saw an explosion of service programs and projects for the community and the world. At home, Rotarians created a wide array of creative ongoing programs to serve the city's young people. Abroad, the club participated in Rotary International's growing number of goodwill and humanitarian programs, including its massive undertaking to end polio worldwide. San Francisco Rotarians conceived and formed three organizations that provide life-changing surgery to indigent children throughout the world.

Chapter Seven ("Always Taking Part: 100 Years of Women and Rotary") takes a century-long view of the active part women have always taken in Rotary club life and good works. San Francisco Rotary took its place in the forefront of change by admitting women as members months before a U.S. Supreme Court decision opened Rotary's doors to women in 1987.

Chapter Eight ("Perspectives") concludes the book with looks back on several points. Three difficult long-term issues are described. Then we recount the club's many time-tested traditions that have nurtured a deep fellowship among Rotarians since the earliest days. Special points of club pride are brought out. Finally, we review San Francisco Rotary's extraordinary accomplishments over a century of dedicated service, and hear a distinguished member's challenge for the new century.

ACKNOWLEDGMENTS

Many people contributed to the writing of this book, and each deserves my thanks and appreciation. SF Rotary President Bill Ecker started the ball rolling on a Centennial history book. The San Francisco Rotary Foundation took up the project and oversaw it to completion during the Foundation

Bill Ecker

presidencies of Bill Sturgeon, Bill Koefoed, Lisa Moscaret-Burr, and Jim Bradley. History Professor Richard Abrams at UC Berkeley offered me the opportunity to undertake the project. From the beginning, Roger Steiner supervised the project and worked to maintain a high level of interest for the new book among the club's membership. Steve Talmadge graciously offered me working space at his office, and kept my energy level up with frequent offerings of his star-quality cooking.

I met Past District Governor Bill Sturgeon my first day on the job, and without his unwavering enthusiasm and support, this book would not have been possible. Bill and Sandra welcomed me to their new home in Arizona, where they shared a library of Rotary information, their boat on the lake, and a newfound friendship. Bill's comprehensive knowledge of Rotary history, his wise guidance, and challenging criticism of each page through several readings were invaluable, and I cannot thank him enough.

My other readers among the club's membership—Kathy Beavers, Jim Bradley, Curtis Burr, Lisa Moscaret-Burr, Dick Rosen, and Roger Steiner—offered positive comments and let me know I was on the right track.

Many Rotarians in the San Francisco club and elsewhere shared their documents and photographs, sat for interviews, and answered my many questions. Helen Abe, Les Andersen, Ron Anderson, Kathy Beavers, Burt Berry, Marsh Blum, Jim Bradley, Marie Brooks, Curtis Burr, Dr. Angelo Capozzi, Marv Cardoza, Rod Carpenter, Cecile Chiquette, Carol Christie, Kay Clarke, Rob Connolly, Vikki Cooper, Helen Daugherty, Mike Davies, Jim Deitz, Dr. Howard Denbo, Past RI President Cliff Dochterman, Lena Dokuchayeva, Cleo Donovan, Bill Ecker, Jim Emerson, Al Feder, PDG Mark Flegel, Dana Gribben, Greg Gutting, Boris Hesser, John Hoch, Harold Hoogasian, Matts Ingemanson, PDG Bob Kane, Past RI President Charles Keller, Jim Kennedy, Bill Koefoed, PDG Pete Lagarias, Eugene Lee, Fred Marschner, Charlie Massen, Stuart Menist, Leni Miller, Zina Mirsky, Lisa Moscaret-Burr, Jim Murray, PDG Virginia Nordby, Jim Patrick, Dr. T. Otis Paul, Scott Plakun, Dr. August Reader, John Ringgenberg, Dick Rosen, Eric Schmautz, Jean Schore, Anita Stangl, Mark Stevenson, Steve Swaab, Steve Talmadge, Pete Taylor, Burton Tregoning, John Uth, Omar Valle, Howard Waits, Bob Wilhelm, Rosey Wong, Sam Yates—all contributed to the success of this book. At the club office, Tessie Reyes and Shoko Valle provided access to club documents and offered help whenever I needed it during my research.

I have received a great deal of assistance from outside the club as well. This book has been built on the previous efforts of club historians William Mountin and Mitchell Postel. Most recently, David Forward showed me what a great Rotary history looks like with his ambitious *Century of*

Service about Rotary International. Jack Selway and the impressive collection of Rotary knowledge made available on the internet by the Rotary Global History Fellowship were the sources of a good many leads for further research. Rotary International's archivists and other staff provided much-needed information—Cyndi Beck, Jesse Ellerton, Francine Keyes, Laura Mills, Lois Robertson, and Wayne Hearn. Archivist Robin Dillow in particular scoured *The Rotarian* and photo archives in response to my never-ending requests.

Members of the Rotaract Club of San Francisco assisted me on two occasions, most recently assembling a historical list of SF Rotarians. I spent several pleasant days enjoying mimosas, and compiling names with these energetic future Rotarians. My thanks to Sofya Bakalova, Lisa Brosterhous, Mandy Canales, Shi Choong, Luci Cline, Kendra Haberkorn, Brent Jarcik, Lauren Knight, Joshua Low, Amanda Nguyen, Jack Olson, Fina Ramialison, Liz Reader, and Beth Ross. Natalia and Oscar Chavez helped with some earlier work.

The staff at the California Historical Society and Carol Peterson at the San Mateo County History Museum archives were especially helpful in locating materials for me.

Karen Miller transcribed hundreds of pages of Rotarians' taped interviews. I would have been unable to make sense of dozens of interview tapes without her professional accuracy and efficiency. Professional book project-manager Carolyn Allison-Holland brought her publishing know-how and timely management to the project. Carolyn and her team—Annette Jarvie, Laura Lind, Christy Phillippe, Charlee Trantino, and Maura Zimmer—made my rough writing look good.

Some personal acknowledgments are in order. Carol D. made sure I kept going. Work days on Mary's boat, movies with Cynthia, art and lunch with Carol, and Lori's eleventh-hour visit—each was supportive in its own way. Jim was a well of limitless support. He made me lunch, cheered me on, and picked over every manuscript word, smoothing out my awkward sentences as he went. Maggi-Su and Barney took me for a walk every day and kept me entertained.

Lastly, my task was only to tell the story of Rotary #2. The greatest thanks of all must go to the thousands of members of the Rotary Club of San Francisco, without whose dedication and service there would be no story to tell.

A Special Acknowledgment

Many of the finest photographs in this book were taken by members of the Moulin family of San Francisco. The Moulins have been some of the city's premier photographers since the late-nineteenth century.

An accomplished photographer from a young age, Gabriel Moulin started his career as an independent photographer on April 18, 1906—the day of the San Francisco earthquake. His reputation as an outstanding photographer was established with his pictures of the earthquake's aftermath. Gabriel was a member of the San Francisco Rotary Club from its early days. *Grindings*, the club's newsletter, called him "Rotary's official photographer," and he took hundreds of pictures of club functions and events.

Gabriel was later joined in the business by his sons, Irving and Raymond—who also became members of San Francisco Rotary. Throughout many decades, the Moulin Studios were commissioned as official photographers for such occasions as the 1915 Panama-Pacific International Exposition and the construction of the Golden Gate and San Francisco–Oakland Bay Bridges.

Raymond's son, Tom (also a Rotarian), began working in the family business in 1949. He continues to operate the Moulin Studios with his wife Jean.

The photographs from the Moulin Studios add an important historical element to this book, and I am grateful to Tom and Jean Moulin for their permission to reproduce the photographs herein.

Thomas, Gabriel, Raymond, and Irving Moulin

A Tradition of Fellowship and Service:

The Rotary Club of San Francisco at 100

chapter one

A New Club for San Francisco: Rotary's Beginnings

Our work was not in vain, for there has grown out of it, not only a world-wide organization known as Rotary International, which is of great usefulness and benefit to mankind, but the entire service club movement of the world as well.

—Homer Wood, 1930

Great happenings often arise from small incidents. On a Sunday evening in June 1908, a young man named Homer Wood walked into the lobby of the Cadillac Hotel in San Francisco, and sat down to write a letter. Homer, a single man of twenty-seven, lived at the hotel. He was a lawyer, and had moved to San Francisco in 1907, the year after the great earthquake and fire. He sat on the opposite side of the writing desk from a man in his twenties, who appeared to be working on his appointment schedule.

The young man, Manuel Muñoz, was in town on business from Chicago, and had checked into the hotel the previous evening. Manuel introduced himself to Homer, and inquired about certain streets and buildings in San Francisco, in preparation for business calls the following day. Homer gave him directions, then the conversation continued.

After they spoke for some time, Manuel casually told Homer of a "new-idea club" in Chicago—a business and civic club called "Rotary." The Rotary Club was like no other. Each type of business was represented by only one invited member, who was the best known in his line, and was recognized by the other members as trustworthy. The absence of competition among members provided a relaxed, jovial sense of fellowship. Each member was eager to trade with and "boost" his fellow members. Rotary members were able to freely describe and promote their occupations, whereas discussions of business matters were frowned upon at other men's clubs. Moreover, the club took pride in its sense of civic responsibility and community service.

Homer Wood

Manuel mentioned the Chicago club only casually, and described it briefly to Homer. But behind his description lay a story of a unique club, founded by Paul Harris, a young lawyer from a village in Vermont.

Beginnings in Chicago

Like thousands of other men who came to Chicago from the country and small towns, Paul arrived in Chicago in 1896, hoping to build a successful small practice in the growing, exciting city. And like many of them, he found the big city an impersonal, often exploitive place. He was lonely, and he longed for the informal sociability of his hometown. For several years, he had contemplated how to bring the friendly fellowship of small-town businessmen, who smiled and greeted each other with a trusting handshake, into his big-city business relationships. He reasoned that a group of men like himself would enjoy meeting others and taking pleasure in sociable fellowship, and might even find trustworthy business advantages in such a group. Why not bring them together?

When Paul decided to act on his ideas in 1905, he considered the character of men he knew. Friendliness and approachability would be important. He introduced and talked the idea over with two men—Silvester Schiele, a coal dealer and client, and Gus Loehr, a mining engineer. They had come to Chicago from small communities, and had built profitable businesses. Silvester and Gus liked each other and liked the idea.

Paul, Silvester, Gus, and a fourth man, Hiram Shorey, held the founding meeting of the new club in Gus's office, on the evening of February 23, 1905.[1] The four men soon discovered

that their backgrounds and personal experiences were quite similar. Paul explained the purposes of the club—"a very simple plan of mutual co-operation and informal friendship such as all of us had once known in our villages." One man from each line of business would be invited to join. As noncompetitors, they would meet in a spirit of fellowship and business helpfulness. Silvester, Gus, and Hiram were very interested, and the four agreed to meet again. A second meeting followed two weeks later in Paul's office, with three new members: a real estate broker and an organ manufacturer, and Harry Ruggles, who supplied printing needs to Paul's office and would go on to become a vital member of the Chicago club and of Rotary's future international organization.

Paul Harris at age 28.
Courtesy RI Archive

More new members quickly joined. Paul recounts how "We grew in numbers, in fellowship, in the spirit of helpfulness to each other and to our city." The lawyer, the coal man, the mining engineer, the tailor,

1. This date is considered the founding meeting of the Chicago club, and is celebrated as the anniversary date of Rotary. The Rotary Club of San Francisco, on the other hand, does not observe its first preliminary meetings, but rather commemorates its founding banquet on November 12, 1908.

the real estate broker, the organ manufacturer, and the printer were joined by a banker and a baker, a parson, a plumber, and a laundryman. In Paul's recollection, together they "discovered the similarity of each other's ambitions, problems, successes and failures. We learned how much we had in common. We found joy in being of service to one another. Again, I seemed to be back in my New England Valley." That return to the atmosphere of a friendlier, more trusting kind of relationship seems to have held a strong attraction for a certain type of man. Like Paul himself, all of these early members had made their own way, and most had come to Chicago from a farm or small village.

At the third meeting in Silvester's coal-yard office, fifteen men attended and made organizational decisions. After considering many suggestions for the new club's name, the members unanimously approved Paul's suggestion of "Rotary." The name referred to the plan to rotate meeting locations among members' places of business, with the leadership of each meeting rotating to the man hosting the gathering. No one would be able to join if any existing member voted not to accept him. Each man's membership would last only one year. Upon expiration, his renewal was subject to approval by three-quarters of the membership. This potential for any member to be "rotated" out of the club was said to lend additional meaning to the name "Rotary." Members would pay no dues. Club expenses would be paid for through a fifty-cent fine collected from each member who missed a meeting. Attendance at meetings was expected, and no excuses were accepted. The men elected a board of directors, and Paul Harris nominated Silvester Schiele for president, after declining the office himself. Silvester became Chicago Rotary's first president by acclamation.

During its first year, the Rotary Club initiated a number of practices, many of which became Rotary's oldest traditions. Besides the club's name and the requirements for a member's unique occupation and attendance, some traditions were put in place to advance fellowship among members. By the fifth meeting, the rotation of meeting places shifted to hotels and restaurants, since the group had grown too large to meet in members' offices. This rotation of meeting places continued for several years, until the club finally settled on Chicago's Sherman Hotel in 1911.

> "One night we had a comedy boxing match between Harry Crofts, weight 250, and Les Lawrence, who barely tipped the scales at 95 pounds. It finished with Harry playing a mouth organ as he carried Les on his shoulders around the room. Kid stuff, sure! It seemed good fun then, though."
>
> —Chicago founding member Harry Ruggles, 1952

From the beginning, Paul sought to bring a sociable casualness to meetings by insisting that members greet each other by their first names; members who used "Mister" were fined. Many members were given nicknames. Silliness was often the order of the day. The early meetings did not usually have official agendas, so activities might include new member initiations, "stunts," or practical jokes—often impromptu.

Rotary's favored tradition of singing began after only a few months, when Harry Ruggles jumped into a lull in the conversation and called out, "Hell, fellows, let's sing!" Thereafter, Harry led the assembled club in singing, printed Rotary songbooks, and took his vocal leadership to district conferences and international conventions until his death in 1959. Gradually, the club began to hold outings and regular "ladies' nights" for wives to attend. A comfortable friendliness among

"To the members of the small group which came together in the big city of Chicago, Rotary was like an oasis in a desert. Their meetings were different from the meetings of other clubs in those days. They were far more intimate; far more friendly. All hampering and meaningless restraint was thrown off; dignified reserve was checked at the door; the members were boys again."

—Paul Harris, in *My Road to Rotary*, 1948

the men—who pledged to ignore differences in national origin and religious faith—was ensured through the prohibition of risqué jokes and political or religious discussions.

Additional practices were introduced to promote the club's other objective—business reciprocity and mutual support. The club published its first roster, so members could find fellow Rotarians from whom to purchase goods and services. Besides the limitation of one member per occupation, business between members was encouraged in other ways. For example, the club statistician tracked and reported regularly on occasions of members' patronage of each others' businesses. Although members traded with members, perhaps the greatest business advantage lay in how the men supported each other in other ways, often without expecting a direct return. One way was in the custom of listening attentively to talks by fellow members, who explained their businesses and displayed their wares at meetings. These were the early practices at Rotary meetings, and many grew into traditions that are familiar to Rotarians today.

Paul Harris was elected club president in 1907, having intentionally spent the first two years outside of the leadership position. As president, his goals were trifold: to advance the growth of the Chicago club; to increase the club's level of community service; and to extend the idea of Rotary to other cities.

The first goal was not easy. At the end of its first year, the Rotary Club had thirty members. Interest sagged in its second year, however, and a handful of members kept the club alive. But the club did grow, and by its third year in 1908, it numbered more than 140, and was a registered nonprofit corporation.

Paul's second goal was to increase the club's level of community service. Service was already under way in the club. A new member had convinced the club to add "the advancement of the best interests of Chicago and the spreading of the spirit of civic pride and loyalty among its citizens" to the club's constitutional objectives of fellowship and business interest promotion. Rotary rendered its first public service a few months later, when the club passed the hat and raised $150 to buy a preacher a new horse, so he could make the rounds of his country parishioners. The Rotarians proved to be enthusiastic about their selfless act.

"The question is often asked, 'Why do Rotary clubs limit membership to one man from each distinct business or profession?' Because our experiment has proved in operation that it makes for congenial fellowship, obviates business and professional jealousies, encourages mutual helpfulness, stimulates pride in the dignity of one's occupation, and broadens one's mind and sympathy with regard to the accomplishments and problems of other occupations."

—Paul Harris, in *My Road to Rotary*, 1948

A few weeks later in 1907, the club initiated a project to install public restrooms—"comfort stations"—in downtown Chicago. It successfully enrolled the city administration and other civic organizations to join in the undertaking. For two years, the proposal was fought by two powerful Chicago associations, representing brewers and department stores. Both contended that the city's saloons and stores already offered accommodations to men and women. The measure's proponents argued in return that "men ought not to have to buy a glass of beer nor women have to buy merchandise to make use of toilet facilities." The proponents prevailed, and Chicago's first public comfort station was established.

At this moment early in its history, Paul Harris later proclaimed, "The Rotary Club was raised to the rank of a civic organization in Chicago, to be counted on, henceforth, as an asset in the city." The head of the YMCA expressed the views of many when he said, "The Rotary Club of Chicago has now shown reason for its existence." With this single act of community service, Rotary became the first of the large modern-day organizations known as "service clubs" in the United States.

Finally, Paul's third goal as club president was to extend the idea of Rotary to other cities. Early in the new club's life, Paul imagined Rotary offering business fellowship and civic service elsewhere. But his fellow Rotarians—the "Doubting Thomases"—did not share his aspirations for "Rotary around the world." They saw no benefit to themselves that would justify spending their time and money for such a purpose.

So Paul set out on his own to establish other Rotary clubs. He began corresponding with former classmates in Vermont, Iowa, and Princeton universities, as well as with other friends he had made during previous travels. His efforts proved fruitless, however, until 1908, when he told Manuel Muñoz about his idea of extending Rotary.

PAUL HARRIS RECALLS THE DOUBTING THOMASES
"The Doubting Thomases were ever present. There's but one way to convince a Doubting Thomas and that is to do the thing he says can't be done.... I soon learned that the best way to get things done was to do them myself."
—Paul Harris, in *My Road to Rotary*, 1948

Paul and Manuel were friends. They had shared a suite of rooms at the Del Prado residential hotel in Chicago, and they had roomed together in Elmhurst, Illinois. Manuel had joined the Chicago club in early 1908. At the time, he was a traveling salesman for Sperry & Hutchinson Company. As Manuel later recalled, he planned to travel to San Francisco and Paul Harris said to him, "Manuel, Rotary is a success in Chicago. Why not, in your travels, drop a seed and see what happens?" Upon meeting and conversing with Homer Wood in San Francisco, it occurred to Manuel that "here was the man to cultivate and a fertile field in which to plant the Rotary seed."

Paul's second and third goals of community service and extension foresaw the future miracle of Rotary. The club would enter a period that Paul later described as a "renaissance"—a revolutionary period when Rotary would expand "from a local group, gathered together in the city of Chicago for mutual advantage and fellowship, to an organization of international vision and nobility of purpose."

Manuel Muñoz
Courtesy of RI Archive

Thus, the message of Rotary was not sent out into the world by the Chicago club. Instead, it originated in the ideas of Paul Harris. True, the ideals of Rotary had been set in motion in Chicago. But it would remain for Manuel Muñoz, the messenger, and Homer Wood, the man of action in San Francisco, to inaugurate the realization of Paul Harris's vision.

Rotary Number Two Is Born

Homer Wood was intrigued—a friendly, noncompetitive club that invited one to discuss his business! Although men's clubs were plentiful in San Francisco, Homer immediately saw the advantages of a Rotary club, where men from various lines of business could meet, enjoying fellowship and increasing each other's acquaintances.

Homer was building his law practice in San Francisco, hoping to make new business acquaintances and to "gain distinction."

In his later recollections of the early Rotary happenings that he termed "the beginning of the growth and development of the entire service club movement of the world," Homer recalled that "I was a pretty good joiner." He was already a member of the Union League Club, the San Francisco Golf and Country Club, and a number of lodges. He was thinking of joining the Commonwealth Club (a five-year-old weekly luncheon club that discussed civic matters, and still does to this day). But the idea of Rotary struck him as something better. He thought that if such a club were organized in San Francisco, it could "be made a force for good."

Indeed, San Francisco in 1908 was an ideal place for such a club. Many of its young businessmen, such as Homer, were recent arrivals. With no connections in the city, they were seeking new friends. Others were survivors of the great earthquake and fire of two years earlier. All were men who saw new opportunities, and looked forward to participating in the exciting, often wild-and-wooly, growing scene as the city rebuilt itself.

The Palace Hotel after the 1906 earthquake. The Palace survived the quake, but was destroyed in the fire that followed.

The Planning Begins

Since Manuel Muñoz had no materials about the Chicago club to give Homer, he gave Homer Paul Harris's address. Homer wrote to Paul, requesting a copy of the Chicago club's bylaws and any additional material. Paul responded by sending Homer the bylaws and weekly bulletins from the Chicago club, along with a cordial letter offering Homer his assistance in forming the club.

Homer was impressed with the Rotary club idea. Over the next few days, he and Manuel had several more conversations at the Cadillac Hotel. Homer immediately set about to persuade other men to join him in forming an organizing group. The first was his doctor, Chester H. Woolsey, MD. Chester later recalled, "Homer came into my office one night, and casually threw a bundle of papers on my desk, saying, 'Doc, look over those papers and tell me the next time I come what you think of the idea.'" When he saw Homer again, Chester told him the idea was "a capital one." Homer replied that they should get together a group of representative men and start a Rotary club in San Francisco. Chester suggested that Homer contact a third man, a wholesale chemist named Rusty Rogers.

Homer discussed the possibility of forming a Rotary club with a few more friends, each from a different line of business. He and several other men met three times in his office at the First National Bank Building. Accounts differ as to the attendees at these first meetings in June, but a core group clearly consisted of Homer, Chester Woolsey, Roy "Rusty" Rogers, John Fraser, Frank Turner, James Patrick,[2] and W. B. Webster. These seven men—a lawyer, a doctor, a wholesale chemist, a painter, a clothing dealer, a rubber-stamp dealer, and a mantle dealer—were joined by more at each new meeting. Together, they formed an organizing committee.

What took place in San Francisco over that summer is hazy, because the only surviving letters of the time that describe events begin in October 1908. In their histories, SF Rotary historian William Mountin (1940) and RI Historian David Forward (2003) both state that for several months between June and October, frequent communications passed between Homer and Paul. Homer asked for assistance with anticipated problems, and Paul replied with solutions and enthusiastic encouragement.

Plans began to take shape in October. Manuel showed Homer letters from Paul, with whom he was in touch, in which Paul praised their interest in forming a new Rotary club in San Francisco. Homer in turn shared one of Paul's encouraging letters with prospective members of the club. Manuel and Homer wrote to Paul, each describing progress in starting the club. Homer wrote that he hoped the club would be successful, because his reputation was at stake.

Homer asked Paul about details of the Chicago club's founding, and for suggestions as to preliminary proceedings for organizing the club. Paul replied by describing the Chicago club's initial meetings. He cautioned Homer not to be discouraged if progress was initially slow. He strongly emphasized the importance of getting "good men" for the initial members, as subsequent joiners would be attracted by the caliber of the early members. He also remarked on the importance of getting the club known early through newspaper advertising, and suggested that this would best be accomplished by addressing issues of interest to the public at club meetings. Although the club's stated main purpose would be to accomplish something for the city, indirectly the members would benefit themselves, "and men of prominence will be glad to ally themselves with you." Alongside this public emphasis on civic matters, however, Paul noted that "Of course, you will find that one

---

2. Throughout most of this book, James or "Jim" Patrick refers to James Patrick I, a founding member of SF Rotary. After October 28, 1975 it refers to James Patrick II, his grandson.

of the readiest avenues to the hearts of prospective members will be the business advantage route, but that would not be the only consideration."

During this time, Manuel also continued to correspond with Paul. He told Paul he had been reviewing the details with Homer, and that a meeting of between fifteen and twenty-four men would be held soon. The attendees were to be given a number of application blanks to give to prospective members. He promised Paul that a subsequent banquet would be held, and that it would be "attended by men of weight, guts, and energy. True descendents of the Forty-Niners."

Homer called a meeting at his law office on Thursday, October 15. A five-man executive committee was to proceed with permanent organization of a Rotary club. In addition, a nominating committee of three was charged with nominating a slate of officers, to be voted upon at the first regular meeting. The first official meeting of the club would be a formal banquet.

These early organizers approached other businessmen in the hope of attracting the city's best business leaders to join the club. Much of the prospecting was done at the prestigious Union League Club, as well as through personal calls on businessmen listed in the classified directory. Homer later recalled that to educate leading businessmen of San Francisco and convince them to join a new kind of civic and booster organization was no small task. Nevertheless, he did not ask anyone a second time, preferring instead to move on and extend the invitation to another man. Their approach worked—San Francisco businessmen were indeed interested in a new kind of business and civic organization. After considerable effort, enough men had agreed to join that plans could become action. It was time for the group to call itself a club.

> "The main object is to create a commercial and business nucleus to boost San Francisco, to boost one another in a commercial way, and to expand the feeling of friendly co-operation among all the industries making up the business life of the city. No one will be urged to join. It will be considered an honor to get in."
>
> —*San Francisco Chronicle*, November 12, 1908, the morning of the club's founding banquet

A Gathering of Founders

On the morning of Wednesday, November 13, 1908, readers of the *San Francisco Chronicle* opened a newspaper that reported the events in a growing, lively city—the largest and most important city west of the Mississippi. Readers of the headline articles on the front page learned that San Francisco voters had approved a plan to create a city water supply by flooding the Hetch Hetchy Valley in the Sierra. *Chronicle* readers also learned that multimillionaire steel magnate Charles M. Schwab had delivered a stirring speech the previous evening at the St. Francis Hotel. In fact, Schwab had addressed the initial dinner meeting of the Rotary Club. The *Chronicle* described the club as "a new organization of individuals representing about fifty separate lines of business, socially combined into a San Francisco boosting society." Schwab (no relation to Charles Schwab, founder of the investment brokerage) spoke to the assembled men about his views of San Francisco's bright prospects "as a great commercial center, one of matchless location and fine climate," and its future as a shipping center second only to New York. He predicted that when the Panama Canal was completed, "the shipping that would pour through that great gateway to and from the Orient would make San Francisco a port of call on the world's marine highway." After a few minutes describing interstate commerce policy and labor conditions, Schwab concluded his inspirational speech, exhorting his listeners, "Let's get together and make San Francisco great!" Leaving to catch a train back East, he bid the group good-bye and waved, as they stood on their feet and cheered.

What an auspicious beginning for Rotary #2! Indeed, the Rotary Club of San Francisco's founding banquet, held in one of the city's most luxurious hotels, had been an upbeat and productive one. Fifty-five businessmen had gathered to inaugurate the second Rotary club in the world. Among them were important business leaders, including General Michael H. DeYoung, owner of the *San Francisco Chronicle*; James Woods, manager of the St. Francis Hotel; and John Britton, vice president and general manager of the California Gas and Electric Company. Homer Wood presided as toastmaster. Michael DeYoung discussed "Community, Cooperation, and the Need of a Get-Together Spirit," and John Britton spoke on "Public Relations of a Public Service Corporation."

As the festivities proceeded, Homer was informed that Charles Schwab was in another dining room downstairs. Homer asked Michael DeYoung to go with him to call on Schwab and invite him to give a talk at the Rotary banquet. Schwab agreed, and accompanied them upstairs, where he delivered his rousing speech.[3]

Homer read telegrams of congratulations from Paul Harris and B. E. Arntzen, Chicago club secretary, on behalf of the Chicago club. The assembled men were unanimous in their desire to complete the organization of a new club, to be called the Rotary Club of San Francisco. The Chicago club's constitution and bylaws were adopted, including the three objectives of business interest promotion, good fellowship, and the advancement of the best interests of San Francisco. The bylaws called for monthly meetings and several standing committees. Homer Wood was elected president, C. M. Wooster vice president, A. S. Darrow secretary, John Fraser treasurer, and George Forderer sergeant-at-arms.

To close the meeting, Rotary #2's first president, Homer Wood, addressed the new Rotarians. He stood alongside a banner proclaiming the new club's motto, "Boost and we all boost with you, knock and you knock alone." He proclaimed SF Rotary to be "a civic organization which is going to accomplish more for the common good of San Francisco than any other club." Its difference from any other type of club would give SF Rotary prominent standing in the city. He praised the notion of a club of noncompeting men, declaring, "It is safe to say that a more harmonious set of men could never be banded together to work for any common good." He described "knockers"—chronic complainers—and made it clear there was no place for them in Rotary. He reminded the businessmen that a large acquaintanceship is a very valuable asset, the same as a college education. Turning to the club's civic-service purpose, he described the Chicago club's effort at community service, and stressed that Rotary could perform community service in San Francisco

---

3. Years later, Charles M. Schwab joined an eastern Rotary club.

as well. He reiterated Charles Schwab's predictions of a shining future for San Francisco, tying SF Rotary's future to a city destined for greatness. After all, San Franciscans had already distinguished themselves in the rebuilding of the city after the earthquake and fire two years before. Finally, Homer urged his fellow members to go out and boost for San Francisco and the distinctive features for which it was famous.

Throughout his inaugural speech, Homer echoed the new club's constitutional objectives. He joined the notions of business advantage, good fellowship, and civic interest, and introduced them into the club's purpose from its very beginnings.

From this first banquet, the Rotary movement began its extraordinary expansion. Paul Harris's renaissance garden was coming into flower. Homer Wood was to spread its seeds.

The Earliest Days

With the first banquet meeting behind him and the new club successfully launched, Homer wasted no time in his efforts to bring the club along. A few days after the banquet, Paul Harris wrote to Homer, congratulating him on the birth of the San Francisco club, and the "live, hustling bunch of men associated with you."

And Homer hustled. He immediately published a club bulletin (a forerunner of the club's newsletter *Grindings*, which has been published continuously from 1913 to today). For the bulletin's masthead, Homer adopted the Chicago club's Rotary emblem—a spoked wheel that stirred up dust to indicate motion.

"Good fellowship among the members should always be foremost. By meeting over a club dinner once a month, each member is enhancing his own business value and education by coming in contact with and knowing influential men in other lines of trade."

—Homer Wood, in the first club bulletin, December, 1908

Homer's first bulletin was packed with information for the new Rotarians. Planning for the next meeting in January was already under way. (December was passed by because of holiday festivities held by the various organizations in San Francisco.) Homer took great pride in the fact that one thousand copies of the *San Francisco Chronicle* article on the day after the new club's first banquet had been printed and distributed by the Rotary Club of Chicago.[4] He happily announced the formation of a new Rotary club, serving the cities of Alameda, Oakland, and Berkeley. Within days of the founding banquet, SF Rotary's Membership Committee had formed a waiting list for membership to the club, in accordance with the club's bylaws. Homer reminded club members that good attendance would enhance their business by bringing contact with influential men in other lines of trade. He also stressed that at future meetings, troubles of particular individuals or contentious civic issues were not to be the subject of discussion, but issues concerning the general welfare in a positive way would be considered.

---

4. Copies were distributed to interested parties in Oakland; Minneapolis; Spokane; New York City; Philadelphia; and Davenport, Iowa.

Homer published another bulletin before the club's second meeting, providing still more news about the brand-new club. Prominent businessmen from occupations not yet represented in the club would be invited to the January dinner meeting so they might understand the aims and objects of Rotary. The speakers would address issues of importance to the city. Homer praised the progress of the recently formed Tri-City Rotary Club across the bay. He dismissed recent inquiries as to whether the club might establish a headquarters, including a grill, with the statement that the club did not need club quarters. Homer did, however, mention that the new Tri-City Rotary Club had established a weekly luncheon, and that he thought the idea a good one. He introduced a system of "tip" cards, which members were instructed to pass out to anyone looking for goods and services. The name of the appropriate Rotarian provider would be entered on the card. Homer said much business had come the way of Rotarians as a result of this system.[5]

An enlarged and enthused group gathered in January for the club's second dinner banquet, held again at the St. Francis Hotel. An orchestra provided music for the gathering. After the dinner, members listened attentively to several speakers, who spoke on issues of local and national importance. They elected the club's first board of directors, which began to meet regularly for luncheon at the Hotel Stewart. Homer proudly distributed SF Rotary's first roster. Fresh off the press, it boasted seventy-eight members, listing each man within his unique business classification.

In the months that followed, the club continued to take shape. Homer announced that his law office in the First National Bank Building would be the regular Rotary office, and the club would be listed on the building directory. By the fourth meeting (held in March), the club experimented with informality. Dinner was held at the Bismarck Café, and members dispensed with the formal attire of the previous banquets, arriving in business suits instead. At that meeting, the members decided to follow the lead of the new Tri-City club, and meet weekly for informal luncheons on Wednesday, at which time no club business would be transacted. The formal monthly banquets would be resumed, with the next one scheduled to take place at the Fairmont Hotel. Members were advised to "BYOC," as the $3 fee included the banquet menu and wine, but no cigars. Singing became a part of the club. At the third meeting in February, the Golden Gate Quartet played old familiar songs, and members joined in the choruses. Thanks to an active Entertainment Committee, musical entertainment became a regular feature at meetings. The formal banquet meeting each month featured a prominent speaker on a public question, in addition to social and musical programs. (The monthly dinner meetings were discontinued in early 1911, with the weekly luncheons becoming the club business meeting.)

During this time, SF Rotary fine-tuned membership and attendance issues, beginning to establish policies and practices that would become the ways of SF Rotary for years to come. The club decided to publish a more elaborate business directory, containing photographs for each member, as a way to help members know each other by sight. The club constitution was amended by unanimous vote to assess each member annual membership dues of $12, and the fiscal year was set at November

---

5. Homer seems to have to exaggerated by saying that this system was already in use by the Rotary clubs in the East, when in fact, there were no such clubs.

"The Rotary Club of San Francisco may well take pride in the way Homer and other charter members of the San Francisco club threw themselves into the effort. Californians are hard to beat, particularly in games calling for cooperation....They are true sons of the 'Forty-niners,' the most intrepid and indomitable of American pioneers."

—Paul Harris, *This Rotarian Age*, 1935

first. At several meetings, attendance was a topic of discussion. In April, the constitution was again amended, adding the provision that any member who missed three consecutive meetings without delivering a written explanation satisfactory to the board would forfeit his membership. By September, since compulsory attendance at the weekly luncheons improved attendance, the club moved its luncheon to a larger venue, Techau Tavern, on the corner of Powell and Eddy.[6]

New members joined the club in rapid succession. The Membership Committee continued its successful work. Within six months of its founding, the club's membership increased threefold, to 171, as listed in a roster of May 1909.

As the club neared the end of its first year, it suffered from growing pains. Although membership was increasing, attendance was not what it should be. Club members were becoming uncertain about the exact purpose of the club—an ambivalence that would create discomfort and change for several years to come. Nevertheless, as it grew in size and prestige, it was clear—for now, at least, Rotary was in San Francisco to stay.

San Francisco Extends Rotary

> As years have rolled by it has given me a great deal of pleasure and satisfaction to note how the Rotary idea has grown and spread wherever it is organized. There are now a great many organizations, such as the Lions Club, Kiwanis, Exchange, etc., which had their inspiration in Rotary and operate along similar lines.
>
> —Homer Wood, 1923

Now commemorating its one-hundredth year, the Rotary Club of San Francisco has scores of accomplishments to celebrate. Most stem from its distinguished role in community and international service. But the singular moment—the source of the club's greatest pride—took place barely two weeks after its founding. Already pleased with its successful creation of a new kind of businessmen's club in San Francisco, the club went on to exceed its claim as "the first extension club of the Rotary world." Homer Wood began to plant seeds.

Paul Harris Tries to Extend Rotary

Since the Rotary Club of Chicago's early days, Paul Harris had attempted to extend the Rotary idea beyond Chicago. But before Manuel Muñoz brought the message of Rotary to Homer Wood in San Francisco, Paul Harris had no success in his efforts to export Rotary to other cities. Although he

---

6. The meetings were held at the Techau Tavern until the club outgrew that location and moved to the Palace Hotel in 1916 (at the same time it took offices at the Palace).

had attempted to promote his extension idea within the Chicago club as early as 1906, Paul's fellow Rotarians were not enthusiastic, and they objected to the use of their time and money to form another club.

Undeterred, Paul stepped up his efforts, just as the preparations for the San Francisco club were nearing their end. Harry Ruggles later recalled that when Paul resigned the Chicago club's presidency in October 1908, he "poured his enthusiasm into extension." Paul shared his hopes with Harry, who warmed to the idea. Later, Harry recommended that Manuel Muñoz be named "Member at Large," charged with initiating a Rotary club in every city he might visit.

But for the most part, Paul was acting mainly on his own, although Homer may not have known it as he went about organizing the San Francisco club. Paul promoted the San Francisco club from his law office, and it appears that the majority of the Chicago club did not know about his communications with San Francisco until Paul advised them that a second club was imminent.

Paul wanted more than separate clubs in other cities; he wanted a national organization as well. In his communication with Manuel Muñoz before the founding of the San Francisco club, he wrote that the planned club should become affiliated with the Chicago club. He asked that it be the aim of all concerned to work so there might soon be "a national body with legislative capacities of its own." Three weeks later, he outlined his plans to Homer, suggesting "a regular National Secretary" to provide "uniformity of action" among clubs. The secretary would be supported by a small levy per Rotary member. He also expressed his idea for meetings of national delegates. While plans for the San Francisco club were under way, Paul notified Homer and Manuel of his establishment of an Extension Committee in Chicago.

Paul had high hopes for the Chicago club's Extension Committee. The month before the San Francisco club's founding banquet, he optimistically announced plans for clubs in New York, Philadelphia, and Boston. After San Francisco's founding, Paul seized on the opportunity to demonstrate to others that another Rotary club could successfully be started outside of Chicago. In his first club bulletin, Homer informed his members that one thousand copies of the *San Francisco Chronicle* article describing the new club's first banquet had been printed and distributed by the Rotary Club of Chicago. Undoubtedly, this was Paul's doing. Two months after SF Rotary came into being, Paul wrote to Homer that Manuel Muñoz was on the verge of opening a club in Washington, DC. He also told Homer the Chicago club would be meeting soon, to establish a national Rotary organization. However, the Chicago club's Extension Committee faltered, due to continuing apathy of the club's members, most of whom were, at best, ambivalent. None of Paul's expectations materialized. After several months, as another Rotarian took over the Chicago Extension Committee, Paul expressed his wish that "this will not prove an illusive hope."

The Wildfire on the West Coast

The new San Francisco club's membership posed no such obstacle to Homer Wood's enthusiasm. In initially adopting the Chicago club's constitution and bylaws, SF Rotary assumed the obligation of maintaining a standing "Publicity and Extension Committee." Along with securing newspaper publicity for the club, the committee was charged with planning "to create and establish similar organizations throughout the United States." However, most of the committee's efforts went toward local publicity. Homer took on the extension mission himself, and with the assistance of founding member Arthur Holman, he set about the task immediately.

Homer and Arthur described their new club to some friends in Oakland, who inquired about it after seeing the newspaper publicity concerning SF Rotary's founding banquet. At Homer and Arthur's suggestion, the Oaklanders convened a preliminary group of representative businessmen, less than two weeks after the founding of SF Rotary. In his first club bulletin to SF Rotary members in December, Homer announced that twenty-five of Oakland's leading businessmen had held two organizational luncheons, and had elected a president. They had invited Homer to attend and to explain the purposes and workings of Rotary. In the process they made him an Honorary Member, "as an expression of goodwill and assurance of co-operation." The club's membership was composed of men from different lines of business in Alameda, Oakland, and Berkeley. Thus the Tri-City Rotary Club, as it was named, might have three members from a single occupation, one from each city.

In the second SF Rotary bulletin the following month, Homer reported that the new Tri-City club was prospering and growing rapidly. That month several SF Rotary members participated in the Tri-City club's noon luncheon meeting. This was the first inter-city Rotary meeting. It established a tradition between the two clubs that has continued for almost one hundred years, and went on to become a custom among Rotary clubs everywhere. The Tri-City Rotary Club—club number three—was officially formed in February 1909. Homer Wood was selected to represent SF Rotary at the new club's February banquet, and it became commonplace for the two clubs to exchange speakers.[7] Paul rewarded Homer for his successful extension work by placing Homer's name and picture in the Chicago club's roster.

Three months after the founding of the Tri-City club, Arthur Holman traveled to Seattle on business. While there and at Homer's request, he approached a fellow insurance man named Roy Denny about the notion of a Rotary club. Homer asked Paul Harris to send Roy literature about Rotary. After holding a preliminary meeting at a candy store, Roy Denny succeeded in forming a club in Seattle in June 1908—the fourth club in the Rotary world.

Having demonstrated again that the message of Rotary appealed to businessmen in other cities, Homer and Arthur continued on. Homer wrote to his brother Walton J. Wood, a practicing lawyer in Los Angeles, about his success with Rotary in San Francisco and Oakland. He asked Arthur Holman to meet with Walton while on a business trip to Los Angeles. Arthur was unable to meet Walton, but he described the new San Francisco club and its promotion techniques to a Los Angeles insurance man, Jerry Muma. Soon thereafter, Walton and Jerry (who had been in college together) met for lunch and planned the organization of a Rotary club in Los Angeles. The new

---

7. Unfortunately, the Tri-City club ran into difficulties, and membership and attendance declined. The main source of trouble resulted from serious talk that the city of San Francisco would attempt state legislation to annex Oakland, in order to gain back the businessmen who had left the city after the 1906 earthquake. The shrinking club did not participate in the first Rotary Convention in 1910, and became insolvent early in the next year. The directors subsequently reorganized as the Rotary Club of Oakland. Businessmen in Berkeley and Alameda formed clubs in those cities several years later.

club came into being at a luncheon with thirty charter members in June 1908, shortly after the Seattle club was organized. It was the fifth Rotary club, the fourth on the West Coast.

Homer's connection with the Los Angeles club did not end there, however. It seems that Walton Wood and Jerry Muma hired professional organizer Herbert Quick as club secretary, promising him a portion of the membership dues from each person he signed up. Quick was fired by the Los Angeles club less than a year later, but he knew an opportunity when he saw it. He immediately formed his own corporation, the "National Rotary Club," beating the authentic club in Los Angeles to secure state incorporation under the Rotary name. Homer Wood was already concerned that several individuals turned down by the San Francisco club had threatened to start another "Rotary Club" in San Francisco. When he heard about Quick's activities, he immediately incorporated SF Rotary (on June 22, 1910), and registered the name "Rotary" as a trademark in California. He also wrote to Paul Harris, suggesting that Paul act as well to trademark the name under federal jurisdiction.[8]

"There have been few, if any, such wild fires of enthusiasm as took place on the Pacific coast at that time; it seemed providential."

—Paul Harris, *This Rotarian Age*, 1935

With Rotary's lightning establishment on the West Coast, success elsewhere now seemed possible. When Paul brought the news of the westward extension to the members of the Chicago club, some began to soften. Many still balked. But Paul persevered.

The real prize in the East, of course, was New York City. Earlier, Paul made his hopes for the largest city in the country clear. New York City seems to have been approached more than once. A month before the formation of the San Francisco club, Paul Harris wrote to Manuel Muñoz stating that he was asking someone to "get a nucleus together" in New York. However, that effort failed in short order. Undaunted, Paul continued in his efforts.

But it would again be the San Francisco club that imparted the right idea to the right man, which ultimately led to success. Paul Harris later recalled that the message of Rotary was first taken to New York by a Chicago Rotarian. But the Rotary Club of New York attributes its founding this way:

> The idea of forming a Rotary Club in New York came in a message to Elmer DePue in New York, not from Paul Harris but from Clarence J. Wetmore, member of the Rotary Club of San Francisco. Elmer was the President of the Eastern Division of the Cresta Blanca Wine Company. [Clarence Wetmore of San Francisco was Cresta Blanca's president.]

Elmer, in turn, spoke to New York lawyer Daniel Cady, who agreed to speak with his close friend Paul Harris. Paul immediately asked Homer Wood to write a supportive letter to Daniel.

Indeed, during this early extension era, Paul and Homer communicated regularly. They agreed both would make efforts to extend Rotary by sending descriptive letters and literature to men

---

8. Herbert Quick subsequently attempted to expand to Seattle as well, but the Seattle club learned of his plan, and headed off his registration. The board in Quick's alternate Rotary club in Los Angeles did not approve of his methods and fired him, and he was not heard from again. Eventually, the two rival clubs merged to become the Rotary Club of Los Angeles.

> "Homer responded instantly to requests from Chicago for help in efforts to win New York and other eastern cities to the cause."
>
> —Paul Harris, *This Rotarian Age,* 1935

interested in forming clubs in other cities. On several occasions, Homer responded to Paul's request for assistance by writing such letters.

Paul sent Chicago Rotarian Fred Tweed to speak with Daniel, Elmer, and Bradford Bullock at a dinner meeting in New York in August 1909. The four agreed a club would benefit them and the city of New York. Six days later, on August 24, 1909, twenty-six men met at dinner and formed Club #6, the Rotary Club of New York—the first Rotary club on the East Coast.

First the Nation, Then the World

After New York was won over, there seemed to be no stopping the spread of Rotary. Work in Boston had already begun, and the Rotary Club of Boston was inaugurated in December. Seattle Rotarian Roy Denny took the Rotary idea to Tacoma, Washington, and a club was formed there in February 1910. February also saw the creation of new clubs in Minneapolis, St. Paul, St. Louis, and New Orleans. Rotary was now in place across the country, and the extension continued. By July 1910, new clubs had appeared in Kansas City; Portland, Oregon; Lincoln, Nebraska; and Detroit. The appeal of Rotary was so strong that there were now sixteen clubs with 1,800 members on both coasts, in the nation's heartland, and in the South.

This evidence of Rotary's strength gave Chicago Rotarians a new appreciation for Paul's vision of a national organization. The proposed national organization would provide assistance and unity of purpose to the local clubs, and would coordinate programs. And by bearing the financial and administrative costs of extension, a national organization would relieve the Chicago club of these costs—a burden that had caused so many in the club to object to Paul's efforts. For Paul's doubters, this represented an acceptable compromise.

The Chicago club issued a resolution and mailed it to Rotary clubs across the country. The two-page document asked the clubs to pledge their "moral and financial support" to a unifying organization, and to work toward extending Rotary to other cities. It also declared that a board of commissioners would arrange for a national convention. The appointed commissioners included Paul Harris and three others from Chicago, Homer Wood from San Francisco, and the presidents of the Los Angeles and New York clubs. Under the direction of Chicagoan Chesley "Ches" Perry, plans were made for a national convention, where the new organization's objectives and rules could be formulated.

On August 15, 1910, sixty enthusiastic delegates from fourteen of the sixteen clubs in existence traveled to Chicago with their wives and guests. They were met at the train by Chicago club members, and taken by automobile to their hotel. SF Rotary had nominated Homer to serve as delegate, but he was unable to attend. He delegated his proxy to Jerry Muma of Los Angeles, and kept in communication with him by telegraph. With Ches Perry as chairman, the delegates debated and negotiated over topics as varied as dues, the new organization's emblem, business reciprocity between members, cities eligible for a Rotary club, and social activities within clubs. They also enjoyed fun and fellowship with others from across the country—all bound by the commonality

The first Rotary Convention in Chicago, 1910. Paul Harris is fifth from right.

of the new Rotary experience. SF Rotary sent a resolution opposing any attempt by the National Association to obligate members of individual clubs to limit their exchange of business outside their clubs' local territories. It also opposed any kind of national roster of members or any limitations or interference with the local clubs. When the convention ended, the delegates had adopted a constitution and bylaws for the newly formed National Association of Rotary Clubs of America. Paul Harris was unanimously voted president. Although he was not present, Arthur Holman of San Francisco was named a director of the new organization. On August 18, 1910, the Rotary Club of San Francisco became a charter member of the National Association of Rotary Clubs.

Paul Harris always credited the San Francisco club for much of the early success of Rotary and the eventual winning over of the Chicago club members to the goal of Rotary extension. In addition to attributing extension on the Pacific Coast to the "splendid efforts" of the San Francisco club, Paul later wrote, "The state of mind both outside and inside the membership was, 'Show me.' The Pacific coast epidemic did that very thing. . . . One after another they dropped into the hopper. There were a tidy sixteen to assemble at the first convention in 1910." Indeed, of the first sixteen clubs, five owe their beginning directly to the actions of Homer Wood and members of the San Francisco club (San Francisco, Tri-City, Seattle, Los Angeles, and New York). Moreover, SF Rotarians' activities were an indirect cause of the Rotary wheel beginning to turn in Tacoma and Portland—Roy Denny of Seattle visited these cities and spread the seeds there.

Now an official national movement, Rotary flourished. By the end of 1911, the Rotary family had grown by fifteen new clubs, located throughout the country. Ever the visionary, Paul Harris was more sure of the soundness of the Rotary ideal than ever. He imagined it even spreading outside the United States. About the triumph of creating a national organization, he wrote, "The success achieved served to stimulate ambitions for greater

"In those early days, the original Rotary idea hit Homer Wood harder than anyone else, for here was the first real missionary of Rotary."

—Arthur Holman, founding member of SF Rotary, 1938

things. The welding of the forces into a national unit encouraged dreams of an international unit to include many, if not all nations."

As early as six months after the founding of SF Rotary, Paul told Homer of a club being formed in Glasgow. However, the new club did not materialize. But in fact, even as Rotary in the United States was spreading after the successful convention in Chicago, Rotary was going international. Ches Perry, the new secretary of the National Association of Rotary Clubs, learned that a former Chicago resident had moved to Winnipeg, Manitoba, Canada, and had started a Rotary club in November 1910. Upon hearing the news, Ches wrote to the club and urged it to join the association. The Winnipeg club joined Rotary in March 1912. When the fact was announced at the Duluth Convention later that year, the delegates unanimously voted to change the organization's name to the International Association of Rotary Clubs. In 1922, Rotary would change its name to Rotary International. (For simplicity's sake, Rotary will be referred to as RI in the remainder of this book.)

At the Portland Convention in 1911, Paul Harris announced he was so confident of Rotary in other countries that he had taken it upon himself to pursue the formation of clubs in London, Paris, Glasgow, Melbourne, and Sydney. With its close cultural ties to America, Britain was the obvious place to start. Paul had enlisted the help of a traveling Boston Rotarian to help start a club in London. They were successful, and the London club coalesced in August 1911, just before the Portland Convention was to begin. Paul also dispatched Rotarians to start a club in Manchester that same month. But Paul was in for a surprise. As he recalled, he was "pluming myself on having initiated the first two British Clubs," when he heard about Stuart Morrow.

Stuart was a San Francisco Rotarian who had returned to his native Ireland early in 1911. A professional organizer, Stuart had established a Rotary club in Dublin in February, but had not told Rotary in Chicago about it. Moreover, by the time the news reached Paul Harris, Stuart was within days of organizing another club in Belfast.

When Paul learned of Stuart's accomplishments, he wrote Stuart and asked him to continue his work in the British Isles. The former SF Rotary member started clubs in Glasgow, Edinburgh, Birmingham, and Liverpool, as well as local clubs in the London metropolitan area. Stuart might have continued on at Paul's request to go to Australia and New Zealand, but he fell out of favor when it was discovered that he was selling Rotary memberships for a guinea each. He disappeared from Rotary and was not heard of again for some time.[9]

9. Later, Rotarians learned that Stuart had returned to Oakland, where he founded the women's service organization called Soroptomist Clubs of America. He reappeared in London again, to present a charter to the Greater London Soroptomist Club.

In 1914, the Rotary clubs in Britain and Ireland announced the formation of the British Association of Rotary Clubs (BARC). It was not initially affiliated with Rotary's international association, but in 1921, BARC became a separate territorial administration unit within RI, called Rotary International in Great Britain and Ireland (RIBI), which it remains today.

As Rotary clubs were being founded in the British Isles, several attempts were under way to establish clubs in continental Europe. But efforts were stalled with the commencement of World War I, and it appeared that the spread of Rotary might plateau. One individual's failed attempt to form a club in Havana, Cuba, led him to inform Paul Harris that Rotary was "an Anglo-Saxon idea that could not be understood or accepted by other races." Three Florida Rotarians proved him wrong, and a Havana club debuted in 1916. South America gained its first club in 1918, and Rotary reached Asia in 1919, with the establishment of clubs in Manila and Shanghai.

Although men had been meeting in Paris since 1918, the first officially recognized club on the European mainland was formed in Madrid after the war. The following year, Canadian Rotarians took the message of Rotary to Australia, and a club was established in Melbourne. When a club was organized in Johannesburg, South Africa, in 1921, Rotary truly became a worldwide organization, with clubs on all of the inhabited continents of the earth.[10]

SF Rotary—The Roots Spread Farther

SF Rotarians continued to play a significant role in extension in California and elsewhere. In 1913, a Sacramento man, Tom Warrington, was a guest at a SF Rotary luncheon meeting at Techau Tavern. He suggested the club start Rotary in California's capital. SF Rotarians agreed, and after a preliminary meeting, a committee from San Francisco went to Sacramento. San Francisco member Joe Thieben had connections in that city, and within one day, the committee signed up thirty prospective members. Within a few weeks, SF Rotary and Oakland sent a joint delegation to help install the new Rotary Club of Sacramento. Early the following year, SF Rotary President Henry "Bru" Brunnier led a group to San Jose to meet with several men interested in Rotary. Only a few weeks later, the charter meeting established the Rotary Club of San Jose. In December, Bru Brunnier (this time as district governor) installed the Rotary Club of Fresno after preliminary work by Oakland Rotarians. The ceremony was attended by Rotarians from San Francisco, Oakland, Stockton, and San Jose. During his year as district governor of the large first western district, Bru traveled to Albuquerque and Reno, and started clubs there—the first in their respective states. District Governor Bru presented other new clubs in his district with their charters as well.

Bru continued to be instrumental in forming other clubs for many years thereafter. In 1920, for instance, Bru and Rusty Rogers arranged the formation and organization of the Santa Rosa club. Bru and two other SF Rotarians helped form a club in Richmond later that year, and he fostered the founding of the Eureka club in 1923. For decades, it was the practice of SF Rotary to send a congratulatory delegation to the chartering ceremony of a new club, whether or not the San Francisco

---

10. Rotary entered Antarctica in 1997, with the chartering of a club at Base Marambio. The Rotary seed was also planted in cyberspace with the chartering of eClub One in 2001. This is Rotary's first club whose operations are supported by electronic communications, phone, and Internet (http://www.rotaryeclubone.org/).

Reminiscing at the thirty-fifth anniversary of the Rotary Club of Los Angeles. (left to right: Walton Wood of Los Angeles; Bru Brunnier, Homer Wood, and Arthur Holman of San Francisco; and Roy Denny, who founded the Seattle Club.)
—The Rotarian, *September 1944*

club was instrumental in the new club's founding. Bru was often present at these ceremonies.

In addition to its contributions to the founding of many clubs, SF Rotary also recognized that its status as Rotary #2 and the largest western club carried a responsibility to smaller, newer clubs. In 1921 it reported the formation of "flying squadrons" of fifteen to thirty SF Rotarians who visited and held programs for fledgling clubs around Northern California. The Inter-City Committee reiterated its commitment to this plan in 1928, as an effort "to carry the life of Rotary, as it is understood in the larger clubs, to the smaller clubs in their surrounding territory."

Although Homer Wood bid farewell to San Francisco in 1911 to resume his earlier career as a newspaperman, he never lost his love for Rotary, nor his ability to get things done. Twelve years later, yearning for Rotary, Homer founded the Rotary Club of Petaluma and became its charter president.

Members of Rotary #2 can look to their place in the history of Rotary extension as unique in all the Rotary world. In this regard, it is worth noting that in 1942, the Rotary Club of Washington, DC, held a meeting program honoring SF Rotary, with SF Rotarian Warren McBryde as Chairman of the Day. In 1977, District Governor Art Agnew estimated that fully one-half of the 17,800 Rotary clubs then in existence could probably trace their lineage back to the early work of Homer Wood, Arthur Holman, Roy Rogers, Clarence Wetmore, Bru Brunnier, and other SF Rotarians.

▨ ▨ ▨

In the broadest sense of service club extension, Rotary has a remarkable distinction in United States and world history. Founded in 1905, it grew to a national, then international association of service clubs—the first and only in the nation and the world—by 1912. The organization's reputation for service and fellowship spread, and others followed suit. Three years after Rotary went international, the Lions Club originated in San Antonio, Texas, in 1915. Two years later, 150 Lions clubs met and named their new affiliation the International Association of Lions Clubs. Kiwanis was started as a businessmen's club in Detroit in 1915. The organization expanded, and it adopted the name "Kiwanis International" in 1924. In the thirteen years after Rotary became an international service organization, fifteen or more national and international service federations were formed. In 2005, Rotary International celebrated its Centennial. Its legacy as the forerunner of organizations that bring millions of volunteers to address humanitarian problems of the world has no equal. As Rotary #2 commemorates its Centennial in 2008, it does so in the knowledge that it has contributed inestimably to this legacy.

chapter two

From Back-Scratching to Service: The Question of Purpose

We must have more in mind, more to plan on than simply our luncheons.

—*Grindings* (SF Rotary newsletter), 1915

Like Rotary clubs everywhere, SF Rotary prides itself mostly on its service to the community and the world. In 100 years, the club's members have accomplished innumerable good works for the city of San Francisco and for less-fortunate souls everywhere. This, however, was not always the case. When Rotary was founded in 1905, it had no model of a "service club" to look to for inspiration. As a different kind of business club, it was striking out on its own. The new Rotary Club of San Francisco faced the same difficulty in 1908. It took a number of years for the way to become clear.

The Rise and Decline of Boosting

As the new club got underway, Homer and the other early members busied themselves putting the basic club mechanics into place. Once that was done, a level of confusion set in. The club had been founded for two seemingly separate purposes: a club for the betterment of San Francisco, and a club to advance the business interests of its members. Which was it to be?

Civic Interest Gives Way to Back-Scratching

The notion of civic betterment was inherent in SF Rotary's purpose from the start. As Homer began his earliest efforts to organize a Rotary club in San Francisco, he emphasized a role for Rotary in civic interest and service. The keynote of his speech at the founding banquet was his vision of a business club where civic boosting and business advantage were closely intertwined. The constitution and bylaws (which were taken from the Chicago club's constitution and bylaws) were adopted at SF Rotary's founding banquet. They included "the advancement of the best interests of San Francisco, and the spreading of civic pride and loyalty among its citizens" as SF Rotary's third Object.[11] To carry out this third Object, a Civic Committee was among the ten standing committees called for in the new club's bylaws.

---

11. In addition to the first two Objects—promotion of business interest and promotion of good fellowship.

This intent to advance the best interest of San Francisco predominated in SF Rotary's activities for the first few months. At the club's second dinner meeting in January 1909, for example, Rotarians discussed and supported ship-subsidy legislation. They also appointed committees to work with other organizations favoring the building of a civic auditorium and to cooperate with plans for a Carnival Week on Portola Drive. A matter concerning the need for fire-alarm systems in the downtown area was referred to the Civic Committee. Homer wrote to Paul Harris that SF Rotary was going on record as the first organization to start the promotion of the Home-Coming Celebration and Carnival—a big celebration to take place on the third anniversary of the San Francisco earthquake and fire. Subsequent monthly meetings featured prominent speakers who discussed matters of civic interest. As a result—and with active effort by Sam Johnston's Publicity Committee—the club consistently received favorable publicity in the press.

As the months went on, however, it became clear that this emphasis did not sit well with the many members who had joined the club for business advantage. Within four months of the club's founding, a member suggested that "Commercial Fraternalism" be included as a subject for meeting talks. The following month, the meeting included a lecture by the local manager of the Sheldon School of Scientific Salesmanship. Club members carried a motion to have an appointed club member speak about his line of business at each monthly banquet meeting.

Many club members were dissatisfied with Homer's failure to lead the club in a more business-oriented direction. Prospective members had been induced to join for the reason given in the club constitution's first Object—"the promotion of the business interests of its members." They expected business reciprocity—"back-scratching"—as a way to increase their business, and they viewed the club as growing away from its original purpose. Enthusiasm waned, and attendance at meetings soon became a problem.

In response to this pressure, Homer introduced an eight-page Rotary Bulletin in June 1909. Its opening remarks included an emphasis on what many members were expecting from the club: "Rotary Club says frankly and plainly—cultivate your fellow members and use them to get business from; they in turn to do the same with you. . . . Influence all the business of your friends and acquaintances that you can for the benefit of your fellow members. The spirit of reciprocity is strong in Rotary."[12] This theme was reflected more and more in the speakers' topics. Presentation and discussion of civic interest declined, in favor of topics of material interest such as "Better Merchandising Methods."

Near the end of the club's first year, back-scratching with one's fellow members had become the business practice of SF Rotarians: You buy from me, I'll buy from you. Chaired by Sam Johnston, the Ways and Means Committee proposed a rather drastic set of suggestions: 1) members should be highly placed enough in their companies "to place business as well as to secure it," and others should resign (thereby securing "live wires" and dropping "dead timber"); 2) a paid assistant should be hired to collect and keep statistics on business given and secured through Rotary membership; and 3) each week should be designated as a "Booster Week" for one of the members, during which each member

---

12. Homer took this from the Chicago club's roster.

would call on local stores and ask for the product offered by the designated member for that week.

As the annual election approached, Homer Wood was nominated to succeed himself. But a contingent of members calling themselves "The Other Ticket" opposed the Nominating Committee's ticket, instead nominating Sam Johnston for club president. The Other Ticket circulated a printed platform that called for an aggressive business-getting policy, including adoption of the Ways and Means Committee's suggestions. The platform stated its intent for the club "to impress on the minds of all members that they must give as well as take business." The last of the platform's eight planks pledged "to keep before us constantly that the Rotary Club is organized for business first and last and business only."

A Business-Only Club

When the annual meeting banquet

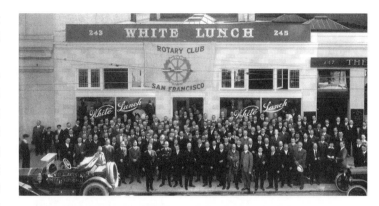

SF Rotarians celebrate the opening of club member Zack White's new restaurant. Courtesy of Moulin Studios Archives

convened in December 1909, Homer was reelected president, over the opposition. Two of the Nominating Committee's opponents from "The Other Ticket," Sam Johnston and James Patrick, were elected to the board.[13]

Soon after the election, Homer and the board acted on the Ways and Means Committee's suggestions by hiring a paid assistant-secretary as a "business-getter." The assistant-secretary was also to present reports on business exchanged between members. Later that year, the club adopted a resolution reflecting the new interpretation of Rotary as a business-only club. It stipulated that the club would work only toward the promotion of members' businesses, and would "eliminate as far as possible any form of civic or other discussion until the actual business interests of its members have been disposed of."

Over the next two years, the club administrations under presidents Homer Wood, Arthur Holman, and M. Louis Wooley initiated various practices designed to enhance members' business

---

13. Despite the opposition, this was not a particularly rancorous election. Two club members appeared on both tickets. Moreover, immediately after the election, James Patrick addressed the club and presented Homer with a beautiful gold watch and fob, "as a token of appreciation from his Rotary friends." Homer carried that watch for decades.

advantage. "Boost Week" generated a demand throughout the city for members' products, as Rotarians (and their wives) descended on stores in the city, asking for those products and insisting they be stocked. Members were encouraged to get to know other members by calling on them at their places of business. SF Rotarians adopted the "roll call"—an on-again-off-again tradition that persisted into the late 1930s. As each member's name was called, he responded with a snappy one-liner that described his business. At some luncheons, members could give ten-minute advertising talks about their goods and services or those of fellow Rotarians. Some members offered merchandise prizes. The luncheon tables were covered with advertising literature, and special shelves were reserved so members could display their merchandise. Self-promotion and reciprocal trading were the order of the day, and few meetings passed without some reference to that fact. Since each member was the sole representative of his business classification, he faced no business competition within the club. All members were expected to trade only with him to meet their needs. Anyone needing accident insurance, for instance, would give that business to Arthur Holman, who held the classification of Accident Insurance;

The first Boost Week on record took place in September 1910, as that month's board minutes suggested that "every member of the Rotary Club buy a bottle of 'Celso' at the drugstore near his residence, and also buy a bottle at some downtown drugstore."

Arthur, in turn, was expected to give as much of his business to other club members as possible. Members were occasionally asked during roll call how many orders they had placed with other members in the past week. One week, Bru Brunnier outpaced other members by placing seventy different orders with his fellow Rotarians. (At the time, he was furnishing his new office in the Monadnock Building.) The Grievance Committee (later called the Adjustment Committee) addressed the complaints of members who felt they did not properly receive other Rotarians' business.

It should be mentioned here that, although SF Rotarians took their businesses seriously, they were jolly fellows. Much of this self-promotion and reciprocity took place in an atmosphere of camaraderie and good fun. Members carried out elaborate "stunts" to advertise their businesses, and often touted their products in silly limericks or puns.

Has the Rotary Club "Made Good"?

This was the question posed by member Ben Dixon in SF Rotary's *Spokes* newsletter in May 1911. Ben listed the business he had gotten from and given to other club members during 1910, "making a total of $58,587.28." He added that this was a "decided increase over 1909."

This intense focus on gaining business does not mean early SF Rotarians were not concerned with their city or were not service-minded—many of them were. On the morning after the club's founding banquet, the newspaper listed several club members among a group of men traveling to Los Angeles by train. They were traveling to a gathering of the California Promotion Committee, an organization formed to convince important city representatives to support each other and to boost for the state of California as a whole. And even as it explicitly took up back-scratching as its stated purpose,

SF Rotary continued to engage in a few matters of civic service. At the December 1909 annual meeting in which the "Other Ticket" opposed Homer Wood over the interests of greater business promotion, the club donated $50 to the city's Portola Festival committee, to help the committee make up its deficiency for the Portola Festival.

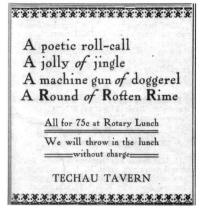

A poetic roll-call
A jolly *of* jingle
A machine gun *of* doggerel
A Round *of* Roften Rime

All for 75c at Rotary Lunch
We will throw in the lunch
———without charge———

TECHAU TAVERN

A Grindings *notice for this week's "Roll Call," 1914.*

One particular club activity for the civic good during this period stands out: SF Rotary's efforts to advance the city's goal of holding a world's fair. The planned 1915 Panama-Pacific International Exposition (PPIE) would celebrate the opening of the Panama Canal, scheduled for 1914 after eleven years of construction. A fierce competition for the privilege of hosting the exposition had narrowed the field to New Orleans and San Francisco. World's fairs could bring enormous economic benefits to cities, and San Francisco's civic leaders had a special reason for wanting to host the fair at that particular time. They hoped to showcase the city's spectacular recovery from the 1906 earthquake and fire, and to show the world that San Francisco was once again a vital, thriving city in which to do business.

Early in 1910, SF Rotary initiated its energetic crusade to bring the fair to San Francisco, in cooperation with the Chamber of Commerce and other civic organizations. Among other measures, the club enlisted the support of the nation's thirteen other Rotary clubs to join its telegram campaign, lobbying Congress and other leaders to choose San Francisco. The club also sent members as part of a California promotional delegation to Washington, DC.

On January 31, 1911, SF Rotary was meeting at Techau Tavern when word reached the club that San Francisco had been chosen for the Exposition. Jubilation broke out, champagne was opened, and the tavern's doors were locked to keep the members from spilling out into the street. The Rotarians voted unanimously to launch a parade down Market Street to celebrate. Although club Secretary Rusty Rogers could not recall ("thanks to the champagne") who had the idea for a parade, he wrote that:

> In the excitement, another good Rotarian suggested a band would be a good thing to lend dignity and noise to the occasion, and a committee consisting of Hoyt, Tooker, and Rosenblum were appointed to secure a band immediately, while Sam Johnston was appointed a Special Collector to extract $1.00 apiece from all those present to defray the expenses. Johnston got the dollar, Hoyt got the band, Wasserman furnished everybody with a flag, Cohen did some rapid-fire work in making two large parade signs. John W. Hoyt was elected Band Master, President Holman was elected Drill Major, and at 2 o'clock the members started down Market Street to the ferry, one hundred strong. The snowball grew as it went down Market Street, and by the time it reached the Merchants Exchange, carried in its wake a great throng!

SF Rotary Club leads a parade down Market Street to celebrate hearing that the 1915 Panama-Pacific International Exposition will be held in San Francisco. —San Francisco Examiner, *February 1, 1911*

Rusty added that Rotarians had secured the services of "four husky policemen," to keep the growing crowd from overwhelming the marchers and band. Despite the inclement weather, the Rotarians and marchers had such a good time, they turned around at the Ferry Building and continued marching (perhaps back to the tavern).

Just before the exuberant Rotarians marched out the tavern door, President Arthur Holman initiated an action to rid San Francisco of vice prior to the fair. He pledged a special committee and the club's 225 members to helping the chief of police stamp out illegal gambling in the city and clean up corruption in the police department. Shortly afterward, the club named a committee to plan a fund-raising effort, to entertain the great numbers of Rotarians expected to visit the fair.

Issues and actions such as these suggest an ambivalence in the new club's membership about the appropriate balance of Rotary purpose from the very beginning. Nonetheless, these moments of civic action by SF Rotary did not overshadow members' larger perception of their club or their reason for joining. Charter members living in 1940 made it clear to historian William Mountin that civic boosting took second place to reciprocal trading as the way to induce businessmen to join the club.

SF Rotary Speaks Out Against Vice

"We are going to have a great fair here, and prosperity. We have got to have a clean city to hold it in, and we are going to have one."

—Arthur Holman, in the *San Francisco Bulletin*, February 2, 1911

The national Rotary organization grappled with the issue of Rotary's purpose during this period as well. In fact, much of the work done at annual conventions formed the basis of Rotary's philosophy today. At the first 1910 Convention in Chicago, delegates debated the extent to which local clubs should address civic betterment, as well as the issue of acceptable business methods. They set five Objectives for the new National Association of Rotary Clubs:

1. To organize new clubs

2. To promote the common good of all clubs

3. To encourage civic pride and loyalty

4. To promote honorable business methods

5. To advance the business interests of the individual members

The following year in Portland, convention delegates from the thirty-six clubs debated a "Portland Platform." Proposed by a national committee, the platform outlined a Rotarian's responsibility for fair and honest dealings.[14] The 1911 Convention delegates also adopted a new motto for Rotary: "He profits most who serves best." Later in 1911, National Association President Paul Harris urged clubs to discontinue the practice of business-trading. A few months afterward, he removed the organization's statistician—who reported on business exchanges—from the organization's list of officers. At the 1912 Convention, delegates adopted the Portland Platform, and gave official approval to five Objects of Rotary, which clearly included aspects of responsibility to civic interests. They also adopted another motto that would become a venerable Rotary tradition: "Service Above Self." These redefinitions of Rotary's purpose came about for a number of commendable reasons. However, they were also in part an acknowledgment of increased public criticism of Rotary's trading practices, which shut out other businesses.

Throughout these distant debates and refinements of Rotary ideals, the San Francisco club members showed little interest in pursuing a direction that would detract from their club's usefulness as a business tool. A little attention to civic issues was acceptable, but when a citizen suggested in 1911 that the club follow the Chicago club's example and establish public comfort stations downtown, SF Rotary's board's response was "that while the Rotary Club is thoroughly in harmony with the suggestions embodied in the letter, the spirit of Rotary is entirely foreign to civic matters." Nor were members interested in discontinuing practices aimed toward generating business for members. Instead, they continued with business interest as their club's foremost purpose (as did a number of other Rotary clubs).

During this time, Homer Wood decided to return to the newspaper business and move to Salinas. He tendered his resignation to the club in January 1911, immediately after his second term as club president. The board regretfully accepted his resignation, and voted him a lifetime Honorary Member of SF Rotary. We do not know today what effect his leaving had on the club, but it surely made a difference in the balance of club sentiment concerning the club's primary reason for its existence.

By the end of M. Louis Wooley's presidential term in 1912, SF Rotary's drive to create mutual business exchange between members was backfiring on the club. It was leading to excesses,

PAUL HARRIS WEIGHS IN

"This business-getting feature of Rotary looks dangerous to me. What will people think of us? I am a member of several clubs and societies all of which rank high in our city and I know it to be a fact that in one of them at least soliciting business is strictly prohibited and in all it is tabooed. In my personal estimation it constitutes the personification of bad form. Clubs are meant for club purposes and not for business purposes."

—Paul Harris, in the first issue of *The National Rotarian*, January 1911

---

14. SF Rotary member Sam Johnston was a member of the national committee.

such as the practice of intentionally embarrassing members who were perceived as not trading sufficiently with their fellow Rotarians. Meetings were becoming semisecret, in an attempt to guard against outside perceptions of a closed system of business trade. Nevertheless, other businessmen in San Francisco and elsewhere were increasingly hostile toward Rotary and Rotarians, from whom they could expect no return for business given. Nationally, Rotarians began to fear an organized boycott against their businesses, and the national leadership sent out instructions on "How to Meet All Boycotts." In 1913, nonmembers in Kansas City actually did boycott Rotary businesses. By 1913, attendance was as low as 50 percent, and members—many of them the club's most prominent businessmen—were resigning. Clearly, it was time for a change.

Away from Back-Scratching

The change that began in 1913 was not a revolution. Rotarians did not discontinue promoting their businesses. They continued with roll call and all the other entertaining gimmicks to advertise their goods and services. And they continued to trade with each other. What did change gradually was the spirit and manner in which it was accomplished.

Historian William Mountin observed in his history of SF Rotary in 1940 that club members began to appreciate and make the most of one of their club's best qualities: it enabled a businessman to develop genuine, close friendships. In 1913, club Secretary Rusty Rogers made up a clever little slogan that appeared periodically in the *Grindings* newsletter for years:

> *Attendance begets Acquaintance,*
> *Acquaintance begets Friendship,*
> *Friendship begets Confidence,*
> *Confidence begets Business.*

Rusty's slogan summed up many SF Rotarians' realization that mutually beneficial business relationships could develop naturally as men came to know and trust one another, not through obligatory, frenetic back-scratching. It was what Paul Harris had envisioned, but was nearly forgotten in the headlong rush to trade business. The key lay in the fellowship offered by the Rotary Club—and attendance at meetings.

SF Rotary directed its efforts toward two matters: improving attendance (which had never been good) and maximizing the opportunity for each member to get to know as many other members as possible. Attempts to improve attendance involved constantly reminding members of their attendance obligation (in 1913, the bylaws required attendance at three meetings out of nine), and explaining the business potential if only they would come to meetings.

The club had a brand-new medium for all of this—the eight-page *Grindings* newsletter. From its very first issue in 1913, *Grindings* was jam-packed with enticing notices about opportunities for members to publicize their businesses and to make new business acquaintances at the weekly meeting. One issue included a picture of a member with the caption, "Who is Doyle? Why doesn't Doyle come?"—a clear message that no one knew Doyle (or would buy from him) because he wasn't at the meetings. Another issue raised the possibility of having members pay for lunch whether they attended or not (an idea that has been resurrected periodically throughout the club's history).[15]

Once Doyle came to the weekly luncheon, he expected to publicize his business and to make new friends. Rotary hit on the means for both. Doyle didn't stop touting his own products, but he started touting the other fellows' products as well. The year 1913 signaled the start of what Mountin has called "The Boosting Era," when SF Rotarians began in earnest to boost for each other.

They boosted in a number of ways. No luncheon program failed to include time for testimonials or other novel ways to praise a fellow member's goods and services—invariably in unrestrained superlative terms. At a "Fellowship Meeting" program, Rotarians gave one-minute talks about other members. At other meetings, a man answered roll call by describing the business of the man sitting to his right, rather than his own.

In addition to getting one's business publicized in this indirect way, the practice of boosting accomplished another goal: that of increasing acquaintance. In order to boost the other fellow, the Rotarian needed to get to know him. In addition to the usual "fellowship" period before the program began, this was accomplished in a number of ways. Sometimes members were given two minutes to converse with the men seated next to them, each knowing he would subsequently be called upon to introduce his seatmate to the rest of the gathering. In 1913 the group tried a rotating lunch for the first time—rotating between the tables at Techau Tavern, with the goal of everyone meeting and striking up an acquaintance with someone new.

Grindings played a central role in the process of members becoming acquainted and boosting one another. The newsletter's first year often included "Boostlets"—small ads for new members written by someone else ("Little Boosts for the New Members who may not have learned to boost for themselves"). The earlier practice of Boost Week continued, and Rotarians were encouraged to drop in to visit the week's designated member—to get to know him in his place of business. The back page of *Grindings* was customarily given over to a paid Boost Week advertisement for the member of the week.

Boosting by no means displaced self-promotion at luncheons and in *Grindings* print. One meeting was entitled "A Megaphone Meeting,"

A Boost Week advertisement on the back page of Grindings, *1914.*

---

15. Whether the enticements actually improved attendance is a matter for debate. Over time, *something* worked. By December 1919, the club of nearly three hundred boasted the best attendance of large Rotary clubs (over two hundred members) in the world. The club's administration credited its program of new member orientation and the high quality of its luncheon programs. Its recommendations for improving attendance subsequently appeared in *The Rotarian* (RI's magazine).

because everyone present was "given an opportunity to blow his own horn." In 1914, a few members each week gave three-minute talks about their businesses. Prizes were given for the best talks. The following year, Rotarians were given the opportunity to pay $10 per minute to give a five-minute promotional talk at a luncheon. In the new world of electrification, SF Rotary held an informative all-electrical meeting, featuring members who were in the businesses of providing lighting, wiring, electrical appliances, and so on. A well-publicized creative variation in 1914 required close cooperation between members. In anticipation of the influx of visitors expected in the city during the upcoming world's fair, several luncheon presentations over three months consisted of an elaborate stunt to demonstrate the breadth of Rotarian business. Dozens of members gave presentations describing how they would build, furnish, and operate a hypothetical fifteen-story hotel. All of the Rotarians who were architects, contractors, electricians, and so on participated, as well as the suppliers of everything a hotel needs, from bedding to signage to flowers to taxicabs. Other Rotarians provided hypothetical management of the project, plus a grand opening complete with music.

Grindings Boosts for Rotarians

To talk of biz, in most of Clubs,
Is extremely infra-dig,
But Rotary for that rule cares not
One solitary fig.

So when at lunch we all sit down
And Roll Call quickly starts,
We hear of Shoes, and Hats, and Stoves,
And Lumber, Lime, and Carts.

We have some members who can talk,
And talk to beat the band,
Even Pratt becomes quite eloquent
About Gravel, Brick, and Sand.

Hot water you can surely get
With economy at the meter,
If you let Basford furnish you
With a Ruud Automatic Heater.

These foolish rhymes have been compiled
To give us all a hunch,
That cheery smile is worth the while,
At Tuesday's weekly lunch.

—*Grindings*, Feb 1, 1916

Despite its intensity through 1913 and 1914, boosting of other members did not go on forever. Members grew tired of it, and their willingness to expend the time and energy it had demanded of them fell off sharply, despite frequent exhortations at meetings and in *Grindings*. Historian William Mountin put it concisely in 1940, when he explained, "In its final analysis, boosting was just a modified form of back-scratching adopted, unwittingly perhaps, as a forced compromise when the idea of using Rotary as a closed unit for business exchange broke down in 1913." Indeed, the old excesses had not been done away with. As late as 1915, one of club Secretary Howard Feighner's duties after everyone was seated at the luncheon was to go out and check every hat band to see that no member had bought a hat from anyone except the man in the club holding the classification of "Men's Hats Retailing."

Years later the business-getting practices of 1909–15 would be looked upon with embarrassment. SF Rotary (and other clubs) became self-conscious about Rotary's image as a gang of back-scratchers—so much so, in fact, that many Rotarians grew hesitant about the perceived propriety of doing business with each other at all. In a widely circulated and republished article in 1923, *Grindings* had to remind club members that, although using Rotary as a means of seeking business was improper, one need not fear that doing business with another Rotarian should be misunderstood as taking advantage of a fellow Rotarian, since all Rotarians have a business service to offer. Membership should not be regarded a bar to ethical business communication.

> THE VIEW BACK TO 1911
> "Yesterday's business procedure was a system of secret rebates, special privileges, control of politics by corporate interests, that had the acceptance of the time in which we lived."
>
> —*Grindings*, August 3, 1926

To be sure, business promotion did not disappear entirely—it never has. For years after the boosting era, *Grindings* shows SF Rotarians actively promoting their businesses, and occasionally those of their fellow members, during luncheon meetings. But never again was it done with the fervor seen in the club's first seven years. Even as boosting started its decline, the club was already undergoing the transformation of its purpose to something new and lasting—and that was service.

A New Outlook—Service for San Francisco

Service in the Rotary Club is not an ideal but a responsibility, and this responsibility lies on the shoulders of every man.

—SF Rotarian Charles Devens Holman, 1913

Late in the boosting era, SF Rotarians deliberated over their club's purpose. Surveys were taken and speeches were made by members, expressing a wide range of opinions. The work done at the national conventions in 1910, 1911, and 1912 had crystallized the Portland Platform, added new Objects to the statement of Rotary purpose, and introduced the motto "He profits most who serves best."

These ideas entered into the thinking of SF Rotarians, as they considered how to give their club meaning, apart from merely serving to attract business. President Harold Basford (1912–13) was an early crusader for the altruistic development of Rotary. He argued that "scratch my back" could not sustain such a club, and the club must develop an unselfish ideal. In 1914, a *Grindings* article suggested that the way to answer "What is Rotary?" would be with a single word: "Service-ness—full of the spirit of service, and the desire and willingness to serve and be of value to others." *Grindings* editorialized that Rotarians must turn their minds to something, and "some specific lines of activity must be adopted. We must have more in mind, more to plan on than simply our luncheons."

Civic Service—For the City

As SF Rotary turned toward service, its first efforts were directed toward civic betterment—service for the good of the city of San Francisco. Rotarians correctly viewed themselves as upstanding citizens, with a personal duty to improve civic life. Their natural impulse for their club was to work for improvements that would bring tourists and new companies—and new customers for themselves. Consequently, their first efforts were aimed at boosting San Francisco—promoting it as an attractive, clean, modern city.

There was no lack of reason or opportunity to boost for the city—the Panama-Pacific International Exposition was on its way. And there was much work to do. From the January day in 1911 when word came that San Francisco was to host the Exposition, SF Rotarians threw themselves into promoting the fair and the city of San Francisco. Club members postscripted their correspondence with phrases such as "We expect you in San Francisco in 1915." In anticipation of entertaining visiting Rotarians at the fair, the club built up a fund with pledges, donations, and a percentage of sales receipts from business between members. SF Rotary had a direct hand in the formation of the Tourists' Association, organized to induce tourists to come to San Francisco and the Bay Area.

From its introduction in 1913, *Grindings* devoted half of its front page most weeks to boosting San Francisco—praising the city's temperate climate, its quality and quantity of restaurants, and its friendly citizens' welcoming spirit. *Grindings* also drummed up evangelical enthusiasm among its members, declaring that "two hundred members of the Rotary Club can educate the whole of San Francisco into a community of chronic boosters, and do the biggest service ever rendered our

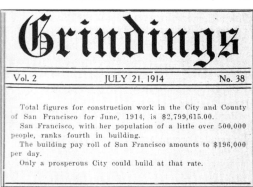

Grindings *boosts for San Francisco, 1914.*

City." It encouraged club members to become knowledgeable about the Exposition, in order to explain it to their friends and colleagues. From *Grindings'* inception until the fair closed in December 1915 nearly three years later, the newsletter maintained a high level of enthusiasm, as it encouraged SF Rotarians to do their part to welcome the world to San Francisco.

Club members participated in most of the city's promotional and ceremonial events. Only weeks before the Exposition's opening, over two hundred SF Rotarians and their wives attended the Exposition Ball, celebrating the opening of the new Civic Auditorium, of which the club had been an early and staunch supporter.

By far, the grandest Rotary promotion for the Exposition was the "Golden Wheel." Conceived and built by the Rotary Club of Los Angeles, the Golden Wheel was a dazzling object—a fourteen-inch-wide cogged wheel containing a smaller wheel for each of the seven California clubs. San Francisco's wheel contained the official seal of the Exposition. *Grindings* reported that the Golden Wheel was made of solid gold loaned by Sacramento and to have cost $10,000, paid for by subscription from California Rotarians. It was initially sent to the Rotary clubs around California. After visiting SF Rotary's luncheon meeting, the wheel was placed in the window of the *San Francisco Call* newspaper, where it attracted such a crowd of viewers that the police were required to clear the sidewalk so pedestrians could pass by.

A Grindings *cover photograph of the "Golden Wheel," 1914. The San Francisco wheel is at the "11 o'clock" position.*

The "Golden Wheel," complete with small Rotary club wheels from cities it visited on its tour prior to the Panama-Pacific International Exposition. —Grindings, February 9, 1915

The wheel was subsequently presented to the International Association of Rotary Clubs at the 1914 Convention in Houston. It then visited the 125 Rotary cities in the United States and Great Britain, as a direct invitation for all who saw it to come to California in 1915.[16] Everywhere it went, it was displayed under police guard, attracting large crowds drawn by newspaper publicity. Arriving back in San Francisco in 1915, it was put on display in the Fine Arts Gallery at the Exposition.

Despite the outbreak of war in Europe, the Exposition opened on schedule in February 1915, with most of the major nations of Europe participating. It attracted nearly 250,000 visitors the first day. The fair was a wonder. It covered 635 acres of what later became San Francisco's Marina

---

16. Both Northern California and Southern California were eager to attract visitors to California in 1915, as San Diego held its own fair—the Panama-California Exposition—from 1915 through 1916.

The Panama-Pacific International Exposition, 1915.

district. Among the palaces, courts, and state and foreign buildings, the grandest was the "Tower of Jewels." Standing forty-three stories tall, the Tower was hung with more than 100,000 colored-glass jewels that dangled individually to shimmer and reflect light. At night, enormous electric spotlights (a novelty) lit the dazzling structure.

Rotarians hosted visitors in their homes and offered transportation. They took schoolchildren on tours of the fair. The Entertainment Committee hosted a 2,500-guest banquet at the Yellowstone Park "Old Faithful Inn" exhibit. SF Rotary's hospitality increased tenfold as club members welcomed Rotarians from all over the world to the RI Convention in July (see chapter 8).

One of the highlights of the Exposition took place in the late afternoon of SF Rotary's seventh anniversary in November. Two hundred twenty-five club members gathered at the Palace of Liberal Arts, in the demonstration hall of the American Telephone and Telegraph Company. Simultaneously, 350 members of the Rotary Club of Albany, New York, were sitting down to an elaborate dinner. The Rotarians in both cities gathered to participate in a long-distance call from Albany to San Francisco, dubbed "The Albany-San Francisco Rotary Transcontinental Telephone Demonstration." Carefully arranged by AT&T, the call was relayed from city to city through thirteen states, over 130,000 telephone poles, and reached San Francisco, 3,400 miles away. The call was orchestrated to last one hour and seven minutes. It started with a roll call of the participants, each with an individual telephone set in front of him. Paul Harris spoke via a tie-in from Chicago. Then the mayors of each city conversed, as did the presidents and officers of each club. Several club members in their respective business classifications spoke to their Albany counterparts. Afterward, Rusty Rogers sang "Albany, Dear Albany" to the Albany club president, who returned with "I Love You, California" (now California's state song) to SF Rotary President Charles Victor. The Albany Rotarians enjoyed a motion picture of the Pacific Ocean filmed at the Cliff House, while they listened to its roar. The call ended with both clubs singing the "Star Spangled Banner" and other songs. This call was not the first such long-distance call for the club; members had earlier enjoyed a recent similar call with the Rotary Club of New York. But it was a very special way of observing the club's anniversary. It celebrated SF Rotary as a modern club, partaking in the most modern of new technology in the early years of the twentieth century. It was a memorable experience for everyone there, each proud to be a part of the history of American progress.[17]

17. Fortunately, Rotary was not charged for the call. In today's dollars, the bill would have been $8,349.17! On the same November date twenty-eight years later in 1943, the Albany club celebrated the historic date "when Rotary was beginning to strengthen and the telephone lines to lengthen." The Rotary Pioneers, with eighteen of the original participants, held a full program that included reading of a congratulatory letter from SF Rotarian and RI President Charles Wheeler, and other letters from original participants Bru Brunnier and Howard Feighner of San Francisco.

Apart from the Exposition, SF Rotary participated in other events and projects for civic good. It promoted various festive events in the city, such as a "Path of Gold Festival," and a celebration of the new electric street lighting, which the city hoped would enable Market Street to compete with the well-known great avenues and boulevards in America and Europe. The club took a broader view as well. It supported such causes as the Good Roads Bond Issue, and saving the California redwoods.

SF Rotarians worked as well to promote good citizenship among the residents of San Francisco. One Rotarian expressed pride in "the great privilege of Rotarians to mold civic sentiment for better community life." Although the club was limited by Rotary's "no politics" rule, it advocated for an informed citizenry during political elections. For years, the Civic Committee's biggest emphasis was its effort to effect a high rate of public voting in the national elections. In 1920, *Grindings* encouraged club members to instruct their associates and employees to promote participation in the U.S. Census, "so San Francisco may retain her place among the large cities."

Community Service—For the People

Rotary says it is not enough to live and let live; we must live and help live.

—Rotarian Harvey Lyon

As the service ethic emerged as a guiding purpose for SF Rotary and the club began its commitment to civic service in earnest, Rotarians soon realized that their efforts to serve the city were incomplete in their scope. They found that working for civic improvements and boosting San Francisco were worthwhile pursuits, but something was lacking—a commitment to serve the people of the community. Rotarians began looking to the less-fortunate people of San Francisco. From its first decision to help where help was most needed, the club set out on a course of service that created the Rotary spirit of community service we see today.

Help for the Poor

SF Rotary's earliest form of community service began in 1914, when the Ways and Means Committee started donating food and clothing to needy families at Thanksgiving and Christmas, a practice that continued for years. The committee located needy families and distributed retail members' donations of clothing, shoes, and other items requested by the families. In one case, the club provided a sewing machine to a mother who expressed the wish "to earn her own way." National attention became drawn to the benefits of milk in helping growing children gain weight and height, do better in school and athletic activities, and steer away from delinquency. In response, the club added donations of a year's supply of milk to the benefits already offered to destitute families in 1920. The following year, SF Rotary furnished milk for luncheons at public schools for one hundred children.

> "Rotary is at its best when engaged in furthering the cause of community service."
>
> —SF Rotarian Charlie Wheeler

In 1922, the Ways and Means Committee studied the club's charitable work and found that four families receiving help had reached self-sufficiency. Despite favorable results in direct help to families, however, the committee believed the club was not in a position to carry on charity work with individual poor families. This work needed to be carried on by more experienced institutions. Instead, the principal work of the committee would be directed to other community-service programs.

It should be noted that many SF Rotarians contributed as individuals outside the Rotary Club toward assistance to San Francisco's needy. In one year alone, the club proudly pointed to the fact that eighty-three of its members worked on the annual Community Chest Christmas drive.

Work Among the Young

During this time, SF Rotary began to focus its charitable works on the most helpless of San Francisco's citizens—its children. In 1917, the Ways and Means Committee reported that its members visited the San Francisco Nursery for Homeless Children at Christmas, showed the children a movie, and donated a pair of good winter shoes to each child over two years old, most of whom owned no shoes. The committee urged club members to "feel they helped to make many little hearts glad at Christmas time." From that time, the club began a long tradition of bringing a measure of joy into small lives in various ways, including Thanksgiving and Christmas activities and parties.

Also in 1917, the club joined with the Rotary Club of Oakland to entertain Bay Area orphans. The outing was so successful that SF Rotary took it up as an annual event, starting the next year with a party at the Orpheum Theater for 2,500 children from orphanages and hospitals. For a num-

A gathering of orphaned and crippled children in Union Square for an Orpheum Cressy party. A Navy band provided entertainment, 1918.

ber of years, the club hosted large annual parties for the city's orphans and poor children, first at the Orpheum Theater, then in Golden Gate Park. These parties were managed by as many as three hundred Rotarians and wives, until they were discontinued.

SF Rotary's measures to bring momentary happiness to poor and orphaned children, while commendable and worthwhile, were short-lived events, without a continuity that many SF Rotarians felt was needed in the club's charitable work. However, one aspect of the club's service to indigent children was different, in that it was continuous and proved to be lasting. It was in these years that SF Rotary began the children's work that would become a major club focus for decades to come—its work for crippled children.

Mending Small Bodies: Crippled Children's Work

> *What situation pulls more strongly at our heart-strings than to witness the pitiable condition and suffering of some crippled child, whose parents are too poor to provide the required treatment?*

—A San Francisco Rotarian, 1920

In the early twentieth century, America's crippled children were desperately in need of compassion and help. Children were at risk from a number of disabling conditions that struck rich and poor alike—chief among these were infantile paralysis (polio) and "surgical" (bone and joint) tuberculosis. Congenital deformities, rickets from malnutrition, and injuries also exacted a toll. The number of crippled children under age sixteen in U.S. cities was estimated at 264,000.

These souls suffered immensely from their afflictions. In addition to physical pain there were other devastating effects. Most such children were socially isolated, unable to leave their homes or to enjoy normal lives in the company of other children. Worse still, crippled children were usually unable to attend school because of their inability to climb stairs, to sit in standard schoolroom seats, and to return home during the luncheon recess. Physical weaknesses interrupted their classroom participation, and most teachers were ill-equipped to deal with the difficulties presented by these infirmities. Although there was an emerging interest in helping disabled children, most went without sufficient assistance, especially those from poor families. Apart from a smattering of small charitable groups, there were no organized private or governmental agencies dedicated to the care and education of crippled children. Nor were there sufficient facilities available for medical treatment.

Rotary found itself faced with this obvious need and took up the challenge in its first decade. The earliest Rotary efforts on record in helping neglected crippled children were in 1913 by the Rotary Club of Syracuse, New York. Syracuse's work was applauded in a *Rotarian* article,[18] and interest soon spread. Rotarians in Toledo, Ohio, began crippled children's programs, and organized the Toledo Society for Crippled Children. Ohio Rotarians took the lead in this work, and would play a key role in the growth of a movement on an international scale.

RI recognized these endeavors as worthy of Rotary civic service. The "Rotary Handbook on Civics" defined aid to crippled children as among a Rotarian's responsibilities for child welfare. As more clubs initiated projects, RI expanded its official role. Inspired by Ohio Rotarians' activities, convention delegates passed a resolution encouraging Rotary clubs throughout the world to initiate similar projects, with RI acting as a clearinghouse for information. As a result, Rotary districts and local clubs increasingly started projects that included surveys, clinics, publicity, lobbying state legislators, and enlisting hospitals and surgeons to join in the crusade. Rotarians also acknowledged that other organizations were beginning work for crippled children as well; Shriners in particular

---

18. *The Rotarian* is Rotary International's monthly magazine.

had voted in 1919 to initiate what would become their international network of hospitals to treat children with orthopedic defects.

SF Rotary began its work not long after Syracuse and Toledo paved the way. The club's earliest activity was in 1916, when it inaugurated the Charity Box to collect members' fines, which were used to finance a bed in San Francisco Children's Hospital at a cost of thirty dollars per month. The first patient in the "Rotary Bed" was an eleven-year-old boy awaiting a second operation for a deformity caused by infantile paralysis. The club expanded its assistance to crippled children a few years later, when it began financing orthopedic corrective cases at St. Luke's Hospital with the help of Rotarian doctors, and furnishing the hospital with equipment.

This activity inspired a member to voice his recommendations for putting the surplus from the Charity Fund to best possible use through a continuous year-round charity. He viewed general or indiscriminate charity work as "highly impractical for a club of this character," and recommended the club confine its activities to "some definite and distinct line." In proposing a crippled children's program as an endeavor worthy of Rotary, he noted that these children were not being cared for by other local organizations, and pointed to the club membership's "exceptional medical and surgical talent."

The Ways and Means Committee agreed, and shifted its spending philosophy to a focus on treating and curing crippled children. Reporting on the worthy work of helping these children with the assistance of five doctors in the club, it recommended that the work be continued and expanded. Most of the club's available charity funds would go toward work in local hospitals. The committee took cases under consideration with the goal of releasing the children after successful treatment.

1924—The Sunshine School

For decades thereafter, SF Rotary's funding for treatment of crippled and otherwise handicapped children, coupled with the generous services of its member doctors, lifted hundreds of destitute children from their painful and debilitating condition. However, the club's greatest legacy arising from this area of community service lies in its founding of the Sunshine School in 1924.

Impressed by the efforts of Rotary in Toledo in opening a school for crippled children, club President Howell Ware (1923–24) envisioned the possibility that SF Rotary might foster such a school as a true Rotary achievement. Howell appointed a committee to study schools for these "small sufferers" in other cities. A survey by the new Crippled Children's Committee formed the basis of the decision to start a school. It would be modeled after one in Dayton, Ohio, whose founders had understood the disadvantages of placing disabled children in schools with healthier classmates. (Sociologists had claimed that such a disadvantage might lead the child into criminality.) Within months, the SF Board of Education took up the matter enthusiastically and resolved to provide the teachers for the school from the city budget, relieving Rotary of an expense that it had expected to bear. If the school proved successful for one year, the Board of Education agreed to take over the school as part of the public school system.

The Sunshine School opened in the fall of 1924, with seventeen children, and a full capacity of twenty-one was expected by spring. The school's city-owned cottage had been renovated with Rotary funds. It was spotless, well-lighted and heated, and furnished with "an air of cheery comfort." Three capable teachers were selected to teach the children academic, manual, and corrective gymnastic work. Rotary provided for a nurse, furnished equipment and supplies, and funded a hot lunch for the students. Transportation to and from the children's homes was provided by a local taxi company. The transportation itself offered a welcome experience for many of these children, who had never before been out of their homes. The school developed such a solid reputation after its opening that Helen Keller visited and spoke to the children near the end of its first term.

The original location of the Sunshine School, 1924.

Only one month after the school opened, the Board of Education was convinced of the necessity for such a school. The Board took over the entire control of the school at the beginning of the next term, and SF Rotary was relieved of any further responsibility for its maintenance. SF Rotary continued to support the school for years, however. It provided special equipment and services to the school. The club's Thanksgiving and Christmas parties featured entertainment and toys for the children, and summertime brought a picnic at Fleishhacker's Playground. Every Saturday SF Rotarians and their wives drove children to and from a gymnasium.

As a tribute to SF Rotary's founding and support of the school, the 1938 RI Convention in San Francisco chose the school for the convention's Crippled Children's Assembly. Because of its success in educating disabled children and relieving them from their isolation, the school was welcomed and nurtured

Children enjoy party clowns at SF Rotary Club Day at the Sunshine School, 1935. Courtesy of Moulin Studios Archives

A Heartwarming Success

At SF Rotary's luncheon meeting, Dr. Markel "held up little Nadine Gilstar and showed us her pitiably twisted little legs, upon which she has never walked, and told us that in a month, thanks to the surgical and hospital care made possible for her by the money of the Rotary Club, she will have known for the first time in her sad little life what it means to walk and run and play like other children." Amid the handkerchiefs, one of the luncheon tables immediately asked to be her Santa Claus and pledged money to enable the corrective orthopedic work to continue. Only a few short months later, the little girl who had never walked appeared again at the luncheon, and smiled as she walked up and down the head table.

—*Grindings*, December 24, 1929

by the city of San Francisco. By 1940, the school had moved to a new building, funded by the city and federal governments, and had an enrollment of 155 children.

In addition to the opening of the Sunshine School, SF Rotary continued its work of supporting and treating crippled children in five local hospitals. The Ways and Means Committee described this as its principal work that year, and reported that most of the children had been discharged after successful surgery and treatment. As time passed, children were treated by Rotarian doctors for damaged and crippled legs, facial deformities, and tuberculosis. In one four-month period, nineteen children were helped with surgery, bone grafting, braces, special shoes,

artificial arms, crutches, and hydrotherapy.

Miracles such as these would not have been possible without the dedication of individual Rotarian doctors, such as Dr. Howard Markel, who gave untiringly of his time and talents to bringing hope and wholeness through his surgeries. Dr. Markel's interest in crippled children led him to organize a chapter among the city's service organizations to carry on the work of rehabilitation started by SF Rotary. Facial deformities also crippled the lives of children. In 1929, a young girl thanked SF Rotary for nine difficult operations to repair her cleft palate. The surgeries were performed by plastic surgeon Dr. Albert Davis. Some of his cases requiring multiple operations took place over a number of years. He performed cleft-palate surgeries over the next three decades as part of SF Rotary's mission to help children, until he became president of the National Association of Plastic Surgeons in 1956. His work was taken up by Dr. Fred West. Other people

OUR LEADING LADY

Little Nadine Gilstar after surgery and recuperation, shown off by Dr. Markel.
—Grindings, *June 10, 1930*

gave generously of their time as well. *Grindings* asked Rotarians' wives to provide transportation for children to the clinics, so the children would not have to take public transportation by themselves.

For years, Rotary continued to sponsor these services with funds raised from member fines, specific donations, and—using a fund-raising technique of the 1920s—collecting tinfoil of all descriptions. Proceeds from sales of the foil were directed to the maintenance of several beds in the Children's Hospital. In addition, the club committed to financially support the local San Francisco Crippled Children's Guild, starting in 1926.

1926—The California Society for Crippled Children and Easter Seals

While SF Rotary was alleviating the suffering of handicapped children in San Francisco, Ohio provided national leadership in the field. Elyria, Ohio was the home of Edgar F. "Daddy" Allen, a wealthy businessman who emerged as the powerhouse in Rotary's international work with crippled children.

Allen lost his son in a disastrous streetcar accident in 1907. Upon receiving the heartbreaking news, he also learned his son's life might have been spared had there been an adequate hospital in the town. He took upon himself the daunting task of raising the money to open a hospital. A few years later, he met and befriended a young crippled boy, and Daddy Allen came to the realization that crippled children needed to be treated in facilities specializing in their specific needs. He spearheaded and partially financed the building of a specialized hospital adjacent to the hospital he had previously opened. It was the first facility in the United States exclusively for the care of crippled children.

Daddy Allen went on to advocate tirelessly for such facilities, speaking at many Rotary clubs. Several clubs opened clinics, and each Rotarian was given the responsibility for following up on two children. With the help of Rotarians, Allen was instrumental in the formation of the Ohio Society for Crippled Children—the first such society in the United States. It generated a wide constituency, actively pursuing legal, medical, and educational assistance for these less-fortunate youngsters.

From that point forward, Rotary clubs in other states and Canada led or participated in the founding of state and provincial societies. The individual state societies were responsible for the enactment of state legislation to help disabled children. The International Society for Crippled Children was formed in 1921, with Rotary founder Paul Harris as chairman, and Daddy Allen as president of the Society. Within a few years, the International Society had begun rapid expansion in Europe, and was coming to the attention of world leaders. Daddy Allen traveled the globe, speaking and advancing the movement. By 1930, more than half of the states in the United States had state societies, and every state had passed laws on behalf of the handicapped. That same year, RI's newly established Rotary Foundation made a donation—its first ever—to the Crippled Children Societies, and Paul Harris presented the award of $500 to Society President Daddy Allen.

From its initial founding by Rotarians, the Society gained support and participation from prominent organizations—including Shriners, Kiwanians, Elks, Parent-Teacher Associations, the American Legion, and the Federation of Women's Clubs—in its work with state and federal agencies.

SF Rotary played a major part in the expansion of the movement to form state crippled children's societies. Based on its earliest work starting in 1916, the club claimed to be the first California Rotary club to undertake a broad and systematic program for the rehabilitation and education of the most helpless in San Francisco. Assuming the responsibility imposed by this history, SF Rotary followed Ohio's lead and, from 1921 on, recommended each year at its Rotary district conference that California should institute a statewide society of all concerned organizations, whereby every unfortunate child would be helped "by this great commonwealth." In 1926, Rotarians gathering at the District 2 Conference resolved 1) that District 2 was on record as favoring such a society, to be sponsored by the Rotary clubs of California, inviting all service clubs and other organizations interested in this humanitarian work to become a part of the movement; and 2) that SF Rotary be asked to undertake the task of bringing together all agencies in the state of California interested in work with crippled children and to organize a California association.

After obtaining assistance and financing from Rotary clubs around the state, SF Rotary formed the California State Society for Crippled Children later that year. SF Rotarians were expected to join and pay dues—"about the cost of one White Owl cigar per week"—to the organization devoted to the cure, care, and education of the state's fifteen thousand disabled children. Under the presidency of SF Rotarian George Davis, the new organization's first order of business was to bring about the enactment of legislation ordering the state board of health to provide treatment and education for these children. Although it was initially organized by Rotary, the California Society was not thereafter purely a Rotary activity. At the first annual meeting of the Society, the officers elected for the next year included a Kiwanian, a Lion, and two Rotarians for the posts of president, first vice president, secretary, and treasurer, respectively. In that sense, Rotary in California fulfilled an RI mandate to bring together a group of concerned men and women into the state organization and then step aside to have it carried on by those interested. SF Rotary continued to furnish its leadership for years afterward, and California Rotary clubs were the Society's largest financial supporters until 1939. SF Rotary's legacy remains as the organizer and chief promoter of the California Society—a part of what became one of the nation's foremost humanitarian organizations.

In 1933, the National Society undertook a fund-raising campaign through the public sale of envelope seals, which people could place on correspondence to show their support. The seals went on sale in 1934, with a ringing endorsement by President Franklin Roosevelt, himself crippled by polio. Public support for the Easter Seals campaign was overwhelming, and it set off a nationwide expansion of the organization and other grassroots efforts on behalf of the handicapped. The International Society for Crippled Children added "and Adults" to its name in 1944. The lily was officially incorporated as the Easter Seals' logo in 1952 for its association with resurrection and new life, and the familiar symbol has appeared on seals every year since. By 1967, the Easter seal and name was universally recognized, and the organization formally adopted the name "Easter Seals."

Until he died at age seventy-five in 1937, Edgar F. "Daddy" Allen served without salary as the directing head of the humanitarian work he had begun. In 1932, he addressed SF Rotary as president of the International Society of Crippled Children. He emphasized the importance of his organization's work in the prevention of the causes of crippling conditions.

Of Rotary's role in the crippled children's movement, Paul Harris later wrote that "it may in truth be said that the International Society for Crippled Children grew out of Rotary. It is a great humanitarian achievement of which we may well be proud, and it should be of interest to those inquiring as to whether or not Rotary is worthwhile." It was one of Rotary's momentous decisions—for years described as "The Brightest Jewel in the Crown of Rotary." This accolade persisted for decades, until Rotary would again confront a crippling disease in 1985, stirring Rotarians to action in its magnificent challenge to end polio worldwide.

1938—The Spastic Clinic and School

With its founding and continued support of the Sunshine School in 1924, its successful organization of the California Society for Crippled Children in 1926, and its ongoing treatment and surgery for children with orthopedic problems, SF Rotary conceived of yet another way to help children. In 1937, the Crippled Children's Committee determined to seek a new channel for its efforts. The result was the Spastic Clinic and School. Ten to fifteen percent of handicapped children suffered from cerebral palsy. Resulting from birth injury to the brain and nervous system, it caused erratic movements, grimacing, and drooling. Some could walk but not talk; others could talk but were not capable of mobility. Despite their physical afflictions, many of these children had normal minds, but required special schooling and rehabilitation to bring out their abilities.

The next year, Rotary opened a spastic clinic in a room at the Sunshine School, and employed a teacher and physical therapist. The clinic's initial enrollment consisted of four preschool children, who had been isolated from normal social experience and had not known other children like themselves. The clinic was the only one of its kind on the West Coast. These children learned that they were not alone in their condition, that they could learn, and that they could begin to do things for themselves and for each other. The clinic's success led the public school system to take over the class after its initial term.

SF Rotary continued its work for crippled children for many decades. The club sent crippled children to camp, and donated a dormitory to the camp. It backed the Shriners in their work in a number of ways, including urging members each year to attend the Shriners' main event, the East-West Game on New Year's Day. For years, Rotarians also donated as many as two hundred East-West Game tickets to the Boys' Club so its members could attend. Most importantly, the club continued its humanitarian efforts. In 1948 alone, eighteen of the thirty-five members of the Crippled Children's Committee were doctors, contributing their time and talent to the repair of small bodies.

Early Fund-Raising

From its beginning, SF Rotary raised small amounts of money, used to fund the club's good works. The levying of fines on members in the spirit of good humor started almost immediately. The "Charity Box"—used to collect the fines—was inaugurated in 1916 to raise money for the club's "Hospital Fund" for indigent children. For many years, the Charity Box was actually a little box at the end of a stick, that was passed among the members.

Within a few years, the club needed to raise more money for its charitable projects. An annual Christmas drive to benefit the needy was instituted. Funds were raised through Rotarians' subscriptions (pledges). Members were quite generous, and the drive raised thousands of dollars annually. When the club's annual drive was announced at a luncheon in 1920, club members responded overwhelmingly, and over $5,000 (in 1920 dollars!) was raised in less than fifteen minutes. At other times, the club called for special subscriptions or pledges during the year. The solicitations were usually made through humorous or clever "stunts"—often as a surprise to the luncheon attendees. Members invariably came through with remarkable openhandedness. In one call for donations to meet the cost of $2,400 for the annual orphaned-children outing, members responded by pledging $4,180. After expenses were paid, the club was able to return almost half of the pledges to the donors.

In 1931, the club had accumulated an ongoing balance in the "Special Service Fund," consisting of collections through the Charity Box and gifts sent in by members. SF Rotary's board decided to separate this charity fund from other club accounts that were used for club expenses. Moreover, they believed that by making it a special corporation for community service, members and others would be likely to contribute larger amounts through gifts and bequests. The new corporation, formed in 1931, was named Rotary Service, Inc. It remains today as SF Rotary's separate nonprofit organization for charitable contributions donated and spent within a year of giving.[19]

※ ※ ※

As SF Rotary's first half-century concluded in 1957, one decade in particular stands out. With the club's founding of the Sunshine School in 1924 and the founding of the California Society for Crippled Children in 1926, the 1920s mark SF Rotary's dramatic expansion of community service for children. This expansion becomes more remarkable when we learn that this work took place even as the club had undertaken a more ambitious project in its work with young people.

---

19. Rotary Service, Inc., is separate from the San Francisco Rotary Foundation (see chapter 5).

Building Better Boys—Boys' Work, The First 50 Years

*What we have a right to expect of the American boy is that he shall turn out to
be a good American man. Now the chances are strong that he won't be much of
a man unless he is a good deal of a boy.*

—Theodore Roosevelt, May 1900

When future president Theodore Roosevelt expounded on "What We Can Expect of the American Boy"
in a popular children's periodical, he tapped into a broadening American concern at the onset of the
twentieth century. Roosevelt declared that the makings of a good boy took three things: a strong body,
a strong mind, and courage. A boy should pursue athletic sports as healthful and beneficial, but above
all, as "preparation for work that counts when the time arises, especially in defense of the country."
He should work hard at his lessons, and he should develop physical and moral courage. Roosevelt told
Americans that the makings of a good boy "should include whatever is fine, straightforward, clean, brave,
and manly,. . . fearless and stalwart, hated and feared by all that is wicked and depraved, incapable of
submitting to wrong-doing, and equally incapable of being aught but tender to the weak and helpless."

As the Rotary Club of San Francisco neared the end of its first ten years and searched for
worthy service work, it responded to this new American concern, and undertook a new community-service pursuit. Without knowing it at the time, the club was embarking on a course that
would represent its longest and most defining service effort throughout its first century.

Americans in growing numbers were turning their attention to the health, welfare, and positive development of boys. They were especially concerned for boys in cities, who were most likely
to encounter distractions from the clean life or to suffer ill effects in the corrosive urban environment. The international scouting movement, begun in Britain in 1907, took hold in the United
States. (SF Rotarians Constant Auger and Frank Turner were two of the three founding directors of
the SF Area Council of the Boy Scouts of America.) World War I in particular focused interest in
the development of American boys as the country's future leaders.

In concert with this growing American interest, Rotary clubs began to initiate "boys' work"
projects. In doing so, Rotarians hoped to turn around rising levels of juvenile delinquency and tru-
ancy through assistance, and, more importantly, through vocational guidance such as mentoring,
providing positive role models, and the "Big Brother" idea.

At the 1916 and 1917 Rotary Conventions, delegates reported on vocational-guidance activities, as well as other issues such as playgrounds, medical and dental assistance for boys, surveys of
public schools, and the efforts of the Boy Scouts and YMCA. The delegates determined that boys'
work activities were widespread, they constituted a challenging avenue of service, and they should
be encouraged. RI formed a permanent Committee on Work Among the Boys to disseminate information on these activities. It emphasized "the personal contact between Rotarians and individual
boys." In subsequent conventions, RI adopted additional guidelines into its *Manual of Procedure*

addressing concerns such as objectives in boys' work, the importance of vocational guidance, ways of coordinating with and supporting outside organizations, and appropriate ways for clubs to initiate new boys' work projects. These guidelines dictated that "Rotary's chief objective in its work among the boys should be the development of good citizens."

SF Rotary had already taken up society's interest in the well-being of boys. Before boys' work had emerged as a distinctive commitment, the Ways and Means Committee helped boys indirectly through its assistance to poor families. As RI and Rotary clubs advanced the interest in boys' work, SF Rotary moved beyond indirect assistance to boys, and reached out directly to local boys in a number of ways.

> "Every Rotary club is a logical vocational guidance bureau. The boys' work program should give Rotarians the opportunity of relating themselves to vocational guidance within their individual classifications."
>
> —The RI *Manual of Procedure*, 1921

The earliest such work centered on imparting guidance to boys— as role models and by providing counseling and advice. In its 1916–17 year, the club began a plan to have members cooperate with the local high schools in vocational assistance to young men, a kind of work widely understood to be "a natural for Rotary." One of SF Rotary's first activities entailed working with the YMCA's vocational-assistance program, which facilitated interviews between Rotarians and boys.

The club began working with more troubled boys as well. Ben Dixon, the first chairman of the Boys' Work Committee in 1917–18, realized during the World War I years that the military uniform held considerable appeal for young boys. He began using military training to replace harsher means of correction at the Ethan Allen School, an institution for boys with discipline problems.

Special emphasis was placed on the relationship between a boy and his father. SF Rotary had initiated a Fathers and Sons luncheon in 1916, in the belief that "luncheon at the Palace Hotel with the Rotary Club will make a lasting impression on boys, and will unquestionably instill a higher ambition into their young minds." The luncheon went on to become an annual December event. A mounting belief in the influence of the father/son relationship on a boy's development was emphasized at luncheon talks such as "A Father's Responsibility to his Son"—described at the time as "the finest talk ever given before the San Francisco Rotary Club." Rotarians at the 1920 District Conference in Oakland cheered loudly after a keynote speech described the importance of "Underwriting Posterity—the Boy."

Club members carried this importance of fatherly guidance over to their service work. They extended their mentorship of young boys to "certain parentless boys in need of a grown man's help and advice." From the first Fathers and Sons Luncheon in 1916, Rotarians were encouraged to "bring a boy, yours or another." Over time, fatherless boys were transported to the luncheon each year, where they were met and "adopted" at the door by a member, who took them inside to enjoy the festivities, entertainment, and gifts.

Early-twentieth-century society's emerging interest in youth, and boys in particular, was largely rooted in notions of the causes of criminality. From early on, Rotarians emphasized a direct connection between a boy's well-being and the likelihood of his rejecting delinquent behavior.

"A penitentiary is nothing more than a monument to neglected youth."

—Warden James Johnston, 1922

"The crime problem is really a boy problem," claimed SF Rotarian James Johnston, warden of San Quentin Prison. This sentiment was echoed in talks by other well-informed club members, such as the chief of police. A number of years later, the Boys' Work Committee voiced its belief that the decrease in number of juvenile court sessions each week was due to the boys' work organizations in San Francisco.

A positive role model was viewed as a vital deterrent to a boy's problems. With the well-being of all boys gaining importance, Rotarians broadened the range of boys who could benefit from their attention and advice. For example, an RI Convention discussion concerned with "Caddie Welfare" noted that golf caddies throughout the world represented the "largest unorganized group of boys today and the one which is in most urgent need of kindly and sympathetic oversight." Adopting the spirit of that discussion, a *Grindings* article gave "the Ancient and Honorable Game" of golf a new purpose by encouraging Rotarians to take time to talk to their golf caddies as they would to their own sons, so as not to miss an opportunity to shape a boy's character. In this spirit, the club began the early forms of assistance and vocational guidance to young people that for nearly a century have formed the cornerstone of the club's service to the community.

As the boys' work movement gained momentum, RI began to formalize its role in providing direction for clubs, adopting a resolution to commit the organization and its clubs to a policy of boys' work. RI amended its bylaws to include boys' work, and began collecting annual reports from individual clubs. U.S. President Calvin Coolidge recognized the importance of Rotary's contributions to boys by serving as honorary chairman of RI's National Boys' Work Committee. The commitment of local clubs to the cause grew to the extent that a *Rotarian* article provocatively asked, "Does Rotary exist for doing Boys' Work, or for bettering the standards of business methods, or what?" SF Rotary remained primarily a business club, but it did respond to RI's policy encouraging boy's work by formally adding its two-year-old Boys' Work Committee to the club's roster.

The year 1920 signaled the start of a decade of explosive growth in the club's commitment to and programs to benefit San Francisco's boys. The club's work centered mostly on the growing worldwide scouting movement—a reflection of society's overall concern with providing strong programs of development for young men. A luncheon speaker for the Boys' Work Committee program underscored the importance of scouting's ability to mold boys into manly, energetic citizens. He stressed this influence as crucial to the postwar emphasis on Americanization. During a Boy Scouts' fund-raising drive, SF Rotarians were the "top-notchers" out of thirty teams in San Francisco.

A major catalyst for the club to coordinate with other organizations came in the form of National Boys' Week, which began with the Rotary Club of New York in 1920. SF Rotary followed New York's lead in the first year of this celebration dedicated to bringing the public's attention to the needs and concerns of "the Nation's Greatest Asset, the potential manhood of tomorrow." The idea gained popularity, and in only a few years, Boys' Week took on a national prominence.

For several years, SF Rotary worked with the Lions and Kiwanis to sponsor Boys' Week. SF Rotarians took the lead in organizing an even broader Associated Boys' Council, by coordinating the various organizations in San Francisco working with boys. These organizations included Kiwanis, Lions, Chamber of Commerce, and Union League, as well as members of the police, judiciary, and other city government organizations. The club predicted the new council would become "the leading factor in boys' work in this city." This organization helped develop events during the National Boys' Week, and was one of over six hundred Boys' Councils in the nation by the middle of 1924. The Boys' Week movement spread throughout the world. (It later became known as Boys' and Girls' Week.)

SF Rotary also added to its programs of cooperation with local schools. The club was hailed in a *Rotarian* article for the success of its Boys' Work Committee in visiting high schools and giving addresses on industrial, business, and professional vocations (to girls as well as boys), and by inviting interested students to visit various businesses. This form of vocational assistance was successful and was repeated over the years. High school students were assigned to individual Rotarians. Each of them hosted the student at his plant, explained his business to him, and brought him to the Rotary luncheon for a special program in the students' honor.

At one point, SF Rotary entertained the idea of electing one or more presidents of high school student bodies to Rotary membership. RI in turn informed the club that high school students were ineligible for membership in the club for business and professional men. But club members knew exposure to Rotary and its philosophy would attract young men who would become the Rotarians of the future. Accordingly, the club began the long-lived practice of hosting two high-school students at the weekly luncheon—a tradition that stood throughout most of the century. At the luncheon, the boys were "thrown into direct contact with men who are leaders in business and social affairs of our community." They were thought to benefit from observing

---

IMPRESSED WITH ROTARY: A FUTURE ROTARY CLUB PRESIDENT

November 10, 1930

Mr. D. I. Bosschart,
San Francisco Rotary Club,
Palace Hotel, San Francisco

My dear Mr. Bosschart: I wish to extend to you and the San Francisco Rotary Club my utmost thanks and appreciation for the manner in which you received me.

I take this opportunity to honestly assure you that I have absorbed and contemplated upon the ideals, the objectives, and the good accomplished by the Rotary movement. The service which your organization renders this community shall remain in my eyes a complete justification for the existence of Rotary.

The four Tuesdays which I spent with you, the leaders of San Francisco, shall remain with me for years to come.

Once more, my sincere gratitude.

Respectfully yours,

Stuart D. Menist*
Judge, Student Body,
High School of Commerce.

*Stuart Menist served as SF Rotary president 1977–78.

the conduct of orderly meetings, and hearing about topics of timely interest.

These worthwhile programs, aimed chiefly at guiding young men toward responsible adulthood, emerged as SF Rotary's foremost community-service commitment over the course of the 1920s. The club's crowning achievement in this field—one that would endure as its mainstay service activity throughout the century—was its sponsorship and leadership of the San Francisco Boys' Club.

> "The men of Rotary have reasoned that if the United States is going to be a better country, first the boy must be made better, and the instrument for his improvement is the man of today."
>
> —*Colliers'* magazine, quoted in *Grindings*, July 15, 1924

1923—The San Francisco Boys' Club

Throughout its history, the San Francisco Boys & Girls Club has reached out to tens of thousands of children, most of whom live in disadvantaged conditions.[20] Many are not enrolled in school. Not only do the children have basic needs, they also face daunting everyday challenges with drugs, violence, and teen pregnancies. The Boys & Girls Club provides a safe haven, and promotes self-esteem and well-being through its many programs, especially the camp experience. The club defines its mission as "helping girls and boys to develop greater feelings of competence, usefulness, belonging and self-esteem." The club serves children from ages six through eighteen, especially those from inner-city and other underprivileged circumstances. Since 1891, it has provided a wide range of "off the street" social, academic, vocational, and athletic programs, including tutoring and other educational services; counseling and job referrals; health examinations and medical services; access to libraries, crafts, and athletic facilities; plus camping and day trips to beaches, museums, and parks. The club's privileges have been the same for everyone; the membership cost is so low that any child can belong.

The Rotary Club of San Francisco has a unique relationship with the San Francisco Boys & Girls Club. SF Rotary has been, for most of the Boys & Girls Club's existence, its major supporter. In turn, the club is SF Rotary's longest-lasting service interest and greatest beneficiary. The Boys & Girls Club has pointed proudly to this relationship, to the influence of SF Rotary, and to the soundness of its policies, shaped by a continuing succession of Rotarian officers and directors—many of them San Francisco's business leaders.

The club was founded in 1891 as the Harrison Street Boys' Club, the first boys' club established on the West Coast. Two years later, it was reorganized as the San Francisco Boys' Club Association. Its original object was described as "the moral elevation of boys in San Francisco and vicinity, by the maintenance of a home, where they may find comfort, sympathy, and assistance in leading the higher life." The Boys' Club's approach of teaching useful skills was similar to that of a nearby girls' organization. But rather than teach girls' home duties such as sewing, the club organized boys'

---

20. In 2001, the club became the Boys & Girls Clubs of San Francisco. For most of this history, however, the organization was called the San Francisco Boys' Club (SFBC), later the San Francisco Boys & Girls Club (SFBGC).

classes in drawing, wood carving, whittling, and hammock netting. The boys gained satisfaction from completing an absorbing, practical project. These crafts were supplemented with exercise, drill, and marching. The club managed the boys' behavior through membership, in which each boy surrendered his membership card to gain entry. Good behavior assured him of getting his card back and being able to return the next time. This time-tested system is still in operation today.

The Boys' Club grew and expanded its activities and services. It survived a move to temporary quarters as a result of the 1906 earthquake and fire. In fact, that year it joined with fifty-two other clubs around the country to form the Federated Boys' Clubs—later to be called the Boys' Clubs of America. In 1920, its director, John Neubauer, opened a second facility at Potrero and 25th Street.

As the nation's interest in boys' work gained momentum, SF Rotary searched for a significant continuous means of serving boys. At the same time, a number of members—becoming aware of strong programs in other Rotary clubs—expressed dissatisfaction that SF Rotary had no "tangible program for regular boys' work." This desire for a strong and continuing program led club President Perry Cumberson (1921–22) to direct Walter Marwedel and his Boys' Work Committee to study the possibility of SF Rotary sponsoring a social and athletic center for underprivileged boys. Walter was inspired when his committee convinced a group of tough neighborhood boys to do much of the heavy work to construct their own athletic field, handball and tennis courts, and a gym, with funds allocated by SF Rotary. Clearly, boys could be guided to work together for beneficial purposes. Walter made an exhaustive survey of all of the boys' organizations in San Francisco, and brought the executive secretary of the Boys' Club Federation from New York to address the club at its weekly luncheon meeting. In the Boys' Work Report to RI later that year, Walter reported on the "desirability" of starting a boys' club. He also recommended that the most important piece of boys' work to be promoted at the next RI Convention should be the sponsorship of boys' clubs by Rotary clubs.

Although the San Francisco Boys' Club was not the biggest nor the best-known of the ten boys' clubs operating in San Francisco, it did claim itself to be "the oldest boy's club in the city." As John Neubauer vied for Rotary support of his club, SF Rotarians could not help but be impressed by the club's showing during Boys' Week in the spring of 1923. The boys marched in an enormous parade, gave drill and calisthenic exhibitions, and played a regulation basketball game that moved down the parade route on Market Street—a stunt that reached across the country in newspapers, newsreels, and *Life* magazine.

Believing the San Francisco Boys' Club Association to be the best organization of its kind in the city, Walter Marwedel and the Boys' Work Committee decided to get behind the struggling club, and to bring time, money, and energy into programs to assist its young members. The committee reorganized the club and incorporated it as the San Francisco Boys' Club, Inc., and the state granted the new club's charter in 1923. In taking this step, SF Rotary joined in a mutually beneficial alliance with Boys' Club Director John Neubauer. Together, Rotary's support and Neubauer's talented leadership would grow the club and its programs far beyond the hopes and imagination of everyone at that moment. It is indicative of SF Rotary's unbroken leadership from the Boys' Club's

Walter Marwedel

early days that three of the first four officers were Rotarians—with Walter Marwedel as president—and thirteen Rotarians were among the original seventeen trustees.

Marwedel headed the Boys' Club board through its first seventeen years of formation and growth, until he stepped down in 1940 and Rotarian Lloyd Bayer took his place. The same year it was organized, the SF Boys' Club was admitted to the Community Chest (now known as the United Way of the Bay Area).

The reorganized club began with two branches in the Mission District under the directorship of John Neubauer. With the support of SF Rotary, the club started responding to requests from various communities in the city, who believed club branches in their neighborhoods would provide a healthy environment for boys and would steer them away from trouble. The month following the club's reorganization, it opened two new branches in the Visitacion Valley and Telegraph Hill. Membership in the first year doubled to 346 members. Another year brought a new branch in Glen Park, and the membership doubled again. In 1928, the Boys' Club lowered its age limit from nine to six years so younger boys could gain from the club's many benefits, further adding to the club's size.

Since its beginning, the club's growth has strained its ability to serve all of the boys wanting to join. More and better facilities have always been needed, and SF Rotary has responded time and time again. Through a building fund drive in 1927, SF Rotary led in raising $44,000 to construct a new and larger Mission Branch building, located at 21st and Alabama Streets, two blocks from the club's original rented quarters. Contributions came from SF Rotary, sale of Boys' Bonds by club boys, funds raised by parents, and public contributions. Two thousand dollars were raised by club boys themselves to purchase the lot. SF Rotary made the largest single contribution of $15,000, and Rotarians donated many of the furnishings. At the groundbreaking ceremony, secretaries operating a battery of typewriters recorded the names of each person who turned a spadeful of earth, including all members of the Boys' Club. The completed list of names was encased in glass and placed in the cornerstone, along with a motion picture of the ceremony and a spadeful of earth. The new building opened in 1928, providing facilities for improved club administration, and larger indoor recreation areas.

Walter Marwedel (center) places a time capsule in the Mission Branch cornerstone at the building ground-breaking ceremony, 1928.

Membership jumped immediately to over 1,200, with individual participations in club events numbering almost 8,000. The following year, four new branches were opened in the Bay View, Portola, Bernal Heights, and Precita Valley districts, bringing the number of branches to nine and the membership to over 1,600, from an original 185 only six years earlier. As the 1920s ended, Boys' Clubs were becoming large multichapter organizations in New York, Chicago, and other big cities. Thanks to SF Rotary's sponsorship, the San Francisco club was no exception, with its well-established and equipped branches, and 2,000 members.

From the beginning, SF Rotarians did not view the Boys' Club as a "charitable institution," nor themselves as "charity-givers." Instead, club branches were described by a SF Rotarian as "outposts of Rotary, where service is taught, and where attendance is rewarded." Rotarians saw their role as that of friends, interested in helping the boys of San Francisco develop mentally, physically, and morally. The boys themselves were viewed as fully capable of becoming good men, citizens, and neighbors. Although the Boys' Club did not limit its membership based on economic distinction, Rotary's interest in sponsoring the club lay in the fact that it served boys who lacked the means to join organizations such as the YMCA, to pay the voluntary Boy Scouts' dues or buy its uniforms, or to pay for fees and transportation to camps. Whenever financial help was extended to an individual boy, it usually placed some form of responsibility on the boy. Upon finding that some boys delayed joining the Boys' Club until they could save some money to purchase gymnasium suits, the Boys' Work Committee established a Rotary Loan Fund at the Boys' Club. A boy could borrow the small amount of $1.25 to purchase his suit, and was obligated to pay back the money in weekly or monthly installments.

Initially, most of the Rotarians' assistance was in athletics, the Boys' Club's main focus. With a growing membership, Neubauer wanted to encourage acquaintanceships among the many members, so he set up team sport games between the branches. In the Boys' Club's first year, SF Rotary provided uniforms for eight basketball teams—the Boys' Club went on to win state titles in two weight classes. Rotary also organized and outfitted eight baseball teams and a league for boys weighing less than eighty-five pounds. Five professional ballplayers emerged from this Midget League, including Joe and Vince DiMaggio. These activities were expanded into more teams, many of which won numerous city and state titles. Within three years, the club sported twenty-eight uniformed baseball and forty-four basketball teams, plus fifteen gymnasium classes. The athletic programs were later expanded to include tumbling, wrestling, boxing, and other sports. Hiking and summer camping at various locations gave boys an escape from the city, good exercise, and the opportunity to

A Boys' Club baseball team, 1952. Courtesy of Moulin Studios Archives

see nature outside of their limited urban environment. SF Rotarians supported director John Neubauer on all of these programs with donations, club leadership, and assistance to the boys.

Within the first few years, the Boys' Club's services were expanded beyond athletics to a broader spectrum of programs—both useful and fun—and Rotary contributed to the success of most of them. In 1925, John Neubauer requested that Rotarians provide one-half day of work for his boys at $2 each, to be applied to purchase camp equipment. Rotarians responded by meeting his request for jobs for 125 boys. Besides providing the boys with work experience, this offered an opportunity to bring 125 Rotarians together with boys individually. A Boys' Club band was formed, with Rotary providing the uniforms and band leader's salary of $50 per month. The club's Big Brass Band thrilled Rotarians and tested the acoustics in the Palace Hotel's Gold Ballroom at the Boys' Luncheon. Club Secretary Ervin Feighner's wife donated a new piano, to round out the Boys' Club's musical activities. Rotarians conducted a book drive and added over 1,200 books to the Club's library. Special social dances were organized for the older boys.

Boys learn woodworking at the Boys' Club, 1935.
Courtesy of Moulin Studios Archives

The Boys' Club added a wide variety of crafts and skills to its educational programs. In 1931, SF Rotary sponsored the first annual Boys' Achievement Exposition, held in connection with International Boys' Week. For five nights, boys competed in three age groups, in such categories as woodwork, models, radio, mechanical devices, weaving, puppets, printing, cooking, drawing, collections, drama, music, and photography. Over 160 Rotarians assisted. Held in the Mission Branch building, the Exposition was attended by more than 7,000 people, including hundreds of special delegates from fraternal and civic organizations.

Some programs were intended to provide moral and social guidance. Boys were rewarded for good works in several classifications by means of an innovative award system, whereby they received bronze, silver, and gold bars through points earned in club activities, home, school, and church. A "personal guidance" program instituted in 1936 provided Rotarian "big brother" advisers to boys, especially delinquent or borderline cases. The Boys' Club also added a new course about courtesy, with each boy awarded a completion certificate after attending six weekly sessions.

Attention to the physical well-being of boys was important, because maintaining good health was a problem for underprivileged boys. A health program with physical examinations and medical advice helped keep these at-risk boys from succumbing to the illnesses that generally afflict the poor.

The boys were given classes in first aid. A dental department saw to it that a volunteer dentist came routinely to clean and check the boys' teeth.

RI was encouraging activities to provide work for boys, and SF Rotary's abiding interest in vocational assistance brought jobs to older Boys' Club members. SF Rotarians began experimenting in a program offering informative industry trips to forty-eight firms where they held executive positions. They started an employment file for boys, and placed seventy-eight grateful boys in jobs.

The Boys' Club's programs were successful in part because boys enjoyed them. And alongside these worthwhile programs, some activities offered boys just plain good fun. SF Rotarians contributed prizes for a citywide treasure hunt that attracted eight hundred boys. A pet show gave boys a chance to show off their best friends.

Many Rotarians stand out in their support of the Boys' Club. When George Whitney joined Rotary in 1930, he immediately turned to community-service work. George and his brother Leo turned over their amusement park—Playland-at-the-Beach (formerly called Chutes-at-the-Beach)—free for a day to more than 1,200 boys, who were transported free of charge to the oceanfront park from all over the city by buses and trolleys. With the assistance of SF Rotarians for the next several decades, thousands of boys—between 2,700 and 3,000 in 1958 alone—enjoyed hot dogs, peanuts, and ice cream. They romped and played on special days at the Whitneys' park until it was sold in 1968.

The Whitneys' generosity went even further than hosting boys at their amusement park. Community Chest cutbacks during the Depression strained the Boys' Club budget. For several years, the Whitneys turned over the proceeds of a week at Playland—several thousand dollars at a time—to the Boys' Club for operating funds. During his Boy's Work Committee chairmanship in 1934, George Whitney led the raising of an impressive $12,000 for the club with a five-night carnival at the Mission Branch. He later raised money to purchase the land on which the present-day Camp Mendocino is located.

A day at Playland-at-the-Beach for the San Francisco Boys' Club, 1930. Courtesy of Moulin Studios Archives

The Depression of the 1930s was particularly hard on Americans on the lower rungs of the economic ladder, and this was equally true for Boys' Club members. During these hard times, the need for assistance to boys extended to their families more than ever. A 1937 survey showed that 74 percent of the boys and their families were receiving some form of charitable aid from the Community Chest. A number of new programs to help financially distressed boys were initiated in 1931. Many young people were homeless and jobless, and the club's Mission Branch opened itself up every morning to transient boys. There a boy could find some respite from the cold streets, and a much-needed boost to his morale. The Boys' Work Committee noted that "the depression exerts an extraordinary pressure upon families, the father of which has been out of employment." It appealed to Rotarians to provide one or more days of work for Boys' Club members, to enable them to help pay for their two weeks at camp. A fourth community-service committee was added to the Rotary roster—joining the Civic, Boys' Work, and Crippled Children's Committees. The new Student Loan Committee provided loan money to boys and girls who proved exceptionally bright and worthy, sending them on through college, the loan to be repaid afterward. Rotary continued with its annual Christmas appeal to members to donate generously for boys' work and crippled children.

Eva Whitney takes a thrill ride on Boys' Club Day at Playland-at-the-Beach.
Courtesy of Moulin Studios Archives

As the Depression wore on, the Boys' Club began giving free memberships to boys whose fathers were out of work, and working with charitable agencies to identify boys from destitute families. Rotarians started a Rotary Sunshine Fund to help the Boys' Club director pay for individual boys' needs, such as clothing, milk for underweight boys, dental work, and eyeglasses. In addition to seeing to the boys' physical needs, Rotary continued efforts to bring some measure of joy into lives filled with hardship. To ensure that all the boys were entertained at Christmas, SF Rotary co-operated in holding multiple Christmas parties—as many as eleven—at the main branch. The boys themselves responded positively to the example set by their benefactors, and they gave back to other unfortunates. One year the boys repaired nearly twelve thousand old and broken toys, which in turn were given to poor children for Christmas. With Rotary support, the Boys' Club continued to grow despite these desperate times. After residents and merchants in the Haight-Ashbury district complained of troublesome youths in their area, the club opened a Haight-Ashbury Branch in 1940. Delinquency dropped immediately.

Although SF Rotary's report in 1929 stated that its most active boys' work was in the Boys' Clubs, Rotary's work did not stop there. After SF Rotary began its sponsorship of the club in 1923, it continued with other general work for San Francisco's boys. SF Rotary reported strong activity in vocational guidance. A Boys' Placement Bureau was created to place boys with Rotarians seeking employees. The Father and Son luncheon had become an annual tradition, and Rotary made continuing efforts to encourage each member to make individual contact with a fatherless boy, preferably as a "Big Brother." The club also sponsored boys to Boy Scout camp.

Proud of its significant role in improving the lives of San Francisco's boys, SF Rotary boasted that "because of Rotary's leadership in every phase of boy activity, the Rotarian has been placed on a pedestal in the boy's life." This sentiment led one boy speaking at the RI Convention in Cleveland to say, "May God help you men to be the kind of heroes we boys think you are."

1930—Camp Mendocino

There should be no doubt in any member's mind that in sponsoring a boy to camp, he is making a "blue chip" investment in the future of our community and of our country.

—Walter Marwedel, 1930

From the Boys' Club's earliest days, when it took boys to a camp in the coastal redwoods called Camp Ha Ha, the club recognized that camping offered unique benefits to poor city kids. Director John Neubauer began camp seasons in 1911, and some of the earliest camping locations included La Honda, Big Basin, and Pescadero, as well as two-week trips to Yosemite. Neubauer organized the club's calendar around the camping season, operating the club from fall through spring, then closing the club entirely for summer camp. He helped his boys find work to pay the small amount needed to attend camp.

When SF Rotarians assumed sponsorship of the club, they began immediately to assist the camping program by contributing time, money, and goods. They provided transportation for one hundred boys to summer camp at La Honda that year, and donated or discounted all of the supplies for the camp. The boys attended at a cost of $2.50 for the three-week camp, and many of the boys were able to earn the money through jobs provided by Rotary members. With the help of Rotarians, the $10 annual trip to Yosemite was extended to three weeks. In an era when poor American children lacked a sufficient amount of protein in their diets, the Boys' Work Committee took pride in the fact that every boy gained weight at camp.

For several years after Neubauer began taking boys on regular camping trips, the Boys' Club made semipermanent use of Camp Olive in the Santa Cruz Mountains. Neubauer also conducted overnight camping at spots all around the Bay Area, as well as more distant trips to Mount Lassen, Mount Shasta, Mount Hamilton, and Yosemite. But as the Boys' Club grew larger, Neubauer needed to consolidate the many trips into a single major summer camp to accommodate more children. As early as 1926, SF Rotary searched for a permanent camping place.

Finally, one was found. Boys' Club President Walter Marwedel negotiated a lease of 250 redwood acres in Mendocino from Union Lumber. Beautifully wooded and secluded, the land bordered on the Noyo River between Willits and Fort Bragg, near the famous "Skunk Train" tracks. The campsite was located on the riverbank, with two large pools for swimming and two fine springs furnishing an abundance of water. It was the ideal location for a permanent camp.

In 1930, the Boys' Club and Rotary opened Camp Marwedel, named in honor of the Rotarian who had forged the bond between the two clubs, and had been so instrumental in the camp's origins. It would later be renamed Camp Mendocino, a name it carries today. The first summer it opened with close to six hundred boys attending. The following summer, the summer camp program was extended from three to four sessions, and 855 boys attended camp. Neubauer was pleased to report that not a single accident or illness marred the entire eight weeks.

This splendid new camp became the central focus of the Boys' Club. Its size and permanence enabled the club to offer an unforgettable two weeks of fishing, swimming, canoeing, riding, hiking, archery, nature study, caring for animals, and other activities. The boys even learned to trap foxes. The camp was a dream come true for boys who knew nothing but the gritty street corners of the city, and who might never have seen a fish, let alone catch one. Each evening boys enjoyed campfires, with songs and skits presented by the boys themselves.

Besides the fun, there was discipline. Boys rose each morning, endured cabin and personal inspection, attended flag-raising exercises, learned to say or lead grace at every meal, attended religious services on Sunday, and took a daily nap. Sleeping in group cabins, they learned to live together harmoniously—a change from the tough combative mentality many knew back in the city. Selected club members, who received hands-on leadership training and later went to work as camp staff, gained experience that would benefit them in their adult lives.

Horseback-riding at Camp Marwedel (Camp Mendocino), 1948. Courtesy of Moulin Studios Archives

In 1933, only three years after the camp opened, a study and examination by the Rockefeller Foundation ranked the new camp among the best boys' camps in America. Whereas earlier camp-outs had been limited to a few hundred boys, the new camp allowed for a dramatic expansion. Only a few years after it opened, the delights of Camp Marwedel were enjoyed by over 1,400 boys during a single summer.

Many boys were able to pay the small fee to attend camp. They were encouraged to save, and the club bank account showed several laying aside fifteen to twenty cents per week for that purpose. Throughout the camp's history, however, some boys have been unable to pay their way. SF Rotarians made certain that boys were able to enjoy camp, regardless of their economic situations. Since the camp's early years during the Depression, Rotary has sponsored deserving boys to camp. For years, Rotarians responded generously to an annual appeal to "send a boy to camp." In 1945, club members individually donated $8,500 to send 350 boys to camp for two weeks, at a cost of only $24 per boy. These "camperships" were awarded every year in a special luncheon program. A sad note: beginning during the Depression, some boys whose families were unable or unwilling to care for them remained at camp for the entire summer. This unfortunate situation still occurs today.

Needy Boys Sent to Camp

Grindings published cases of boys being sent to camp through the generosity of SF Rotarians:

Harry—13 years old. Father is in Folsom Prison, mother is divorced and will have nothing to do with the children. A small sister is in an orphan asylum and neighbor has been caring for Harry since family difficulty.

Al and Paul—These boys are brothers 12 and 13 years of age. Father was divorced by mother for cruelty. Five boys in the family. Mother does odd jobs. Only one boy old enough to work. Both of these boys need camp.

Dan—11 years old. Next to oldest in family of five. Father died five years ago. Mother receives "Widow's Pension." At present is in the hospital recovering from an operation. Girl of 14 looks after the house with occasional help from relatives.

Angelo—13 years old. Orphan and lives with aunt who makes a living working in a bag factory. Angelo has been both spoiled and abused and needs the discipline and good-fellowship of camp.

Boating at Camp Marwedel (Camp Mendocino), 1945.
Courtesy of Moulin Studios Archives

Ten years after Camp Marwedel opened, the Boys' Club hoped to make its ownership of the land permanent, and SF Rotary stepped in to raise funds. George Whitney raised money to purchase the 250 leased acres, and an enormous tract of surrounding watershed—a total of 2,000 acres—plus $40,000 of improvements. In 1942, at a luncheon meeting "full of drama and human interest," Rotary presented the deed to an enlarged and improved Camp Marwedel to a grateful Boys' Club. Today, that gift stands out as SF Rotary's signature legacy to the San Francisco Boys & Girls Club.

The first year the Boys' Club owned its own camp proved a difficult one. Transportation problems caused by the wartime rubber shortage were keeping many visitors away. Nevertheless, John Neubauer reported the camp was flourishing, albeit with a smaller staff than in earlier years. The following year, Neubauer reported that the U.S. Government recognized the urgent necessity for operation of the boys' camps of the nation, and supported their opening again for the summer despite transportation limitations.

After the war, the camp underwent significant improvement, with Rotary's continued support. In 1956, thirty-four new buildings were added in a complete rehabilitation of the camp. During that same period, SF Rotarian I. W. Hellman contributed most of the funds to purchase Cragmont Ranch in Sonoma as a nature-study center, which remained open for eight years.

In the 1950s, the Boys' Club was able to claim Camp Marwedel as "the finest boys' summer camp in America." Reflecting the

Cold War emphasis on American ideals, the Boys' Club proudly called the camp "a proving ground for real Americanism, . . . a fine training in citizenship."

On the more practical side, for many years the Boys' Club emphasized the real improvements in the health of otherwise impoverished boys, who thrived on the camping experience. Boys were given all they could eat, and they gained weight. In one year two new records were set: the campers gained an average weight of five-and-a-half pounds, and—in a related case—a record of twenty-six pancakes was eaten by one boy in a single sitting.

The camping experience evolved, but in many ways it remained as it had been at the beginning. The objectives for camp supervisors as counselors for several hundred boys were concisely stated at a Rotary luncheon meeting:

> No race, creed, nor color is barred from attendance. Group activities replace attempts to form "cliques" or "clans." The financial status of any boy is not a determining factor in his acceptability at camp, nor is lack of funds a deterrent from the enjoyment of a happy camp period and the opportunity to share equally in all camp functions. Many boys arrive in poor physical condition, however, the outdoor activities in which all engage plus regularity of routine result in an average weight increase of five pounds per boy.

After Rotary's presentation of Camp Marwedel to the Boys' Club in 1942, SF Rotarians continued to support the Boys' Club in its other fine work, much of it related to the war. Despite difficulties brought about by the war, the boys themselves were eager to help from the home front. Among their many activities, they assembled first-aid kits, made splints, planted victory gardens, collected scrap materials to make necessary items for servicemen, and sent chests of games to American prisoners of war. They corresponded with servicemen overseas, and participated in Victory Bond drives. They also borrowed movie films for Boys' Club entertainment during blackouts. Older boys went off to war, and the club posted service unit banners, and sewed a gold star for each member who died for his country. George Whitney's annual day for boys at Playland-at-the-Beach was limited to daylight hours due to wartime "lights out" regulations.

At the war's end, the Boys' Club resumed buying, building, and renovating club branch buildings. It purchased a building for the Portola Branch in 1947, and rebuilt it with Rotary help, adding a game room, craft shop, locker room, office, and a new lobby. Rotarians donated time, talent, and money to help plan, engineer, construct, and furnish a new debt-free building for the Haight-Ashbury Branch, which opened on Page Street in 1952. The showcase building—designed at no cost by Rotarian Al Roller and engineered by Bru Brunnier—was dedicated by former President Herbert Hoover, chairman of the board of the Boys' Clubs of America. It was renamed the Ernest Ingold Branch in honor of Rotary's past president (1948–49) who was serving as president of the Boys' Club's board of directors. A new indoor swimming pool was added the following year by SF Rotary.

BUILDING RESPONSIBLE BOYS

Mission Club Center of the Young Women's Christian Association
Mr. J. C. Neubauer, Director, San Francisco Boys' Club

Dear Mr. Neubauer:

We wish to express our appreciation to the San Francisco Boys' Club for the return of the $20.00 in currency which was found in the dressing rooms by two of your boys, and returned to us.

We feel that this act is a fine example of the training and spirit of the boys in your organization; and the Y.W.C.A wishes to take this opportunity of expressing its appreciation to the boys.

The money was the property of one of the girls from the Telephone Company, and you may be sure that the return of her week's salary meant much to her.

Sincerely yours,
Alberta L. Baumberger,
Secretary Mission Center

The 1950s saw boys' work programs continue.[21] The short-lived Student Loan program that was begun in 1931 was restarted with a modest fund, to "extend help in meritorious cases" for third- and fourth-year and graduate students in Bay Area colleges and universities. Rotarians were invited to participate by recommending and sponsoring students, and by acting as counselors.

Juvenile delinquency came to the forefront of Americans' worries in the 1950s. Just as Rotarians emphasized the crime-reducing effects of boys' work in general, the Boys' Club had always taken pride in its role in preventing crime. During SF Rotary's initial search in the 1920s for a worthy boys' organization to sponsor, the SF Boys' Club's president had stressed the club's effectiveness in reducing juvenile delinquency in the neighborhood around the club by providing a different kind of "gang" for boys to join. Walter Marwedel remarked that "it is better to form character than to reform it." After Rotarians began their sponsorship of the club, they had continuously paid close attention to the correlation between the Boys' Club and lowered delinquency rates. In 1927, a survey by the Boys' Work Committee had mapped the homes of hundreds of boys referred to the Juvenile Court, and found no cases of delinquent boys in the neighborhoods where a club branch was located. Three years later, SF Rotary's board had cited reliable sources claiming that wherever Boys' Clubs had been established, juvenile delinquency decreased by 75 percent.

As the public's worries increased in the 1950s, the Boys' Club publicized its role in fighting delinquency. Citing dramatic ten-year increases in delinquency, city congestion, broken homes, and households with unsupervised children, the club's brochure appealed for monetary and personal support with police testimonials and statistics demonstrating the impressive local effects of club branches in neighborhoods.

When SF Rotary celebrated its fiftieth anniversary in 1958, it also celebrated the growth of the Boys' Club from its original 185 members to almost 4,300. This represented a remarkable achieve-

---

21. In the early 1940s, RI established a Youth Committee, to encourage local clubs to extend their services to girls. For the most part, SF Rotary's work remained primarily with boys until later years.

ment, for Rotary and for the Boys' Club. Throughout its first fifty years, the commitment of the Rotary Club of San Francisco to the well-being of the city's boys brought hope and a new direction to thousands of vulnerable youngsters. It firmly cemented a relationship that benefited Rotarians as well, offering them an unparalleled opportunity for meaningful and enduring community-service work in its truest sense.

LES ANDERSEN—A SUCCESS STORY

The SF Boys & Girls Club boasts of club members—many of them lacking in direction when they joined as children—who went on to lead successful lives. Among the most well-known are men such as Joe DiMaggio, who played Boys' Club baseball, and Edmund G. "Pat" Brown, who later became governor of California. Closer to home, SF Rotarian Les Andersen's story is an exemplary tale of Boys' Club success.

When Boys' Club Executive Director Harold Meyer found Les at age eleven, Les was a tough young San Francisco kid hanging out with a Portola District gang of nine brothers, whose mother was gang-leader. As his rite of passage, she ordered him to enter a store ten times and shoplift dozens of items. Meyer convinced Les to come to the club, but it was a hard sell. When Les didn't show up, Meyer followed him to his home, demanded that he help around the house, and sided with Les's mother in arguments. Finally, Les not only joined the club, but became one of its most loyal converts and began working for it. He went on to go to City College, then joined the Army and served during the Korean War. Returning, he continued college at University of San Francisco night school, then to New York University on a Boys' Club scholarship. Afterward, he worked his way home at boys' clubs across the country. He worked delivering supplies at Camp Mendocino, considered becoming a fireman, then

Les Andersen

took a job at the Boys' Club Ingold Branch at half the fireman's pay. After a time as assistant executive director, Les succeeded Joe Daugherty and became the club's executive director in 1968. He joined SF Rotary two months later. Les guided the club as Boys & Girls Club executive director until his retirement in 1997. Today, as executive director emeritus, he continues his work for the betterment of San Francisco's children.

The Four Avenues of Service

As SF Rotary transformed itself from a back-scratching and boosting club to an organization with a mission to serve, it gained new ideas about what the words to serve could mean. Some thoughts came from club members themselves, others from the broader Rotary movement.

In 1927 and 1928, Rotary International advanced a new "Aims and Objects Plan." Under the plan, Rotary clubs would organize their operating committees under four Avenues of Service:

- Club Service—service to one's Rotary club, to make possible the club's functioning and to encourage fellowship among the members;

- Vocational Service—service to others through one's vocation by the pursuit of ethical and excellent business practices;

- Community Service—service to the local community through good works;

- International Service (the last to be added)—service to the world by advocating international peace and seeking to eliminate hunger, suffering, and disease.

Under the administration of club President Charlie Wheeler, SF Rotary adopted the Aims and Objects Plan in 1930. The club reorganized its various committees by appointing one coordinating committee for each of the Four Avenues of Service. The new Club Service, Vocational Service, Community Service, and International Service Committees were placed under the general oversight and coordination of the Aims and Objects Committee, which replaced the club's Ways and Means Committee.

Although this plan—based on four ways to serve—had taken over two decades to formulate, its roots go back to the earlier days of Rotary, when the movement departed from "back-scratching" and business advantage as its primary purpose, and turned instead toward service. SF Rotarians had already begun Community Service for the people of San Francisco, by acting for the civic good and performing charitable works through the club's Civic Service Committee. But it is clear that SF Rotary members were also beginning to take a broader view of what service meant, beyond serving one's community. By then, Rotarians were becoming aware that service in a broader sense could also mean serving one's club and one's customers. By 1915, an inkling of two additional forms of service—Club and Vocational—had taken shape. International Service would come later.

Club Service

At its first meeting in November 1908, SF Rotary put Club Service into action—although its new members did not think of it as such at the time. The new Rotarian's first act of club service occurred when he fulfilled his responsibility to the club by joining one or more of the newly established committees. SF Rotary's Membership, Judiciary, Finance, Publicity & Extension, Grievance, and Nominating Committees were designed by the club's bylaws to make the organization function effectively. The Fraternal and Entertainment Committees were created to nurture group cohesiveness among the members through fellowship. The Ways and Means Committee coordinated the work of the other committees, so they would function together to advance the club's original objectives of promoting members' business interests and fostering fellowship among the membership. In 1910, an Educational Committee was added, to inform new members on the philosophy and workings of Rotary.

In addition to contributing to the functions of the various committees, club service also entailed being present at the club's meetings, taking part in its programs, and bringing in and welcoming new members. It involved representing the club through outside speeches, visiting other clubs, and attending inter-club functions such as annual conventions and district conferences once they were instituted. When the permanent newsletter *Grindings* was started in 1913, club service also meant editing, contributing items, and reading the newsletter to remain informed.

One club institution that has lived on as a tradition is the sectioning of members into divisions. At first in 1910, club membership was divided into two sections, as a way to increase administrative efficiency. As the club grew, so did the number of sections. Various ways were tried to balance the number of members in the sections, including sectioning by alphabet and geographic business location. In 1927, the club settled on the present-day system of sectioning the membership by members' birth months. For many years, the Birthday Divisions represented a major aspect of club service, as the "Birthday Babies" were called upon to provide entire luncheon programs. Because they were permanent (one's birth month didn't change), the Birthday Divisions became a focus of fellowship within smaller groups, which has continued as their primary function throughout the club's history.

As other service clubs—primarily Lions, Kiwanis, and Optimist—came into being, one issue of club service was loyalty to one's club. In the early 1920s, Rotarians grappled with the proper attitude toward clubs with similar or kindred purposes. The question centered around "the loyal Rotarian's duty to give all his energy to his own organization." SF Rotary passed a Resolution on Dual Memberships in 1921, and distributed it to all the clubs in the district and to RI headquarters. By 1922, organizations for which dual membership was prohibited included Kiwanis, Lions, Optimist, the Exchange Club, Business League, and the National Progress Club. Membership was not discouraged in such organizations as the Commercial Club, the Bohemian Club, the Commonwealth Club, the Downtown Association, and others.

Rotary's prohibition against its members joining other service clubs did not preclude San Francisco's various service/business clubs from cooperating with each other. They occasionally held joint meetings and worked together on projects such as Boys' Week. During Paul Rieger's presidential year (1922–23), he inaugurated a council of presidents and secretaries of twelve service clubs, which periodically staged a big meeting featuring nationally known speakers. When Lions International held its convention in San Francisco, *Grindings* asked SF Rotarians to furnish automobiles to the visitors for sightseeing trips. In 1930, club President Charlie Wheeler invited the entire membership of the local Kiwanis Club to join the SF Rotary luncheon, and to provide the entertainment with its chorus. The two clubs then listened to a lecture about the service club movement.

Vocational Service

Many Rotarians point out that it's easy to define the ways that Club Service, Community Service, and International Service function. However, as SF Rotarian Bob Rockwell pointed out in 1979, "Vocational Service eludes us, probably because we lack established organizations that call for our talents." He went on to explain that Rotary opens opportunities for each member to express their sense of vocation.

The notion that a man could serve others through his vocation had a precedent before Rotary. In a 1902 Fourth of July speech to his town of Bodie, California, at the young age of twenty-one, SF Rotary's founder Homer Wood expressed his belief that the character of a man ennobles his vocation: "In America, it is the man who makes the position honorable, and not the position which makes the man honorable. In America, a miner who digs in the earth, provided he is noble in character, is just as high in the estimation of the people as he who walks the halls of legislation."

Homer's belief is reflected in the emergence of a Rotary sense of business ethics. In this process, Rotarians—who viewed themselves and their fellow Rotarians as men of high caliber and trustworthiness—began to consider the idea that how one conducted his profession or trade was an indicator of the man's personal character. Furthermore, Rotary should embrace and nurture the development of these good qualities. Since a Rotary club was limited to one man from each business classification, the man could act as an example of his vocation to the other members. Rotary could, in turn, encourage all of its members to follow these demonstrations of good business practices.

These ideas developed over the course of a few years. At its formation in 1910, the new National Association of Rotary Clubs adopted as one of Rotary's Objects, "To promote progressive and honorable business methods." The following year, the national Rotary convention brought forth the Portland Platform of 1911, which contained the seeds of what would become "vocational service" through one's occupation. It also introduced the motto "He profits most who serves best."

SF Rotarians received the rudiments of these ideals even as back-scratching and boosting were in their ascendancy. In 1909, the president of the Tri-City Rotary Club addressed the San Francisco club on "Rotary Ethics." He emphasized that "if everything Rotary means is properly carried out," each member will gain business value and success.

In 1913, when the limitations and harmful effects of Rotarians' reciprocal trade practices were becoming evident, the new *Grindings* newsletter editorialized that "being in business is not merely trying to accumulate wealth. Let us place before us such ideals and have such high aspirations; establish for ourselves such a reputation for good, honest, and straightforward dealing, that it will be worthwhile; and let us as Rotarians use our individual efforts to hasten the time when to be a member of a Rotary Club shall be deemed a higher rating than an A1 rating in Bradstreets or Duns."

The early process of promoting business ethics as Rotary philosophy reached a new height at the 1915 RI Convention in San Francisco. Out of this convention came the adoption of the Rotary Code of Ethics. It expressed an analogy to the Golden Rule, a prescription for fair and just business practices, and a declaration that a Rotarian should set the example for non-Rotarians in his same vocation. These principles added to SF Rotarians' reconsideration of the meaning and purpose of their club and their place in it.[22]

After the adoption of the Rotary Code of Ethics in 1915, Rotarians began to expand their philosophy of service through one's vocation. They could use their vocational ethics to serve the public good. At a time when fraudulent and deceptive business practices were rampant, and there were no consumer-protection laws, Rotarians realized they could take positive steps to restore the public's faith in business. One way was for them to communicate the principles of their sound business practices to others in the same occupations. The Rotary Code of Ethics admonished each Rotarian to "use my best endeavors to elevate the standards of the vocation in which I am engaged, and so to conduct my affairs that others in my vocation may find it wise, profitable, and conducive to happiness to emulate my example." In 1920, SF Rotary's Education Committee announced its intent to promote Rotary ethics to other organizations, such as trade associations. The real push came three years later, when SF Rotary followed the leadership of RI President Guy Gundaker and established the Business Methods Committee—the club's first committee dedicated to vocational service. Thus began the "code-campaign"—an effort by SF Rotarians to exercise leadership in formulating ethical standards of conduct with members of their respective professional and trade associations. SF Rotary continued its code-writing efforts for almost five years, with mixed results. The club's historian William Mountin explained in 1940 that although club members joined trade associations and wrote some trade codes of ethics, they also encountered resistance when trying to impress their views on other members of their occupations.

> ## BRU BRUNNIER RECALLS
>
> "Something that happened in 1915 convinced me that we were nearly over the philosophical hump. In that year, we adopted a code of ethics and began printing it on pocket-sized cards. As men began to carry this code, they began to read it, and reading it, they began to believe it. Thus a Rotary trend developed which, I think, played a major part in changing 'Let the buyer beware' to 'The customer is always right.'"
>
> —SF Rotarian and RI President Bru Brunnier, 1952

The Four-Way Test

During the 1920s, Rotary's declarations of vocational idealism were disseminated as policy throughout the Rotary world. One of the district's criteria for club excellence was whether club members spoke at meetings about their experiences in trying to apply the Golden Rule to every business and professional transaction. In its annual report to the district in 1929, SF Rotary reported that its members did.

In 1932, a Chicago Rotarian applied the Golden Rule to what has become the crowning touch in Rotary's philosophy of business ethics. As the Great Depression ravaged America, a Chicago Rotarian named Herbert Taylor was asked to take charge of a company that was facing bankruptcy.

---

22. Although the Code of Ethics addressed the issue of business practices, one member of the SF Rotary Business Methods Committee later pointed out that Rotarians must apply the same high standards in their social relations as well.

THE FOUR-WAY TEST

Of all the things we think, say, or do:

1. Is it the TRUTH?

2. Is it FAIR to all concerned?

3. Will it build GOODWILL and BETTER FRIENDSHIPS?

4. Will it be BENEFICIAL to all concerned?

He encountered angry creditors, disaffected customers, and fearful employees. Herb called upon his Rotary background, and wrote down four inspired questions, which he called the Four-Way Test. With these questions as the company's guiding principles, within months creditors were paid, customers were back, employees were productive and confident, and the company eventually returned to prosperity. Herb credited his Four-Way Test for the company's turnaround. RI officially adopted the test in 1943. Today, the Four-Way Test is the mainstay of Rotarian ethics the world over, and is recited at the weekly meetings of many clubs, including SF Rotary.[23]

Vocational Service for Others

Within their club life, SF Rotarians found other ways to put their vocations to good use. In 1917, the club founded a Business Counsel Committee to offer business help in a number of ways. Committee members held private advisory meetings for members who needed help solving business problems. *Grindings* notified the membership of the committee's willingness "to counsel and advise any member who thinks that a confidential chat with ten business men, fellow members who are all his friends, may be of some benefit to him." The committee also offered to help widows in looking after the business affairs of deceased members when called upon to do so, and to render services to members in case of emergencies. The idea of the Business Counsel Committee spread to a number of other clubs, and it was commended in RI's monthly magazine *The Rotarian* in 1926. The committee was in place for three decades.

Outside SF Rotary, boys' work and the Boys' Club offered ample opportunity for Rotarians to use their vocations for altruistic purposes. Since the club began its work with boys in 1917, club members have counseled troubled children, mentored young people, helped them with career counseling, and found them jobs.

■ ■ ■

Club Service, Vocational Service, and Community Service: once SF Rotarians realized their club offered these avenues for helping others and gaining the inner satisfaction that comes from doing so, they never looked back. Yes, their Rotary club still offered business opportunities. SF Rotarians still promoted their businesses at meetings and advertised in *Grindings*. But the inner views of Paul Harris, Homer Wood, and others concerning the nobility of service had been given a voice and had prevailed. Rotarians and San Franciscans would reap the benefits of SF Rotary's turn to service.

---

23. Herb Taylor later served as RI President, in 1954–55.

Three Men of Rotary

T he Rotary Club of San Francisco honors members who have given special support and service to Rotary and to the wider community. There are three such honors: the Paul Harris Fellow, the Homer Wood Fellow, and the Bru Brunnier Fellow. It is fitting that these honors are named after the three men whose historic contributions to the history of SF Rotary outshine all others. Paul Harris, the founder of Rotary; Homer Wood, the founder of the Rotary Club of San Francisco; and Henry "Bru" Brunnier, a longtime club member who led the Rotary world as RI president, deserve the club's gratitude and respect. No history of Rotary #2 would be complete without their stories.

Vision of a World of Friends—The Story of Paul Harris (1868–1947)

The best thing in life has been the enjoyment of friendships. How ridiculous to assume that friendship can be confined by national boundary lines, religious faiths or political affiliations; friendship is not anemic; it over-rides such considerations; it is one thing of which there can never be too much; it is the ever faithful hand maiden of happiness, and it broadens and sweetens life. My fervent and oft expressed hope is that I may live until the coming of the day when I can number my personal friends in every civilized country in the world.

—Paul Harris, in *The Founder of Rotary*, 1928

Paul Harris was born April 19, 1868, in Racine, Wisconsin, into modest, middle-class beginnings. Paul's father, George, was chronically unsuccessful, and both he and his wife, Cornelia, were extravagant spenders. They were frequently rescued financially by Paul's thrifty, responsible, paternal grandfather. But George's business failed, and Paul's parents separated. At age three, Paul was taken with his older brother, Cecil, to the country home of his grandparents in Wallingford, Vermont. The time with his brother was all too short, as Paul's parents reunited temporarily and took Cecil back to live with them. Except for short visits, Paul was never united with his brother

Paul Harris as a young boy.
Courtesy RI Archive

again during their childhood. (Cecil would, however, serve later in life as assistant secretary of Rotary's international organization.)

Paul lived for the rest of his early life with his grandparents in Vermont. He grew to love Wallingford, his home, and the "wonderful yard with its apple, pear, and butternut trees; the old cow and its youngest daughter; the chickens, the orchard with its ample garden and bit of hay land, and in the distance were the splendid mountains." His closest bond was with his grandfather, who took over the role of father and instilled in him qualities that would serve Paul again and again in his adult life. Grandfather Howard had a limited education, but he valued education above else. He and his wife, Pamela, gave Paul a home where thoughtful conversation turned to literature, philosophy, and nature. They taught Paul religious and political tolerance, high ideals, and set the example for a strong work ethic.

Paul's dominating characteristic was a love of fun and companionship. He made close friends with other boys. His group called themselves the "Rapscallions"—and together they climbed trees, fished, ice skated on the pond, hiked in the local mountains, and of course, looked at girls. In fact, it was one such girl, Josie Lilly, who, for an all too brief time, set his heart to palpitating as they "coasted" in the snow. Paul had a streak of mischievousness. His many pranks included sneaking out at night after he was supposed to be in bed, meeting his friends, and riding the steel cowcatcher in front of a locomotive for a thrill.

> "The genealogy of my contributions to the Rotary movement goes back to my Valley, the friendliness of its folks, their religious and political tolerance."
>
> —Paul Harris, *My Road to Rotary*, 1948

Grandfather Howard was determined not to let Paul fail in life, as Paul's father had done. Paul, however, was disinterested in school as an annoying hindrance to his childhood interests. His grandfather persevered, and sent Paul as a teenager to an academy in Vermont. Paul's preference for silliness and pranks did not go over well at the school, and he was soon expelled. His grandfather then sent him to a military academy where Paul changed his behavior, and did well academically. Later, he was accepted into the University of Vermont. There he was wrongfully accused of misconduct and was subsequently expelled. (Many years later, the school absolved him of wrongdoing, and conferred on him a B.A. degree in physical culture, followed later by an honorary Ph.D.) Despite this accusation, Paul gained admission to Princeton and performed well. His time there was cut short when his grandfather died suddenly. After completing the year, he returned home to care for his grandmother.

His education interrupted, Paul worked sweeping floors, but his work ethic won the admiration of his employer, and he was promoted to more responsible duties. While he worked, Paul had time to contemplate his future. His grandmother implored him to honor his grandfather's memory by working hard and succeeding in life. Recalling his grandfather's admiration for a lawyer friend,

Paul decided to pursue law as a career. At age twenty-one, he entered law school at the University of Iowa in Des Moines. On his way to Des Moines, he had to change trains in Chicago. The burgeoning city, with its frontier atmosphere and huge skyscrapers, thrilled him, and he spent a week there. He decided that when he was ready to start a career, he would settle in Chicago.

After his brief stop, he continued on to the university. During his time there, he received notice that his grandmother had passed away. She was buried in the small family plot in the land where she and Paul's grandfather had spent their lives.

Paul Harris playing football as a young man. Paul is fourth from the right with his foot on the ball. Courtesy of RI Archive

Paul completed his law degree in two years. At that point, he felt a strong desire to learn about people everywhere—in his own country first, and then elsewhere in the world. His practical sense urged him to stick to the conventional rules and follow the sane and sensible paths of his classmates, who would be practicing law within sixty days of graduation.

But his visionary side won out, despite his knowing "folks back home would think he had gone stark crazy." Paul set out on a "fool's errand"—to see the world before settling into a career. He traveled to the Northwest, where he hunted and fished. When his money ran out, a college friend found him a temporary job working as a reporter for the *San Francisco Chronicle*. Soon, he resumed his journey. While traveling throughout the United States, he walked hundreds of miles in the mountains, climbing in Yosemite and Colorado's Pikes Peak. He visited cities from Fresno, to Denver, Philadelphia, and Washington, DC. As he traveled, he worked as a fruit picker, a teacher, an actor, a newspaper reporter, a hotel night clerk, and a cowboy. Answering a newspaper ad in Philadelphia, he went to work as a cattleman on a cattle boat to England. In the course of the voyage he experienced nearly unbearable privations—horrible food and depraved, vicious boatmates. But, after his return, he set out again on another ship to London. Upon his second return to the United States, he traveled to Chicago to see the World's Columbian Exposition in 1893. The added presence of visitors from across the United States and the world lent another dimension to this already exciting city.

After the fair, Paul continued his adventure, going first to New Orleans. While he was employed picking oranges there, he survived a massive hurricane estimated to have killed two thousand people. Paul nearly drowned as he held a little girl over his head, carrying her through water that rose rapidly until it reached his shoulders. As the storm continued through the night, Paul joined others in wielding axes and crowbars trying to open a dike to let the flood through to the river. Throughout his life, Paul never forgot the horror and suffering he witnessed there.

He resumed traveling in the United States, working as a salesman for a marble and granite company in Florida. His job took him to the southern states, the Bahamas, Cuba, and to the British Isles and Europe, where he bicycled all over the Continent. During his wanderings, Paul learned the value of travel as a means to broaden the mind to the people and customs of other places—if one could set aside one's "mental near-sightedness."

Throughout his travels, Paul always made his own way, either by paying his own fare or by working. He attributed his success in finding employment in strange places to several things: he always made it a point to look well-dressed and groomed, he was willing to undertake any kind of work, and he always gave his work his best effort.

> "The vision of a world-wide fellowship of business and professional men had not yet come; there were experiences of a different nature yet to be had; but a wonderful foundation had been laid. Is it any wonder that an impressionable mind which had found so much good in the midst of evil, so much friendliness in places that might have been barren, so much reason for confidence and faith in business men, should be receptive to such a vision?"
>
> —Paul Harris, *My Road to Rotary*, 1948

After five years, Paul's wanderlust was satisfied. He turned down a partnership offer in the granite business from his Florida employer, choosing instead to return to Chicago to begin his adult life in earnest. He was now almost twenty-eight years old. He had experienced hunger and loneliness, and he had learned to rely on himself and his mental and physical skills to survive. He had gained an understanding of human nature and of the differences and similarities of people everywhere. His journeys had infused him with the seeds of knowledge and yearnings that would be fulfilled later, but first he had to begin a career.

Paul hung out his shingle in Chicago in 1896, during a nationwide financial panic and recession. He thought his travels and experiences in survival would prepare him for hard times, but he underestimated the difficulties to be faced by a young stranger to the city. He would have been far better advised to take a job with a well-established firm, but new to the huge city, he had no idea how to begin.

Having difficulty finding work at first, he gradually acquired clients. Many had experienced fraud, embezzlement, and bankruptcy in the tough, dog-eat-dog climate of Chicago, where fraud, corruption, and commercialized vice were rampant. Paul joined the Chicago Association of Commerce and the Bar Association. He was known by his colleagues to conscientiously prepare every case he took on. The ethical conduct of his law practice would stand as a portent of his emphasis on the ethical conduct of business that later became a foundation of Rotary principles.

Despite his growing practice and accumulation of clients, Paul suffered intensely from loneliness in the large city. He longed for the green fields of his New England childhood and for "the voice of a kindly old friend." He gave in to his yearning for Vermont, and revisited his old home. The streets, the homes, the greenery, and the friendly people were as he recalled them. But he discovered a new perspective: the core of his being was intact and had not changed since his childhood. That core had been fashioned by his grandparents. He later wrote, "Their ideals had become my ideals.. . . . The principles of my grandparents had been made crystal clear; they could not have been made more clear if the words *integrity, frugality, tolerance,* and *unselfishness* had been carved in gargantuan letters on the bare face of majestic White Rocks."

He returned with a newfound clarity, but the loneliness persisted. His travels had left him with an instinct for learning about all sorts of people, so he frequented restaurants of every ethnicity he could find, and attended church services of many denominations and religions. In the fifteen years after he arrived in Chicago until his marriage later, he lived in more than thirty locations in the city and surrounding suburbs. He did learn a good deal about people, but his yearning for good friends went unabated. Interactions with his law-practice clients during the week kept his mind off his solitary life, but the weekends and holidays were nearly unbearable. He frequented churches, city parks, and beaches, and he took boat excursions across Lake Michigan to popular resort areas, but he experienced only crowds, without a familiar face.

Paul has written, "Betterment in human affairs comes through travail. Someone first has to visualize the need, and suffering clarifies the vision." Through his loneliness, he understood humanity's intense need for companionship as he would not have otherwise. He wrote later that he pondered the question of finding a way to increase his acquaintance with young men like himself, who had come to Chicago from farms and colleges, "who knew the joys of friendliness and neighborliness without form or ceremony." He knew there were hundreds, perhaps thousands. In fact he knew a few himself. Perhaps he might try to arrange a gathering. *If the others were longing for fellowship as I was,* he thought, *something would come of it.*

During the summer of 1900, Paul dined with a lawyer acquaintance. After dinner, they took a walk in the neighborhood, calling on several stores and shops of various kinds, where Paul's friend introduced him to the proprietors, greeting each by name. The interactions were pleasant, without the formality and indifference of business relationships that he had experienced in the city, and they reminded him of his New England village.

Paul was impressed. Clearly, his business friend had made many friends of a different sort among the businessmen of his suburban neighborhood. Paul did not have such social friends among his own business relationships. Business interactions in the city were typically not friendly; instead they were competitive, often suspicious and calculating. He wondered how he could make social friends of his business contacts. The idea of a social group of businessmen could satisfy his need for informal contact with people like himself. Moreover, if each member were the sole representative of his particular trade or profession, the alliance would be mutually advantageous to all concerned. And, unlike other social clubs where business talk was frowned upon, such discussion would be welcomed by fellow members. Although he did not act at once—several years passed— he kept the idea in his mind. That idea, of course, came to fruition in his founding of the Rotary Club of Chicago. Paul did not know it at the time, but he would never lack for friends again.

Paul enjoyed the fellowship of the Rotary Club from its start. And for Paul, fellowship included good fun. In addition to taking an active part in the jovial club meetings, he often promoted

> "When there was fun to be had, Paul was usually the ringleader. He would keep a poker face, until the right time, then laugh until his whole body would shake. Nobody ever enjoyed fun more than Paul."
>
> —Harry Ruggles, founding member of the Rotary Club of Chicago

weekend picnics with his fellow Rotarians at areas around Lake Michigan. Throughout his life, he retained his boyish sense of fun and penchant for pranks—there was nothing of the stuffed shirt about him.

With his lifelong love of hiking, Paul became a charter member of the new Prairie Club of Chicago. The club sponsored hikes in the countryside on the outskirts of the city, and Paul spent many Saturday afternoons hiking with friends. On one such day in 1910, at age forty-two, he ripped his jacket climbing over a barbed-wire fence. Jean Thomson, another hiker who had moved from Edinburgh, Scotland, three years earlier, offered to mend it for him.

Three months later, Paul and Jean were married. After two years he bought a home for Jean on top of a wooded hill in the Morgan Park district, fourteen miles south of Chicago. Several years earlier, he had seen some boys coasting down a hill in the area. The scene brought back memories of his boyhood in Vermont, and he had decided he would like to have a home there. He named their home "Comely Bank," for the street in Edinburgh where Jean was born. It was the last time he would ever move.

In the seven years after he founded the Rotary Club, Paul served two terms as club president and two as the first president of Rotary's national organization, completing the second term in 1912. He stepped down at the end of the Duluth Convention, at which the Rotary Club of Winnipeg was admitted and Rotary was renamed the International Association of Rotary Clubs. The Convention named Paul "president emeritus" of the international organization, a title bestowed on him for the rest of his life.

Paul and Jean Harris. Courtesy of RI Archive

As his term ended, Paul was exhausted. His extensive Rotary duties and travel as national president had taken a toll on his marriage and law practice, as well as on his health. Ches Perry recalled that Paul "suffered a serious physical breakdown, from which he recovered only because of his indomitable will to do so." For the next decade, Paul absented himself from Rotary. He sent only greetings to Rotary conventions, and occasionally visited clubs of interest. Much of his mail was answered by RI headquarters. His absence was often noted, and was a matter of regret for his fellow Rotarians. He did not return to active Rotary work as president emeritus until the early 1920s.

After his return, his Rotary work was extensive. Paul and Jean traveled the globe in the service of Rotary, visiting conferences, conventions, and club assemblies. In 1926, the RI board of directors extended an invitation for Paul to make a trip around the world on Rotary's behalf. In several trips within two years, Paul and Jean visited Rotary clubs in all parts of the United States, and in Bermuda, Mexico, and Cuba. They journeyed to the British Isles, Ireland, and the Continent, then to South Africa. Later, their travels took them to the countries of the Pacific, to Canada, and to countries in South America. He wrote of his travels in a series of books he called *Peregrinations*. On most occasions when an RI board asked him to make a trip, he accepted, and strove to make himself and Jean ambassadors of goodwill. He began a custom of planting "friendship trees" wherever he went. The tree plantings were ceremonial events, with the participation of Rotarians and national and local government officials. Monuments and plaques

Paul Harris planting a friendship tree in Long Beach, California, 1941. Courtesy of RI Archive

were often placed to commemorate the event. In his memoirs, Paul took enormous pride in the fact that he had planted trees "in the parks and playgrounds on all the five continents of the world and even on some of the major islands of the seas." Describing his trees as symbols of international understanding, he explained, "Our tree plantings are merely gestures of goodwill but they are intelligible to all the citizens of the various countries, whatever language they speak."

When not traveling, Paul and Jean welcomed scores of Rotarians from around the world to their home, sometimes hosting guests from as many as eight countries at one time. To honor their guests, they often planted trees in their friendship garden at Comely Bank, as lasting memories of good friends.

Much of Paul's travel and work on behalf of Rotary was accomplished despite mounting health problems—including heart attacks, breakdowns, and possibly a stroke—that began in his forties and struck intermittently.

Paul also kept up an active, if somewhat curtailed, law practice. Although he was the senior member of his law firm, his partners and associates took over many of his responsibilities. Their generosity enabled Paul to keep up with Rotary, but at somewhat of a financial cost. He was active in many organizations including the Chicago Association of Commerce, and for several years he maintained memberships in the city, state, and national bar associations. He served five years as a member and chairman of the committee on professional ethics of the Chicago Bar, where he welcomed the opportunity to carry Rotary ideals to his profession.

As the visionary and founder of Rotary, Paul received a wealth of honors. While in Nice, France, for the 1937 RI Convention, Paul was made an *Officier de la Légion d'honneur* (Officer of the Legion of Honor decoration). Created in 1802 by Napoleon, it is still France's highest decoration. It is given to any person regardless of status, for bravery in combat or for twenty years of distinguished service. He was also decorated with Ecuador's Order of Merit, Peru's Order of the Sun, Brazil's Order of the Southern Cross, Chile's Order of Merit, and the Dominican Republic's Order of Cristobal Colon. He received the Boy Scouts of America's highest award, the Silver Buffalo Token. Paul had served as the first chairman of the board of the National Society for Crippled Children in 1922, and later of the International Society. In 1942, he was presented with the national organization's Extra Mile Medallion, for his years of service on behalf of crippled children. Paul was honored twice by SF Rotary. He visited in 1925, and attended a luncheon in his honor at the Palace Hotel. While in California, he also visited Homer Wood in Petaluma. In 1935 (RI's thirtieth-anniversary year), Paul was honored at a large luncheon held at the Palm Court in the Palace Hotel. The luncheon was attended by members of all Rotary clubs north of Bakersfield, with special guests Homer Wood and RI President Bob Hill.

Throughout their thirty-seven-year marriage, his "bonnie Scottish lassie," Jean, supported him in all of his responsibilities as Rotary's honored founder. Paul later wrote that had Jean been a different type, his course as a Rotarian could not have been successful, for she made "material though inconspicuous contribution to the cause of Rotary."

Time passed for Paul and Jean at Comely Bank. They found themselves no longer in the countryside, but in a community with new apartment buildings where oaks, wild crab trees, and sumac had once stood. However, his friend and Rotary cofounder Silvester Schiele lived nearby, and the atmosphere in the neighborhood remained friendly. Jean and Paul spent many evenings reading together. While Paul read aloud, she fashioned garments for the fatherless children born at Cook County Hospital. Later in life, Paul and Jean made annual visits back to his valley in Vermont. Although people and industry had begun to encroach, Paul never tired of the beauty and friendliness of his childhood home. He also continued to retreat to the countryside outside of Chicago, particularly when he suffered physical problems. He looked upon these visits as restorative.

In his autobiography, *My Road to Rotary*, written at the end of his life, Paul described "the end of the journey." He and his beloved wife, Jean, sat daily at the fireside, drinking a cup of tea—"One who marries a Scottish lady must acquire the habit of sitting at the fireside and drinking black tea. . . . It's a good way to end the day." He recalled, "At our fireside scores of friends from all corners of the globe have delighted us by their presence. They have come as the result of my planting a sapling in 1905. The first Rotary Club was that sapling. It has grown into a mighty tree, in whose shade it is delightful to dwell."

After several months of illness, Paul Harris died at age seventy-eight, on January 27, 1947, at Comely Bank. Three days later, past RI presidents and directors who were able to come to Chicago were among a host of mourners who attended his funeral service in Morgan Park. Paul had requested that no flowers be sent, but that contributions be made to The Rotary Foundation. After the church service, the gathering slowly walked two miles through a January snowstorm to the cemetery. His casket was carried by the president and past presidents of the Rotary Club of Chicago. Throughout the world, Rotarians and others attended religious and secular services in his memory. At the time of his death, his club—conceived by one man out of his loneliness—had grown to 5,638 clubs with more than 259,000 members in seventy-five countries. Eight years later, in a tribute to RI in commemoration of its fiftieth anniversary, Eddie Arnold starred in the role of Paul Harris in a Hallmark Hall of Fame production—"The Story of Paul Harris and the Founding of Rotary International."

Ches Perry—Paul's longtime friend and the man whom Paul described as the "builder" of Rotary—penned a gentle poem in tribute:

Paul Harris, founder of Rotary.

> *He was a friend whose heart was good,*
> *Who walked with men and understood.*
> *His was a voice that spoke to cheer*
> *And fell like music on the ear.*
> *His was a smile men loved to see.*
> *His was a hand that asked no fee*
> *For friendliness or kindness done.*
> *And now that he has journeyed on*
> *His is a fame that never ends.*
> *He leaves behind uncounted friends.*

Rotary's Missionary—The Story of Homer Wood (1880–1976)

Perhaps had it not been for Homer Wood's action to bring Rotary out of Chicago,
Rotary might still be a one-club organization or perhaps might no longer exist.

—Rotary International President Rajendra Saboo, 1992

Homer Winfrey Wood was born October 18, 1880, in the mountainous Feather River gold-country town of Oroville, California. He was the youngest child of Jesse and Alice Wood. The couple had been married nineteen years, and had nine children before Homer's birth. Homer's oldest sister, Magnolia, remembered slaves in the Wood household in Alabama.

Jesse and Alice moved west from Alabama in 1868, via steamboat to Panama and by railroad across the Isthmus of Panama, then to San Francisco. Alice was still a nursing mother of a baby boy, Tison, and three very young daughters when they made the arduous, dangerous journey. By the time of Homer's birth twelve years later, the family had settled in Oroville, and his father was a prosperous Oroville citizen. He served as superintendent of Butte County schools, was part owner of the *Oroville Mercury* newspaper, and owned a fruit ranch, where he built a fine home called Eyrie Villa. He was also a fiery fundamentalist, and had been pastor of various Methodist and other congregations.

When Homer was eight, everything changed. His older brother Tison was killed jumping from a slow-moving train in San Jose. Homer's grief-stricken father viewed his eldest son's death as a sign from God, ordering him to devote his life to the ministry. Jesse sold everything and moved the family to Stockton, to take over a ministry. He came to Stockton with funds from the sale of his Butte County assets, but his meager minister's salary eventually plunged his family into poverty. Homer described himself as a "Free Thinker," and resented the fundamentalism that guided his father's decisions and caused so much hardship in the family.

As a boy, Homer loved to hike and camp in the Sierra Nevada mountains. He wrote about having made a trip to Yosemite with an older companion when he was fifteen. Their adventures there included an encounter with Indians that cost them most of their supplies. Nonetheless, the trip instilled his love for the outdoor life. One of his greatest pleasures for the rest of his long life was singing around a campfire with friends.

After several years in Stockton, the family moved to Visalia. While he went to school, Homer worked picking fruit and at other odd jobs. He applied himself to his studies and graduated as president of the Visalia class of 1899. After graduation, Homer applied and entered Stanford in the fall, as his two older brothers had. But shortly after he started, he began to suffer from eye problems, and found himself financially unable to remain at Stanford.

His plans for college thwarted, Homer took off for the gold country, in the area where he had spent his childhood. He found a job as a miner in Angels Camp, where he worked briefly, then he crossed the Sierra mountains to Bodie, California. Now a ghost town located 8,300 feet high in the Sierra, Bodie in 1900 was an isolated remnant of the Old West. It was regarded as the roughest and toughest of the remaining California boom camps, where shoot-outs were real and commonplace.

Bodie, California, now a ghost town. Photo by Dave Thompson

For a short time, Homer worked for $3 per day, underground in the Standard gold mine (which was managed by a brother-in-law).

Bodie was a roaring mining town, dotted with saloons. Homer had been raised as a strict teetotaler, but it conflicted with his love of socializing. Rather than join in with his hard-drinking friends, however, Homer's ploy in a saloon was to ask for a cigar instead.

Shortly after starting work in the mine, Homer was injured when he drove a pickaxe through his foot. Unable to continue mining, he decided to follow in his father's newspaperman footsteps. He bought a struggling weekly newspaper from two sisters by acquiring its debts. He was able to turn a profit publishing the *Bodie Miner*, and at nineteen, Homer was said to be the youngest newspaper editor and publisher at the time in the United States.

He became active in Bodie civic and community affairs. He played cornet in the town band and sang in impromptu choirs. When he was only twenty-one, he stirred the citizens of Bodie with a rousing Fourth of July speech. The following year he ran unsuccessfully for public office.

Homer also adapted to the tough side of Bodie life. After he published a story about a saloon brawl in which a man was killed, he was threatened by one of the town bullies. Homer bought a six-shooter and a box of ammunition, and practiced shooting at one of the dumps outside of Bodie. Word spread through town that the young editor was prepared to defend himself, and before sundown, rumor had it that he was a dead shot. The bully who had threatened Homer took the evening northbound stage and disappeared for parts unknown. Homer kept the six-shooter for the rest of his life.

> HOMER'S FOURTH OF JULY "ORATION"
> "There are other cities of America greater in population, greater in pomp and parade, greater in their sights of waving plumes, prancing steeds, martial music, and other indicatives of patriotism, but other cities greater in spirit of celebration, greater in patriotism today—there are none!"

Three years after arriving in Bodie, Homer left, crossing westward back over the Sierra to Sutter Creek. He became proprietor of the weekly *Amador County Record* in 1904 and, again, he was successful in his venture. As a newspaper publisher, he socialized with a number of influential men in Amador County. This led to an interest in the field of law, and he began to study law intensively in his spare time. While he studied, he was offered and accepted an appointment as clerk of the Court of Appeals in Sacramento. The year following his arrival in Sutter Creek, Homer leased the newspaper and left for Sacramento. For two years Homer worked as a court clerk, earning $200 per month. He continued to study law under the tutelage of a judge in the court, and passed the state bar exam. In early 1907, he resigned his job as court clerk and moved to San Francisco, only a year after the city's devastating earthquake.

Homer established himself in an office in the First National Bank Building, and began to build a law practice. A little more than a year later, at twenty-seven, Homer met Manuel Muñoz, and founded SF Rotary.

After four years of practicing law in San Francisco, Homer realized the newspaper business was more to his liking. He jumped at the opportunity to buy a part-ownership of the *Salinas Morning Democrat* in Salinas, California, and regretfully bid his fellow Rotarians good-bye. In his resignation letter to SF Rotary in 1911, Homer explained that his business in Salinas would not permit him to do justice to his club membership, and that he certainly could not continue in the classification of Lawyer. Although the club's board accepted his resignation, it voted him an Honorary Member of the club. Thus ended Homer's short six-year career in law. He never practiced law again, except in his own business matters, but he remained a member of the California Bar Association until his death sixty-five years later.

Salinas had three newspapers, and the competition was intense. Nevertheless, Homer made a go of it, with the same energy he had exercised managing his earlier papers. Happy to be back in the vocation he loved, he determined to settle down. In 1912, he married Cora ("Sunny") Sundberg. The following year Homer purchased the *Petaluma Daily Courier*, a morning newspaper with dilapidated equipment. The newlyweds moved to Petaluma, and remained there for fifteen years. They had a son, Homer Jesse, and a daughter, Peggy.

Homer Wood
Photo by Hammond, Porterville, CA

Homer never forgot his love for Rotary, nor lost his industriousness and skills for organizing, and he offered to start a new Rotary club in Petaluma. Twenty-four business and professional men responded, and agreed that a club should be formed. With the help of the Santa Rosa club as sponsor, the Rotary Club of Petaluma received its charter in March 1923. It was the 1,397th Rotary club in the world. Homer Wood served as the club's first president until July the following year.

Besides Rotary, Homer was active in the Masonic Lodge and several civic organizations. His newspaper and civic work led him to become involved in local, state, and national politics. He served as president of the Sonoma County Press and North Bay Counties Press associations. He was also active in the California Newspaper Publishers and California Press associations.

From a struggling publication, Homer had worked tirelessly to built up a respectable newspaper. But after fifteen years, he saw changes coming, and he sold the paper. Homer and Cora made their last move in 1928, this time to Porterville, California. Homer had purchased Porterville's *Evening Recorder* (later the *Porterville Evening Recorder*) after making a careful survey of various newspapers in the state.

The Rotary Club of Porterville immediately accepted and welcomed Homer. He also continued his previous professional, fraternal, civic, and political activities in Porterville. He gained prominent friends, including two California governors and two state senators. Among his political activities, he made significant efforts in the location of the Porterville State Hospital and the building of the Success Dam on the Tule River.

When radio advertising appeared as competition for newspapers in the 1930s, Homer decided to expand his business interests. He formed a partnership with newspaper publishers in Tulare, Visalia, and Hanford, and established KTKC, a successful radio station.

In his middle age, Homer was a prosperous businessman. He was publisher of the *Evening Recorder* and part-owner of the radio station. He owned a fine home in Porterville, and considerable other real estate, plus a summer home in the Sierra. Homer actively managed the *Recorder* until he retired and sold the paper in 1960, at age eighty. For the rest of his life, he retained a keen interest in the paper, and visited his office almost daily.

> "He always published newspapers that were highly influential and of high standard. He was a major supporter of all worthy civic events."
>
> —From Homer Wood's Newspaper Hall of Fame award, 1984

Homer Wood at the desk he used throughout his life as a publisher.

After his retirement, Homer turned to one of his long-standing interests—"Simplified Spelling." Growing from the Simplified Spelling Board established in 1908 by Andrew Carnegie, it was an idea that had been advanced by Noah Webster, Benjamin Franklin, and Theodore Roosevelt. Homer recalled struggling with the vagaries of the English language in his boyhood days. Simplified Spelling would spell words as they sounded: "brite" for "bright," "fone" for "phone," "bot" for "bought," and so on. After he sold the *Recorder*, Homer kept an office in his Wood Building, which housed the newspaper. He published pamphlets and wrote letters daily, corresponding nationally and internationally. He distributed literature, and relied on the *Recorder* to proselytize for this cause. The California State Senate passed a resolution for reformed spelling, calling for the president to implement it. A U.S. congressman introduced a bill in Congress, but the bill was tabled.[24]

All his life, Homer kept up with his earliest Rotary friends. In 1925, as a past president of SF Rotary, he traveled to San Francisco to meet Paul Harris at a luncheon given in Paul's honor. Eight years later, Homer visited Chicago. Unfortunately, Paul was out of town, but Homer was introduced to Silvester Schiele—a meeting of the first presidents of Rotary Club #1 and Club #2. In 1935 (RI's thirtieth-anniversary year), Homer again met Paul at a large SF Rotary luncheon in the Palm Court of the Palace Hotel. Homer gave the concluding speech, reminiscing about what had grown forth from the meeting in his office twenty-seven years before. In 1952, SF Rotary presented Homer with a special medal. Homer continued to make occasional appearances at his beloved San Francisco club, with rare visits into his eighties. In 1965, five hundred Rotarians honored him with a standing ovation at the club's celebration of Rotary's sixtieth anniversary. The following year, he made a generous contribution to the San Francisco Rotary Foundation.

Rotary clubs he founded continued to honor him. The Rotary Club of Oakland commemorated Homer's first success at Rotary extension at their fortieth-anniversary dinner. Homer's last visit to the Petaluma community was in 1967, for a dinner honoring all past presidents of the Rotary Club of Petaluma. After dinner, he gave a brief history of Rotary and the Petaluma club. He had attended meetings of the

Homer Wood presented with Paul Harris Fellow award by the Rotary Club of Petaluma, 1973. Courtesy of RI Archive

24. The Simplified Spelling movement continues today.

Porterville club regularly until he was seventy-three years old, when the club made him an Honorary Member. On his ninetieth birthday, the Rotary Club of Porterville thrilled him with a birthday party at his home. Three years later, Homer was unable to attend the Petaluma club's fifty-year banquet. In his absence, the club voted to award the pioneer Rotarian their first Paul Harris Fellow award. Members of the Petaluma and Porterville clubs visited him at home to present him with the award.

Homer received many honors outside of Rotary. During his years of publishing, he was cited by Army Emergency Relief, the American Heart Association, the U.S. Navy, the Bureau of Naval Personnel, the U.S. Treasury Department, and numerous others. In a short biography of his father, Homer's son concluded that these honors "were based on a philanthropic, ethical, and patriotic philosophy of business conduct stemming from the moral outlook of his family environment." In Homer's eightieth year, the California Senate unanimously issued a resolution, congratulating him on his lifetime achievements as one of California's colorful characters and founder of Rotary in the West. It described Homer as "devoted to the welfare of his fellow man, a follower of the good life, a sportsman, and philanthropist."

> "Homer Wood will be remembered as a quiet man of firm convictions and high achievement."
>
> —From Homer Wood's Newspaper Hall of Fame award, 1984

Homer enjoyed remarkable health, living out his life in the house he bought when he moved to Porterville. He joined hunting parties with friends into his nineties. He outlived Cora, who passed away in 1970 after fifty-eight years of marriage. Following a ten-day hospitalization for heart infirmities, Homer Wood died on July 18, 1976. He was almost ninety-six years old.

When Homer died, he was recognized as the oldest member of the California Bar Association, with its longest tenure of membership. He was also posthumously elected to the California Press Association's Newspaper Hall of Fame.

Members of the Rotary Club of San Francisco mourned their club's founder, as did Rotarians worldwide. Homer Wood has been remembered in a number of ways. His granddaughter Victoria Wood was introduced to the San Francisco Rotarians as an Honorary club member in 1999. SF Rotary's RI District 513 (now 5130 and 5150) created its annual Homer Wood Award for the club that has done outstanding work in World Community and International Service over the past year. As its own tribute, SF Rotary created its Homer Wood Fellowship to honor individuals who have contributed to the San Francisco club's Foundation. In 1995, club President Bill Koefoed presented the new award to nine charter members, for their Foundation support. Since then, more than thirty individuals have been so honored.

SF Rotary also conceived of a more public way to commemorate its esteemed founder. On January 4, 1992, members of Districts 5130 and 5150 gathered at the site of the old Kezar Stadium in Golden Gate Park. They dedicated a newly planted Homer Wood Grove and Bench. Most of the clubs in the two districts contributed to the project. Rotary International President Rajendra Saboo and his wife attended the dedication ceremony and a dinner. Of Homer Wood's place in Rotary history, President Saboo said, "Perhaps had it not been for Homer Wood's action to bring Rotary out of Chicago, Rotary might still be a one-club organization or perhaps might no longer exist."

■ ■ ■

Amid so much to celebrate, there is a sad aspect of Homer's life in Rotary. On many occasions, he read or heard it said that Manuel Muñoz founded the Rotary Club of San Francisco "with the aid of Homer Wood." Proud of his role in the magnificent growth of Rotary, Homer wrote letters periodically to Paul Harris and RI Secretary Ches Perry, asking that the attribution in official Rotary literature be corrected. The problem persisted, however, despite Homer's repeated attempts. In a letter written in 1959, Ches Perry

Members of District 5130 and 5150 dedicate the Homer Wood Grove and Bench in Golden Gate Park, 1992. RI President Rajendra Saboo and his wife are at left. Courtesy of Pete Taylor

surmised that "the tradition probably developed among us Chicago Rotarians that a man named Muñoz had gone to the Coast and organized several clubs there."

At long last, Homer's pioneering effort as the man who brought about Rotary extension was fully recognized. Two years before Homer died, the Petaluma and Porterville clubs launched a concerted effort to set the record straight. Based on their work, and with information provided by the San Francisco club, *The Rotarian* magazine featured a story titled "He Seconded the Motion." It was sixty-five years since Homer had founded Rotary #2, and Rotary had grown to over sixteen thousand clubs in the world. Homer finally had his story told as he believed it should be.[25] Since then, several publications, such as *The Golden Wheel* and David Forward's *A Century of Service*, now give Homer the honor due him.

Based on the letters and documents available, it does seem that the credit belongs largely to Homer Wood, but Manuel Muñoz is certainly due his share. Indeed, without Manuel Muñoz bringing the message of Rotary to San Francisco, and his chance meeting and conversation with a young San Francisco businessman, the triumph of being the second club in the Rotary world—and the one most responsible for the early spread of Rotary—might instead have gone to another club.

The Rotary Club of San Francisco has never wavered in its support of Homer Wood as its true founder. Founding members of the club wrote letters to RI confirming that it was Homer who organized and brought the club into being. The club honored him as its only longtime Honorary Member from the time of his resignation from the club in 1911 to his death in 1976. In his history of the club in 1940, William Mountin acknowledged the controversy surrounding Homer's claim. He also dedicated the book to Homer, "Founder of the Rotary Club of San Francisco, President during its first two years, early missionary in the establishment of Rotary on the Pacific Coast."

25. For more about this issue, see Source Notes.

Integrity and Leadership—The Story of Bru Brunnier (1882–1971)

The world is a better place because of Rotary, and we all know Rotary is a better place because of Bru.

—Stan McCaffrey, former SF Rotary club member and RI Past President, 1971

There are diamonds in the rich history of the Rotary Club of San Francisco. Homer Wood is honored as the founder of the second Rotary club in the world, and the club that sent Rotary out to the rest of the world. On the other hand, Bru Brunnier is unquestionably the club's most illustrious member. He left a legacy of service that has no equal. Henry J. Brunnier was renowned for his professional expertise and achievements, and for the many positions of honor he attained throughout his life. But he was simply called "Bru" by friends and colleagues, and has been respectfully known all over the world by that nickname ever since.

Bru Brunnier at one year. Courtesy of Mike Davies, H. J. Brunnier Associates

Bru was born in 1882 on a farm near Manning, Iowa, of second-generation parents. He went to a one-room country school, then graduated to Manning High School. While in high school, he worked for a contractor during summer vacation, and decided to become a contractor because his employer was one of the wealthiest men in town.

One of his early lessons in personal integrity came about when his uncle encountered financial difficulties in his general merchandising business. Bru recalled that "in those days a family name meant something," so the older brothers sold their farms to pay the debts and moved to town to help with the business.

Very few country boys went on to college in those days, and Bru was the first boy in his town to attend Iowa State College in Ames. He paid his own living expenses with his savings. While in college, he formed a longtime friendship with his professor Dean Anson Marston that was to prove invaluable to Bru time after time.

In his college years, Bru already demonstrated the foundations of his leadership. While still a freshman, he learned that the Manning town council was contracting with a blacksmith for a tall water standpipe (a vertical pipe used to maintain uniform pressure in a water-supply system). He immediately went to the mayor and then to the town council and recounted one of Dean Marston's lectures about a standpipe failure that resulted in collapse. After hearing the college freshman's story, the council asked him if he could design a tank tower. He suggested Dean Marston, who was delighted to do the job. Bru made the drawings for that project, which started his lifelong interest in design. Afterward, Marston said, "Any freshman who could go out and sell an engineering job can work for me anytime." He subsequently gave Bru all the drafting work Bru could handle.

The tank tower designed by college freshman Bru Brunnier in Manning, Iowa. —The Rotarian, November, 1952.

Bru's innate sense of integrity no doubt helped his relationship with Marston. Bru recounts how Marston took him aside during his last term and suggested he take some time out to enjoy himself socially. He offered Bru a loan of $100, which Bru could pay back later. Bru took out his first life-insurance policy as soon as he found his first job after college, so he could be sure Marston would get his money back.

Despite Marston's efforts, however, Bru had little inclination for outside social activities. Lacking time and money, he didn't date. However, he developed an appreciation for fellowship during these years. Although he "didn't do much with it," he joined the local literary society "for a little relaxation and fellowship." He preferred the Friday-night meetings of the society to a night out on the town.

Bru graduated with honors as a civil engineer from Iowa State University in 1904. His lifelong accumulation of honors started early, with memberships in several honor societies and fraternities.

Bru's first contracting job was with the American Bridge Company in Pittsburgh. However, his life as an engineer nearly didn't come about. He had always played baseball and had a strong right arm and a good fastball. In the early 1900s, baseball was becoming wildly popular. While at his first job in Pittsburgh, he pitched in semipro games. The Pittsburgh Pirates tried to sign him, but the professional ballplayer's itinerant life was not what Bru wanted. He continued to play semipro ball for several more years, saving the earnings as a nest egg. He pitched with the Flatbush team in Brooklyn, which later became the Dodgers. He set a number of records, and at one point pitched a no-hitter. For most of his life he thought he could throw a baseball better than he could swing a golf club.

His job at American Bridge lasted a little less than a year. In 1905 he joined the Edison Company in New York and began to work in design. At first he lived in boardinghouses and tried the New York big-city life. He played long poker games with the men who lived there, sometimes using slow time at work to figure out the probabilities involved in poker. But, as he recounts, one day he asked himself, *What are you trying to be, a gambler or an engineer?* He decided he would rather work on developing a new theory in reinforced concrete than waste his time and mathematics on "this gambling stuff." He quit poker, breaking up the boardinghouse group and making his poker-playing landlord furious in the process. Bru had to move from the boardinghouse and swore he would never play poker again.

Later that year he decided he would rather get married and be "a home man" than to continue the life of "the bright lights people" in New York. He had known Ann Weideman when she was a young girl in Manning, but "wouldn't

Bru Brunnier in his baseball uniform at Iowa State College, c. 1904. Courtesy of RI Archive

look at her" because "her mother kept her in long dresses and short pigtails." She looked a lot younger than she was, which was three years younger than Bru. He met her again one Christmas while he was in college and liked what he saw. So began Bru's sixty-five-year marriage to his "Little Ann" in 1905. They lived at a boardinghouse for a few months, then found an apartment and set up housekeeping.

Ann appreciated Bru's interest in buildings from the start. She enjoyed watching construction, and on Sundays they would take time and go to watch large projects such as the huge tunnels to the Pennsylvania Terminal and New York subway projects. For his part, Bru was getting a feel for those kinds of jobs by observing.

In 1906, San Francisco was rocked by the earthquake and largely consumed in the resulting fire. New York Edison loaned Bru to the engineering company for United Railroads, which operated several cable-car and trolley routes in San Francisco. The earthquake had destroyed the Powell Street cable line and car house, and damaged other routes. The engineering company desperately needed engineers to work on reconstructing the lines, and made a generous offer to Bru, which he accepted. With no idea where he would sleep, Bru arrived in the devastated city two weeks after the earthquake and experienced the extreme conditions of every aspect of San Francisco life.

Ann returned to Iowa to wait for Bru, finally joining him a few weeks later. In a city where forty thousand people were still living in tents, the couple was fortunate to find an apartment. They had two children in their adopted city. After a succession of apartments, they eventually settled for a number of years in Oakland, and Bru commuted to San Francisco by ferry. In later years Bru and Ann returned to live in San Francisco, where they lived in several locations as his success grew.

In the years following the 1906 earthquake, the job Bru had been sent to San Francisco to do—rebuilding the railroad—had not gone far due to railroad strikes and ongoing prosecutions of railroad officials for bribery and graft. Instead, Bru worked on detailed drawings for an ironworks, and learned more about engineering work. Bru observed the buildings that had withstood the quake, especially the Palace Hotel. His observations led to his basic theory of structural resistance to stress. This theory led to his international reputation as a specialist in earthquake stability.

In 1908, Bru decided to go to work for himself, two years after he had arrived in San Francisco. He opened an office of three rooms in the Monadnock Building on Market Street. What distinguished this ambitious young man of twenty-five from the very start was the nature of his practice and the service he provided. Unlike the few other structural engineers in town, Bru provided a more complete design product that was immediately usable as delivered. The client did not need to figure out the details for himself. And Bru had no conflicting commercial interests or obligations to specific manufacturers, so he could choose the quality products for his designs.

From the beginning, Bru placed a value on his services. He kept his prices high and he resisted pressure to lower them. He took pride in the fact that a few years later he won the contract to build the three-thousand-foot Santa Cruz Wharf because he held his ground during negotiation, stating that he would not lower his level of service just to save the builder some money.

Bru struggled in his new practice, taking part-time work at first, but five months later he was able to hire his first employee. In his first year, he won an important contract for all the structural work on the San Francisco waterfront development. He established such a reputation as an experienced engineer with high-quality service, that his youthful appearance startled people who met him in person.

Several months after opening his office in 1908, Bru learned, through a good friend, about a new organization for business and professional men. Bru was invited to become a member of the Rotary Club by member A. E. Hornlein. It was the first organization Bru joined after college, and he embarked on an adventurous journey with Rotary that lasted for his lifetime. Since the new Rotary Club limited its membership to businessmen considered of high caliber, the fact that he was chosen for membership was satisfying to the young man of twenty-six years. Bru was just three years out of college, in business for only a few months, yet he had already earned a solid reputation as a good engineer.

SF Rotary may seem a strange choice for Bru. After all, his business classification of structural engineer was referred to as a "long shot"—the kind not likely to receive patronization from other members. Nonetheless, he actively patronized other club members' businesses, and "boosted" for them at meetings.

Bru Brunnier's application for membership in SF Rotary, April 27, 1909.

As an early member, Bru was instrumental in shaping the club. He was an active member, serving on the Grievance Committee, the Publicity and Extension Committee, and the Adjustment Committee. He served as a director in 1912–13. On the lighter side, he indulged his love of baseball by organizing and promoting several games with the Oakland Rotary club.

Bru's career in Rotary began in earnest when he was elected club president in 1913. According to Bru, it came about because the contentious election the previous year "sort of split the club up," and they were looking for a neutral president for 1913. At the annual meeting, one of the members rose and nominated him for president. "Somebody seconded the nomination, somebody moved the nominations be closed, somebody else seconded the nominations be closed, and the next thing I knew, I was president. I was so scared,. . . I had never been president of anything, and here, to be president of the San Francisco Rotary Club was just unthinkable!" What Bru modestly omitted from this account was that the vote was unanimous and by acclamation, one of the club's few such votes at the time. Riding home on the ferry later that day, he realized that this was an opportunity, and he had better get to work.

An Early Gift from Rotary

"They had a little blow-in down at the waterfront just before a Rotary lunch one day, and I didn't like to miss the luncheon or the fellowship that was there.... So I got on the hook and went down the hole without putting on any coveralls. It didn't take me long to tell them what to do, then I cut out and went to the lunch.

"When I got to the luncheon,...a lot of questions came up, and first thing I know I'd given them a good education on caissons and foundations, and they liked it.

"Well [Homer Wood] was without a speaker the next Tuesday, so he called me up and said 'Bru, I want you to tell that story of the caisson to the club next Tuesday.' I said 'Homer, you're crazy, I can't even answer roll call. I'm scared to death when I do that, and you can't hear me ten feet away.' He said 'You're a good Rotarian and you'll be there next Tuesday.' And he hung up on me.

"Then Monday rolled around and I called Homer. I said 'Homer, I am'—I didn't say 'I have to'—'I am going to San Jose tomorrow,...and I can't possibly get back for lunch, so you'll probably have to get someone else.' I didn't want to lie to him, so I actually went to San Jose.... I just wasted the day, but I didn't make the speech.

"Several weeks later,... he said 'Bru, I'm without a speaker today, so come on up here and tell them about that caisson.'... I could have crawled through a knothole—just scared stiff to get up and talk to a group. I can talk around a table, but to talk to a group? Yet there I was—I couldn't help myself. I had to go up.

"I stumbled around a little while, but all of a sudden I got the feeling that these fellows wanted to hear what I had to say.... First thing I knew, I was talking to the whole group and telling it to them. That's how I learned I could get up and think and talk. I've always been grateful to the San Francisco Rotary Club for developing me so I could do that."

—Bru Brunnier, 1959

And work he did. Bru focused primarily on fellowship, the problem with attendance, and with preparation for the upcoming 1915 Rotary Convention in San Francisco. The leadership that marks his Rotary career was visible that year. As club president, he had each member involved in a program. He believed in designing all club activities to develop the individual so each Rotarian could better serve his vocation and community.

One of his earliest obstacles was a perception that he—among the youngest men in the club—was in over his head. However, he won over his worst critic, Past President M. Louis Wooley, by ordering him to "lay off me" or he would take up with the club the question of who was really the president. They became good friends after Wooley "finally decided maybe the damn kid had something."

After his presidential year, Bru increased his efforts to make the approaching Rotary Convention in San Francisco a roaring success. As executive chairman of the 1915 Convention Committee and also chairman of the Iowa Building for the concurrent Panama-Pacific International Exposition, Bru overextended himself. When he found it difficult to get his fellow members to help with the planning, he had to take a room at the Palace Hotel for three weeks so he could work on this enormous undertaking day and night. He and the club secretary wrote out the whole plan for all of the committees, including a seven-course banquet for an unprecedented attendance of 1,900 at one sitting at the Palace.

On the convention's opening day, without time for dinner or breakfast, Bru was exhausted. When he collapsed from a dizzy spell, a Rotarian doctor took charge and prevented him from working any more that day. The doctor suggested that Bru take time off for a trip to Hawaii, where no one could reach him. Bru thought it was a good idea, but the trip had to wait. However, he would soon get his chance.

Bru didn't rest for long. At the convention, Rotary's constitution and bylaws were revised, and the new district concept was adopted to create an administrative link between the International Association of Rotary Clubs and the individual clubs. Bru was charged with defining each district geographically. Bru has been widely credited with the original concept for the district plan. He is said to have had the idea while traveling from a six-city meeting he attended in Tacoma. He defined the geographical system based on the shortest distances for railroad travel between groups of the original one hundred clubs, so that each district governor could visit his clubs, and the clubs could be represented at an annual district conference. The next month, the "Around State" meeting in Oakland furthered his idea that contact with nearby clubs was a strengthening process. When he took the need for a district organization to the International officers, they presented it at the San Francisco Convention in 1915, where it was adopted.

Bru took pride in the convention—rated as the best yet—and acknowledged that when the convention week came, everyone on the committees worked long and hard. When his fellow SF Rotarians recommended him for Rotary's president later in 1918, they praised his "heroic work" on the San Francisco convention—which included inaugurating a system of management and handling conventions that was followed in large measure for years afterward.

During the convention Bru was also elected first district governor of the newly created District 13. It covered New Mexico, Arizona, Nevada, California, and Hawaii. At first, there were only nine clubs in his district: San Francisco, Oakland, Los Angeles, San Diego, Stockton, Sacramento, San Jose, Phoenix, and Honolulu. Taking his doctor's advice, Bru and Ann took a boat to Hawaii to give the Rotary Club of Honolulu its charter.

Through a chance meeting on the boat to Hawaii, Bru met the chairman of the Harbor Board of Honolulu. Thus on his first day in Honolulu, he started a consulting job about harbor facilities throughout the islands. He returned home $2,500 richer, and regarded his service to Rotary as the source of business opportunity.

During his year as district governor in 1915, businessmen in Fresno and Berkeley formed new Rotary clubs. There were no clubs in New Mexico and Nevada, so Bru traveled there himself and started clubs in Albuquerque and Reno. He visited every club in the district, including Honolulu, traveling ten thousand miles during the year. He held the new district's first conference in Fresno in February 1916, the most attended district conference in RI that year.

For the next few years, Bru's Rotary career advanced rapidly. In 1917 he chaired the important Constitution and Bylaws Committee at the Atlanta RI Convention. He was elected a second

Bru Brunnier in 1918, the year he was first nominated for RI president.

vice president of the International Association (one of the five directors on the board), in a "spur of the moment" action that took place without consulting him.

The Rotary Club of Tacoma paid him the honor of placing his name in nomination for International president for 1918, declaring that "whenever Rotary has had a particularly hard and disagreeable job on hand, they would send the bell-boy out to page Henry J. Brunnier." Once again, Bru was caught by surprise, as he was away on a wartime job in Washington, D.C., and couldn't be reached when the nomination was made.

He was approved as candidate, but his nomination ran aground on the shoals of "dirty politics" in the election at the 1918 Rotary Convention. As he explains it, a member confronted him with literature sent out by the Tacoma Club promoting him for president. Bru denied knowledge of the literature, or even that he was running for president. He said, "That's news to me, I'm not going to ask anyone to vote for me—I never have, and I'm not now." Evidently there were enough available votes to elect him, so the promoters of another candidate tried to eliminate him by running headline rumors in the newspapers that Bru "Can't Run" because of his war work. The headlines cost him the election. Bru claims that the tactics were considered by many to be "raw." He points to the *Convention Proceedings* in which then-President Leslie Pidgeon condemned the newspaper reporting, and declared that "Vice-President Brunnier has some reason to complain" about the reports, adding that a "statement of regret is due" from the chair. "It must have been pretty bad or he wouldn't have said that," Bru reasons. "And I'm glad getting elected didn't happen then. Because later on, I did become president when it was a much bigger and much better job, and I could do much more than I could have at that time."

1n 1922, he had been so helpful in designating districts earlier that Rotary again called on Bru and appointed him chairman of the Redistricting Committee—"Everything had grown, . . . you just had to put everything back into the hat and reshuffle." Bru was

> "Rotary was like a religion with him, and it was his only religion."
>
> —Brunnier associate Charles De Maria

faced with making difficult recommendations to divide several of the largest districts into smaller ones. Many clubs objected so vehemently that Bru lost several friends. But he was able to divide all of the districts except his own, where the objections were especially bitter. It was so bad that Ann told him, "You're never going to talk redistricting in this district again." And Bru said, "I won't—I've had enough of it." "So all these jobs are not glory," he warns.

Bru by no means gave up on Rotary. He continued doing committee work, both for RI and actively in his San Francisco club. In 1926, the Pan-Pacific Rotary Conference—a biennial conference of clubs in countries bordering on the Pacific basin—was established, to maintain amicable relations between the several countries in that part of the world. Bru represented SF Rotary at the second conference. For decades, he attended every district conference for his district. In 1938 he repeated his role as chairman of the Host Club Executive Committee for the second RI Convention in San Francisco.

Bru and Ann Brunnier relaxing in Palm Springs after Bru's year as RI president, 1954. Photo by Edward Canby; Courtesy RI Archive

Bru was known to travel widely, starting early in his Rotary career. By 1918 alone, he had attended six consecutive RI conventions, either as a delegate or international officer; and as district governor he had traveled ten thousand miles in the service of Rotary. In his later positions in RI—before, during, and after the year of his presidency in 1952–53—he would add hundreds of thousands of miles traveling on behalf of Rotary, and in his business life. Bru looked upon travel as an opportunity for fellowship. He rarely traveled without Ann, an ambassador of friendship and goodwill—and a tireless traveler. Bru recalls that "she nearly killed herself because she kept a diary all day long." She stayed up late writing after long, tiring days, because, "tomorrow there will be some more stuff, and once I quit I'm lost."

There seems to have been no limit to Bru's energy and drive. While working unceasingly for his much-loved Rotary, he grew his company into one of the most successful and prominent engineering firms in the country. In the process, he left his mark throughout San Francisco and the western hemisphere. He served his country on strategic projects in wartime. In World War I, he organized and managed the concrete ship department for the U.S. Emergency Fleet Corporation. During World War II, he worked for the Navy on air-base structures and submarine bases. He designed transport docks in the Panama Canal Zone for the Army, and was involved in many other military installations along the Pacific Slope.

Bru contributed to plans for construction of RI's headquarters in Evanston, and turned the first four spadesful of earth during his RI presidential year. Closer to home, his name is associated with dozens of major structures, for which H. J. Brunnier Associates was responsible for earthquake stability and safety, and which led to his reputation as "the acknowledged dean of West Coast engineers." One of his early commissions was the design work for the elegant Sharon Building in 1912—

"All of his life he stood like a giant redwood in a valley of second-growth timber. The evidence of his work is all around us in the structures he designed, the organizations he founded and built, and the people whose lives he touched."

—Brunnier associate Charles De Maria

where he subsequently moved his firm (and where it remains today, one floor away from the present-day office of SF Rotary). Other prominent landmarks include the former De Young Museum, the old Seals Stadium, the San Francisco Public Library (now the Asian Art Museum), and skyscrapers on the early San Francisco skyline such as the Shell Building, Standard Oil Building, Federal Reserve Bank, the Russ Building (which remained San Francisco's tallest building until 1964), and the Crown-Zellerbach Building, as well as the low-level Broadway tunnels between Alameda and Contra Costa Counties.

The most famous jewel in Bru's crown is indisputably the San Francisco-Oakland Bay Bridge, which was completed in 1937. In the planning stages for the bridge, his structural expertise and his abilities as a public speaker served him well. These skills led to a prestigious appointment to the five-member Consulting Engineers Board for the bridge, chosen from the United States at large. His presentations to over eighty organizations garnered public support for the bridge. As one of the five engineers who oversaw design of the bridge, Bru was memorialized in a caisson named for him beneath one of the bridge suspension towers.

In 1963, he incorporated his firm, and gave all the stock in the company to six engineers, keeping none for himself. He remained president of the firm, and never retired. Ever the proponent of vocational service, he served as president of five engineers' associations. In 1941 he was awarded the first Iowa State University Marston Award. Named for his old mentor, it is the highest honor from the engineering department of his alma mater. He received honorary membership in the American Society of Civil Engineers, the highest award given by the society.

Bru carried his profession into his community involvement. He believed "there is nothing more important for engineers than to take a hand in civic affairs. Most community activities involve some phase of engineering, and it is about time that we stop depending upon our businessmen, our doctors, and our lawyers to make these important engineering decisions. . . . Engineers are slow to pick up their share of the load." When engineers' claims of professional status were continually challenged, he emphasized support for the U.S. Chamber of Commerce. He viewed the Chamber as the best venue for an effective public-relations effort, through which engineers could make their most important contributions to progress on the local, state, and national levels. Bru's love of design extended to organizations of all sorts. While chairman of a San Francisco Chamber of Commerce committee, he guided a new model charter for the city and county.

His keen interest in service was not limited to Rotary and trade organizations. After serving as director for the California chapter of the American Automobile Association in 1924, he went on to become its president, and later the national president of the AAA in 1945–47. In this capacity, he worked tirelessly, advocating for motorists and combating driver-unfriendly legislation. He served in countless other organizations and state and local boards and committees. He was Past Master of the Mt. Davidson Masonic Lodge.

Besides his lifelong love of baseball, Bru found time in his busy life for golf. He was the organizing president of the Lake Merced Golf and Country Club in San Francisco, and members in District 5150 vied for the Bru Brunnier Golf Trophy.

Bru and Ann were also avid collectors of fine decorative arts—porcelain, jade figurines, carved ivories, glass, snuff boxes, and dolls—accumulated over forty-seven years during their travels. In 1963 the Brunniers donated their extensive art collection to Iowa State University, where a special building was constructed to house it. The donated art objects arrived in two semitrailers and took nine months to unpack.

Bru continued to garner respect throughout the Rotary world. His storehouse of experience and passionate obligation to service lifted him to the highest honor that is bestowed on a Rotarian, the office of international president for 1952–53. The introductory article in *The Rotarian* that year summed up his spirit:

> Perhaps one key to all Bru's activities has been his training as an engineer in the best and largest sense of the word—a quality now smoothed and polished into an easy ability to go to the heart of all he approaches, to analyze and sort out what he deems to be best, and to put principles into a foundation on which can be erected things of beauty as well as utility. He never forgets that structures, whether of stone and steel or men and organization, are built to serve mankind.

One of the hallmarks of his presidential year was his travel itinerary. Like other RI presidents before him, he traveled the globe. But he set aside most travel to Europe, which had been covered extensively by former presidents. Instead, he went where his immediate predecessors hadn't been, visiting Australia and New Zealand thoroughly, and contacting all the clubs there through inter-city meetings. He went to Indonesia, India, Burma, the Philippines, and Japan. He traveled 75 percent of the time in that year—and he was seventy years old.

Still, he paid attention to detail. While charged with responsibilities all over the world, he thrilled the small town of Manning, Iowa, when he returned as RI president. He was greeted by most of the townspeople and a brass band, and Bru realized his ambition to present a charter to a new Rotary club in his hometown. *The Rotarian* favored the event with a four-page feature, publicity that brought hundreds of congratulatory letters from all over the world to the Manning club and community.

During his presidential year, he presided over the RI Convention in Paris. It hosted over ten thousand

Bru and Ann Brunnier ride a ceremonial elephant during his presidential year. Notice the Rotary emblem on the elephant's forehead.
Courtesy of RI Archive

French President Vincent Auriol (right) presents Bru Brunnier with the Order of the Legion of Honor decoration, 1953. This still hangs in Bru's old office in San Francisco. Courtesy of Mike Davies, H. J. Brunnier Associates

Rotarians and families from seventy-six countries, making it the largest RI Convention held outside the United States to that date.

Many certificates of high honors still hang undisturbed on the wall behind Bru's desk in the Sharon Building office of H. J. Brunnier Associates. A few stand out most prominently. While in Paris for the 1953 RI Convention during his presidential year, he was awarded the *Légion d'honneur* (Legion of Honor). The award was presented by the president of the French Republic, Vincent Auriol, at his Elysée Residence. He was also awarded the Belgian *Officier de l'Ordre de la Couronne* (Officer of the Order of the Crown), presented by the crown prince. Bru was honored in his profession by *El Instituto de Ingenieros de Chile* and the Civil Engineering Society and Architectural Institute of Japan.

The year after his RI presidency, Bru served as an RI director, and on the RI Headquarters Committee. He also served as a Rotary Foundation trustee for six years. He resumed activities in his home club as well, serving on the Adjustment Committee and the Vocational Committee. Bru was a proponent of the SF Rotary Foundation. He served on the first SF Rotary Foundation board when it was established in 1959 and served in the eighty-ninth year of his life. When Ann died at age eighty-five in 1970, he requested that memorial contributions be made to the SF Rotary Foundation. He continued to attend club meetings until his advanced years. He was an honored guest on several occasions during the final years of his life.

In 1971, with sixty-three unbroken years of Rotary service, Bru had longer club service than any of the 700,000 members in the Rotary world.[26] On the sixty-sixth birthday of Rotary that year, he participated in a telephone conversation with Bill Oppenheimer, at age eighty-seven the second-longest Rotarian and a charter member of the tenth Rotary club in the world in St. Paul, Minnesota. Moreover, he outlived all of Rotary's original nineteen district governors.

At age eighty-nine he still had a golf handicap of twenty-nine and played every week. Although he no longer drew a salary from his firm, he remained its president, and he kept current on technical and professional matters. As recently as the construction of the Bank of America

---

26. Homer Wood was a Rotarian a few months before Bru, but his service was discontinuous.

World Headquarters in San Francisco (completed in 1969), he was involved in developing a test section and actually "walked the beams."

SF Rotary recognized his eighty-ninth birthday at the last meeting he attended on November 23, 1971, and he spoke about the history of Rotary, sharing Rotary with the newest members from its oldest.

Bru died on December 10, 1971 while napping at his desk, after a typical morning of work, an appointment with his barber, and lunch with his associates in the Palace Hotel Garden Court. A note of detailed plans for a dinner party he was hosting that evening was found on his desk. Bru expressed the wish that there be no service or tributes of any kind, but a brief memorial service was held by local Rotarians, with fellow SF Rotarian Charlie Wheeler as RI's official representative. In keeping with Bru's wishes, only a few words of thanksgiving were spoken, followed by a moment of silence as each attendee pondered Bru's contribution to the world of Rotary.

Charles Wheeler later said of Bru that in early Rotary days, "he joined forces in the historic battle to change the Rotary practice of business exchange to a program of 'He Profits Most Who Serves Best,' thereby laying the foundation of his worldwide identity as Mr. Rotary."

Bru has long been regarded as a San Francisco Rotary Club treasure. Four years before he died, Rotary District 513 established a Bru Brunnier Award for Distinguished International Service, given each year to the club determined to have the best International Services program. Earlier in the year he died, the club named him "Rotary's Number One Member," in its nomination statement for Bru to receive District 513's first Distinguished Individual Service Award. It is fitting that the SF Rotary's most honored members should be called Bru Brunnier Fellows. In Jim Patrick's thank-you to the club upon being named a Fellow, he said "Bru has set the highest of all Rotary standards for all of us to follow. I'm moved to be in his shadow." Former club member and RI Past President Stan McCaffrey said before Bru died, "The world is a better place because of Rotary, and we all know Rotary is a better place because of Bru."

> "It's been a long time. . . . You do a little [volunteer work] now and a little then. After a while it adds up."
>
> —Bru Brunnier, 1959

chapter four

Difficult Decades:
Three Calls to Serve

S F Rotary's entry into service in its early years—Community Service, Club Service, and Vocational Service—did not come about in a vacuum. Three decades, from 1914 through 1945, brought about unimaginable events at home and abroad. Twice, the world experienced war, as freedom battled tyranny and emerged victorious. Between the wars, Americans suffered through a period of fear, loss, and hardship. Throughout these crises, SF Rotary answered calls to serve, and Rotarians gained an understanding of how they could join together and work to make their community and their world a better place in which to live.

World War I—The Dawn of International Service

As the war drums were beating in Europe, club President Charles Victor expressed—for the first recorded time by a SF Rotarian—the idea that there might be a role for Rotary in bringing about the international harmony so sorely needed in the world. Charles was speaking at the 1914 RI Convention in Houston about the upcoming Panama-Pacific International Exposition, scheduled to open in San Francisco in 1915. "The Exposition was planned with one mighty sentiment. . . ultimate peace in the world." He envisioned Rotary extending around the world one day. And Rotary, he declared, sought nothing so much "as to bring the nations of the world in closer bonds of fellowship and love, and a realization that wherever we are from, we are men and we are brothers."

Less than six weeks after Charles's impassioned speech, country after country entered into the terrible conflagration that was World War I. *Grindings* first mentioned the hostilities after Germany, Russia, France, and Great Britain entered the war in August. It informed SF Rotarians that a member traveling to Switzerland had not been heard from, and the editors hoped he was not among the hundreds of thousands of stranded Americans across Europe. Within a few days, the member's family cabled that they were alive and well in London.

Under U.S. President Woodrow Wilson, America remained out of the war for almost three years. SF Rotarians went about their business, as did most Americans. During 1915 and 1916, there was almost no mention in club records or *Grindings* of the war raging across the Atlantic. One of the few exceptions was a luncheon speaker—an attendee of the Ford Peace Exposition, convened to encourage a peace conference based on humanitarian, rather than military achievement.

President Wilson's efforts to maintain a position of neutrality failed. The U.S. was drawn into the war, as American lives were lost through German aggression in the midst of British and German naval warfare. Early in 1917, the United States severed diplomatic relations with Germany. With America's entry into the war a near certainty, SF Rotary club President Jim Lynch declared in *Grindings* that the highest form of Rotary service "is shown to be a man's fidelity to his own country." He urged every fellow Rotarian, as an American citizen, to "give expression to his patriotism by a direct and immediate offer of service to his country." He closed with an announcement that he would offer his employees a promise that their positions would be held during their voluntary service for America. On April 2, U.S. President Wilson asked Congress to declare a state of war. Congress responded swiftly, and the United States entered World War I.

The club went on record as approving the president's message to Congress. The Publicity Committee recommended that each Rotarian wear a small flag on his coat, and to fly the Stars and Stripes at home. Soon thereafter, *Grindings* began to carry a wide banner emblazoned with a patriotic message across the entire front page of most issues. The message most often used was a pledge of "Rotary's Duty—Keep Business Normal." *Grindings* asked each SF Rotarian to do his duty to keep the American economy strong by maintaining a robust business and buying American goods and services.

As promised by President Lynch, most luncheon programs adopted a patriotic theme, in an effort to "leave undone nothing that will arouse the latent spark of patriotism that smolders in the heart of every American citizen." Many luncheon programs focused on the war itself. One speaker, for instance, was a decorated British soldier, who spoke of Anglo-American relations during the war. Other programs addressed broader patriotic topics, such as a reflection on the human ideals embodied in the Declaration of Independence and the U.S. Constitution.

World War I brought about "total mobilization," in which Americans not only served in the military "over there," but in all aspects of everyday life on the home front. SF Rotary set about to support the war effort in every way possible. Members collected and donated such materials as tinfoil and scrap metal, and grew "victory gardens." On June 5, the club cancelled its weekly meeting in recognition of "U.S. Registration Day," a one-day national lottery that resulted in the signing of over 9.5 million American men for military service.

> "The service of righteous living and honest business will now receive its supreme test in patriotic endeavor. This test may now be on the field of battle or in the field of industry, for patriotic service will be demanded in all our efforts to win the Battle of Humanity."
>
> —*Grindings*

Throughout the war, the U.S. Government raised enormous amounts of money to finance its wartime operations overseas and at home. Soon after war was declared, the government issued its first in a series of "Liberty Bonds." Within weeks, SF Rotary bought a Liberty Bond to kick off the campaign, and began promoting Liberty Bonds among its members. And club members responded.

At one week's luncheon with 200 members present, 185 subscribed for $56,000 in Liberty Bonds. Canvassing of members not present netted another $10,000. For the remainder of the war, SF Rotary members pounded the streets soliciting for the Liberty Bond campaign. By war's end, SF Rotarians had bought and raised more than $125,000 in Liberty Bonds. Later in the war, the government issued War Savings Stamps, also called "Thrift Stamps." Americans were urged to adopt cost-cutting measures, and to buy the stamps with their savings.

"How do you feel when a boy stands before you totally blind and bearing the scars of bayonet wounds, and says that he is always fit for further service? Does it make you feel that you have done enough? If you smoked an expensive cigar as you listened, did you resolve to get along with less expensive ones and buy a few Thrift Stamps? Did Tom Skeyhill's talk make you ache to do something— and start doing it right away?"

—*Grindings*, March 26, 1918

SF Rotarians also contributed to the American Red Cross. When club President Thomas Doane became president of the local Red Cross chapter, the members began to donate even more generously. Two teams of members worked on the Red Cross drive and raised over $47,000.

The club supported the government's wartime intelligence effort. *Grindings* announced that, at the U.S. War Department's request, the American Protective League had "undertaken to procure for immediate use for intelligence purposes photographs, drawings, and descriptions of bridges, buildings, towns, and localities" in Germany and German-occupied areas of France, Belgium, and Luxembourg. The club office would forward any contributions to the War Department.

Conditions during the war brought about an opportunity for Rotary service in the club's work with boys. Agricultural operators desperately needed workers to fill vacancies left as young men went to fight. The U.S. Boys' Working Reserve was created by the government to place millions of unemployed boys in farm labor. Only eleven days after the United States entered the war in 1917, RI issued a detailed recommendation of the program to Rotary clubs, and instructions for working with the State Defense Committee. The Rotary Boys' Working Reserve attempted to place boys in such work in Northern California, but was unable to locate suitable agricultural jobs for more than a fraction of these urban boys living far from farmlands. But the attempt proved beneficial another way. The effort toward organizing the boys sensitized SF Rotarians to the issue of boys in the streets of San Francisco.

Rotary took its service overseas. By 1918, twelve thousand Rotarians were fighting throughout France. The Allied Rotary Club of France was formed with officers from Rotary clubs in Allied countries. SF Rotary counted a number of men in uniform among its members. A "roll of honor," displaying the names of club members fighting for their country, hung over the head table at luncheons. *Grindings* instituted a weekly feature—an "Honor Roll"—featuring the names of Rotarians or members of their families who were serving America in the armed services. The 1918 club roster devoted a page to each of its active servicemen commissioned during the war, with details of their service records. The club supported the nation's men overseas in various ways, such as sending shipments of books and toiletries addressed to servicemen.

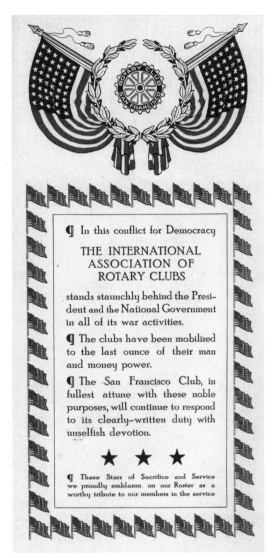

¶ In this conflict for Democracy

THE INTERNATIONAL
ASSOCIATION OF
ROTARY CLUBS

stands staunchly behind the President and the National Government in all of its war activities.

¶ The clubs have been mobilized to the last ounce of their man and money power.

¶ The San Francisco Club, in fullest attune with these noble purposes, will continue to respond to its clearly-written duty with unselfish devotion.

★ ★ ★

¶ These Stars of Sacrifice and Service we proudly emblazon on our Roster as a worthy tribute to our members in the service

A page from the club roster during World War I, 1918. The roster also listed the military service record of each active-duty club member.

SF Rotary also provided assistance to servicemen who were in San Francisco. The club office distributed windshield-display cards that read "Army and Navy Men Invited to Ride." Members were also encouraged to invite one or more soldiers for Thanksgiving dinner. Past President Arthur Holman led SF Rotarians in support of a national effort called the "Smileage Campaign," by raising over $30,000 for a library and recreation hall at Fort Fremont on the Peninsula.

The nation's war with Germany imposed hardships on German-Americans. The government's potent wartime propaganda fueled anti-German sentiment throughout America. Viewed with considerable suspicion or denounced as traitors by other citizens, German-American Rotarians faced a dilemma. Like many other Americans of non-Anglo descent, they had belonged to civic-minded German-American clubs and society centers, whose membership— although thoroughly patriotic—had been sympathetic to the Kaiser's cause before Germany became America's enemy in war. Now they were pressed to prove themselves "100% American" and loyal beyond question to the United States. SF Rotary historian Mountin describes the German-American Rotarians' efforts as "handsome." They enthusiastically bought Liberty Bonds, War Savings Stamps, supported the Red Cross and the Smileage Campaign, and chaired the club's patriotic committees. For the most part, these actions successfully calmed the suspicions of their fellow Rotarians.

In 1918, America suffered an additional hardship—the flu. An influenza epidemic encircled the globe, killing between fifty and one hundred million worldwide—550,000 in the United States. Named the Spanish Influenza, the flu lasted from 1918 through most of 1919, striking San Francisco hardest in October 1918, the month before the armistice ended the war. SF Rotary cancelled its weekly luncheon on October 22. The Board of Health announced that it

GRINDINGS
ROTARY CLUB OF SAN FRANCISCO

VOL. 6. OCTOBER 29, 1918. No. 50.

NO TUESDAY LUNCHEONS
UNTIL FURTHER NOTICE
THE OFFICE HAS BEEN CLOSED
SEC'Y. FEIGHNER CAN BE REACHED
AT PACIFIC 9327
WEAR YOUR MASK AND WATCH YOUR STEP

THERE MUST BE NO COMPROMISE PEACE

The greatest conflict in the history of Nations is being fought to determine the destiny of the world. We are fighting for the rights of humanity. America is not in this war for the conquest of land, for industries, for commercialism, but for the safety, well-being, and liberty of the people of the world.

It will be a violation of the principles and honor of America and a disgrace to her people to give the lives of our boys in No-man's land for a compromise peace with Germany.

When Germany cries, "We want peace"—
Let us remember the Lusitania.
Let us remember Belgium.
Let us remember the blood of Poland and Russia.
Let us remember the millions of lives that have already been given by England, France, and Italy.
Let us remember our own boys who have given and are still giving their lives in this great struggle—and all this—for what?
A compromise peace?

Let there be no compromise peace—no premature peace—no peace without a crushed Prussianism and a repentant Germany. Such a peace would be a violation of American principles. It would be a retreat of the flag. We must not let Germany chloroform us into inaction by her treacherous peace talk. We shall not give the lives of our boys for a dishonorable peace. No peace shall be entered into or even discussed until it is made absolutely impossible for Germany to repeat her offense against humanity. Let us fight the next war now.

On to Berlin!

P. G. HOLDEN.

THE FOURTH LIBERTY LOAN

As we go to press the Committee is still hard at work counting up the pledges given for bonds of the Fourth Loan. Undoubtedly the drive in this district was a success, and it only remains to find out how far "over the top" it went.

Very little publicity has been given the fact that this splendid success is due largely to the efforts of the Sales Manager's Committee, consisting of nineteen members. Our own Jim Lynch was chairman of this committee. Each member was designated a Colonel, and served with one of the eighteen Generals who had charge of the various divisions in the city. It was the business of these Colonels to put salesmanship with a big "S" into the campaign, which they very evidently did. It is interesting to note the names of some of the members of Jim's Committee. They are: C. H. Victor, F. W. Aust, J. V. Shepard, H. T. James, O. Boldemann, Ransom Pratt, W. S. Greenfield, J. G. Decatur, D. E. Harris, R. F. Haegelin, R. M. Alvord, H. H. Ware and Jack Bierma.

Besides the above, there were a large number of Captains and Lieutenants selected from our membership by the Generals and Colonels who should not be overlooked when credit is given for good salesmanship.

Moral: If you want something done — get a busy Rotarian to do it for you.

ASSEMBLÉE ANNUELLE DON'T FORGET IT

A Grindings front page during the 1918 worldwide influenza epidemic. Club luncheons were cancelled, and members warned to take precautions. Also note the editorial about Germany.

would take about two more weeks to wipe out the Spanish Influenza in San Francisco. In the meantime, the club office remained closed, and meetings remained cancelled until late in November. SF Rotarians pitched in. They donated their automobiles for use by the Red Cross.

For several months, *Grindings* asked for volunteers to drive nurses around the city to visit the ill, even as it reminded Rotarians to remain vigilant and wear their masks. Members and their families did not escape illness or death. Most illnesses, however, were not fatal, and San Franciscans came through the deadly times.

The German war effort collapsed and the armistice was signed on November 11, 1918, ending hostilities. The deadly war was over. Rather than return to normal life, however, Americans faced new difficulties. One of the greatest challenges in the war's aftermath was veteran rehabilitation. To address a dismal employment outlook for the thousands of maimed and disabled soldiers, the government established the Federal Board for Vocational Education. SF Rotarian Harry Bostwick chaired the club's Vocational Occupations for Wounded Soldiers Committee. Its purpose was to work with the government to provide counseling for soldiers by Rotarians. Within weeks of the armistice, the club entertained one hundred wounded soldiers at a Christmas luncheon. Each serviceman sat near a Rotarian who could be helpful because of his knowledge about the industry in which the soldier worked before he was drafted. Work with American veterans continued for nearly two years after the armistice. In 1920, SF Rotary reported that its Vocational Committee was working with a local hospital to help restore servicemen to a peacetime basis. The club's efforts to help did not stop with the soldiers themselves. SF Rotarians were also called on to help the Red Cross in its work of caring for the dependents of killed or wounded soldiers.

■ ■ ■

Although SF Rotary began its efforts to lessen the suffering of the poor, the orphaned, and crippled children before America entered the war, the need brought about by the war was impressed deeply into the hearts

MARSHALL ROTARY BLUM TELLS HIS STORY
Marshall Rotary Blum, a member of SF Rotary from November 21, 1950 to June 8, 2000, served as club president in 1986–87.

"My father came here as an immigrant in 1906.... He joined the San Francisco Rotary Club in 1914. After the war there was the influenza epidemic. People were afraid to go out on the street, and my father was in Mount Zion hospital with the flu, not caring whether he lived or died. The Sunshine Committee from the Rotary Club put on masks—you know, for the danger—to see how he was doing. He said later that if they thought that much of him, he was going to get better. That was the turning point. Then when he started to leave the hospital to go home to recuperate,... my mother was in the same hospital to have a child. And he said, 'I don't care if it's a boy or a girl, I want that child named "Rotary," because it means service to your fellow man.' And that's what my dad was in—the service business. So that was my introduction to Rotary. And I think when I was about 2 years old, they brought me in and stood me up on the podium, introduced me to the club— just one of the boys, I think. He paid a helluva fine, five dollars."

of Rotarians. It brought home the importance of working to improve the physical welfare and moral upbringing of boys, who would be called on to serve America should the need arise again. War gave SF Rotary its first large-scale service opportunity, and led to the realization among SF Rotarians that working together to serve the community and the nation was a far greater purpose for their club than the advancement of individual members' business interests. Out of the war and the understanding it brought of the tragic consequences of misunderstanding between the nations of the world came the beginning of notions of an even greater purpose for the international Rotary movement.

International Service

> *May Rotarians continue to be ambassadors of goodwill to high and low, rich and poor, to all races, to the devotees of all religious faiths and to members of all political parties, purveyors of tolerance, forbearance, justice, kindliness, neighborliness and friendliness to the inhabitants of this snug little world, the best little world of which we know.*

—Paul Harris, *This Rotarian Age*, 1935

The opportunity for SF Rotarians to go beyond helping their community and nation was not long in coming. International Service for SF Rotary started immediately after the war's end, as a shattered Europe sounded desperate pleas for help. In early 1919, club members began collecting clothing for Europe's millions of refugees. The following year, *Grindings* urged members to give to the Jewish Relief Fund. In its appeal for members to help the Fund assist the starving women and children in Europe and Eastern Mediterranean countries, *Grindings* reminded them that "charity the world over has but one language and knows no creed."

As the immediate need for emergency international relief subsided, Rotary International turned its attention to an even greater need. Rotarians everywhere were beginning to view themselves as part of a movement that could transcend borders and advance the cause of peace among nations. In 1921, delegates to the RI Convention in Edinburgh added International Service as a Sixth Object in Rotary's statement of purpose. As Rotary's statement of purpose evolved, International Service became the Fourth Avenue of Service in 1928. Since its last revision, the Fourth Avenue is stated as "the advancement of international understanding, goodwill, and peace through a world fellowship of business and professional persons united in the ideal of service." Throughout the 1920s, Rotary's work toward the cause of international peace occupied a significant place in its growing service efforts. Year after year, RI Convention delegates debated and weighed the possible ways that Rotary could play a beneficial role on the world stage.

Rotary's early work was recognized, and began to garner praise. Soon after International Service was named as one of Rotary's Objects, King Albert I of Belgium opened the 1927 RI Convention at Ostend. He declared that "the great Rotarian ideal, essentially a humanitarian ideal of brotherhood, may have an efficient application in the broad sphere of international relationships."[27] In the United States, Rotary's strong championing of world peace changed the minds of some of its most outspoken critics. Sinclair Lewis's 1922 book *Babbitt*, about a small-town "booster" club member, was a scathing critique of clubs such as Rotary. One critic referred to the book's complacent Babbitt as one "whose individuality had been sucked out of him by Rotary clubs, business ideals, and general conformity." Only six years later, Sinclair Lewis observed Rotary clubs at close range while lecturing, and was quoted as saying, "I have been accused of saying nasty things about the Rotarians, but I assert that the growth of Rotary in Great Britain. . . is more important for world tranquility than all the campaigns of the reformers put together."

Like most local Rotary clubs, SF Rotary applauded international service mostly from a distance, as RI shaped its plans to be a contributor to the cause of world peace. After RI established International Service as one of four Avenues of Service, SF Rotary commended "Rotary's latest great ambition, the furtherance of international goodwill." At the same time, the club announced its hope that newly elected U.S. President Herbert Hoover would stir a sentiment of interest in international harmony. In 1929 the club reported to the district that it had no International Service Committee, but stated that it did stand in its community for the advancement of goodwill, and that it took tactful steps to correct wrong impressions regarding other countries given through editorials or news reports. Past District Governor Bru Brunnier emerged as SF Rotary's first ambassador of goodwill. He wholeheartedly endorsed RI's developing international service programs and represented SF Rotary at the biennial Pan-Pacific Rotary Conference, beginning in 1928 and continuing for decades thereafter.

When the club adopted RI's Aims and Objects Plan in 1930, it formed an International Committee, and reported on its efforts to put on luncheon programs "of an international character," with a focus on the entertainment of foreign visitors. Indeed, SF Rotary's Committee for Entertainment of Visitors from Foreign Countries was the club's first—and until 1945, only—committee under the new heading of International Service. In his 1940 history of SF Rotary, William Mountin described SF Rotary's International Service policy during this time not so much as an ongoing program, but one of "day-to-day performance of little services, amenities, and courtesies" to visiting Rotarians from foreign lands. Mountin's view of SF Rotary's early contributions to international goodwill centered on SF Rotary's unique geographical location in a world port, "through which come and go the men and commerce of all nations." Welcoming visitors to this beautiful cosmopolitan city was not new to SF Rotary. As early as 1916, *Grindings* reported that the club had hosted visiting Rotarians from Edinburgh, Honolulu, London, and Holland. For decades, the tradition of hosting foreign visitors gave SF Rotarians the chance to meet and learn something about their guests. In turn, thousands of visitors left with a favorable impression of Americans and SF Rotary.

SF Rotary occasionally found opportunities to engage in other international-service activities. In the early 1930s, club members opened their hearts and wallets to help others overseas. Following a severe earthquake in New Zealand, SF Rotarians collected and donated money for

27. In 1919, King Albert I of Belgium honored SF Rotary as a luncheon guest, and was named an Honorary Member of the club. When Rotary was later introduced in Belgium, King Albert was influential in its development.

emergency relief. Two years later, they responded again, this time to the Japanese victims of another massive earthquake.

An interesting event in 1931 may have been the club's first opportunity for what would become a mainstay of Rotary International Service—cooperation between Rotary clubs in different countries. The Rotary Club of Mallorca bought the building and land comprising the birthplace of Father Junípero Serra in Petra, Spain. The Mallorcan Rotarians then contacted SF Rotary, asking for the club's assistance in making a gift of the property to the city of San Francisco. After some deliberation, the SF Rotary board determined that the gift could better be transacted through a semi-public organization. The club helped the Mallorcans establish contact with the California Historical Society to work with the municipal authorities in Spain. The following year, representatives of the Rotary Club of Mallorca traveled to San Francisco and presented the title to Father Junípero Serra's birthplace to city officials.

Although SF Rotary wholeheartedly embraced the principles of International Service and welcomed opportunities to participate, the club remained essentially a community-service club at heart until its second half century. It would take time for SF Rotary's outstanding role in International Service to blossom fully, but the seeds had taken root.

Boom and Bust—The 1920s and 1930s

For two decades after the war, Americans turned their thoughts inward, to matters at home. Likewise, SF Rotarians involved themselves with American issues. The club's focus during the 1920s and 1930s reveals the extent to which SF Rotary and its members are an inseparable part of the fabric of society. America's concerns were SF Rotarians' concerns, and as America struggled with anxiety, prosperity, and an economic cataclysm, so would the Rotarians themselves.

In 1919, RI passed a resolution recognizing the urgent task of stimulating public discussion and "right thinking for the general public good," hoping that the people of all countries would be able to more effectively combat the "enemies of democracy." Although the resolution was directed to Rotarians worldwide, it held a particular meaning for Rotarians in the United States. For Americans, the enemies of democracy were not limited to overseas threats. In the wartime and postwar years, fearful citizens perceived many such enemies here at home. Among them were radicals and Bolshevik conspirators, labor organizers, and immigrants. This led to what has been termed "Americanism"—a national sentiment that emerged during the war and persisted well into the 1930s. Americanism was reflected in the native-born public's insistence that citizens be "Americanized," or "100% American," which meant thoroughly loyal and fully assimilated into American culture and civic values.

The greatest source of intense postwar American anxiety was the vast wave of eastern and southern European and Russian immigrants who flocked to America in the early twentieth century, bringing their Old World ways with them. Native-born citizens adamantly demanded and pursued the Americanization of these foreigners. American Rotarians—including SF Rotary members—supported the principles and ideals expressed in Americanism, and regarded its advancement as their civic responsibility. At the 1920 District Conference, the keynote speaker addressed "The Patriotism of Peace," with his theme reflected in an accompanying women's pageant. Major conference discussions endorsed the "Americanization of those elements now in the country requiring education and assimilation." SF Rotarians came away from the district conference prepared to promote the Americanization process, having attended sessions on such topics as Jury Service, Registration and Voting, and the Necessity of Education in a Republic. *Grindings* items and luncheon speakers routinely addressed the need for Americanization and how Rotarians could help. One *Grindings* article announced that it was every Rotarian's duty to study the American Constitution, to enable him to answer "questions of civic and official affairs of state and country, and to be able to explain to others what Americanism really is."

SF Rotary's concern about unassimilated immigrants entered into the club's new work with boys. A *Grindings* author worried in 1920 that thousands of non-English-speaking boys were "poisoned" by reading material from their parents' native countries. Until they became old enough to read American publications and associated with "real-blooded Americans," they could learn little of American ideals, so "the problem of making the right kind of citizens of these boys is just that much more difficult." To move the Americanization process forward, the writer suggested an Educational American Program on the Fourth of July, as a way to reach out and save these boys. Although many suggestions were not taken up, it is clear that early SF Rotarians recognized the importance of steering boys toward good American citizenship and patriotic thinking—values no different than those they held as responsible businessmen and postwar American citizens. *Grindings* items and luncheon speeches about the dangers of immigration and immigrants subsided rapidly in the late 1920s, after Congress enacted a series of immigration quotas, placing severe limits on the numbers of southern and eastern Europeans permitted to enter the United States.

■ ■ ■

As America's anxieties of the 1920s played out, a combination of dire conditions gradually developed in the American economy. The popular view of America's first postwar decade is that of the "Roaring Twenties"—a decade of wild prosperity and economic optimism, unrestrained consumerism, strong government support of business, and excess in the financial markets.[28] The 1920s began with the United States reeling from a severe economic decline as Americans slowed their buying. SF Rotarians considered it their patriotic duty to help revive the nation's economy. Recovery began in 1922, and Americans embarked on a wave of consumerism (much of it on credit) and unregulated financial-market speculation built on a shaky economy. There were warning signs. In 1926, SF Rotarian Sid Schwartz (president of the San Francisco Stock Exchange) warned club members of a "break" from the remarkable bull market, and again in 1928, he warned against speculating

---

28. —and Prohibition. Although members complained, the club weathered Prohibition (1920-1933). *Grindings* notes a "not dry, rather intoxicating New Year's Eve party" in 1922.

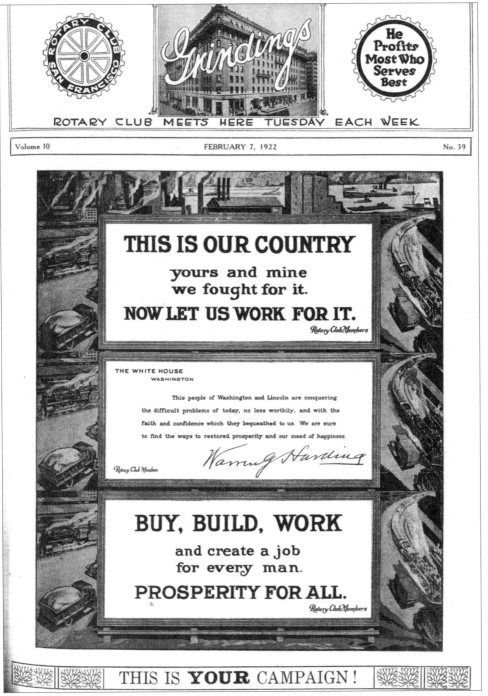

THIS IS OUR COUNTRY

yours and mine
we fought for it.

NOW LET US WORK FOR IT.

Rotary Club Members

THE WHITE HOUSE
WASHINGTON

This people of Washington and Lincoln are conquering
the difficult problems of today, no less worthily, and with the
faith and confidence which they bequeathed to us. We are sure
to find the ways to restored prosperity and our meed of happiness.

Warren G Harding

Rotary Club Members

BUY, BUILD, WORK

and create a job
for every man.

PROSPERITY FOR ALL.

Rotary Club Members

THIS IS **YOUR** CAMPAIGN !

An early-1920s patriotic-themed Grindings *front page, urging SF Rotarians to do their parts as the economy recovers, 1922.*

on borrowed money, explaining that "loans usually are not called one by one but in a great mass." Generally, however, such forecasts went unheeded in the financial markets. The Roaring Twenties' party would not continue forever.

The Great Depression

In September and October of 1929, a series of massive stock-price drops rocked Wall Street. After the first crash, stock prices continued to fall until the market bottomed out in July of 1932, with the Dow down 89.2 percent (from 381.17 to 41.22). The stock market would not fully recover for twenty-two years. America was plunged into the Great Depression of the 1930s.

Like most Americans, SF Rotarians did not foresee the devastating consequences of the 1929 Crash. The following month, a luncheon speaker described "The Effect of the Readjustment of the Stock Market on General Business." He surmised that the "deflection of money and credit from Wall

Unemployed men in a bread line in San Francisco, 1933.

Street to the regular channels of trade portends a brilliant future for general business." He closed with a prediction that 1930 would be "the best business year the country has ever seen."

Over the next four years, a human tragedy unfolded. More than one hundred thousand businesses went bankrupt and corporate profits declined by 90 percent. Banks were badly weakened, resulting in a national panic. Nine million savings accounts were lost. Jobs vanished, and by the time President Herbert Hoover left office in 1933, thirteen million—25 percent of the American work force—were unemployed, and millions more were reduced to working part-time.

For the first few years, Rotarians across the nation mirrored President Hoover's hopeful message of rapid recovery. They strove to increase optimism and encourage spending to counter the Depression's debilitating effects. *The Rotarian* urged members, "Let's buy now, but let's buy wisely." President Hoover appealed to Rotary to help stop currency-hoarding, and *Grindings* carried his message. In early 1932, *Grindings* perceived a somewhat improved economic forecast, with recovering manufacturing, higher agricultural prices, and a moderate bond and stock rally. It predicted that "1932 will bring release from the fears of 1931, and make the 'light ahead' discernible to the man who is now skeptical."

Because this is America GIVE

To feed . . . . . . our hungry
To shelter . . our homeless
To protect . our fatherless
To care for . . . . our sick
To cherish . . . . our aged
To guide . . . . . our youth

COMMUNITY CHEST
OCT. 26 — NOV. 18

A Depression-era notice in Grindings, 1931.

Like Americans everywhere, Rotarians across the country were stunned by the collapse of 1920s prosperity and the depth of the crisis in its early years. Ill-equipped to cope with the ferocity of the Depression, they were helpless to provide adequate local community assistance. However, they did what they could. *Grindings* carried advertisements for the Community Chest, urging SF Rotarians to donate.

Club President Harold Porter made an appeal at the Ladies' Christmas Luncheon in 1931. He thanked his fellow Rotarians for their "magnificent response" to the Community Chest Campaign. He asked each club member "to make careful investigation in his immediate neighborhood, to locate those unfortunate individuals who until recently were able to provide for their families and hold their heads up as we do today, but through circumstances beyond their control have been bowed with distress." He closed by reminding club members that "if we can locate such and do something for their Christmas which will add to their pleasure, it will tremendously enhance our own."

AN APPEAL TO SF ROTARIANS

"It occurs to me, as we are seated here in this colorful and pleasing atmosphere, with its delightful decorations and delicious luncheon and fine musical program about to be presented, that we should not be unmindful of the conditions surrounding us."

—President Harold Porter at the Christmas luncheon, 1931

SF Rotarians carried on their work with children. They participated individually in Citizens' Training Corps activities for the encouragement and leadership of itinerant boys. Throughout the Depression, club members continued to give generously. In 1935, pledges to Crippled Children and the Boys' Club topped $7,300.

From the onset, Rotarians and their families were not immune to the ravages of the Depression. In his first message to Rotary upon being elected RI president, Almon Roth expressed his understanding that "not all men can meet the taxes, fees, and dues which Rotary imposes equally, because of different personal circumstances." In SF Rotary's report to the district governor, the club stated that insofar as enforcing regulations respecting attendance, "more leniency is shown in strenuous times." *Grindings* published items such as one asking club members to donate a suit of clothes, for "a former member of the club having met with reverses."

In 1932, Americans expressed their distress and unhappiness with the government's inability to bring the economy back to life and end their suffering. President Herbert Hoover was unable to retain his presidency and newly elected President Franklin D. Roosevelt took up the challenge. SF Rotarians shared the nation's hopes for Roosevelt's policies. After FDR took office, club members unanimously instructed President Jim Patrick to telegraph him, extending the full support and cooperation of the club's membership in carrying out his program for recovery. As the years passed and the Depression continued, however, many were disappointed. Conservatives in particular became disillusioned with FDR and many of his New Deal economic interventions. As businessmen, Rotarians grew resistant to the intrusion of New Deal policies and bureaucracy on local business.

Perhaps surprisingly, the Depression did not result in losses to Rotary membership. After a sharp drop during the early years, Rotary grew to a new worldwide high by the end of the 1930s.

SF Rotary also weathered the Depression decade—ending at more than 420 members strong, up more than 120 in ten years.

A Dual Threat

During the 1930s, Americans faced another source of national anxiety—the infiltration of Communism in the United States. The perceived threat of Communist influence arose a decade earlier, in the "Red Scare" of 1919 following the war's Bolshevik Revolution. An address in 1923 by RI President Frank Mulholland mirrored Americans' postwar fear of Russian-inspired radicalism in America. The Communist threat was overshadowed during the 1920s by Americans' greater fear of immigrants, then increased during the depression decade. Despite the fact that the Communist Party in America never rose above a few thousand members, "Americanism" turned its focus on the godless Communists bent on destroying the American way of life.

The national perception of Communist influence and radical activity went hand-in-hand with an explosion of labor organizing and strikes across America—fueled in part by Depression conditions. Following enactment of legislation increasing workers' rights in 1933, more than 1.5 million additional workers joined unions. A wave of strikes—many of them violent—swept the nation. Among the largest were the West Coast Longshoremen's Strike and the simultaneous four-day general strike in San Francisco in 1934. The Longshoremen's Strike began in San Francisco in May and lasted eighty-three days, during which an emergency was declared and the National Guard and U.S. Army were called out to restore order. The strike turned deadly on July 5—"Bloody Thursday"—when two strikers were killed and sixty-four people were wounded in a street battle with police, during an attempt to bring cargo through the picket line.

As generally conservative businessmen, SF Rotarians sided with business and attempts to put down the strike. In the wake of Bloody Thursday, Past President Paul Rieger wrote to RI headquarters of a related incident involving strikers. Describing it as "a volatile situation involving a Communist demonstration," Paul applauded the fire chief for maintaining order by turning fire hoses on demonstrating Communists. He also commended the mayor and chief of police, who entered "a situation filled with dynamite" and "handled the communists without making martyrs of them." Praising the three—all SF Rotarians—for exhibiting leadership in a time of unrest, Paul reported that the club attributed their leadership to personal development through membership in Rotary.

A confrontation between a policeman wielding a nightstick and a striker during the San Francisco General Strike, 1934. Photo: National Archives

Following Bloody Thursday and the general strike, the club stepped up its civic efforts to work against the chaos created by the twin influences of Communism and organized labor. Alameda District Attorney Earl Warren addressed a SF Rotary luncheon audience about Americanism. His speech was among the frequent—almost weekly—luncheon talks for the rest of the year on how to combat radical activities in America, the meanings of the flag and national anthem, and the importance of voting. *Grindings* praised "Rotary's movement to bring about a deeper consciousness of the fundamentals upon which this great nation was founded and has prospered." The club established a new Americanization Committee. In turn, the committee expanded to form the Americanization Group of San Francisco Rotary, whose purpose was to promote Americanization through education.

■   ■   ■

In 1939, the city of San Francisco opened its second world's fair—the two-year Golden Gate International Exposition. Located on Treasure Island (a newly constructed artificial island), the fair celebrated the dedication of two grand new bridges—the San Francisco-Oakland Bay Bridge in 1936, and the Golden Gate Bridge in 1937. Like its forerunner in 1915, the Exposition was a spectacular affair, with dazzling nighttime lighting, fantastic buildings, and a "Tower of the Sun" that rose four hundred feet into the sky.

As it had in 1915, SF Rotary supported the Exposition—a welcome respite from the debilitating dreariness of the Depression. The club participated in a "Rotary Day" of Bay Area clubs, which ended with a banquet for 1,200. During the fair's first season in 1939, SF Rotary welcomed over one thousand luncheon visitors in a three-month period, and established the practice of giving away a pair of fair tickets to the visitor from farthest away. The club sponsored more than one thousand Boys' Club members to the fair, providing box lunches and reserved seats for Exposition events.

Like their predecessors in 1914, the Exposition's planners hoped the fair, a meeting of exhibiting countries from around the world, would forestall the gathering storm in Europe. But it was not to be. By the time of the fair's opening in February 1939, Hitler had annexed parts of Czechoslovakia and Austria. The European situation had deteriorated to the point that Rotary clubs in Italy had been forced to disband. SF Rotary luncheon speakers warned of the approach of a seemingly unstoppable disaster. The director of the League of Nations Association asked, "Can the world avoid another war crisis?" One month after the fair opened, a speaker described a Europe darkening under the "Shadow of the Swastika." Another speaker denounced the rise of totalitarianism, and pressed the need for vigilance to preserve the proper relationship between the government and the individual. In September, Germany invaded Poland. Once again, Europe was at war.

World War II

Like most Americans, SF Rotarians generally favored neutrality in the early years after Germany's initial incursions into neighboring countries. Although President Roosevelt was providing limited arms assistance to Britain and France so they could stop Hitler themselves, Americans wanted to remain out of the war. But following France's collapse in July 1940, *Grindings* editorialized that "everyone recognizes that eventualities are crowding in upon us, and we must do something about it." SF Rotarians began to act. The club started preparations to carry out RI's plans for the prospect of placing British Rotary children with local Rotary families, and to endorse non-Rotarian families who wished to receive a Rotarian child. RI encouraged contributions to the Rotary Relief Fund, established in 1940, to be used exclusively to aid Rotarians and their families. SF Rotarians were kept informed of developments in Europe by guest speakers, who explained "The Lesson of French Defeat," and "England Under Fire."

On a Sunday in December 1941, SF Rotarians turned on their radios and listened to the stunning news that Japan had attacked the United States in a daring raid on Pearl Harbor. The next day, Congress voted to declare war on Japan. Three days later, Germany and Italy declared war on the United States. America entered World War II.

Over the next year, RI defined numerous ways local clubs in the United States could help in the war, civilian defense, and relief efforts, and SF Rotary threw in its full support. Soon after America went to war with Japan, the club formed a National Service Committee. One of the Committee's actions was to broadcast a club luncheon featuring speakers from Civil Defense, who explained the very real possibility of a nighttime Japanese attack on San Francisco. The speakers urged members having homes in view of the sea to cooperate with the civil-defense efforts in the "dim-out"—the light-restriction ban. SF Rotarians participated in activities recommended by the Local Defense Council, which was well-represented among the club's membership. More than 50 percent of the club's members took courses and qualified to become air-raid wardens, auxiliary police, fire watchers, and other wartime civil-defense positions. The club offered its services and manpower to the council for any defense work the council wished to assign. SF Rotary also sponsored public meetings for the purpose of educating San Franciscans about various topics, including civil defense and the USO (United Service Organizations).[29]

In addition to its work on the defense effort in San Francisco, SF Rotary assisted the United States overseas. As it had in 1917, the club urged members to buy the government's U.S. Savings Bonds—called "Victory Bonds"—to help finance the United States' entry into the war. The club collected books for servicemen, and SF Rotarians were requested to comply with the government's request for businessmen to voluntarily sell their newer standard office-size typewriters to the government. Members also collected donations of service knives and radios.

During World War II, Rotary wives were encouraged to save bacon drippings and fats, because the glycerin used to make gunpowder could be extracted from the grease. "Who knows, maybe that little bit of bacon grease you save will save the life of one of our boys."

Opportunities to serve in the war effort were many. SF Rotarians served on the Community Chest's board of directors, and the club actively supported the organization. Proceeds from the Chest's War Chest Drive, with a goal of $3 million, would help maintain vital health and welfare services needed on the war and home fronts. The club asked Rotarians to donate blood, to help meet San Francisco's quota of nearly three thousand pints per month. As America's young men went off to fight, *Grindings* asked members to help the War Manpower Mobilization Committee in its intensive campaign to bring thousands of unemployed women into essential defense-industry jobs. Shortly after the first anniversary of America's entry into the war, the visiting Rotary district

29. Founded by President Roosevelt in 1941 to provide recreation services to U.S. military personnel.

"Our whole planet today is a crucible. In it we are running a test—whether freedom shall be taken from mankind. Many of our sons and daughters are on the front lines where blood is flowing. We, too, are called for service—all-out service at home. And who can better hold the front line of the home front better than Rotarians?"

—SF Rotarian and RI President Charles Wheeler, 1943

governor spoke at the club's luncheon about how Rotarians were supporting the war effort in over one hundred wartime activities.

Several of SF Rotary's younger members served in the armed forces. Rotarians who remained behind turned to how best to serve the nation's brave servicemen and women. *Grindings* editorialized that the National Service Committee's ambition "to entertain and be helpful in any way they can to Rotarians or sons of Rotarians who may be stationed here or passing through" merited the enthusiastic support of every member. The committee maintained a list of servicemen, for any member who found himself in a position to assist someone. On "Fathers and Sons Day," President Herb Shuey announced that the club would provide Rotarians' sons overseas with cards of introduction to any Rotary club in the world. The sons would also receive a subscription to *Reader's Digest*. The club established an honor plaque with the names of SF Rotarians and sons serving in the armed forces, and created a Rotary Service Flag, decorated with stars for the sons of members. Lists of the club's men in service were posted at the luncheon tables so members could write letters to them.

RI heartily endorsed Rotary work in the local USOs. Under the direction of the club's National Service Committee, SF Rotarians served at the USO on O'Farrell Street. U.S. servicemen and women stationed near San Francisco or passing through were provided with food and entertainment, and made to feel at home and appreciated. The club accepted the responsibility for staffing the USO one day per month, rotating among the Birthday Divisions. On one Saturday night, January Division members fed and entertained four thousand servicemen.

Many of SF Rotary's luncheon speakers discussed wartime events and conditions on the fronts, and club members were reminded of the stark reality far away. In 1942, Rotarians left one meeting shaken after a visiting Rotarian colonel told the tale of his personal ordeal in the Bataan Death March in the Philippines, and appealed to members to try to find a way to help the twenty-

RI President Charles Wheeler serves U.S. servicemen at the San Francisco USO. Mrs. Wheeler, SF Rotary President Herb Shuey, and club Secretary Ed Whitney are also behind the counter, 1944. Courtesy of San Mateo County History Museum

Princess Juliana of Holland greets Rotarians and service-men at an SF Rotary–sponsored night at the USO on O'Farrell Street, 1944.

seven thousand who remained in "a bitter prison camp in pestilence and literal starvation." Later the same month, a visiting young man from Norway spoke of his experiences as a Nazi political prisoner and of his countrymen's bravery. The luncheon audience listened attentively to the president of the Rotary Club of Manila, himself an escapee from a Japanese prisoner-of-war camp.[30] Others spoke on a variety of topics—the development of radar, provisions for California's defense, how to assist the FBI during wartime, and what to do in case of firebombing in San Francisco.

Within the war's first year, a few modest hardships made themselves felt, but the club adapted to the stresses and inconveniences of wartime. *Grindings* announced that U.S. Postal Service conditions made its timely delivery each week an uncertainty. Gasoline rationing and the mandatory thirty-five-mile-per-hour speed limit forced SF Rotary's Sports Chapter to suspend many of its golf trips, and threatened the club's annual Del Monte golf weekend in Monterey.[31] Nevertheless, the Sports Chapter determined to carry on for 1943, and made occasional forays to country clubs in Marin County and the East Bay. A distant inter-city meeting in Los Angeles was cancelled, but the Sacramento inter-city meeting hosted an overflow crowd. The 1943 inter-city meeting in Oakland went on as it had for so many years, with more than eighty SF Rotarians making the transbay trek. After D-Day in 1944, transportation restrictions were tightened considerably. Traveling SF Rotary members were warned they could be "bumped" without notice anywhere and any time, because all or part of a train might be taken over to provide space for wounded servicemen. The club cautioned Rotarians not to travel except when absolutely necessary. In early 1945, at the government's request, all conferences in the United States were cancelled. RI subsequently notified district governors to cancel their district conferences for the year.

In January 1943, the RI Nominating Committee telegraphed SF Rotary's Past President Charles Wheeler, requesting that he serve as RI president in 1943–44. The committee advised him that "we are convinced that you have those qualities of leadership so desperately needed in these trying times. Your intimate knowledge of world problems, combined with your complete understanding of Rotary problems in a world at war, make you our unanimous choice." Charles accepted the honor, and began his leadership of the Rotary world six months later.

---

30. *Grindings* made no mention of the issue of the internment of Japanese-American citizens during the war.

31. The Del Monte weekend became a moot point after the government took over the Del Monte resort in 1943.

During his year as RI president, Charles was constrained by acute travel restrictions. SF Rotary made office space available to him as a temporary RI headquarters in San Francisco, and provided the services of the club members and office staff. A presidential assistant and secretary were moved from Chicago to San Francisco, and Charles conducted his many RI meetings in the SF Rotary directors' room. The club benefited from his frequent presence at the weekly luncheons, and particularly enjoyed having its visitors introduced by the president of RI.

In 1943, RI announced its adoption of the "Work Pile Project" as its number-one objective for 1943–44. The program was designed to encourage large and small businesses throughout the country to develop and commit to postwar work orders that would stimulate production and create private-enterprise jobs for twelve million men and women upon their discharge and return home from the war.

This impressive international program is one in which SF Rotary can justifiably take great pride. It was the brainchild of SF Rotarian (and later club president) Ernest Ingold, who was acutely aware of the nation's postwar employment needs. Ernest understood that without advance planning, the nation faced disastrous consequences at the war's end. The U.S. Government would discontinue defense-industry business with firms providing war work. Simultaneously, the massive and sudden discharge of servicemen would overwhelm an unprepared job market. The resulting widespread unemployment would throw the nation's wartime prosperity back into a national recession. Ernest envisioned a "shock-absorber" for the crucial transitional period after the war and before civilian business could begin to flow again. The idea was simple: every community would gather up a pile of work orders to begin when the war ended. Ernest surveyed his own retail automobile business and located customers willing to commit in advance to buy immediately after the war. He amassed a "pile" of postwar work orders amounting to $75,000. As president of the San Francisco Chamber of Commerce, Ernest convinced his Rotary friends in the Chamber of the program's viability, and initiated it as a Chamber project early in 1943. Soon afterward, two hundred Chamber of Commerce committees reported a $2,000,000,000 "work pile" of future postwar work orders.

Upon assuming the RI presidency in July 1943, Charles Wheeler immediately telegraphed Ernest and SF Rotary President Herbert Shuey, offering his support by giving the plan RI's top priority. In its monthly "Work Pile Driver" section, *The Rotarian* magazine reported on the project's progress and Rotary's leadership in making it work. Across the country, Rotary clubs worked with their Chambers and other civic organizations, conducting consumer surveys and providing businesses with "leads"—the names and addresses of people who would need goods and services as soon as the war ended. The plan was enthusiastically backed by the press. One national newspaper chain officially endorsed the plan, and pledged to throw its huge circulation and editorial influence into helping local Rotary clubs move the plan along.

Locally, *Grindings* urged SF Rotarians to get behind the effort and pledge orders for postwar work. One *Grindings* article argued that the plan "will do more than any other one thing to put an end to regimentation by the State and restore the opportunity of a free economy." Another essay worried that "unless mass unemployment can be eliminated under a system of private enterprise, private business will be supplanted by some other arrangement for the production and distribution of goods and services." SF Rotary's Vocational Service Committee worked in full cooperation with the Chamber of Commerce and the local press to build a "work pile" in San Francisco. Other nations adapted the program to meet their needs. Work-pile projects were organized in Canada and in other countries, from Australia to Southern Rhodesia.

Adoption of the Work Pile Project was not President Wheeler's only Rotary action in anticipation of potential problems facing businesses at war's end. In December 1943, Charles invited the national commander of the American Legion, the president of the U.S. Chamber of Commerce, and the Kiwanis International president to join him in the SF Rotary's directors' room. He was prompted to call the meeting because Rotarians from many nations expressed their concern over a worldwide campaign to nationalize industry. Together, the four leaders enacted "The Specific Charter." The document linked the 2.6 million members of their service and patriotic organizations in a pledge to help speed victory, facilitate an orderly demobilization at war's end, and maintain individual liberty "to plan, work, and live without fear of exploitation from any source."

As Charles Wheeler's presidential year neared its end in May 1944, he presided over a unique RI Convention. It was initially scheduled for Omaha, but was relocated to Chicago to enable RI officials to attend without traveling. In a drastic wartime measure, the Convention was pared to the bone. Attendance at the streamlined affair was restricted to Rotarians of district-governor rank or higher, a decision that was widely applauded in the press. Total attendance was 266, the smallest convention since Rotary's second Convention in 1911.[32] Rotary clubs around the world voted by proxy. A high point of the Convention was the announcement that Rotary had continued to grow. During Charles Wheeler's RI wartime presidency, over 160 new clubs were formed in the United States and other countries where men were still free to do so.

Two weeks after Charles Wheeler's 1944 Convention concluded, two hundred thousand Allied troops pushed their way ashore on the beaches of Normandy. The Allies began their liberation of German-conquered Europe, and Germany surrendered in May 1945. Japan surrendered in August, after the United States unleashed the weapon that would define the shape of world power for the second half of the twentieth century.

As America rejoiced over the war's end, SF Rotarians joined in to celebrate. Early in 1946, the club held a Johnny-Comes-Marching-Home Day for the fighting SF Rotarians. There was still cause to celebrate in late 1947, when the International Service Committee observed the re-entry into Rotary of many clubs worldwide that had involuntarily disbanded or been closed down during the war.

The world's nations had laid down their arms, but the aftermath of war remained. It would be years before everyday life could return to normal. Like Americans everywhere, SF Rotarians complained about ongoing food rationing and shortages of household goods, but understood that these inconveniences were but small sacrifices for what had been achieved.

---

32. The 1945 Convention in Chicago was smaller still, at 141. To comply with a U.S. Government directive, no single meeting at the Convention exceeded fifty attendees.

SF Rotarians continued to serve where they could. There was immediate work to be done to relieve the suffering in Europe and Japan. Soon after the war, the U.S. Government asked RI to assist in a national collection of used clothing for overseas civilian relief in war-devastated areas. The goal was 150 million pounds of men's, women's, and children's clothing. RI strongly endorsed this most worthy and humanitarian purpose. Of particular note here is the individual service rendered to the world by SF Rotarian Harry McClelland. Harry headed the commission that administered the postwar Marshall Plan in Italy.

At home, SF Rotary took steps to assist discharged soldiers and sailors. As early as 1943, the district governor pointed out that Rotary's job would not be over when hostilities ceased. Rotarians would have to take the lead during "reconstruction"—helping the returning boys reorient themselves. To this end, SF Rotary had established a Postwar Planning Committee in 1944. As one of its activities, the club continued to host one day per month at the USO, until the USO was closed in December 1946.

■ ■ ■

The greatest service of all for Rotarians was that which could help achieve what was needed most—world peace. Over the next sixty years, Rotary became a formidable force in the world for international peace and humanitarianism. For SF Rotary, the opportunity to contribute arrived in the summer of 1945, even before the last shots of the war had been fired.

The Founding of the United Nations—A Point of Pride for Rotarians

The true partnership of Rotary and the United Nations is not tied to a date in time. It is tied to the commonality of our causes and our ideas.

—Past RI President Charles Keller, 1995

Perhaps no single world event is more aligned with the Rotary Object's fourth point—"the advancement of international understanding, goodwill, and peace through a world fellowship of business and professional persons united in the ideal of service"—than the founding of the United Nations in San Francisco in 1945. By the time of the UN's founding, Rotary International was prominent as one of the major nongovernmental organizations (NGOs) in the world. As such, Rotary was to play a significant role in the events leading to and culminating in the formation of the United Nations.

Rotary's involvement with what would become the world's largest institution for global peace did not begin in 1945. In an early proposal for a postwar world, RI enacted a "Respect for Human Rights Resolution" during its 1940 Havana Convention. RI initiated and chaired discussions in 1942 for an international educational and cultural exchange to promote cooperation between nations. The results of this conference in London are reflected in the constitution of the United Nations Educational, Scientific, and Cultural Organization (UNESCO). In its capacity as a major NGO, Rotary had observers present and actively involved at several international conferences, including 1943: Food and Agriculture, Relief and Rehabilitation, and 1944: Monetary and Finance, International Security, and Civil Aviation. Rotary's proudest moment, however, was its participation in the United Nations Conference on International Organization in San Francisco (1945).

Seeking a way to peacefully manage international affairs in a postwar world, delegates from fifty nations came together at the Opera House and Veterans' Building on Van Ness Avenue in San Francisco on April 25, 1945. They met to deliberate on proposals for an international organization called for by President Franklin D. Roosevelt in 1943. A preliminary agreement had been hammered out in 1944, at the Dumbarton Oaks mansion in Washington, DC by representatives of the United States, the United Kingdom, the Soviet Union, and China. The 1945 Chartering Conference occurred at a crucial point in the war. President Roosevelt had died only thirteen days earlier. Two weeks after the conference began, Germany would surrender, and Japan would follow in August after the bombings of Hiroshima and Nagasaki.

Delegates to the conference drew up the 111-article charter. It was adopted unanimously two months later on June 25, 1945. On the following day, the charter was signed in the Veterans' Building Herbst Theater by the representatives of the fifty countries. (Poland would sign later and become the fifty-first of the original Member States.) On October 24, the charter was ratified by the five permanent members of the Security Council and a majority of the other chartering nations. History's boldest experiment for world peace and cooperation came into being.

Rotary's role in the founding of the United Nations is noteworthy for its remarkable representation at the conference itself. Of the fifty nations who sent delegations, thirty-two had Rotary clubs, and seven more European countries had a Rotary presence before the German invasion that began the war. Rotarians served on half of the delegations, five of them as delegation heads. Three of the United States' eight delegates were Rotarians.

RI President Richard H. Wells hosts a dinner at the Bohemian Club for UN Conference participants. —The Rotarian, *July 1945*

In addition, the U.S. State Department extended an invitation to forty-two NGOs to send advisers and consultants. These included organizations as varied as the Congress of Industrial Organizations (CIO), the American Jewish Committee, the American Bar Association, the League of Women Voters, the National Association for the Advancement of Colored People (NAACP), Kiwanis International, and Rotary International. RI was represented in this capacity by eleven Rotarians, including RI President Richard H. Wells and five past RI presidents. In all, fifty Rotarians participated in the conference.

The extent of Rotary's presence was evident at a festive dinner May 1, hosted at the Bohemian Club by RI President Richard Wells for all Rotarian delegates and observers (although not all were present, as they were attending a plenary session of the conference).

One such Rotarian who served in the efforts for a world peace organization before and during the conference was SF Rotary's own Charles Wheeler. As an immediate past RI president in 1945, Charles participated as one of the consultants to the United States delegation during the UN Chartering Conference.

Charles Wheeler also extended an invitation to *The Rotarian*'s editor to make use of SF Rotary club headquarters as an office for *The Rotarian* during the conference. Alongside his other duties as immediate past RI president, Wheeler took on a role closer within his home club. He chaired the committee to provide transportation for all visitors. Charles and the committee were charged with determining ways for the club to extend hospitality to visiting delegates and their staffs.

SF Rotary's tradition of fellowship served it well during the conference. As the host club, SF Rotary members gave generously of their time and hospitality behind the scenes. Six weeks before the conference, a visiting luncheon speaker from the U.S. State Department had emphasized the importance of helping the country, U.S. allies, and the world during "this most important event in the world's history," by showing "open-handed western hospitality to the individual delegates." He requested those gestures of hospitality that Rotarians worldwide are so accustomed to offering—"invitations to dinner in our homes, automobile rides, personal individual contacts"—as important to the successful functioning of the conference. Among its other responses, SF Rotary solicited members' cars for long trips, and help from those who spoke foreign languages.

Rotary's early connections to the United Nations did not stop with its founding. Carlos P. Romulo (past RI vice president, 1937–38), the chairman of the Philippine delegation to the Chartering Conference in 1945, went on to become the fourth president of the UN General Assembly in 1949. He has been followed in that position by other Rotarians. Eight years after its enactment, RI's "Respect for Human Rights Resolution" of 1940 served as a model for the United Nations' powerful 1948 "Universal Declaration of Human Rights."

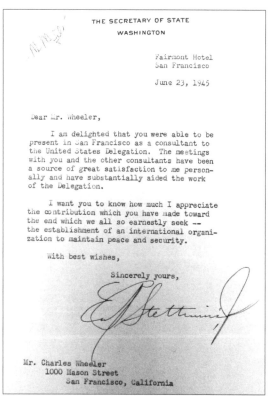

THE SECRETARY OF STATE
WASHINGTON

Fairmont Hotel
San Francisco

June 23, 1945

Dear Mr. Wheeler,

I am delighted that you were able to be present in San Francisco as a consultant to the United States Delegation. The meetings with you and the other consultants have been a source of great satisfaction to me personally and have substantially aided the work of the Delegation.

I want you to know how much I appreciate the contribution which you have made toward the end which we all so earnestly seek — the establishment of an international organization to maintain peace and security.

With best wishes,

Sincerely yours,

E. R. Stettinius

Mr. Charles Wheeler
1000 Mason Street
San Francisco, California

A letter from U.S. Secretary of State Edward R. Stettinius Jr. to Charles Wheeler, thanking him for his service as consultant to the U.S. delegation at the UN Conference, 1945.

Since then, Rotary has frequently worked on peacemaking efforts with UN agencies, as well as such disparate programs as conducting revolving-loan programs for Bangladesh fish farmers, AIDS education in Burundi, and literacy training for women in Guatemala.

Justly proud of its impressive presence at the UN's founding, Rotary has since celebrated the historic moment in 1945 on several occasions, and honored the Rotarians who participated in the historic moment. The first large commemorative event in San Francisco took place in June 1955, exactly ten years after the signing of the UN Charter, in conjunction with a weeklong Tenth-Anniversary Conference. Conceived by a San Francisco oil-company executive and gradually endorsed and financed by the city of San Francisco and the United Nations, the conference drew a delegation from every one of the member nations, plus observers and guests from nonmember nations as well. Prominent Rotarians attended, including many who had participated in the founding events a decade earlier. SF Rotary held one of the many concurrent meetings as its regular luncheon, featuring Nobel Peace Prize winner and Under Secretary General of the UN Ralph Bunche as speaker. Charles Wheeler coauthored *The Rotarian*'s coverage of the conference.

The next great celebration took place in 1995, when dignitaries from across the globe again convened in San Francisco to commemorate the United Nations' fiftieth anniversary. Rotary celebrated as well. RI President Bill Huntley initiated a formal Presidential Conference in San Francisco. Chaired by RI Past Director Mike Kutsuris, the Conference Committee consisted of SF Rotarians Bill Sturgeon, Bill Koefoed, Pete Taylor, and Bob Wilhelm, as well as Bill Mayhood (PDG District 5170) and Werner Schwarz (PDG District 5160). Under their leadership, SF Rotary again played host club— this time to a three-day conference at the Fairmont Hotel, termed the 1995 President's Conference of Goodwill and Development. Rotarians once again enjoyed the opportunity to extend a warm welcome, providing homes, transportation, and fellowship to their visitors. The conference included over a dozen well-attended plenary

SF Rotary President Clyde L. Chamblin greets Under Secretary General of the UN Ralph Bunche, 1955.
Courtesy of Moulin Studios Archives

and breakout sessions on such varied subjects as shared goals and cooperation between the UN and RI, community development opportunities between the UN and RI, RI's leadership in eradicating polio, UN opportunities within grassroots communities through partnership with RI, and RI's involvement in environment, literacy, and education programs. Keynote speakers included Roberto Romulo, son of the 1945 representative General Carlos Romulo, and Madeline Albright, United States Ambassador to the United Nations.

One of the first events of the conference was a four-hour Model United Nations Assembly for high-school students. In a session moderated by SF Rotarian Jim Bradley, and featuring a keynote address by former San Francisco Mayor George Christopher, Rotary hosted an international group of young people. They participated as UN delegates—debating realistic problems and finally adopting a

High-school students participate in a model UN session at the UN's fiftieth-anniversary celebration conference, 1995. Courtesy RI Archive

resolution to call for an end to nuclear testing in the Pacific. After vehemently arguing their countries' positions on nuclear testing, the delegates representing France and Australia shared a soda and a friendly hug, making peace between nations. Some of the delegates remained to attend other conference events.

A highlight of the conference was a dinner at the Bohemian Club in San Francisco, which recreated the Bohemian Club dinner hosted by SF Rotary in 1945. In his address to the gathering, Past RI President Charles Keller described RI's earlier efforts on behalf of world peace and human rights. Recalling there was no United Nations before 1945, no organized staffing, and few world-class NGOs capable of providing assistance, Keller said it is not surprising that Rotary observers were present and actively involved in the earlier international conferences before the 1945 UN Chartering Conference. Past President Keller closed his talk citing H. G. Wells: "Human history is essentially a history of ideas." and he spoke of the challenge in recognizing the commonality of RI and UN causes and ideas. Madeleine Albright closed the conference with a stirring speech on the UN's next fifty years. Recognizing that the UN had been hampered by the Cold War, she felt the UN was becoming a strong voice for human freedom by helping new countries draw democratic constitutions and by increasingly using sanctions to control aggressors.

One disappointing moment during SF Rotary's celebration of Rotary's long-standing relationship with the UN came when the club's plans to erect a monument at the Opera House to commemorate the charter signing ran aground on the shoals of San Francisco politics. The funds were set aside, however, and used during the sixtieth anniversary of the signing on June 25, 2005, which provided an opportunity to once again celebrate Rotary's role in the UN founding. At a ceremony to dedicate the new San Francisco Rotary Meadow on the Mount Sutro summit, Jim Bradley spoke of the enduring relationship between Rotary and the United Nations, and the two organizations' mutual goal of harmony between nations.

chapter five

The Service Club Matures: The Second Half Century

The things that are worthwhile take time, and it is not the I's of the world but the We's who achieve them.

—Rotary International President Bru Brunnier, 1952

S F Rotary's second half century brings us to the story of how SF Rotary emerged as an extraordinary service organization. Already a very large club of more than five hundred in 1958, it would grow to its high point of 604 members within a decade. We've seen in the first fifty years how SF Rotary found a lasting reason for being, not in its members' individual self-promotion, but in their ability to join hands and render service to their community. The second fifty years has brought about the maturing of this generous organization.

This process began in 1959, with the formation of a SF Rotary endowment to provide sustained support for service activities. The San Francisco Rotary Foundation would grow into a powerful source of major contributions to the club's service projects. The second aspect of SF Rotary's maturation took longer, but unfolded as a grand expansion of the club's service programs. As a result, SF Rotary continues today as a remarkable force for service to the residents of San Francisco.

The Means to an End—The San Francisco Rotary Foundation

In its first fifty years, the club performed acts of service using several forms of relatively small-scale funding. Funds for charity projects were raised informally (as in fining and collecting for the Charity Box), or through an "annual appeal," when members were asked to show their generous spirit during the Thanksgiving and Christmas holidays. A pool for the club's charity funds was formalized in 1931, in the establishment of the separate nonprofit Rotary Service, Inc. The Rotary Service monies were short term in nature, because money donated was distributed for various service purposes soon thereafter.

For several years SF Rotarian Russell Bowell had considered the idea of a more permanent source of funding for charitable purposes. It would be an endowment similar in purpose to RI's Rotary Foundation, which was created in 1917 and grew dramatically in size following Paul Harris's death in 1947. As president in 1958–59, Russell discussed his concept with SF Rotary's past presidents, who formed a

*Stuart D. Menist,
SF Rotary President
1977-78*

committee among themselves to develop a plan. Articles of incorporation and by-laws were drawn up and approved by the past presidents and the club's board.

The corporation was to be a nonprofit organization, "authorized to accept donations and bequests for carrying on various types of worthwhile projects." The foundation would distribute grants only from earnings on its investments, while its principal would remain permanently invested, thus guaranteeing that any individual's contribution would go toward perpetual good works. The foundation board would consist of nine directors. Membership requirements for the board were set forth to ensure that the fund would remain under the control of active members of SF Rotary. Upon hearing President Bowell's presentation, club members were favorably impressed and voted unanimously in March 1959 to establish the San Francisco Rotary Foundation (hereinafter called the SFR Foundation).

SF Rotary's new foundation was successful from its beginning. Only a year after it was established, the Foundation's first memorial fund came from contributions upon the death of District Governor Francis Whitmer, the member who had drawn up the Foundation's legal papers. Club member Stuart Menist replaced Francis on the board within the first year of the Foundation's existence. Stu went on to serve on the Foundation board for twenty-five years. In 1967, the Foundation's assets of $50,000 were tripled, with a $100,000 bequest from longtime member Grayson Dutton.[33]

This early growth made it possible for SF Rotary to give to a wider range of worthy organizations. For decades, the club's contributions were mainly limited to the Boys' Club and the Society for Crippled Children. By 1966, contributions to the SFR Foundation helped support the National Aid to Visually Handicapped Organization, the San Francisco Hearing and Speech Clinic, the Recreation Center for the Handicapped, the Girl Scouts, and the Red Cross. From 1959 to 1970, the SFR Foundation distributions and the club's Rotary Service giving totaled over $250,000.

Donation of a van to the Recreation Center for the Handicapped by SF Rotary President Larry Walker (right), to Janet Pomeroy, founder and director of the Recreation Center. SF City Supervisor Peter Tamaras is on the left, 1966. Courtesy of Moulin Studios Archives

---

33. At the time of his death, Grayson was one of the four oldest Rotarians in the world—a member since 1909.

Upon Bru Brunnier's death in 1971, the Foundation's assets again increased substantially. Bru had left $81,000 to the organization. In 1995, the Foundation received another substantial bequest from Past President Chet MacPhee (1974–75).

Over the past thirty years, the Foundation has enjoyed phenomenal growth. This growth has been due in large part to skillful management by the Foundation's Investment Committee. Twenty years after it was started, the fund's principle stood at $450,000, mainly invested in stocks and bonds. In 1985, only six years later, the fund total reached over $1 million, under the direction of Al Barnston's committee. To celebrate, Ed Thompson and Chet MacPhee each donated $10,000. "Black Monday" struck the stock market in October 1987, sending the Dow Jones Industrial Average plunging by 22 percent. Al Barnston and the Investment Committee were credited with having protected the portfolio by investing defensively

Al Barnston

in a period of dangerous speculation. During the next few years of market turmoil and the boom years of the 1990s, the fund gained 22 percent one year, and enjoyed an annual increase of over 16 percent in one five-year period.[34] Indeed, during the time Al chaired the Investment Committee, scarcely a Foundation board meeting passed without words of praise for the "magnificent job" the Investment Committee brought to the financial returns of the Foundation's fund. After Al's death in 1996, he and his committee were credited for achieving $2 million growth in the fund's assets in only twelve years—despite distribution of all dividends and interest to local charities.

> "The Investment Committee during that period has never received the credit it should have. The Foundation would not have been able to provide the funding over the past fifteen years if it weren't for the growth of the fund."
>
> —Past District Governor Bill Sturgeon, 2007

Club member Sam Yates stepped into Al's shoes and the Foundation has continued to grow, reaching its high of over $5 million in 2000. In 2002, a surprised committee chair Sam Yates received the Homer Wood Fellow award for his outstanding service to the Foundation. Bill Koefoed remarked that SF Rotary owes a tremendous debt of gratitude to Sam Yates, Al Barnston, and the dedicated Foundation Investment Committee. Since the Foundation was established in 1959, donations and bequests to the Foundation had totaled less than $500,000, but astute investing over the years had increased the corpus tenfold, even after providing over $2.3 million in grants for charitable and educational service. Since reaching its high of $5 million, the fund lost some value in the "dot-com bust" of the early 2000s, although the balance still stands at over $3 million due to significantly increased giving.

Sam Yates

As the Foundation endowment grew over the years, a number of changes were made. Investment strategy changed constantly as market conditions varied. In order to provide for rotation

---

34. During this period, the committee members included Al Barnston, Marsh Blum, William Brennan, Marv Cardoza, Hal Gray, Chet MacPhee, Al Maggio, Stu Menist, Varnum Paul, Lloyd Pflueger, and Sam Yates.

Robert B. Wilhelm,
SF Rotary President
1993–94

and fresh viewpoints among the directors, the bylaws were changed to impose term limits on board members. One topic under periodic review and revision has been the philosophy governing the amount of money to be distributed to service projects each year. The original idea was to distribute earnings only, thus preserving the principle to increase through growth. When the fund grew larger, some board members thought the annual distribution of earnings too small to be fair to the club and community. Today, the annual amount of earnings available for distribution is based on a percentage of a three-year average of fund assets. This has enabled the Foundation to make larger amounts of money available to club presidents for use in their yearly programs.

SF Rotarians continue to help their Foundation grow. Most of the fund's corpus has come from past and continuing member bequests. Contributions also come in other ways. For example, club Past President and Hotel Executive Bob Wilhelm has, on more than one occasion, presented the hotel's luncheon receipts from a club meeting to the Foundation.[35]

In recent years, the SFR Foundation has devised three forms of recognition for club members. The first is the Homer Wood Fellow, established to honor individuals contributing $1,000 or more to the SFR Foundation.[36] The Fellow also serves as a method of providing memorial recognition and honoring friends, relatives, and outstanding individuals, through a $1,000 contribution in the individual's name. The first awardees were announced in 1995, and many Fellows have been awarded since. To date, Homer Wood Fellows honored by SF Rotary are:

SF Rotarian Gary Wollin performs card tricks to raise money for the SFR Foundation.

Art Agnew	Grant Hundley	Bill Sturgeon, PDG
Al Barnston	Bill Koefoed	Sandra Sturgeon
Herb Bergren	Charles Massen	Libby Swope
Burt Berry	Lisa Moscaret-Burr	Carroll Tornroth
Marsh Blum	Dick Newburgh	Howard Waits
Curtis Burr	Don Parachini	Bob Wilhelm
Dick Buxton	Tom Parry	Gary Wollin
Dr. Scharleen Colant	Linda Pavia	Rosey Wong
Bill Ecker	Scott Plakun	Sam Yates
Allan Herzog	Everett Price	Jason Yuen
Harold Hoogasian	Dr. David T. Shen	

35. Bob also contributed several times to Rotary Service in the same way.

36. Note that this SF Rotary award is not the same as District 5150's Homer Wood Award for the club that has done outstanding work in World Community and International Service over the past year.

In 2005, the Foundation board announced the Diamond Circle—those individuals who pledge a bequest to the SFR Foundation in their wills. To date, Diamond Circle members are:

Alfred Alessandri	Kun Sam Kim	Richard Rosen
Tiffany Birch	William Koefoed	Anita Stangl
Thomas Brunner	Frederic Marschner	Joseph S. Talmadge
Curtis Burr	Lisa Moscaret-Burr	John Uth
Dr. Scharleen Colant	Richard Nelson	Shirley Victor
Christina Harbridge-Law	Donald Parachini	

SF Rotary's highest award of recognition is the Bru Brunnier Fellow.[37] The Fellow is an award to a SF Rotarian who is jointly recognized by the boards of directors of the club and the SFR Foundation for rendering substantial service to the cause of Rotary. Established in 1980, the award was initially presented as recognition of a $2,500 contribution to the SFR Foundation. But in 1996, the club and Foundation boards agreed that the club's highest award should recognize exceptional service as well. The SF Rotary boards must jointly consider any Fellow nominee's service to the club and SFR Foundation. Then when contributions from other members in the nominee's name reach $2,500, the nominee is named a Bru Brunnier Fellow. In recent years, the Bru Brunnier Fellow is awarded at the annual Holiday Party luncheon. To date, Bru Brunnier Fellows honored by SF Rotary and the SFR Foundation are:

1980 James Deitz	1995 Peter V. Taylor
1980 Bill Tolson	1996 Dr. Angelo V. Capozzi
1980 Ed Thompson	1997 Robert B. Wilhelm
1980 Bradford Swope	1998 Richard C. Volberg
1987 Richard Saxton	1999 Thomas C. Paton
1988 PDG William B. Sturgeon	2000 William A. Koefoed
1988 Chester R. MacPhee, Sr.	2001 John Uth
1991 James M. Patrick, II	2002 Dr. Scharleen H. Colant
1992 William H. Ecker	2002 Ernest J. Colant
1993 Henry C. Todd	2004 Curtis Burr
1994 PDG Peter C. Lagarias	2004 Anita Stangl
1994 Marshall R. Blum	2006 James Bradley
1995 Alfred J. Barnston	

■ ■ ■

Even as SF Rotary established and grew its SFR Foundation fund, it continued to raise short-term money for service projects through Rotary Service, Inc. As before, the funds came from longtime

---

37. Note that this is not the same as the District 5150 Bru Brunnier Award for Distinguished International Service, given to a club for outstanding international service.

Thomas C. Paton,
SF Rotary President
1982–83

traditional sources, such as member fines, on-the-spot contributions for various causes (especially to send emergency relief outside of San Francisco), and the "annual appeal" during the holidays.

In 1982, club President Tom Paton had an innovative idea. Needing to raise money for the club's seventy-fifth-anniversary celebration in 1983, he decided upon an auction and dinner-dance, and announced that Bill Koefoed would plan and carry out the event. Plans called for a shift to lower-cost gifts for members' wives at the annual Ladies' Christmas Luncheon giveaway. Major gifts contributed by members and others would instead be emphasized for the spring auction.

SF Rotary's first auction/dinner-dance was called the Rotary Charities Dinner-Dance. Bill Koefoed and his committee created excitement several weeks in advance at weekly luncheon meetings, with acting-auctioneer Jim Patrick auctioning off such items as a single share of IBM stock.

The evening itself was a gala affair at the St. Francis Hotel, attended by several hundred SF Rotarians and their ladies in formal attire. The dinner was preceded by a silent auction. After dinner the live auction began. A professional auctioneer from the Rotary Club of Oakland drew excited bidding that exceeded opening bids for most items. After the auction, attendees enjoyed a grand raffle drawing, and the evening concluded with dancing. Tom Paton's auction idea was a winner. SF Rotary's first auction/dinner-dance netted $60,000 ($126,000 in today's dollars) for Rotary Service.

Following its stunning success, the club held the formal auction/dinner-dance to benefit Rotary Service for many years. Jim Patrick continued his auctioneering, sometimes as coauctioneer with club member Ken Baggott. The club received donations of big-ticket items for the event, such as round trips to Europe and cars. In one year alone (1993), the club auctioned off ten overseas air trips and a $17,000 cruise. These auctions brought substantial funding for Rotary Service. By 1988, the auction had made $350,000 available for the club's charitable projects, and the event's net profit increased for several years

Jim Patrick promotes the auction by auctioneering from a trampoline during a luncheon meeting, 1985. Courtesy of Pete Taylor

after that. In 1993, the auction grossed $110,000, netting $80,000 for use in good works.

Since 1995–96, the club's president-elect has chaired the annual event, specifically as a fundraiser for the upcoming year's service projects. These events have been possible only through hard

Joanne Ireland

work and contributions by SF Rotarians. The 2000 "Monte Carlo Madness" was held at Marie Brooks's donated auto-dealership showroom. Professional event-planner Joanne Ireland donated staff time to make the big event run smoothly.

This annual spring fund-raiser has undergone many changes with the times, such as including tables for those attending solo, and changing to "not-formal" or "black-tie optional" attire.

Seeking a way to revitalize the event in 2004, Bill Koefoed, Curtis Burr, and Lisa Moscaret-Burr hit upon a new idea. With help from Rotarian Steve Revetria of the San Francisco Giants baseball team, a party and auction was held at San Francisco's new baseball park. Called "Grand Slam at the Ball Park" in 2004, and "Diamonds to Diamonds" the following year, the ball-park parties received rave reviews and brought in substantial funds for Rotary Service. More than an auction and dinner, the events offered fun for the whole family. Club member Rev. David Stechholz relished the opportunity to hit one from a major-league park's home plate, as did his handicapped son, who hit one off the delivery of a former Giants pitcher.

Although the SFR Foundation and the club's annual spring fund-raiser have made far more money available for philanthropic work, they have not eliminated the club's many other ways of generating money for charitable and educational programs. Sale of the "Entertainment" discount book in the 1980s and '90s lasted for several years. Other fund-raisers are more sporadic, such as the spontaneous auctions of concert and sports tickets, prizes, or other goods by members at the luncheon meetings. Several that are done in the spirit of fun at meetings (such as fining and "ringing the bell" for $100) have become club traditions. One recent innovation was "Burr's Bogus Bucks," a feature of the weekly luncheons during Curtis Burr's presidential year in 1996. By "selling" two-dollar bills for five dollars, and entering part of the proceeds into a progressive weekly raffle, Curtis raised funds for Rotary Service. The drawing proved to be an effective fund-raiser. The initial fund continued over six months and reached $4,400. Upon restarting after a member drew the winning token, the fund raised almost another $4,000 by the end of Curtis's presidential year. "Burr's Bogus Bucks" was continued by the next club president, John Uth, as "Rotabucks." After

Curtis almost wound up afoul of the law. He "upgraded" the two-dollar bills with a gold portrait of Aaron Burr pasted over the front of Thomas Jefferson's face. During one memorable luncheon meeting, Curtis was confronted and nearly arrested by a gun-toting "Fed," who charged Curtis with defacing U.S. currency. Curtis thought the situation might be real, until SF Rotarian Police Chief Fred Lau rescued him at the last minute.

several years, President Dick Rosen revived the game as "Dick's Devalued Dollars" in 2003. Succeeding presidents continued it, as Grant Hundley's "Grant's Greedy Greenbacks," Steve Talmadge's "Chief's Wacky Wampums," Anita Stangl's "Fat Cats Cash," and John Hoch's "No-Name-Drawing."

These new sources for funding revealed the true generosity of SF Rotarians, as the club's second half century unfolded. Club members were eager to provide the means to make "Service Above Self" a reality, and to nourish the expanding areas of service that would define the club as it matured.

Community Service—The Club Broadens Its Good Works

A young thirty-year-old Rotarian coming in to the club has seen a need, let's say, for a safe house for children in a particular bad area of San Francisco. If that new Rotarian comes in and suggests that project, and convinces the board to do it—here is somebody who has an idea that can have an impact on the community.

—Past District Governor Bill Sturgeon, 2001

In the club's century of service, San Francisco's children have remained the focal point of members' service interest. From the 1920s until the early 1970s, the club's only continuous community-service committees were for Civic Service, Boys' Work, and Crippled Children's work. The club established a popular tradition—its annual program in which the Boys' Work Committee and Crippled Children's Committee reported to the membership on the club's good works.

Ed Imhaus and Ron Imhaus emcee a Sunshine School Christmas Party, 1959. Courtesy of Moulin Studios Archives

Handicapped Children

Handicapped children—SF Rotary's oldest area of youth service—remained prominent, with a Crippled Children's (later Handicapped Children's) Committee in the club roster through 1980. Each year, SF Rotarians held the traditional Christmas Party at the Sunshine School. As the 1980s began, the Sunshine School was closed for budgetary reasons and because less severely handicapped children were "mainstreamed" into public schools. Children not mainstreamed were served at the LeConte School. SF Rotarians continued to donate toys at Christmas to children at the school, and in 1985, the club revived the Sunshine School–type Christmas party that had brought joy to so many little lives in the past. For several more years, SF Rotarian Marsh Blum officiated at the Christmas party held at the Louise Lombard School for Handicapped Students.

The club provided other assistance to handicapped children throughout the 1980s. SF Rotarian doctors helped indigent children by occasionally taking charity orthodontia cases. The club supplied large-print books to partially sighted youngsters, and contributed to the San Francisco Aid for

Marsh Blum Remembers

"When I came into the club, Ed Imhaus had a beautiful voice, and he would emcee a party for the kids. We'd get contributions from the other Rotarians. We'd get chocolate candy from Boldemann chocolate and ice cream from Spreckles Creamery—anyone in the club who could give something, did. And we'd have a Santa Claus. Ed Imhaus was Santa for years, and then his son Ron did it, and then Ron asked me to be Santa Claus. It would bring tears to my eyes, because I remember as Santa Claus, there was a little boy, a child who wanted to stand up and touch my face."

Retarded Children's fund. Gradually, SF Rotary assistance specifically for handicapped children diminished, as this kind of aid was increasingly done by various organizations that help the disabled of all ages, such as the Recreation Center for the Handicapped.

The Boys & Girls Club

SF Rotary's proudest tradition of community service has been with the Boys & Girls Club,[38] and the club has continued to thrive with Rotary's help. For decades, the Boys' Work Committee was one of SF Rotary's largest, and nearly all the work done by this committee was with the Boys' Club itself. Rotarians participated in the longtime annual day at Playland-at-the-Beach, helped the boys raise money for their club, and upheld the tradition of having members "adopt" a fatherless Boys' Club boy at the annual Fathers & Sons luncheon. The Boys' Club remained SF Rotary's primary community-service focus through the 1970s.

SF Rotary also kept up its generous financial support to the club in a number of ways. Throughout the years, SF Rotary has donated vehicles for use at Camp Mendocino and for transporting children in San Francisco. Among its many other contributions, SF Rotary brought music to the Boys' Club Mission Branch in the 1960s, in the form of a music department—complete with music lessons, instruments, and uniforms. The department produced fine young musicians, good enough to march in the Rose Parade for three years. The club also continued its impressive program of funding improvements to Boys' Club buildings. In the 1970s, three branches were renovated with SF Rotary's help, and the club provided furnishings for a new Richmond Branch.

The Boys' Club Band, with uniforms and instruments donated by SF Rotary. Courtesy of Moulin Studios Archives

38. Changing with the times, the Boys' Club admitted girls. It first tried the idea in 1974, with an experimental three-month official program. The club's board voted to continue the project for two years at the Mission Branch. The Ernest Ingold and Mission Branches were subsequently opened to girls on a permanent basis, and in 1985, the name of the club was officially changed to the San Francisco Boys & Girls Club.

> "At our camp, the boys eat like men, play like boys, and sleep like babies."
>
> —Joe Daugherty, executive director of the Boys' Club in 1959

Since its creation in 1930 (as Camp Marwedel), Camp Mendocino has remained the Boys & Girls Club's central program, and an enormous source of pride for SF Rotary. For nearly eight decades, the camp has provided the happiest two weeks an underprivileged child might see in a year.[39] SF Rotarians continued generously supporting Camp Mendocino as they did in the camp's earlier days, with their time, money, and materials. In the early 1980s, Rotary helped remodel the camp's entire kitchen, dining hall, and staff quarters.

Despite many improvements since the camp opened, one glaring problem persisted into the 1980s: the camp remained inaccessible to vehicles during the winter because of increased water flow on the Noyo River. This inaccessibility greatly limited off-season use of the camp, and hampered winter maintenance efforts. Again, SF Rotary stepped forward. In celebration of its seventy-fifth anniversary in 1983, the club committed to build a bridge across the Noyo. Dick Connell, a Rotarian and retired brigadier general of the Army Corps of Engineers, conceived the type of bridge—a portable "Bailey bridge"[40]—and eliminated red tape through the Corps, enabling the project to go forward. Professional planning, engineering, and construction supervision services valued at over $200,000 were donated. SF Rotary raised the remaining $45,000. President Jim Patrick launched the fund-raising campaign at the weekly Rotary luncheon by cutting the ribbon on a Tinkertoy model of the bridge. SF Rotarians rode the Skunk Train to the site with volunteers from the Boys & Girls Club and the Purple Kumquats (a volunteer Boys & Girls Club alumni group). They set the Bailey bridge in place over a weekend. A well-attended official dedication of the "Rotary Bridge of Friendship" was held several months later, in June 1985. The bridge has been a valuable addition to the camp. It has enabled Camp Mendocino to become a year-round facility, making it usable for kids' "mini-camps" in the winter.

Rotary Bridge of Friendship at Camp Mendocino, donated by SF Rotary, 1985.

One cannot visit the camp without seeing SF Rotary's good work everywhere. The club has rebuilt the laundry after it was destroyed by fire, donated an entire camp-administration office building, and helped rebuild a pedestrian swinging bridge and a water-treatment plant. After the SFR Foundation donated funds to renovate and upgrade the

---

39. The camp has also hosted other youngsters over the years. They range from boys and girls who visit from around the world through various international exchange organizations, to a group of children from San Francisco's rough Tenderloin area.

40. The Bailey bridge was the type used by the Allies in Germany during World War II. The bridge was purchased from army surplus.

SF Rotary work day at Camp Mendocino. Courtesy of Boys & Girls Clubs of San Francisco

camp's corral, it was named the Alfred J. Barnston Corral, to memorialize Al and "his devotion to the Foundation, to the Boys & Girls Club, and his love of horses." The SFR Foundation continues to donate to specific capital needs at the camp.

SF Rotarians' openhandedness has also benefited kids directly. Throughout its early history, the club sponsored hundreds of boys to attend camp. In more recent years, SF Rotary's expansion into a wide array of community-service interests limited its ability to provide camperships at the same rate as in earlier decades. For many years, the Ed Detrick Memorial Fund, created by members and Ed's widow Shirley upon his death in 1986, sent a few children to camp each year. During SF Rotary's ninetieth-anniversary year in 1998, the SFR Foundation's donation to the Boys & Girls Club included the sponsorship of many additional camperships for the summer.

SF Rotarians have also contributed their own time and energy to the camp's upkeep. The Boys & Girls Club has invited Rotarians to visit its camps since the 1920s. During many of those years, Rotary club members participated in "work weekends," painting, cleaning up, and doing other maintenance chores. Although the working visits were discontinued in 2001, SF Rotarians and their families continue to enjoy a long tradition of "Host Ourselves" fun weekends, where they have the camp to themselves and enjoy all it has to offer.

Today, Camp Mendocino is a comfortable haven, with cabins, and a lodge. Campers enjoy the dining hall, amphitheater, canteen, recreation hall, nature-study cabin, swimming pool, and—of course—the river. The infrastructure, which includes a kitchen, an infirmary, an office, directors' cabins, a caretaker's home, laundry facilities, maintenance buildings, a power plant, and primary and secondary water supplies, enables the camp to keep functioning—a self-sufficient "city" in the forest. A large part of the credit for the camp's success as one of the best and most beautiful children's camps in the United States belongs to SF Rotary.

Besides contributing money to the Boys & Girls Club directly through Rotary Service, Inc., and the SFR Foundation, Rotarians have historically assisted

"Les Andersen always knew there were little kids that needed more than just a couple of weeks away from home. They needed to spend the summer up there—maybe there was trouble at home or no parents were available. So Les would get them up there to the camp, and keep them there for the summer, or send them back, depending on the environment at home to come back to. I can remember some of the 'invisible' kids—this one was playing in the petting zoo that Les keeps up there. And this was a kid who lives in Hunters Point and had never seen a duck before, and he just adopted this duck."

—Past President Jim Bradley

SF Rotarian Dick Dixon helps a Boys' Club member sell flowers, in an annual Boys' Club Flower Day fund-raiser, 1978. Courtesy of RI Archives

the club financially by leading and participating in various fund-raising activities. For the better part of the twentieth century, SF Rotary was the Boys & Girls Club's biggest fund-raiser. Early efforts included fund-raising for building purchase, construction, and renovation projects; the Whitneys' contribution of Playland-at-the-Beach receipts; and a series of talent shows and carnivals. In recent decades, Rotary has engaged in a number of innovative and often fun activities to raise money for the Boys & Girls Club. Each year since 1963, Rotarians manage teams of boys and girls who sell flowers during the Flower Day benefit.

In 1990, SF Rotary helped put on a fund-raising "Rubber Ducky Race" at Aquatic Park. Phone callers were able to "adopt" a duck entry, and the first hundred ducks to finish the race were awarded prizes. The event was well-promoted, with a roving "Duck Truck," shopping-center events, local radio coverage, and a full "Farley" comic strip in the *San Francisco Chronicle* on race day. The Boys & Girls Club's most profitable fund-raiser has been the annual Golf and Tennis Tournament, begun in 1972. SF Rotarian Ed Thompson was for many years a generous contributor, underwriting several Golf and Tennis Tournaments. He also donated $10,000 for the Camp Mendocino bridge project, and by 1986, Ed had contributed $90,000 in nine years. Another SF Rotarian, Harold Kilpatrick, left a large bequest of $100,000 to the Boys & Girls Club in 1980.

SF Rotary's involvement with the Boys & Girls Club lessened somewhat after the 1980s. SF Rotarians have spread their community-service contributions and efforts over a wider range of projects, and the Boys & Girls Club board diversified as well. The two organizations have continued their strong relationship however. SF Rotary maintains a Boys & Girls Club Liaison Committee, chaired for many years by Ron Anderson

The Boys & Girls Club game room provides a clean, fun, after-school environment.
Courtesy Boys & Girls Clubs of San Francisco

Ron Anderson

John Dissmeyer III

Mike Davies

Rob Connolly

and more recently by John Dissmeyer and Mike Davies. John Dissmeyer sits on the Boys & Girls Club's board, and its executive director, Rob Connolly, is an SF Rotarian.[41]

Although it is no longer the Boys & Girls Club's largest supporter, Rotary continues to give generously to the club. In 1996, SF Rotary helped bring the club into the computer age. For President Curtis Burr's signature project, Kathy Beavers chaired Rotary's venture into "an electronic barn-raising"—the creation of a computer/Internet learning center in each of the Boys & Girls Club's five branches. Funded jointly by SF Rotary and corporate contributions, the multimedia computers—including sixteen monitors donated by Allan Herzog—were installed with educational and career-oriented software, and connected to the Internet. The project also included implementation of learning-center staffing and plans for innovative and informative learning programs, and won the district's Best Youth Service award for the year. By providing technology to the 4,100 underprivileged young people served by the club, Rotary has helped them pre-

Computers help Boys & Girls Club members with their homework. Courtesy Boys & Girls Clubs of San Francisco

Marie Brooks

pare for higher learning and professional careers, and enhanced their confidence and knowledge of the world around them.

During SF Rotary's ninetieth-anniversary year in 1998, Rotary gave the Boys & Girls Club $25,000 and bought the club a van—in part a donation from club member Marie Brooks's auto dealership. The van sported a personalized

41. In 2001, the Boys & Girls Club merged with the Columbia Park Boys & Girls Club. The Columbia club had been formed as a boy's club in 1895, four years after the founding of the San Francisco Boys' Club. The new name of the merged organizations is the Boys & Girls Clubs of San Francisco. Today the club consists of nine clubhouses in the city of San Francisco.

plate—"Les One"—to recognize longtime Director Les Andersen's many years of dedicated work for the Boys & Girls Club.[42]

To celebrate its one-hundredth anniversary in 2008, SF Rotary is honoring its historic ties to the Boys & Girls Club with an ambitious project to rebuild the club's Mission Branch building, which Rotary originally helped build in 1928. SF Rotary is working to raise $1.7 million for

Les Andersen behind the wheel of a truck donated by SF Rotary to the San Francisco Boys' Club in 1973.

its sponsorship of the project through fund-raising events and recruiting of individual and corporate donors. The new facility will be vastly improved over the old building, which has been vacant for nearly four years. It will include a teen room, a larger gymnasium, a new rooftop play yard, a game room, an updated full-service kitchen, a stand-alone multimedia center, and a new learning center. The project is most appropriate for SF Rotary's Centennial, as it symbolizes Rotary's longtime contributions to the well-being of the children of San Francisco.

> "The Boys & Girls Club gave me a new direction and a positive outlook on life, and for that I am very grateful. I was a lonely and angry kid. Boxing is very physical and I was able to channel that raw energy into a positive outlet."
>
> —Past President Steve Talmadge

■ ■ ■

SF Rotarians and Boys & Girls Club members celebrate the ground-breaking for the new Mission Branch clubhouse, 2007.

The story of SF Rotary's present-day levels of community service has its start in the 1980s, which began a period of rapid new advances in service. These advances are seen in three major changes, starting during the presidency of Tom Paton. First, the new annual auction/dinner-dance instituted in 1983 made substantially more money available to the club's Rotary Service, Inc. Although the SFR Foundation was also distributing money to service projects, the days of very large annual grants from the Foundation were still to come in the

42. In 1997, longtime Executive Director Les Andersen stepped down, and Ron Anderson took his place. Today the club is in the capable hands of another SF Rotarian, Rob Connolly. Les continues his valuable service to the club as Executive Director Emeritus.

late 1990s. But in the 1980s, the auction/dinner-dance made a significant difference in what could be accomplished during a club's year. This is illustrated by the fact that annual giving from the SFR Foundation and Rotary Service, Inc. totaled $65,000 in 1980, whereas in 1986 it totaled over $140,000, much of the increase coming from auction/dinner-dance profit.

Second, the early 1980s began a period of substantial expansion in SF Rotary's range of service interests. The club's main focus on the Boys' Club and handicapped children gave way to the multitude of new projects and programs the club sponsors today. As always, the majority of new programs benefited young people, but SF Rotarians developed innovative new ways to help them.

Third, despite the new availability of service money, the 1980s saw a shift away from SF Rotary's role as a "checkbook club" toward its present-day preference for "hands-on" service activities. This is not to say that members had not been involved in club activities before. Rotarians had always given generously of their time to the club, where as many as eighteen Club Service committees consisted of 50 percent of the membership. And certain aspects of Boys' Club work had always involved hands-on work by club members. But for the most part, the club members wrote checks—these were their chief contribution to the well-being of San Francisco. One reason for the shift in emphasis lay in the fact that the club worked hard to attract young members in the early 1980s. Hands-on projects were viewed as attractive to younger members, who were less able to "ring the bell" or contribute substantial amounts of money. But older members became involved as well. Rotarians were active in a wide variety of community-service projects, from planting trees in Golden Gate Park and painting a preschool center to sponsoring large youth projects involving dozens of students. In 1988, Past President Tom Paton reported that the emphasis on member involvement had evolved SF Rotary from a checkbook club into a hands-on club, "where priority goes to projects requiring a Rotarian's input rather than money donations alone."

> "When I came into the club it was a checkbook club and it did very little charitable work, almost no projects at all. Within just a few years, it became quite a different operation. Then in rapid sequence we started several programs—Camp Enterprise, Academic Decathlon, and so on. I'd say the big change came in Tom Paton's year, when he established the auction—a program that resulted, for the first time, in our really having some money available to spend on charity."
>
> —Past President Bill Ecker, 2001

Much of the credit for this explosion of new and different community-service programs that began in the 1980s belongs to a succession of imaginative club presidents. It also belongs to the hundreds of SF Rotarians who chaired and staffed the committees that turned good ideas into realities with lasting benefits to the people of San Francisco.

Youth Service in the 1980s

By the end of SF Rotary's first decade, young people emerged as the club's foremost community-service interest. Subsequently, the 1920s witnessed an explosion in the club's youth-service work. In only two years, the club's efforts expanded from a few charity cases to the opening of the Sunshine

School and the assumption of responsibility for the struggling Boys' Club. These two areas (handicapped children and the Boys' Club) represented the majority of SF Rotary's philanthropic work through the 1970s. Then came SF Rotary's broad expansion of community service in the 1980s—with most of the new work serving young people. The decade between the mid-1980s and mid-1990s ranks as a time when SF Rotary reached out to San Francisco's children with a sense of purpose and excitement not seen since the 1920s.

Camp Enterprise

Since its inception in 1985, Camp Enterprise (CE) has been SF Rotary's largest continuing hands-on youth program. Junior- and senior-year high-school boys and girls from San Francisco, Marin, and San Mateo counties attend an annual two-and-a-half-day camp adventure. They are introduced to a firsthand understanding of entrepreneurial business and the free-enterprise system. With guidance from Rotarian business and professional leaders, the students learn to apply this knowledge in the development of a hypothetical business of their choosing. In doing so, they benefit from a valuable aspect of education not provided in schools, where teachers rarely have extensive business backgrounds. For students who are thinking about careers and opportunities, the camp provides a forward-thinking experience, and helps them shape their college plans.

James M. Patrick II, SF Rotary President 1984–85

In 1984, President-Elect Jim Patrick attended the Rotary Club of Oakland's Camp Enterprise-84, held at a YMCA camp in Marin County.[43] Jim returned inspired by the enthusiasm he had seen in students and Rotarians at the camp. He designated Camp Enterprise as the club's principal project of his presidential year, and appointed Warren Eggert as the project's committee chairman.

By early 1985, Jim had gained the support of high-school principals and school counselors for the project. Students would attend the camp at no expense. The cost of $75 per student for the three days would be absorbed mostly by sales of sponsorships to Rotary club members and their firms.

The planning effort was tremendous. Camp Enterprise is a considerable undertaking, requiring volunteers to serve in a wide variety of functions, including camp speakers and discussion-group leaders, school relations, medical assistance, recreation, camp operations, food, registration, transportation, dormitory counselors (Rotary wives were encouraged to serve in the girls' dorm), and sales of sponsorships.

SF Rotary's Camp Enterprise-85 opened in the Point Bonita YMCA camp, at the entrance to the Golden Gate and San Francisco Bay. It took place over a Sunday, Monday, and Tuesday morning, under the direction of Jim Deitz, Bill Sturgeon, and Roane Sias. Buses, vans for luggage, and Camp Bonita facilities were given or provided at reasonable or no cost to the club by outside organizations. Forty-two SF Rotarians and their wives participated.

---

43. The same year, other Rotary clubs, including San Jose and Beaumont, Texas, also sponsored camps. The San Diego Rotary Club's Camp Enterprise promotion had garnered the participation of the Lieutenant Governor of California as kick-off speaker for their program. Several of these clubs planned to continue Camp Enterprise as a yearly event.

The Camp Enterprise winning team presents its business plan at the SF Rotary luncheon.
Courtesy of Eric Schmautz

Students from thirteen high schools were chosen by their teachers to attend the camp. Under the guidance of SF Rotary's business leaders, the students developed an understanding of the business world. They explored management functions such as financing, production, product sales, and advertising. These topics were introduced to the students within the principles of the Rotary Four-Way Test. The students were divided into teams, each team using the knowledge gained to conceive, plan, and develop a hypothetical company to produce and sell goods and services.

Afterward, the entire entourage was bussed back to SF Rotary's Tuesday luncheon at the Palace Hotel, where they were the club's special guests, dining with their individual sponsors. The two-and-a-half-day seminar was highlighted by the winning group presenting a skit about its business during the luncheon program.

The initial camp was judged so successful that school administrators convinced SF Rotary to establish Camp Enterprise as an annual program. The newly minted young entrepreneurs—who had been skeptical at first—enthusiastically promoted CE among their student friends. From the experience gained in 1985, the CE committee established an outline for the program. The plan would direct the various committees, individual leaders, and counselors, yet give the students plenty of latitude to develop their own ideas. With sixty-five students, the 1986 camp was again judged very successful. The San Francisco school district thanked SF Rotary for the unique CE experience, acknowledging it as a program that "has the potential to positively change a life and career path."

SF Rotary has repeated Camp Enterprise every year since 1985, and it continues to be successful. Schools are not asked to send their brightest students. Instead, teachers are encouraged to send the students who show a spark of promise that needs development. At the start of the weekend, the students are grouped into teams of eight, with as much ethnic diversity as possible. They are assigned to their teams by Rotarians, rather than letting them group themselves by school, where the students already assume who their leader is. The team members do not know each other, or who's "smart," so leaders surface naturally. Some of the students are shy or speak little English, but the teams are not permitted to ignore anyone. They are encouraged to work with everyone, because every member of the team must be in on the final presentation. Over the weekend the students develop a team spirit, and approach the Camp Enterprise challenge determined to be the winning team.

Beginning the first day, Rotarians give presentations, motivational speeches, and mini-classes on topics such as public speaking, team building, goal setting, and elements of a successful

DANA GRIBBEN, A SF ROTARY COUNSELOR AT CAMP ENTERPRISE
"I know these junior boys in high school don't care about Dana Gribben and what she's done in the grown-up world, so I go in on a motorcycle with my motorcycle gear, and I have a pretend job interview with another Rotarian. And I put on this attitude. Then I stop and say, 'Okay, what's wrong with this picture?' And the kids tell me. Then I switch to a personality that's got jewelry and bracelets and nail polish in my pocket and chewing gum, and go on with the interview as though it's a different inter- view, different person. I say, 'What's wrong with this picture?' That's the way I figure to gain their attention, because they don't give beans about me coming up in some business clothes and going blah, blah, blah at them. They like my approach."

Dana Gribben

business. Typical of many such talks, Jean Schore brought "Creating a Business" to the stu- dents. Jim Deitz mesmerized the students as he encouraged them to look forward to the future as they grew from consumers to pro- ducers, from takers to givers, and from reliance to self-reliance.

Then the students set to work. Each team develops and presents a viable business based on hypothetical conditions, such as obtaining a $10,000 loan from the school board and payment of rent for school space. They cre- ate materials to demonstrate and display a resulting business pro- posal, financial statements, and a marketing strategy. Examples of businesses that have been formed by camp participants include an "I Spy" video yearbook, a mobile used-clothing store, a dating service, "COMP Enterprise" (computer training), a dance club, and a homework tutoring service. At the end of the second day, the students compete for the best business design, presenting their new businesses to the Rotarian counselors.

The students and counsel- ors also have fun with hiking and games. The evening campfire fea- tures a hot-dog roast, toasted marsh- mallows, and singing. On the last night of camp after the competition ends, the students are treated to a dance and wrap-up party.

After the weekend, the win- ning team presents its business proposal at SF Rotary's luncheon meeting. The club awards cash scholarships to the students whom Rotarian counselors believe have made the greatest advance in per- sonal growth.

A team-building session at Camp Enterprise. Courtesy of Eric Schmautz

SF ROTARY PAST PRESIDENT JIM BRADLEY ON CAMP ENTERPRISE

"Up until that point, my only experience with high-school kids had been seeing them skateboarding and just hanging out—not doing anything productive. And I was really concerned about it. What's the future going to be if this is what the kids are?... And all of a sudden, here were these bright kids.... And they're standoffish. They're unsure. The way they've been taught is the teacher's going to give you the instructions: 'Start at A. End at Z.' And Rotary comes to them and says, 'You're a smart kid. Find A and work your way to Z. You figure out how. You think this thing through.' You throw them into groups and they don't know how to form a group and how to become a leader and how to get a group moving. By the end of the project, you've got kids doing things that in the first day, they would have said, 'I'll never do that.' And that's the interesting part of it.

"Then they come back and make a presentation at Rotary.... One of my greatest experiences was when my group won. They came back to the Rotary meeting, and sitting at the table, they realized they had left all their notes on the bus, so they had nothing. Their first thought was, 'Let's make a run for it.' But I said, 'They're counting on you guys. You gotta do it.' So they got up there and did it almost word for word the way they had done it the night before at the competition. These kids just came through perfectly."

Although its underlying function and process have remained much the same, Camp Enterprise has undergone some changes over the years. Early women members Anita Stangl and Leni Miller became involved with Camp Enterprise as soon as they joined the club. They eliminated some of the standard business speakers and added hands-on team-building exercises.

There have been organizational changes as well. After the San Francisco school administration discontinued official school participation in overnight trips in 2003, recruitment for students to attend Camp Enterprise has taken place through individual teachers, coaches, parents, and student groups. In an effort to expand the pool of potential attendees, Past District Governor Pete Lagarias and club member Eric Schmautz were instrumental in introducing Marin County Rotarians and students to the program that year, and CE became a District 5150 program.

By any measure, Camp Enterprise has been a rich undertaking. In the two decades since Jim Patrick envisioned a large, hands-on project to benefit San Francisco students, CE has given an exciting and memorable experience to over 1,600 young people. It continues to receive high praise on student evaluations. Camp Enterprise offers students tools to help in their career planning. The program has broadened youth and adults alike, by improving relations between the generations. It involves more than Rotarians and

Eric Schmautz, SF Rotary President 2008–09

spouses. Successful Camp Enterprise alumni are often invited to return as counselors, to assist and work alongside Rotarians, and to help recruit for the next year's event.

Rotarians gain from the program as well. The camp offers expanded fellowship opportunities for club members, working together in a few short but intensive days. Participants report the experience as giving them enormous feelings of satisfaction and personal reward. Camp Enterprise has worked as a hands-on project for Rotarians and students alike because it goes beyond community service. It involves Rotarians in vocational service—bringing the strengths of their vocations into service for others. Camp Enterprise follows in a historical tradition of SF Rotarians mentoring and counseling young people, helping them find their way along by providing strong role models as successful businesspeople. And—because it draws on what businesspeople already know—the vocational-service program has been one of the best ways for new Rotarians to get involved in the club's work for the community.

Academic Decathlon

Not surprisingly, many of SF Rotary's other new youth programs of the 1980s and 1990s have been built on the strengths of vocational service. The Academic Decathlon—the second of SF Rotary's two major hands-on programs—succeeded for the same reasons.

Academic Decathlon is a national program for high-school students that develops and rewards scholastic achievement and public-speaking skills. Modeled after the Olympics, the Academic Decathlon is a competition of mastery in ten academic events. In the one-day competition, each student is interviewed; writes an essay; gives a speech on a current topic; completes written exams in art, math, science, history, music, and literature; and competes in the "Super Quiz"—a college bowl–like test on a preannounced major topic. The program is not academically elitist; it includes A, B, and C students. Public and private city high schools enter teams of nine students—three each of A, B, and C grade level—who compete in a citywide Decathlon. The winning team from the city advances to the California Academic Decathlon, and the winning state team advances to the national competition. Stimulating the same sense of school spirit and pride as athletic competitions, the Academic Decathlon sends a message that perseverance, study, and teamwork can bring personal rewards and that academics can be as exciting as any athletic competition.

Academic Decathlon was developed in 1978 in Orange County, to encourage and recognize academic excellence. It became a statewide event the following year. Three years later, the competition became a national event, and more than four thousand schools in the United States and Canada participated. The program was brought to San Francisco schools in 1988, through a partnership between SF Rotary and the San Francisco Unified School District.

In 1987, President-Elect Bill Sturgeon saw an article about the Decathlon in his local newspaper. Thinking it might be a worthwhile program for SF Rotary to sponsor, Bill and his wife, Sandra, a former teacher, traveled to Sacramento to interview a state school official involved in the program and to see an Academic Decathlon event for themselves. What he saw was an exciting statewide competition that challenged students to excel.

When Bill returned home with a video and a sample medal from the event, he showed Bill Koefoed the video and asked him to chair a Rotary committee to sponsor Academic Decathlon in San Francisco. Since San Francisco high schools were not participating in Academic Decathlon at the time, Sturgeon and Koefoed met with School Supervisor Ramon Cortines and outlined the program to him. Cortines was aware of the program, and agreed to work with SF Rotary.

Bill Koefoed put together a team of his motivational-speaker contacts, and SF Rotary hosted an introductory cocktail party for the city's high-school teachers, with Koefoed educating them about the program. To be successful, the program needed an intensive commitment from teachers willing to act as coaches. Wanting to demonstrate the importance of academic coaching, SF Rotary paid the teacher-coaches at the same rate as the school district paid athletic coaches.

William B. Sturgeon, SF Rotary President 1987–88; District Governor, 1989–90

San Francisco's first Academic Decathlon was funded $25,000 by SF Rotary, with additional funding from several corporate sponsors. Teams from the participating San Francisco high schools trained for the event many months in advance. In a typical school, contestants met two days a week during class time to prepare. They also held study sessions on Saturday nights, becoming friends in the process. With the teacher-coaches emphasizing the academic side, SF Rotary provided coaching in public speaking and interviewing.

> "The enthusiasm for this event is what makes it so special. When I arrived at 7:30 in the morning, there must have been fifty kids at the school already, studying and preparing notes with their teammates. It was great!"
>
> —Bill Koefoed, Academic Decathlon Chair

The Academic Decathlon took place on a Saturday in February 1988, as students from all over the city converged on the Philip and Sala Burton School. There were ninety-nine students—six team members and three alternates from each of eleven public high schools. Moving from classroom to classroom, the contestants were interviewed, gave their current-topic speeches to Rotarian judges, and completed their essays and examinations.

In all, SF Rotary provided over one hundred volunteers to plan and publicize the event, judge speeches, provide test proctors during the exams, correct tests, and decide upon the awards for the winning teams. The club provided box lunches for the contestants.

At the end of the day, the students met in the gymnasium for the final and most exciting Decathlon event—the Super Quiz. While their fellow students cheered them on, the contestants answered questions on the year's preannounced topic, "The History of

High-school students apply themselves to the Academic Decathlon, 2000.

Flight: From Daedalus to Kitty Hawk to Voyager." SF Rotary's speaking-skills training was put to good use, as the students grappled with the questions posed by local television news personality Fred LaCosse.

Winners of the competition were not announced until the awards banquet, a lavish affair in the Gold Room at the Palace Hotel with Bill Koefoed as emcee. The audience included parents, school officials, teacher-coaches, and sponsors. Music was provided by the Touch of Class band from Burton High, and trumpeters from McAteer High. As each proud student stepped forward, Fred LaCosse presented the awards. Top achievers at each grade level in each event were announced and presented with custom-designed gold, silver, and bronze medals, while their fellow students cheered. Lowell High School carried the night as the winning school, with the highest overall performance. Lowell competed for San Francisco County at the statewide event later that year.

A resounding success in its first year, President-Elect Kline Wilson committed SF Rotary to sponsor the event again in 1989. The club recruited team sponsors from individuals and companies, at $250 per sponsorship. The Academic Decathlon continued as an annual event in San Francisco for seventeen years. SF Rotary remained its primary source of funding and provided organization and volunteers, as it had its first year. Unfortunately, the program ended in 2005, when the San Francisco school district discontinued the program, primarily because the district chose to focus on less-gifted children. SF Rotary continued for one more year by sponsoring Lowell High School at the state competition.

Of the many youth programs sponsored by SF Rotary in the past century, the Academic Decathlon has been one of the club's most rewarding and successful programs for young people, and a great source of pride for the club. The Rotarian volunteers found it exciting and worthwhile. They benefited as well, because the program's large need for volunteers offered opportunities for Rotary fellowship, in the spirit of helping others.

Like SF Rotary's other hands-on youth programs involving Rotarian volunteers, the Academic Decathlon provided strong, positive role models for students. By stimulating a desire for knowledge, pride in learning, and skill in public speaking, the program served as an effective vehicle for training the leaders of tomorrow.

Career Day

SF Rotarians have continued a strong tradition of vocational service with such programs as Career Day, held for several years in the 1990s. As is the case with so many of SF Rotary's projects, Career Day has roots in the past. "Careers Day" was part of the national Boys and Girls Week in the 1920s, and SF Rotary has steadily sponsored programs for student career counseling since then.

In 1992, club President Pete Lagarias thought that Rotarians could offer helpful counseling to more young people than those served by Camp Enterprise and the Academic Decathlon alone. A Career Day would give any high-school student the chance to participate in an exploration of career choices. It would also help compensate for diminishing numbers of school counselors due to school budget problems.

With Anita Stangl as chair, the four San Francisco Rotary clubs held the first Career Day. More than one hundred Rotarians hosted nearly three hundred students. Described as an "occupational smorgasbord," the day included breakout sessions based on twenty-one career areas, including police officer, lawyer, engineer, and teacher. Many of the career mentors were Rotarians. The students had the opportunity to ask questions such as, "How long does it take to become a lawyer?" or "What qualities make a good social worker?"

For several years, the annual Career Days enabled high-school students to see that their career possibilities were endless, leaving the event inspired to stay in school, motivated to study, and thinking about goals they wanted to achieve in life.

Throughout its history of work with youth-oriented community service, SF Rotary has conducted much of its work in conjunction with San Francisco's schools. At its inception in 1917, the Boys' Work Committee assumed this role. From the 1920s to the 1980s, however, this committee focused primarily on the club's association with the Boys' Club. At the same time, SF Rotary was beginning to develop its many student-oriented programs, all of which required close contact and cooperation with school officials. To this end, President Pete Lagarias initiated a School Liaison Committee in 1992. First chaired by Jim Bradley, the committee's intention was to improve the club's communication with schools. Its members worked directly with the school district, and with the administration and guidance counselors of each school. By getting school officials to recognize the results of Camp Enterprise, the Academic Decathlon, Career Day, and smaller projects, Pete and Jim hoped the committee would help project the club's image as an organization dedicated to community service, rather than simply a business club.

*James W. Bradley,
SF Rotary President
1998–99*

As club president several years later (1998–99), Jim introduced his major program for the year—a "Character/Counselor Project." Its objective was to enhance school counselors' skills in proactively imparting the ethical concepts sorely lacking among young people. Jim reasoned that many parents looked to schools to help emphasize trust, fairness, goodwill, friendships, and concern for the benefits of others—the very concepts that Rotarians hold dear through the Four-Way Test. Working with the San Francisco school district, the club sponsored two-day training sessions for school counselors focused on guiding young people toward making ethical decisions and habits to benefit their character development. The club provided books and manuals, and paid for the instructor, meeting rooms, and lunches. In addition, volunteer Rotarians participated in the training, interacting with the counselors and monitoring the

"I remember one of the counselors said, 'I've got a kid that's in trouble after school every day. He's got no parents at home. He just basically wanders around and gets into little bits of trouble and he's not a bad kid.' And the Boys & Girls Club said, 'We've got a club right there.' So the counselor made it mandatory that this kid was to stay out of trouble and join the club. The kid found an after-school place to be, where there were computers and there were kids. And he went from having nowhere to go, to having somewhere to go.... To think the counselor had been doing this job for years, and didn't know there was this community resource out there that's looking for kids—and to fit those two together!"

—Past President Jim Bradley

training. Club members Christina Harbridge-Law and Nick Carlson chaired the project, which was developed on the model of consultant Stephen Covey's "Seven Habits of Highly Effective People" program. In addition to training counselors and teachers, the project brought in speakers from several youth service groups—including the YMCA, Boy Scouts, and the Boys & Girls Club.

SF Rotary has continued its work for disadvantaged students in San Francisco Schools. It has given particular attention to the special needs for financial and hands-on assistance in inner-city schools. During John Uth's presidential year (1997–98), the club sponsored a program called Adopt-a-School, chaired by Leni Miller.

The program formed alliances with the Detwiler Foundation (a supplier of donated computer equipment to schools) and Junior Achievement of the Bay Area. SF Rotary "adopted" two inner-city public schools—Bessie Carmichael and the Filipino Education Center. The Detwiler Foundation enlisted California business leaders to donate computer equipment. AT&T provided networking and Internet connec-

tions. Rotary volunteers, or "Rotabuddys," supported the students by teaching classes, becoming mentors, and supplying equipment. The club also provided Junior Achievement with funding to cover the expense of putting Rotarian and other volunteers from the business community into classrooms to teach economic education programs. SF Rotary continued to support this Junior Achievement program with funding and volunteers for several more years.

Every year, SF Rotary contributes to the success of students—in large and small ways. One year, a new Head Start Program was sponsored in the Tenderloin area under the leadership of Bob O'Conner and Carol Boman. In

Leni Miller

another year, students at middle schools were provided with student planners, to help introduce them to time management, goal setting, study skills, and the precepts of the Four-Way Test, which was prominently displayed on the back cover. Aware of widespread discontinuance of school arts programs—a vital aspect of education—the club has provided assistance for such programs in schools. During Bill Ecker's presidential year (1999–2000), SF Rotary sponsored several programs that made music available to children of limited-income families, including the San Francisco Children's Chorus production of *Kids on Broadway*. Today, the club participates in a district-wide distribution of dictionaries to third-grade students.

One of SF Rotary's most enduring sources of assistance to students has been in its scholarships, given by the SFR Foundation in the names of Bru Brunnier, Brad Swope, and Marsh Blum. The Bru Brunnier Educational Scholarship has been given in Bru's name each year since 1976, to honor Bru's generous bequest to the SFR Foundation and his appreciation of higher education. Upon the death of its respected former secretary in 1980, the club founded the Bradford Swope Rotary Memorial Scholarship Fund. SF Rotary members quickly raised over $11,000 to seed the fund. The following year, the club's board sent $35,000 to the SFR Foundation to establish

Past President Tom Paton leading the "Band from Ben," a SF-Rotary-sponsored band from the Benjamin Franklin Middle School, 1999.

a permanent fund in Brad Swope's name. The SFR Foundation added $15,000 to bring the fund to $50,000. The fund's first scholarships were presented in 1982. A third scholarship—the Marshall Rotary Blum Scholarship Fund—was established with $10,000 seed money, plus over $3,000 raised at a luncheon meeting in the weeks following Marsh's death in 2000. During their lifetimes, the three funds have provided scholarships to several San Francisco colleges and universities. Today, three scholarships—valued at $5,000 from each fund—are given each year to students attending the University of San Francisco (USF).

Interact

Since SF Rotary's early days of community service, club members have introduced young people to the joy of helping others. Early SF Rotarians helped boys provide entertainment, including a puppet show, at the annual Crippled Children's Thanksgiving Dinner. Later in the 1950s, club members worked to bring an understanding of the Four-Way Test and Rotary service ethic to high-school students, hoping to stimulate young people's interest and a desire to develop their abilities and character. The program worked so well that the students gave their vacation time freely to hospitals and social agencies. Under Rotary guidance, young people have more recently cleaned and painted the Audrey L. Smith Development Center, a preschool in the Tenderloin area, been involved in litter cleanups at Baker Beach and Union Square, participated in an antigraffiti project, and helped with repairs for sixty senior-citizens' homes.

SF Rotary has not been alone in encouraging young people to serve their community. For the ninety years since boys' work was taken up by U.S. Rotary clubs in the late 1910s, Rotarians have held the belief that students should be introduced to the satisfaction that service offers. In 1962, a Florida Rotary club formed a Rotary-affiliated service club for young people. The idea was taken up by an international committee of Rotarians, and today, more than eleven thousand Interact (for International Action) service clubs for students are sponsored by Rotary clubs worldwide. While providing over 250,000 young people aged fourteen to eighteen with ways to serve their communities, Interact clubs also give them the opportunity to make new friends. At the same time, members gain insight into the Rotary ideals of service, personal integrity, teamwork, and self-development. Each Interact club around the world is sponsored by a local Rotary club that provides guidance and inspiration, but the clubs are self-governing and self-supporting.

Since 1990, SF Rotarians have worked to form and sponsor Interact clubs in San Francisco. The first in the city, at St. Ignatius High School, remained intact for several years. In succeeding years, several clubs have gone through the formative stage, but have not managed to remain self-sustaining because students leave upon graduation from high school.

*Joseph S. Talmadge,
SF Rotary President
2005–06*

In 1994, a club was started at Archbishop Riordan High School (a Catholic boys' high school) through the efforts of SF Rotarian Doug Hiemstra. Under SF Rotary sponsorship, the group became a flourishing club, successful enough to earn its charter from RI in 1997. Past President Steve Talmadge is presently the SF Rotary liaison to the club, which is open to all Riordan High students who maintain a satisfactory or better grade level. It has nearly thirty members. Club member Carol Christie has recently founded another Interact club at the S. R. Martin College Preparatory School (for grades five through twelve). Drawing from the private school's very small population of about fifty students, the club presently has eight to ten members. It received its RI charter in 2005–06.

Carol Christie

The young members of SF Rotary's two Interact clubs are remarkably self-sufficient. With some guidance from their Rotarian advisers plus a school liaison, the students choose their own projects. They raise money for operating the projects, so they can receive matching funds from Rotary—up to $3,000 for each club.

Interact clubs are expected to carry out at least two service projects a year—one to serve the school or community, and the other to further international understanding. San Francisco Interactors have assisted the Larkin Street Youth Center by collecting and delivering winter coats and clothing for runaway children. They have supplied toys and games for the waiting room at St. Luke's Hospital Children's Clinic, and held toy drives for the San Francisco Fire Department's Toys-for-Tots Program. As their Rotarian counterparts have known for a long time, the most rewarding service efforts are those that provide hands-on activities. For several years, Interactors collected toys for children at the Wu Yee Children's Center in the Tenderloin area. They put on a Christmas party, dressed as Santa Clauses, and gave each child a big bag of toys. The children enjoyed cake, ice cream, and a magic show.

Interactors also serve frequently with SF Rotarians on Rotary projects. They help recruit students for Camp Enterprise, and work with SF Rotarians during the camp. For Career Day, they registered students and hosted a continental breakfast for guest speakers. They have also assisted with Rotary projects as varied as the organ/tissue donor registration program, the book drive, and the auction/dinner-dance; and they have participated in the AIDS Walk.

The other annual service project is of an international character. For their international-service project one year, Interactors raised funds (matched by SF Rotary) to send school notebooks, pencils, pens, and other much-needed school supplies to Afghan students, particularly to girls.

SF Rotary provides the Interact clubs with guidance and matching funds for their projects. It also hands out $6,000 in scholarships each year, divided among several students in each of the two Interact clubs. This is Rotary money well spent, as an investment in young people's sense of service and Rotary ideals.

Rotaract

While the Interact club offers a first-rate opportunity for service and friendship in the teen years, young adults are usually not yet professionally qualified for membership in a Rotary club. To bring continuity to this line of service opportunity, RI began an organization called Rotaract, open to young men and women aged eighteen to thirty.

Rotaract has a historical predecessor in the "20–30" clubs—Rotary-sponsored service clubs for junior professionals and university students aged twenty to thirty.[44] Begun in Sacramento in 1922, approximately 125 20–30 clubs were located in California and elsewhere at one point. SF Rotary sponsored the fourth club in the United States. Before he joined SF Rotary in 1949, Past President Bob Lee belonged to a 20–30 club.

Present-day Rotaract began as a club in North Carolina in 1968, and today has 163,000 members in more than 7,000 clubs around the world. Through the Rotaract program, young adults develop their teamwork and leadership skills, and enjoy the company of others who find satisfaction in serving the needs of their communities. Rotaractors are also committed to promoting world understanding and peace through Rotary ideals of international friendship. Rotaract clubs are usually community based or university based. They are sponsored by a local Rotary club, and have access to the many resources of RI.

Howard R. Waits,
SF Rotary President
2002–03

Upon hearing of the new Rotaract idea in 1968, SF Rotary's board considered sponsoring a Rotaract Club for San Francisco, and in succeeding years, several clubs were formed—at the University of San Francisco (USF),[45] Golden Gate University (GGU), and the Weller School of Management. For a time, each club conducted community-service activities, but—as was the case with the several Interact clubs—they did not survive because, when their members concluded their education, they often moved out of the area. In 1995, SF Rotary's board decided to establish another club, hoping that a community-based club would fare better. Such a citywide club was chartered in 1998, but did not last. Another was formed in 2004. Natasha Valentova, its first president, had been a member of the earlier club while she was an Ambassadorial Scholar. SF Rotarians Howard Waits

---

44. During World War II, a shortage of eligible members forced a raising of the age to thirty-five for the duration of the war.

45. The new USF club formed in 1978 named its newsletter *Shavings* (after SF Rotary's *Grindings*), as a tribute to the SFR Foundation for its sponsorship.

Rotaract Club of San Francisco members with SF Rotarian Howard Waits, 2007. Courtesy of Liz Reader

and Tom Purcell attended meetings of the new club and helped it gain its footing. Howard hosted biweekly meetings at his company's office space in the Financial District. The Rotaract Club of San Francisco received its RI charter later that year.

The new Rotaract club took up community service immediately, working with the East Rotary Club of Oakland to rebuild a widowed woman's home in Oakland. For its first international-service project, it produced and sold business cards to raise money for scholarships and school supplies for disadvantaged children in Goma, Congo. Rotaract members also helped SF Rotary with its book drive and other programs.

The Rotaract club has gained new members and progressed well. Rotaractors now work on several projects at a time. Their latest community-service projects included partnering with two other nonprofit organizations to introduce the fun of filmmaking to medically challenged children. For their most recent international-service project, club members held two fund-raising events. The money raised—more than double the anticipated amount—was given to help fund a SF Rotary-sponsored microcredit project in Nigeria.

Rotaract members participate regularly in SF Rotary's projects and functions, such as the AIDS Walk and the annual spring fund-raising auction. They are very involved with Camp Enterprise, working alongside Rotarians as camp counselors. Although sponsored and advised by SF Rotary, they extend their service efforts to projects by other Rotary clubs as well. Recently, the Rotaract Club helped renovate a small preparatory school in Oakland. Rotaractors also attend the RI convention, district conference, and district RI Foundation fund-raiser each year, as well as other Rotary events. Representatives from North American Rotaract clubs attend the United States, Canada, and Caribbean Conference (USCC), an annual regional event of more than four hundred Rotaract clubs that work together to develop within the framework of "Service Above Self." Rotarians and an RI representative advise the conference and help the hosting Rotaract clubs conduct plenary sessions, workshops, social events, and a community-service event.

Most Rotaract members join to meet people and have fun in addition to service. Many have made close friendships, and the club enjoys regular events for socializing. The club is particularly ethnically diverse, and makes

"Rotaractors know how to have fun, make friends, and make the world a little better in the process."

—A Rotaract motto

a point of having dinners at restaurants that are representative of the cultural backgrounds of its members. In addition to service and sociability, Rotaractors are concerned with self-development. Guest speakers at club meetings talk on such topics as career development and communication. Rotarians speak at the club's meetings on the history of Rotary and other Rotary-related topics.

Together, Interact and Rotaract complete Rotary's chain of providing opportunity to serve others. SF Rotaractors recently mentored young people in a "College & Beyond" panel and workshop with the Interact Club at S. R. Martin school. Rotaractors strive to strengthen the relationship between the two groups and to provide insight to Interact members as to what Rotaract does. Through this effort, they hope to encourage the Interact members to join Rotaract when they reach the appropriate age. Rotary in turn looks upon Rotaractors as the Rotarians of the future.

> "Our Rotaract club's success is tied to the tremendous support we receive from the Rotary Club of San Francisco. And personally, I'm a better person and professional because of the support and opportunities Rotary has given me through Rotaract."
>
> —Amanda Nguyen, District 5150 Rotaract Representative and charter member of the Rotaract Club of San Francisco

■ ■ ■

Since the 1980s, SF Rotary has had much to be proud of with its major new youth programs. Alongside these programs, SF Rotary has maintained a consistent level of continuing ties to various other youth organizations, including Junior Achievement, Boy Scouts, Girl Scouts, and the Easter Seal Society. The club occasionally funds small projects for the Larkin Street Youth Center for homeless and runaway kids. Other children were helped when the club provided funding to leaders of the Boy Scouts' "Operation Bootstrap," a program for inner-city boys. Toys for Tots has benefited from Rotarians' generosity, as have the Big Brothers.

SF Rotary has a strong and continuing interest in YMCA programs and facilities. Rotarians have been involved in mentoring programs, and have provided computer assistance at all local YMCA branches. After a SFR Foundation-sponsored remodeling in 1989, the Mission YMCA named its new multipurpose room the "Chester R. MacPhee Sr. Social Center," as a tribute to the SF Rotary past president (1974–75). In 1998, Chet was honored again by the YMCA. To celebrate the relationship between Rotary's Camp Enterprise and the Point Bonita YMCA, the "Chester R. MacPhee Dining Hall" at Point Bonita (where Camp Enterprise is held annually) was formally dedicated. The hall and its surroundings were refurbished as a joint venture by the YMCA and SF Rotary in memory of Chet MacPhee, for "his many contributions of time, expertise, and money to the YMCA."

*Allen S. Feder,
SF Rotary President
1985–86*

For much of his time in SF Rotary, Past President Allen Feder has had a strong presence in the club's work with young people. During Allen's presidential year (1985–86), SF Rotary contributed to the Oakes Children's Center. The center provides a temporary residence for homeless children, or a "home away from home" for children coming with psychological problems brought on by their dysfunctional families. SF Rotary contributed to the center to build additional bedrooms, which enabled children to stay for a longer period of time.

The Immunization Project

In addition to its long-term programs for young people, SF Rotary has initiated large shorter-term projects that have yielded impressive results. One such project was the effort to provide much-needed immunizations to San Francisco's children, launched during Bill Koefoed's club presidency in 1994–95.

SF Rotary had considered pursuing an immunization program for children for several years. Then in the mid-1990s, media attention stepped up public interest in the need for improved childhood immunization in the United States. A three-year national epidemic of measles had resulted from widespread failure to vaccinate preschool children on time. To prevent a recurrence of such an epidemic, and to eliminate other childhood diseases, U.S. President Bill Clinton offered support for a comprehensive initiative. Its goal was to achieve immunization coverage for 90 percent of the nation's two-year-old children by 1996. The Centers for Disease Control (CDC) looked to organizations such as Rotary to play a major role in the development of coalitions to get the job done.

In the meantime, Bill Koefoed was looking for a community-service project for his upcoming presidential year. In a chance conversation, SF Rotarian Zina Mirsky—a retired Navy captain and nurse—described the difficulties involved in getting vaccinations to all San Francisco children, particularly in poorer areas of the city. Also by chance, then-President Bob Wilhelm learned of an RI program that would pay the cost of vaccine for Rotary-sponsored immunization programs in the United States.

William A. Koefoed, SF Rotary President 1994–95

At the start of his presidential year, Bill Koefoed announced his goal of immunizing 90 percent of all San Francisco's children under age two against polio, measles, whooping cough, and diphtheria. Appointed to chair the effort, Zina referred to it as "PolioPlus in our own back yard."[46] She visited the other San Francisco Rotary clubs and convinced them to join in the immunization effort in the city. In addition, a coalition was formed to enable the project to go forward; it included Rotary, the mayor's office, the health department, and other organizations.

For the program to be successful, it would need to reach out to the many parents who had not previously known of the need for immunization, or who had not been convinced to bring their children in for the series of vaccination shots. SF Rotary worked to attract a media blitz, using all available publicity avenues, including Rotaract, Interact, schools, and churches to educate the public. The club worked with the San Francisco Health Department to establish a tracking system developed by the CDC and California State Health Department. Rotarians were asked to perform phone duty by calling on new mothers to provide information and encourage them to bring their babies and older children for timely immunizations.

---

46. PolioPlus is RI's long-term program to end polio in the world. (See chapter 6.)

Other club functions included scheduling physicians, nurse-practitioners, and other health-care providers to conduct education sessions periodically in the Tenderloin, Mission, Haight-Ashbury, and Hunters Point neighborhoods. SF Rotary provided funds for multilanguage materials to encourage immunization, as well as extra medical supplies. To attract sponsors for these expenses, Zina offered club members their business logo on immunization notices, calendars, posters, growth charts, magnet reminders, and other related products.

To maximize the citywide coverage, the immunizations were given in several highly publicized events throughout the city. The kickoff event took place at several city locations in August 1994. The obvious purpose of these events was to immunize children. But a second and equally important goal was to attract San Francisco's parents so they could be connected with health-care providers and made aware of the free or low-cost immunizations available for their children. The hope was that parents would continue to bring their children to clinics for other required shots in the future. For that reason, the events were given a happy, carnival-like atmosphere, with games, face painting, toys, and SF Giants souvenirs provided by the baseball team.

At the events, babies were started on their immunizations or given follow-up immunizations, while their older siblings received back-to-school shots. Rotary volunteers set up the event and supported the health-care professional volunteers with duties that included registering families and verifying their immunization and approval forms, keeping the families happy while waiting, and presenting proud mothers with Polaroid photographs of the happy kids. Rotarians with skills in other locally spoken languages assisted as translators.

The program was successful; with thousands of immunization shots administered, it met its goal of reaching 90 percent of San Francisco's children under age two. Parents came in from throughout the city, and their awareness of the importance and availability of additional immunizations was increased significantly. Andy Kirmse, the succeeding SF Rotary president, continued the program with Zina chairing it. SF Rotary held annual immunization days through 1997–98. Zina presented the project to the District 5150 governor for consideration as an Outstanding Community Service Project, with photographs, letters, video tapes, and posters. Her innovative work led to SF Rotary winning the prestigious RI Significant Achievement Award in 1995.

The Boeddeker Park Revitalization Project

Large projects such as the Immunization Project demonstrate SF Rotarians' impressive talents for making things happen. Another large community-service project took place three years later, under the club presidency of John Uth (1997–98). The Boeddeker Park Revitalization Project is an apt example of Rotarians building a broad coalition of outside interests and putting together an impressive amount of donated money, materials, and services.

Boeddeker Park occupies a two-and-a-half-acre site on Eddy Street in the gritty Tenderloin neighborhood. Funded with city money, the park was initially dedicated in 1985 by Mayor Dianne Feinstein, and named Father Alfred Boeddeker Park for the priest who founded the nearby St. Anthony Dining Room. The park was intended to provide the Tenderloin area's seniors and

Southeast-Asian families with green space and recreation, safe from the area's drug dealers and vagrants. The park's design did not prove to be safe enough for children, however, and the park was plagued by drug traffickers, substance abusers, blight, and disorder.

As one of a succession of efforts to "Save Boeddeker Park" in the 1990s, the SF Rotary-sponsored Boeddeker Park Revitalization Project made major improvements during John Uth's presidential year in 1997–98. Chaired by Doug Hiemstra and Allan Herzog, the project created a secure fenced-off playground with a new entrance through a Recreation-and-Park building. It made the park disabled-compliant, added new shrubbery, and replaced the park's existing sand (a magnet for glass and spent drug needles) with safe rubber matting.

John Uth chose his project for its visibility as a community-service effort. Asked for his ideas, Rotarian Police Chief Fred Lau urged Rotary to lead a coalition consisting of the SF police department, the Recreation and Park Department, and the San Francisco Boys & Girls Club to facilitate the cleanup and restoration of Boeddeker Park. Knowing this project would rely on diverse groups for support, John shared his vision with more than twenty Tenderloin community leaders and asked for their input in a series of meetings. These leaders agreed the park renovation was a good idea—to provide a safe place for the kids. Out of this planning emerged a partnership with the police department, which agreed to put a station on one corner, "so they could keep an eye on it." The Recreation and Park Department would staff the park properly. Rotary would provide the funds to make it happen. The mayor's office agreed to support the project. The resulting coalition also included fourteen community organizations representing populations as diverse as those served by the YMCA; Glide Memorial Church; service groups for seniors, women, children and others; and various neighborhood planning and development groups. Local community leader Reverend Cecil Williams of Glide Memorial Church expressed strong reservations about outsider intrusion into an area where homeless members of his congregation gathered. But in the end, he endorsed it and gave SF Rotary the go-ahead.

"I really believe Rotary needs to have their name in the paper. You know, you need to do something to bring awareness that there is a Rotary Club and that we are a service club. So I met with Police Chief Lau and I said, 'What can we do in this town that will get your support?' And he came up with Boeddeker Park."

—Past President John Uth

John began SF Rotary's fund-raising efforts, turning first to the club. Fifty thousand dollars was allocated to the project from the 1997 auction/dinner-dance proceeds, and the SFR Foundation matched that amount. Of the $500,000 final cost of the project, this $100,000 was Rotary's cash contribution. Then John approached the business community: "We wrote probably a hundred letters, from PG&E to the banks to hotels, which brought awareness. You know, all of a sudden somebody hears about Rotary." Businesses, foundations, and individuals responded with pledges for another $105,000. The remaining $300,000 would come as donated services, mostly from Rotarians' businesses.

Besides providing services, volunteers pitched in at fund-raising events and worked at the site itself. The YMCA and Boys & Girls Club wanted kids involved. Neighborhood children

John Uth,
SF Rotary President
1997–98

were recruited to do some tile work and to create a puddle pond. Rotary volunteers held a pre-construction cleanup in anticipation of the groundbreaking ceremony, which was attended by over forty Rotarians and a good cross-section of the press. After planning for almost a year and construction, the project was completed and the park officially opened in June 1998.

In addition to the media presence at the opening, the project received the publicity John had hoped for. Four months after the park's opening, the local cable company broadcast "Taking Back Boeddeker Park." Early the following year, the Tenderloin Task Force of the San Francisco Police praised the park's benefits for the area's five thousand children, and Chief Lau presented an award of appreciation to the entire club.

While the park reemerged as a community center, Rotary continued its investment in the park with monetary and volunteer support through events like the Fund-Raiser Golf Outing. The city voiced its need almost immediately, for continued help with replacement or repairs of overused equipment and worn materials such as the rubber matting. With Joe Lamberson chairing a Boeddeker Park Programs Committee through 2001–02, the club went on to sponsor festivals for children of the Tenderloin, bussed them to the Boys & Girls Club for swimming, and held a Tenderloin Mini-Olympics at the park. Some of SF Rotary's Camp Mendocino camperships were given to kids from Boeddeker Park. Rotary worked with the city to provide a computer program at the park center.

Along with the Boys & Girls Club, Rotary created "Boeddeker Buddies"— a peer-to-peer mentoring program for the Tenderloin's young people. Teenage "Buddies" from the Boys & Girls Club provided homework and academic assistance, practice with computers, and the friendship of good role models. SF Rotarians participated in the Buddies program by hosting field trips to Rotarians' businesses. Boeddeker Buddies continued for several years, providing enrichment for the Boys & Girls Club teen mentors, and the young Boeddeker children as well.

Boys & Girls Club members mentor Tenderloin youngsters as "Boeddeker Buddies".

■ ■ ■

Timeline: SF Rotary Works with Young People

1916—SF Rotary initiates Charity Box to support Children's Hospital

1917—SF Rotary commits to Boys' Work

1923—San Francisco Boys' Club is chartered; SF Rotary assumes sponsorship

1924—Sunshine School for crippled children is opened

1926—California Society for Crippled Children formed—part of future Easter Seals

1930—Camp Marwedel opens on leased land

1938—Spastic Clinic opens

1942—Camp Marwedel permanently expands with purchase of two thousand acres

1976—First Bru Brunnier Educational Scholarship is established

1980—Bradford Swope Rotary Memorial Scholarship Fund is established

1985—Rotary Bridge of Friendship is built at Camp Mendocino

1985—Camp Enterprise is founded

1988—Academic Decathlon is founded

1992—Career Day is founded

1994—Archbishop Riordon High School Interact Club is begun

1994—Children's Immunization Project is begun

1996—Computer/Internet Learning Centers for Boys & Girls Club are established

1998—Boeddeker Park revitalization is initiated

2000—Marshall Rotary Blum Scholarship Fund is established

2004—Rotaract Club of San Francisco is founded

2008—Rebuilt Boys and Girls Club Mission Branch clubhouse is dedicated November 10, 2008

SF Rotary's many programs and projects to aid San Francisco's young people should not obscure the fact that the club has a long record of service to the needy of all ages. In 1918, members donated a Victrola to the Relief Home for the Aged and Infirm, and solicited members for donations of used records. Since then, the club has continued to help bring hope and cheer to the city's senior citizens. In later years, for example, the club's sponsorship of two major theatrical performances brought holiday entertainment to 450 patients at the Laguna Honda Hospital, and SF Rotarians worked with the Little Brothers–Friends of the Elderly to make life brighter for senior citizens living in the Tenderloin area. The club organized a special program on Thanksgiving morning, put on a cheery Christmas party, and gave a computer to help the Little Brothers keep track of the elders and volunteer helpers. Club members have also worked on impoverished seniors' homes—doing basic carpentry and electrical work, cleaning up their yards, and other tasks.

Neediness touches people in dozens of ways, and the club has been responsive to many of them. SF Rotarians have helped the Recreation Center for the Handicapped extensively, with contributions of items such as a van, a barbeque, dishwashers, and picnic tables. The club has

Burt Berry

contributed generously to the Rose Resnick Center for the Blind and Visually Impaired, and sponsored training of a puppy in the Canine Companions for Independence program. A Book Drive program started by Burt Berry in 1994 collects books for delivery to local San Francisco hospitals, clinics, and rest homes. Each book is stamped "A Gift from the San Francisco Rotary Club," and nearly nine thousand books have been collected and delivered to date.

Among the needy in America's large cities, the last three decades have seen a dramatic increase in one group in particular—the homeless. One of the most difficult and intractable urban troubles in the last quarter of the twentieth century, homelessness afflicts young and old alike, including families and children. As homelessness worsened, SF Rotary and the SFR Foundation began to consider the problem in the late 1980s. The club was already contributing Rotary Service money to St. Anthony's Dining Room, and club members enthusiastically rang Salvation Army bells during the holidays (which they still do today).

SF Rotary's specific programs to aid the homeless began in the early 1990s. Members Anita Stangl, Cleo Donovan, and Larry Townsend created a Birthday Division project called Helping Hand for the Homeless. The club facilitated the construction of a child day-care center in the Tenderloin area, and donated one hundred pounds of toiletries to St. Anthony's.

At the district governor's request, clubs became more involved in addressing the homeless situation, and Anita and Cleo began a project in 1995 to work with the Salvation Army. Its Gateway House (now called Harbor House) takes in single-parent homeless families with a parental drug or alcohol addiction. Many have had their children removed from them by Child Protective Services. The family remains for a two-year period in safe transitional housing.

Kathy Beavers rings the bell for the Salvation Army, 1999.

While there, the parent breaks the desperate cycle of addiction and homelessness and learns good-parenting skills, while preparing to become a self-sufficient member of the community.

SF Rotarians connected directly with the families at Gateway House to provide these often-forgotten people with a link to mainstream life. They showed the families what education and careers were available, and taught them job-search skills. Cleo obtained several rooms of furniture that would help outgoing families set up and furnish their new homes, and the club donated furniture, bedding, clothing, and household supplies.

Cleo Donovan

SF Rotarians prepare Thanksgiving turkeys and baskets for Salvation Army Harbor House residents, 2006.

SF Rotary Executive Secretary Tessie Reyes and club member Greg Gutting of the Salvation Army entertain children from Harbor House at a picnic at Golden Gate Park, 2007.

For the children, club members planned trips to the zoo and the aquarium, barbeques, and an Easter festivity. They provided arts and crafts supplies, and assisted parents with gift giving on Christmas and Easter. SF Rotary occasionally provided funds matched with donated services by the club's participating dentists and doctors, who provided dental and medical help for the resident children of the House. The program continued for a number of years, and was the club's largest community-service contribution during Bill Ecker's presidential year (1999–2000).

In 2006, President-Elect Anita Stangl reinitiated the club's assistance to the homeless at Harbor House. SF Rotary adopts a family at "graduation time," making sure the family has what it needs to be successful as it leaves its transitional home. The club provides a mattress and bedding, linens, pots and pans, and other household needs. During the holidays, SF Rotarians help all the residents of Harbor House, with turkeys and food baskets for Thanksgiving, and shopping gift cards and poinsettias in December. The club recently hosted the Harbor House families at a spring picnic with food and games in Golden Gate Park.

Habitat for Humanity

For some San Franciscans, the only impediment to escaping a substandard living is the lack of decent affordable housing. By partnering with Habitat for Humanity, SF Rotary engaged the problem of affordable housing by making homes available for two fortunate families able to provide their own labor.

Habitat for Humanity International seeks to eliminate poverty housing and homelessness. Through Habitat's program of home ownership, thousands of low-income families have found new hope in the form of affordable housing. Habitat for Humanity homes are built almost entirely by volunteers and are funded completely by donations of money and materials. Selected families partner with Habitat by contributing hundreds of hours of work for the construction of their own houses and the houses of others. Family selection is based on level of need, willingness to become partners in the process of building, and ability to repay an interest-free mortgage. Once completed, the homes are sold to the families for no profit.

*Kathleen L. Beavers,
SF Rotary President
2000–01*

SF Rotary President Kathy Beavers chose Habitat for Humanity as her presidential-year major project in 2000. Habitat had already purchased building sites, and had located eligible families for two houses on Oakdale Avenue in the Bayview District of San Francisco. The future owner of one of the houses attended a Rotary board meeting, and explained how he would feel to move out of the housing projects and into a home of his own. The SFR Foundation provided $100,000 toward the cost of building the houses. SF Rotary arranged for volunteers and publicity for the project.

The club recruited volunteer construction workers in several ways. In an effort to raise club members' awareness of the program, project chair Shawn O'Hara challenged Rotarians at each luncheon table to build a house from graham crackers, frosting, and other supplies. Although no Frank Lloyd Wrights emerged from the process, a good time was had by all. The club worked to attract volunteers from outside SF Rotary as well. The club invited the San Francisco Bayview Rotary Club to participate in the building of the two houses, since they were to be built in the Bayview club's area. Kathy invited the San Francisco Chamber of Commerce to participate, offering a $100 contribution in the name of any Chamber member who came out to help on the project. SF Rotary also reached out to Interact Clubs and other youth organizations. The inclusion of young people was viewed as an important element of the project, because it put the young volunteers in a position to help others, and gave them an opportunity to experience an aspect of the construction industry.

SF Rotary organized the groundbreaking ceremony, which was well attended by city officials and the press. During the construction of the houses, volunteers came on specified workdays. After receiving an orientation and safety training, Rotarians and other volunteers of many skill levels put in a full day of building and cleanup. When the houses were completed, the club organized the final dedication ceremony. The generosity of SF Rotarians helped make home ownership a reality for two low-income San Francisco families.

In 2007, SF Rotarians revisited the excitement of helping families realize a dream, by sponsoring a "Rotary Day" in December. Rotarians and their families, Interact members, and Rotaract members came together to help finish building a new Habitat for Humanity home in San Francisco's Outer Mission District. It was a wonderful gift for a San Francisco family—just in time for Christmas!

Rotaract President Liz Reader wields a jackhammer for Habitat for Humanity, 2007. Courtesy of Jim Murray

Work for AIDS Victims

Throughout the century, SF Rotary's community-service programs for the underprivileged have focused on problems that are always with us—the poor and homeless, the disabled, and at-risk young people. More recently, a new need has arisen: the men, women, and children of San Francisco who are stricken with AIDS. First identified in 1981, AIDS is the most devastating epidemic in world history, killing over twenty-five million people worldwide. An estimated forty million people are now living with the disease. California has 140,000 cases among the 1.2 million cases in the United States. San Francisco became an early center of national focus as the disease slowly gained the attention of Americans during the 1980s.

SF Rotary's involvement in humanitarian work for people with AIDS started in 1993. Following the lead of the Rotary Club of Los Altos, SF Rotary formed an AIDS Task Force Committee during Bob Wilhelm's presidency. Chaired by Arlene Kaplan, the committee worked with the San Francisco AIDS Foundation and initiated two projects in its first year. A team of SF Rotary volunteers began staffing a meal-delivery route for San Francisco's Project Open Hand—an organization that provides hot meals to AIDS patients. Rotarians delivered hundreds of meals to shut-ins in the city's Tenderloin area. The club's second project was devoted to SF Rotary's most enduring interest, children. The AIDS Task Force adopted "Bridge for Kids"—a day-care program providing up to four hours of care per week for children with AIDS. The club's involvement included cosponsoring a summer day camp for two days per week, and planned outings to Marine World Africa/USA and the Exploratorium. SF Rotary has also contributed to the University of California at San Francisco for HIV-related and AIDS-vaccine research.

SF Rotary's AIDS Walk team, 1996.
Photo by Ainis Nollendorfs

For more than a decade, club members have participated in the annual San Francisco AIDS Walk—a 10k fund-raising walk to benefit the San Francisco AIDS Foundation and other Bay Area AIDS service organizations. Rotary's participation in the walk has usually raised more money than any other non-AIDS organization, resulting in as much as $10,000 annually going to this worthy cause. Since 1998, the SFR Foundation has matched donations, such as those by top-earning SF Rotarian Robert Weinberg in 2006.

Blood Drive

In its second fifty years, SF Rotary has expanded its community-service efforts in many ways. Besides delivering continuing help to youth and the needy, SF Rotarians have contributed by giving of themselves and encouraging others to do so as well.

Dr. Howard Denbo

For forty years, SF Rotarians have given the gift of life through the SF Rotary Blood Reserve Fund. In 1967, SF Rotary members overwhelmingly approved the establishment of a club blood fund. Members of each Birthday Division were encouraged to donate in their respective month. New SF Rotarian Dr. Howard Denbo became involved with it immediately upon joining the club that year, and has continued ever since, running the club's annual blood drive and overseeing the blood reserve fund. In addition to its own annual drive, SF Rotary has, for many years, partnered with the Elks Club for other blood drives.

In 2004, the club cosponsored (with the Herbst Foundation) a mini-Bloodmobile for use by the Blood Centers of the Pacific. It was the first mini-Bloodmobile in Northern California. The traveling blood-donation center serves four donors at a time, with three donor stations and an intake station. The mini-Bloodmobile with its prominent Rotary emblem was inaugurated with its first blood drive in front of SF Rotary's headquarters at the Marines Memorial Club & Hotel.

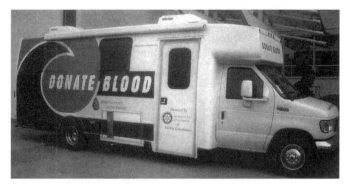

"Mini-Bloodmobile" cosponsored by SF Rotary in 2004.

Organ & Tissue Donor for Transplant Registration Program

Besides its forty-year-old Blood Donor Program, SF Rotary more recently formed an Organ & Tissue Donor for Transplant Registration Program. Its purpose is to promote awareness of the critical shortage and need of organ donations, and to encourage people to register themselves as organ/tissue donors. Only a very small percentage of Americans who die each year are properly registered as organ/tissue donors. Meanwhile, tens of thousands of people nationwide are awaiting organ and tissue donations, and many may die before help can reach them.

In 1999, SF Rotarians took the message of the urgent need for organ and tissue donor registration to heart. The club began participating in the "Share Your Life—Give of Yourself!" donor-education program. Started by several Rotary districts a year earlier, the program was created to provide Rotary clubs and districts with a "turnkey" program. It provided the resources necessary for a club to conduct its own donor-awareness program, and then to expand into the local community with Rotary in a leadership role. The purpose of a club's organ and tissue donor education program is to educate individuals in Rotary, and the public at large, of the desperate need for people to add their names to the Living Bank—a national organ donor registry. The SF Rotary board enthusiastically endorsed the program, and brought it into the club at the start of Bill Ecker's presidential year in 1999. The program was acknowledged in Green Ribbon Awareness Week—an annual event that was recognized by the mayor of San Francisco. SF Rotary has held Green Ribbon Awareness Day luncheon programs. Their purpose is to honor those involved in organ and tissue donation—donors, recipients (including people awaiting organ transplants), families, and physicians. On one such day, SF Rotarian Cleo Donovan was honored for her compassionate decision to sustain life in others after the death of her daughter, Leslie.

Besides raising awareness within the club, SF Rotary's program went outside as well. Led by Ernest and Scharleen Colant, SF Rotarians worked to bring about organ and tissue donor registration drives in several other Rotary clubs and districts, schools, and other organizations. Club members also successfully encouraged San Francisco-based companies such as Bank of America to set up in-house donor programs and registration drives. Steve Talmadge involved the local Interact clubs in San Francisco, and programs at several high schools were set up to promote the national organ-donor registry.

Most recently, SF Rotary has promoted the Donate Life California Organ & Tissue Registry, the first statewide online registry that will provide an official record of a person's wish to be a donor. The registry offers a simpler, paperless way for individuals to record their choice to become organ/tissue donors.

Disaster Relief

For one hundred years, San Francisco Rotarians have maintained close ties with their city and the needs of its people. Perhaps the single most dramatic moment of need in SF Rotary's history arose in 1989. On October 17, the Loma Prieta earthquake struck in the Santa Cruz mountains south of San Francisco, with a Richter magnitude of 7.1—the largest earthquake in the San Francisco area since the great earthquake of 1906. Many communities in the region, including neighborhoods in San Francisco, suffered heavy damage.

Loma Prieta earthquake damage in San Francisco, 1989. Photo by C. E. Meyer. Courtesy of U.S. Geological Survey

President Dick Volberg initiated SF Rotary's response immediately. Within two days, the SFR Foundation pledged $25,000 to be split between the Red Cross and Salvation Army. In the weeks that followed, the club added an additional $56,000, including $15,000 directly from club members, $10,000 from Rotary Service, and $25,000 received from Rotary clubs around the world. A number of SF Rotarians were in a position to offer special assistance. A committee that included the police and fire chiefs, as well as other members knowledgeable about earthquake relief needs, made recommendations about how best to help.

As the club representing a world-famous city, SF Rotary was a central point of attention by Rotary clubs everywhere. But San Francisco was not the only area in need. Accordingly, District

*Richard C. Volberg,
SF Rotary President
1989–90*

Governor Bill Sturgeon immediately formed a joint committee between Districts 5150 and 5170 to benefit quake-stricken communities from San Francisco to Santa Cruz. Much of the money raised by
SF Rotary was sent to the district, and the club directed donations
from elsewhere to the district fund.[47] This money was divided among
several charities in the areas most affected. A substantial amount
went for such work as refurbishing of schools in several districts,
and bringing in trailers for temporary school classrooms. By sending
its members' contributions to the larger fund, SF Rotary was able to
help many smaller organizations that did not receive large sums from
other sources.

Another major disaster struck the Bay Area almost exactly two
years later. The Oakland Hills firestorm, a massive urban fire, devas-
tated the hillsides of northern Oakland and southeastern Berkeley on Sunday, October 20, 1991. It
killed twenty-five people and destroyed more than 3,200 homes. Of twenty-five Rotarians who lost
their homes in the fire, four were from the San Francisco club. SF Rotarians responded generously at
the following Tuesday luncheon, by "ringing the bell" over and over.

As one would expect, SF Rotarians' bigheartedness has not been limited to emergency help in
the Bay Area. Club members help people in distress everywhere, nationally and globally. The club
has sent emergency money for flood damage in
places as near as Guerneville, as well as across
the country to help hurricane victims in Florida.
When an earthquake struck Los Angeles only
four years after the Northern California Loma
Prieta quake, one hundred SF Rotarians raised
$6,000 to help.

Nothing in recent history awakened
Americans' sympathy more than the plight of
the residents of the ravaged Gulf Coast after
Hurricane Katrina of 2005. In a very short time,
the club contributed $13,000 to help, includ-
ing matching fund offers by Carroll Tornroth
and Allan Herzog. The club held the money
in a bank account until a suitable relief project
could be found. In 2006, President Anita Stangl

*SF Rotary is helping with the rebuilding of the public library in
Pass Christian, Mississippi, after it suffered major damage in
Hurricane Katrina, 2005. Courtesy of Wyoming State Library*

attended a large national Rotary meeting (a "Rotary zone institute"). While there, she saw a display
by Rotarian D. H. Short from Pass Christian, Mississippi. He was looking for help rebuilding the

---

47. This joint-district fund was especially fortunate to receive an amazing gift of ninety-three million yen—$750,000—from Rotary
clubs in Japan.

public library in his town of 6,600, which was nearly leveled by Katrina. Anita brought his request back to San Francisco, and the SFR Foundation decided to help the small town by adding $15,000 to the fund. A sister-club to SF Rotary—the Rotary Club of Wanchai in Hong Kong—contributed another $10,000. With an RI's matching grant, the fund will reach close to $70,000, enabling SF Rotarians to reach out to the people of this little town across the country.

▩ ▩ ▩

On Tuesday, September 11, 2001, people across the United States awoke to horrific images and news of the terrorist attacks on New York City, Washington DC, and on board United Airlines flight 93.

The weekly luncheon meeting of SF Rotary was not held that week. When the luncheon resumed the following week, SF Rotarians responded like shocked Americans everywhere, with an overwhelming desire to "do something." They opened their pockets generously, immediately raising $10,000, an amount that was promptly matched by the SFR Foundation and sent to the Rotary Club of New York's Foundation.

Although still in shock and disbelief that such an event could happen here in the United States, SF Rotarians tried to continue the club's normal life of service and fellowship by holding their regular club events. The week after September 11, the luncheon speaker—the president of the San Francisco Convention & Visitors Bureau—predicted how the attacks would affect tourism in San Francisco. He feared that tightened airline security and travel fears would "cocoon" San Francisco. A major effect would be on San Francisco hotels. Since the city's hotel tax goes to such things as youth programs, the arts, low-income housing, and the general fund, SF Rotary would face new service challenges.

With the passage of time, it became clear that September 11, 2001, has changed the world. It delivered a stunning reminder of what Rotarians everywhere have known for decades: service at home is not sufficient to fulfill Paul Harris's dreams for Rotary. Only through sustained international efforts can peace among all nations be achieved. More than ever, individuals must continue their efforts—large and small—to promote world understanding and peace. For Rotarians, the clearest way is through Rotary's fourth Avenue—International Service.

chapter six

Service Throughout the World: The International View Expands

Governments can make war, and governments can enter into peace treaties. If,
however, the world is ever to enjoy a true and lasting state of peace, it will be
because a sense of understanding has been implanted in the minds of individuals.
We can dream all we please about a bright, new world, but unless we are willing
to work for it as individuals, we shall never realize our ambition.

—SF Rotarian and RI President Bru Brunnier, at the Paris RI Convention in 1953

W hen asked what Rotary does, most Rotarians describe some aspect of their club's service work. And as often as not, that description includes some mention of Rotary's
impressive international-service work. But this was not always the case. From Rotary's
inception through the end of World War II and the founding of the United Nations, international
service remained in the background of Rotary's work. True, the Object of Rotary had been revised
in 1921 to include the ideal of international goodwill through service, and International Service had
been added to Club Service, Vocational Service, and Community Service as the fourth Avenue of
Service in 1928. But although most Rotarians had come to view themselves as part of a worldwide
fellowship dedicated to peace and international understanding, "Rotary," for the most part, still
meant business friendship and local community service.

SF Rotary had created an International Service Committee in Charles Wheeler's presidential
year (1929–30) as a result of the club's adoption of RI's Aims and Objects Plan, which organized
service work according to the four Avenues of Service. But with few exceptions, such as providing
hospitality to foreign visitors and occasional disaster-relief contributions, club members would not
view international service as a major aspect of club activity until RI began to initiate programs in
the 1960s. Since then, SF Rotary has grown its earlier interest in the world's well-being into today's
remarkable array of programs and projects.

Hands Across Borders—Goodwill Toward All

Through Rotary, one can open any door, anywhere in the world. The spirit of Rotary is love—and it reaches out across space, race, religion, nationality, and creed to serve mankind.

—SF Rotarian George Mardikian, 1966

Rotary's concept of itself as an international-service organization was at first focused on the ideal of spreading international goodwill and promoting peace between nations. This view had its first stirrings during World War I, and developed into a common Rotarian notion through the next World War and afterward. The emergence of Rotary as a force for worldwide humanitarian work would come later.

From the early days after Rotary became an international organization, SF Rotary prided itself for its role as host to hundreds of foreign visitors each year. Hospitality took many forms. The club maintained a practice of making Rotarians from outside the United States welcome at its meetings. Members generously opened their homes to Rotarians and their families, as well as to other foreign visitors who came through a Rotary connection. A typical case of SF Rotary's hospitality is seen in the club's response to a letter from fifteen French Rotarians, who asked for help in seeing San Francisco in the early 1970s. The Housing and Hospitality Committee arranged for a bus tour with a French-speaking tour guide. The committee also invited the visitors to the weekly luncheon, where they were seated with the club's French-speaking members and members of the French Consulate. Tours to outlying areas were arranged, Rotary wives took the women shopping, and Rotarians took the entourage to cocktails and dinner at the Top-of-the-Mark. "This is how it's done," the *Grindings* editor remarked. "This is what Rotary is all about."

Carroll Tornroth

SF Rotarian Carroll Tornroth assumed the leadership of this kind of international service in the early 1980s, as club members assisted young foreign students while they were in San Francisco. During Bob Lee's presidential year (1981–82), Rotarians hosted seventy students in their homes. The International Service Committee identified the foreign-language skills of club members, along with the kinds of hospitality and assistance they were willing to provide. Wanting to extend a "welcome to San Francisco" to all young people, Carroll and the committee strongly supported the American Youth Hostel at Fort Mason.

For decades then, welcoming visitors was the club's primary form of international service. Members reached their hospitality high points as they hosted four RI Conventions in 1915, 1938, 1947, and 1977; and welcomed foreign Rotarians during the UN founding in 1945. In the long run, however, providing a warm reception to San Francisco visitors would not remain SF Rotary's primary international activity. In the postwar years, other ways of reaching the hand of friendship across borders took shape, initially through RI's Rotary Foundation.

The Rotary Foundation

The Rotary Foundation is the magnificent offspring of the Rotary family that began in 1910, when the National Association of Rotary Clubs came into being. The Foundation was started seven years later as a very small fund, with an initial contribution of $26.50. RI's sixth president, Arch Klumph, proposed "an endowment fund for Rotary . . . for the purpose of doing good in the world in charitable, educational, and other avenues of community service."[48] In 1928, the fund was named The Rotary Foundation, and was established as an entity separate from Rotary International. It is funded entirely by voluntary contributions from all over the world. The mission of The Rotary Foundation is to enable Rotarians to advance world understanding, goodwill, and peace through the improvement of health, the support of education, and the alleviation of poverty. Although The Rotary Foundation's first check was written in 1930 to benefit the International Society for Crippled Children, its initial long-term function was to serve as a scholarship fund. Today, nearly all of the Foundation's vast humanitarian work is in the developing world.

The Paul Harris Fellow recognition was established in 1957 by the Foundation, as an appeal to potential donors. Anyone who contributes—or in whose name is contributed—a cumulative gift of $1,000 or more is recognized as a Paul Harris Fellow. Since it was begun, the program has been an enormous success. Today, about 80 percent of the annual donations to The Rotary Foundation come from individuals who contribute toward being named as Paul Harris Fellows, or who are naming other people as Paul Harris Fellows.

SF Rotarians have historically been strong supporters of The Rotary Foundation, contributing toward their own Paul Harris Fellow awards and on behalf of others. Many members give additional Paul Harris Fellowships to their spouses, children, and other relatives. Carroll Tornroth, Bill Sturgeon, and Jim Patrick were among the first SF Rotarians to make their wives Paul Harris Fellows. Occasionally, a surprised member is presented with a Paul Harris Fellow award by the club for outstanding club service. The club has also conferred Paul Harris Fellowships for ceremonial purposes to honor various individuals outside the club. With a large contribution by member Mike Sander in 1997, the club presented awards to "eight of the people who help make San Francisco such a wonderful and livable city." The honorees were a city supervisor, the fire and police chiefs, the sheriff, the city protocol chief, a local news anchor, and the heads of two major local nonprofit organizations.

Paul Harris Fellow contributions are solicited in a number of ways. One is by encouraging members to become Sustaining Fellows with an initial contribution of only $100, which is applied toward the full fellowship. A particularly effective means of encouraging members to become Paul Harris Fellows has been through matching contributions. In 1995, club President Andy Kirmse matched $100 contributions for Paul Harris Fellows for two months.

Since then, several club members—Ernest and Scharleen Colant in particular—pledged to match specified amounts contributed by other SF Rotarians. The goal was to achieve 100 percent

---

48. SF Rotary Past President Harold Basford declared that "any idea by Arch Klumph is bound to be a good one," and contributed $10, "just to start the ball rolling."

club participation in Paul Harris Fellowships. On November 14, 2006, at the luncheon meeting celebrating SF Rotary's ninety-eighth anniversary, the club reached a milestone in the Rotary world. Thanks to the Colants' program of matching contributions, as well as other club leaders who pushed for full member participation, and all the members who contributed, SF Rotary became the first major club in the Rotary world to attain 100 percent Paul Harris Fellow participation. The club received special recognition from The Rotary Foundation, and District Governor Mark Flegel presented a unique RI banner to the club in commemoration of the event.

Ernest and Scharleen Colant

Rotary Foundation funds are also raised in other ways. SF Rotary participates in the long-standing annual District 5150 fund-raiser—the Rotary Foundation Benefit. Usually in the form of a dinner, family picnic, or other outing, funds are raised with a raffle or auction. Fred Marschner brings fun into fund-raising with the annual Super Bowl football pool. Through the sale of one hundred chances at $100 each, the pool raises $10,000 for the Foundation each year. The purchaser's contribution is applied toward a Sustaining Paul Harris Fellowship, and the four pool winners receive a full Paul Harris Fellowship.

Fred Marschner

Where has the money raised by SF Rotarians for The Rotary Foundation gone? The answer should be a source of pride and inspiration to all Rotarians. In the decades since its founding, the Foundation has performed untold good work throughout the world, with an expanding array of humanitarian and educational programs. Initially, The Rotary Foundation chose to send representatives of Rotary out into the world, to make friends across borders and cultures. In 1962, SF Rotary began to participate in The Rotary Foundation's oldest international goodwill program—the Ambassadorial Scholarships.

Ambassadorial Scholarship Program

Of the many international programs in which SF Rotary now directly participates, perhaps none exceeds the international prestige of the Ambassadorial Scholarships. The program is the RI Foundation's oldest and best-known program. (Hereinafter, The Rotary Foundation will be referred to as the RI Foundation, to clearly distinguish it from the San Francisco Rotary Foundation.) The Ambassadorial Scholarships program provides opportunities for university or language/cultural-immersion studies in a foreign country for third- and fourth-year undergraduates, graduate students, and professional people pursuing vocational studies. Like Rotary's other international-exchange programs, the purpose of Ambassadorial Scholarships is to promote friendly relationships between people of different countries. In addition to combining education and training of potential leaders, the program involves students by having them describe their country to citizens of another nation, and in turn describing their experiences upon their return to their own homeland.

The Ambassadorial Scholarship program (formerly called Rotary Foundation Fellowships) was founded after Paul Harris's death in 1947. RI asked that Paul be honored with small contributions from individuals and clubs to the RI Foundation. In a short time, over $1 million had been contributed in his name. The following year, the RI Foundation awarded eighteen scholarships for one year's study abroad. In Rotary's fiftieth-anniversary year seven years later, 494 young men and women from 57 countries were awarded scholarships. Today the Ambassadorial Scholarship program is the largest privately funded international scholarship program in the world. Since its founding, 38,000 scholars from one hundred nations have participated, and over one thousand comprehensive scholarships are presently offered each year to study in countries where Rotary clubs are located.

Ambassadorial Scholars benefit from a comprehensive support network of Rotarians at home and abroad. Local Rotary clubs participate in the program by submitting candidates to their district. The sponsoring club of an accepted candidate assigns a sponsor and a host counselor. They provide the scholar with orientation, advice, and assistance in preparing for and successfully completing their study. While abroad, the scholar benefits from assistance and the friendship of a Rotary family.

SF Rotary sponsored its first scholar in 1962. Since then, the club has sent many scholars abroad through sponsorships, including a number of full monetary "named scholarships" by the club and individual members such as Ernest and Scharleen Colant and Henry Alker. Each year, the club hosts visiting scholars, and SF Rotarians serve as counselors. Besides actively submitting, funding, and hosting candidates, the club has publicized the scholarships at local universities and colleges, and with public service announcements.

The club has enjoyed many past successes in its sponsorship of Ambassadorial Scholars. Danielle Gordon, a scholar sponsored by SF Rotary in 2003–04, spent her postgraduate year at the Edinburgh University in Scotland, where she was hosted by the Corstorpine Rotary Club. In addition to successfully completing her study abroad, Danielle was expected to devote considerable time and energy to furthering international understanding. She spent her year representing Rotary and the United States as an ambassador of goodwill during her studies. She gave presentations about the United States at Rotary clubs and other groups throughout her host district in Scotland, and she attended numerous RI cultural, community, and social events. As an American, she learned about the culture and politics of Scotland, and in turn she learned to have constructive conversations with people who did not agree with U.S. foreign policies, particularly the war in Iraq. Danielle founded a Rotaract Club in Scotland with the help of nine other Ambassadorial Scholars, and served as its first president. The club received its charter in a ceremony attended by the RIBI (Rotary International in Great Britain and Ireland) president. When she left Scotland, the club had a substantial number of members, was meeting two nights a month, had a bank account and a Web site, and was developing a community-service project. Upon her return to San Francisco, Danielle shared with Rotarians and others the experiences that led her to a greater understanding of Scotland. She arranged several speaking engagements, and planned to keep her ties with Rotarians in her sponsoring and host countries. She also offered advice to new Ambassadorial Scholars and participated in their orientations. Danielle treasures her year abroad, and the gift of understanding another country and its culture.

Past President Jim Bradley and his wife, Kathy, host visiting Ambassadorial Scholar Natasha Valentova at a district picnic, 2001.

Natasha Valentova, a visiting scholar from Siberia, was hosted by SF Rotary. During her year here in 2001–2002, she formed a Rotaract Club. After she completed her study at San Francisco State University, she remained in San Francisco and served as the club's president. Some scholars eventually join Rotary. Lena Dokuchayeva, a former Ambassadorial Scholar from Russia to Santa Monica, is a recent addition to the SF Rotary family.

Rotary's Ambassadorial Scholar program was but the first of several RI programs that foster good relationships around the world by sponsoring individuals to travel abroad to learn about others.

Group Study Exchange

Rotary's Group Study Exchange program (GSE) provides a unique opportunity for a cultural experience between people of two countries. A four- to six-person team (one Rotarian leading a group of non-Rotarians age twenty-five to forty) visits a Rotary district in a foreign country for four weeks. The RI Foundation pays for transportation, while the host district and local Rotarians pay for other expenses directly related to the visiting team's study tour. The visitors travel within the host district, living in Rotarians' homes. The host district arranges sightseeing and opportunities for the visitors to learn about the cultural, business, and civic institutions of the country. The visitors learn about the culture, and meet with people in their same professions. They also attend Rotary meetings in the host district, and speak before other groups. When they return, they give talks about their experiences to Rotary clubs and other organizations within the sending district. Later (usually in the same year), the exchange is completed, when the visited district sends a team to the original sending district.

The first Group Study Exchange teams were organized in 1965, between districts in California and Japan. The program's precursor was a Rotary project of exchange initiated in New Zealand, dating from 1950. The GSE program has proven so successful, it claims sixty thousand alumni. Many GSE team members join Rotary. Twenty percent of Rotary clubs have Group Study alumni among their membership.

SF Rotary has been an active supporter of Group Study Exchange since the 1970s. Members have participated as group team leaders and have graciously hosted visiting teams from abroad. In a typical Group Study Exchange, a team from the Philippines visited District 5150 in 1995. They stayed in the homes of SF Rotarians for five days. Members arranged a tour of the University of California's San Francisco Medical Center to observe patient care and state-of-the-art technology, tours of the Pacific Stock Exchange and Bank of America as an introduction to American financial markets and banking systems, a tour of city government at city hall, and the judicial system at the sheriff's and public defender's offices. The visitors were also treated to a boat ride on the bay, and dinner and entertainment with SF Rotary's "Under-35 Group." Afterward, the visiting team moved to another location in the district. Earlier that year, SF Rotarian Mike Sander had led a district GSE team to the Philippines. Most recently, club member John Tornes served as the district's San Francisco host coordinator for an inbound group from Germany. Later, member Roger Steiner led the five members of District 5150's team on a reciprocal visit to District 1820 in Germany.

Roger Steiner leading a District 5150 GSE team, in front of the Kurhaus in Wiesbaden, Germany, 2007. Courtesy of Roger Steiner

Rotary World Peace Fellows

One of Rotary's recent advances in promoting world peace in our complex era has been the establishment of the Rotary Centers for International Studies in Peace and Conflict Resolution. This program aims to train leaders, policy makers, and workers in the vast field of international relations. The worldwide program was conceived in 1997 to commemorate the fiftieth anniversary of Paul Harris's death. The RI Foundation established seven (now six) Rotary Centers for International Studies around the world, to offer two-year master's-level programs in international relations, peace studies, and conflict resolution. Rotary World Peace Fellows have applied their studies to work in the private sector, nongovernmental organizations, the UN, and the diplomatic corps. The University of California at Berkeley was selected as one of the Rotary Centers. In 2002, UC Berkeley welcomed its first ten Fellows to begin their studies.

Rotary World Peace Fellows receive host support from surrounding Rotary districts. The five Northern California Rotary districts are host to the Fellows at UC Berkeley. Each district provides one or two host counselors. SF Rotarian Roger Steiner has served as District 5150's chair for the program since its inception. He works with local clubs in the district, coordinating support activities and speaking about the program to clubs, district assemblies, and district conferences. Roger organized a district reception dinner for the UC Berkeley Fellows. The dinner featured a potluck of their dishes from around the world, and was such a success that it has been adopted by the other Northern California districts.

A Rotary district may also submit candidates for Rotary World Peace Fellowships. SF Rotary sponsored the program's first successful candidate application from District 5150. Kathy Brown was interviewed by club member Henry Alker, who has contributed generously to the program. She was accepted into the program by RI, and began her study in Tokyo in 2005.

World Wide Rotary Day

As part of its commitment to the Rotary ideal of international understanding, SF Rotary also celebrates Rotary's universal fellowship in one of its most successful luncheon programs of the year. World Wide Rotary Day is a festive day featuring the San Francisco Consular Corps as guests. The club has a history of paying tribute to the ambassadors and consuls of the world as a means of promoting international goodwill. In the 1920s, RI began to encourage local clubs to observe the national holidays of other countries by inviting the consular representative of a country to the club's meeting that week. Although SF Rotary did not take up the practice immediately, it did honor consuls by welcoming them as members of the club.

SF Rotary's long tradition of inviting its local consuls to celebrations began on the eve of World War II, when the club began a series of periodic "Pan-American Solidarity" luncheon programs. These programs reflected a new international spirit of Pan-Americanism—a development of mutual understanding of the common problems the countries of the Americas faced in the oncoming European crisis. After the onset of the war, RI encouraged club activities that would "promote western hemispheric solidarity." In response, SF Rotary held meeting programs hosting the Latin American consuls, and speakers who educated club members about their neighbors in Latin America. The club also sent a letter of greeting—written in Spanish—to the president of each club in Chile. The program received considerable praise from RI.

In the decades following the war, SF Rotary continued its luncheon programs about the Americas. During SF Rotary's fiftieth-anniversary celebration in 1958, the International Service Committee held a program about Central America, with music, costumes, and the local consuls from the Central American countries. Several years later, the committee's program celebrated our neighbors to the north and south, featuring the consuls of Canada and Mexico. In more recent years, SF Rotary has been proud to claim consuls among its membership. In keeping with RI President (1981–82) Stan McCaffrey's theme of "World Understanding and Peace Through Rotary," the club awarded year-to-year Honorary memberships to several San Francisco consuls. In 2000, the SF Rotary board voted to invite consuls to join the club, and agreed to waive the initiation fee.

SF Rotary can trace the roots of its present-day World Wide Rotary Day back to 1961, with the club's celebration of a "World Understanding Week" in a special program. Later in the early 1990s, the club acknowledged World Understanding Month, so designated because RI celebrates

its founding on February 23—known as World Understanding and Peace Day. In 1993, club President Pete Lagarias welcomed San Francisco's consuls to a World Understanding and Peace Day program. The program was repeated the following year.

A few years later, longtime SF Rotarian Eugene Lee had an idea. These earlier programs that focused on consuls did not emphasize the worldwide fellowship of Rotary. Eugene envisioned a "Rotary Around the World" celebration. With an outstanding committee, he was the driving force behind

Eugene Lee

the first World Wide Rotary Day in 1997. The day's purpose was "to increase the club's awareness of its wider fellowship, which spans the globe and crosses the international dateline."

The club team that planned and organized the day included members who were born in countries such as China, Germany, Italy, Singapore, and Switzerland. Twenty-eight consuls ac-cepted the club's invitation to attend as special guests. For its first celebration, the club invited Frank Devlyn (RI Trustee and future RI President, 2000–01) to speak on the RI Foundation's thou-sands of projects resulting from partnerships be-tween clubs from countries around the world. Devlyn greeted the consuls at a special recep-tion held in their honor.

Entertainment trio in the hospitality room before the World Wide Rotary Day luncheon, 1998.

The luncheon itself was packed with 240 attendees, including members, consuls, cur-rent and past district governors, Group Study Exchange team leaders, Ambassadorial Scholars, and representatives from other Bay Area Rotary clubs. Arriving guests were greeted with music from around the world. The room was decorated with foreign banners and travel posters, and tables to which the consuls were assigned were deco-rated with their countries' national flags. At each table was a list of world Rotary clubs that had already met that day at each hour since midnight, a newsletter outlining SF Rotary's international activities, and a letter written to a club in the consul's country signed by everyone at the table. After singing and the invocation, the visiting consuls, Group Study Exchange team leaders, and Rotary scholars were introduced. In addition to the luncheon, the club sent out personalized let-

World Wide Rotary Day

ters to clubs throughout the world. The letters described the program and invited the clubs to share in a world-wide Rotary day by recog-nizing the day in the follow-ing year with celebrations of their own. SF Rotary's highly successful program was recognized by District 5150 as the most outstand-ing program of the year, and earned the district's World Community Service award.

Club President John Uth continued the popular program the following year, and it has been celebrated each year since, under committee chairs Eugene Lee, Roger Steiner, and Jim Kennedy. World Wide Rotary Day has become the best attended luncheon of SF Rotary's year. Several clubs around the world have adopted the program and have similar meetings the same week.

Beyond its active participation in these programs of friendship, SF Rotary has fostered international goodwill in a number of other ways. For example, over the years, the club has established "Sister City" relationships with more than a dozen clubs around the world.

One of Rotary's strengths is the eagerness of its members to extend the hand of friendship to people of nations that are considered enemies or former enemies. A case in point is an elaborate exchange of greetings between SF Rotary and clubs in Japan that took place only six years after the end of World War II. In 1951, Japan signed a peace treaty with the Allied powers and several other members of the United Nations. Because the signing took place at the Opera House in San Francisco, SF Rotary took the opportunity to celebrate international Rotary fellowship with America's former foe. The club extended an invitation to all Japanese Rotarians who might be in San Francisco at the time to avail themselves of SF Rotary's offices and to any service the club might render. In reply, members of the sixty-three Rotary clubs in Japan sent each SF Rotarian an Emblem of Friendship—a tie clasp with a pearl in the Rotary emblem—in honor of the signing. The Rotary district governor in Japan sent greetings as well. To celebrate the peace treaty signing, SF Rotary held its annual International Program luncheon honoring the Rotary Clubs of Japan. The two Japanese Rotarian speakers—including one from Hiroshima—had attended the peace conference. One of the Japanese guests was an Ambassadorial Scholar in Washington. SF Rotarian Charles Wheeler, the president of RI in the midst of America's war with Japan, brought greetings from Rotary International. Club President James Holbrook sent a copy of the luncheon program and a letter of appreciation to each club in Japan. As is the case in so many Rotary efforts, small details demonstrate the effectiveness and cooperation that are brought about by the hard work of Rotarians behind the scenes. A Japanese-language newspaper in San Francisco printed the meeting program, and Pan-American Airways arranged delivery of the Emblems of Friendship from Japan at no cost.

More recently, SF Rotarians have reached out to Russia. After the collapse of the Soviet Union in 1989, club members immediately began a series of interactions with the Russian people. In the fall of 1990 (the same year that Mikhail Gorbachev visited San Francisco) six members toured four cities in Russia. They "made-up" their missed luncheons by attending a meeting of the newly formed Rotary Club of Moscow—the first club in what had been the USSR since 1917. The next year, the Moscow club's first vice president visited SF Rotary and reported on his club's status. SF Rotary also hosted a contingent of visiting Rotarians from the St. Petersburg club, which had been formed in 1991.

In the past few years, SF Rotary has welcomed and assisted Russian business professionals through its participation in the Productivity Enhancement Program (PEP). This program is administered by the Center for Citizen Initiatives, a San Francisco-based nongovernmental organization working in the field of citizen diplomacy. Utilizing volunteer services from civic organizations such as Rotary, PEP provides training to Russian small-business owners to boost production of domestic goods and services and help ease Russia's transition to a market economy. The visitors will return to Russia and share their knowledge with their peers. Hundreds of Rotary clubs in the United States have hosted and educated thousands of Russian visitors.

SF Rotarians meet with a delegation of visiting Russian dentists, 2007.

The first visitors hosted by SF Rotary under PEP was a group of eleven attorneys, who visited during Harold Hoogasian's presidential year (2001–02). At the request of District Governor Pete Lagarias, club member Don Parachini chaired a joint arrangement with the Golden Gate Rotary Club to provide the Russian attorneys with a study in reducing corruption through a review of legal traditions in the United States. The group also educated the Russians in Rotary values, to help them combat corruption by way of the Four-Way Test. Since then, SF Rotary has teamed with other San Francisco Rotary clubs to host groups of visiting accountants, senior business executives, dentists, builders, and investment bankers, for a transfer of knowledge and ideas in their respective fields. In 2007 alone, the club hosted three such groups of Russians.

■ ■ ■

From the club's early tradition of hospitality to visitors from abroad to wide participation in RI's successful exchange programs of today, SF Rotary's interest in friendship and service to the world has grown steadily through the century. The Rotary ideal of extending the hand of friendship across borders has evolved as a logical extension of the fellowship found in the Rotarian's local club and community. It is just as Paul Harris hoped it would be.

Help Across Borders—International Humanitarianism

Rotarians do not ask, "What's in it for me?" They derive satisfaction from the multitude of ways they can improve the lives of others, especially children. That is enough to keep us in Rotary forever.

—Ernest and Scharleen Colant, 2002

Alongside its offer of international friendship, Rotary's hand often reaches out to lend much-needed assistance. The many ways in which Rotarians in one country can bring relief and hope to fellow humans around the world has grown from humble beginnings to today's grand array of humanitarian service.

SF Rotary has a rich tradition of international service to others. Since the club's days of sending wartime relief during World War I, the past half century has given ample opportunity for SF Rotarians to help. They have never failed to volunteer, in ways that range from the simple to the extraordinary.

Grant Hundley,
SF Rotary President
2004–05

Many of SF Rotary's contributions to international service have been in the form of emergency humanitarian response to disasters. Club members have responded generously and spontaneously to calls for help after major earthquakes in Mexico City, Kobe, and El Salvador. Many calls come from RI. Rotarians worldwide were asked to help child victims of the Chernobyl nuclear power plant accident, and to reach into their pockets for hurricane relief aid to Central America in 1999.

One of the greatest disasters in recent history was an enormous tsunami that struck coastal communities in Southeast Asia in December 2004. SF Rotary President Grant Hundley and SF Rotarians rallied to the cause, to the tune of $26,000. The SFR Foundation contributed another $20,000. The money was used to build sixteen steel-reinforced concrete-block homes in Sri Lanka for displaced families.

In addition to disaster response, SF Rotary has helped distant people in numerous other ways, some chiefly through funding, and others through the kindness of club members who give of their time and energy in distant lands around the world.

Many of SF Rotary's international-service projects for the past four decades have been conducted through the World Community Service (WCS) program. WCS is an RI concept, created in 1962 to provide the means for local Rotary clubs around the world to become involved in humani-

"You know, we're going to be building homes in Sri Lanka. And that is so neat to me. We know what they are going to look like. We know they're going to have the Rotary wheel and it's going to say, 'Donated by the Rotary Club of San Francisco.' The families are going to be living in a concrete-block residence that will be there for years and years and years."

—Past President Bill Koefoed

A house built in Sri Lanka for the Priyantha family, after theirs was destroyed by the tsunami in 2004.
Courtesy of PDG Eric Shapira

tarian activities in distant communities. Through a WCS Projects Exchange Database, a local club seeking an international-service project can be "paired" with a Rotary club in a developing country. In this manner, the local club can send volunteers, technical and professional expertise, and financial and material gifts, to help solve the asking club's problems in health, education, agriculture, and industry. The local club's funding is often matched with district and RI Foundation money.

SF Rotarians sponsored an early World Community Service project during club President Jim Huckin's year (1970–71) by sending a hemodialysis system and surgical instruments to hospitals in the Philippines and Columbia. In another instance, the club contributed money for a six-hundred-gallon rain-storage tank that was part of a new modular "Rotahome" for a poverty-stricken family in Fiji.

SF Rotarians inspecting surgical instruments donated to a hospital in Columbia as a World Community Project in 1971.

Although many of SF Rotary's international-service activities take place within the World Community Service structure, many do not. The past four decades have seen a dramatic increase in Rotarians' generosity to the less fortunate in distant places. The following are only a few of SF Rotary's international-service projects around the world during the past fifty years. SF Rotary donated one ton of books to the Rotary Club of Pago Pago in Samoa. Books and medical supplies were sent to Turkey. The club joined with a Rotary club in the Philippines to buy pairs of goats for farmers, and funded an ambulance for small Chilean town. Chile benefited again when Rotarians Kay Clarke and Mark Oei successfully obtained and donated a fire engine from the Catalina Island Fire Department. In 2003, during Dick Rosen's presidential year, SF Rotary supported two projects in Asia. One was sponsoring a new playground and overall upgrades in a rural orphanage by a foundation called "Half the Sky." The other was funding of the containerization, shipment, and distribution of donated up-to-date textbooks, valued at nearly $2 million, to Afghanistan, Thailand, and Vietnam.

Richard B. Rosen, SF Rotary President 2003–04

Some SF Rotary projects are the result of a single member's idea, proposal, and perseverance through the grant process. One such Rotarian is Boris Hesser, formerly a Rotaract member in Heidelberg, Germany. For over a decade, Boris has worked with the Rotarian Action Group for Population and Development, a worldwide network of Rotarians that works toward population stabilization. In 2005–06, Boris collaborated with the Rotary Club of Ibadan West in Nigeria to gain SF Rotary sponsorship of an

Boris Hesser

SF Rotarians Henry Alker and Eric Schmautz (second and third from left) present a tricycle-type wheelchair to a young boy, Bharat. His grateful mother looks on, 2008.

international-partner "Reproductive Health/ HIV-AIDS Awareness and Microcredit Financing for Women" project, using matching-grant funds from District 5150 and the RI Foundation. The project was a two-pronged effort to combat the root causes of hunger and poverty in a sustainable way. First, in the knowledge that lifting women out of poverty reduces population growth, the project established a microcredit revolving-loan program for Nigerian women. In a nationally publicized presentation at a Rotary meeting in Ibadan, thirty-six women with existing trades received repayable loans of approximately $100 each. Such a loan is sufficient to establish a woman on the road to economic self-reliance. Second, the program funded an education and awareness campaign to educate adult women and over two thousand Nigerian high-school students about reproductive health, using dramatic presentations and lectures that were presented live and on radio and television by Rotarians and health-care providers.

Another venture that came about as a result of personal inspiration is a wheelchair project, in conjunction with the Rotary Club of Agra, India. Conceived by club member Rosey Wong, the project sponsored the presentation of wheelchairs to 130 children in the city of Agra. Several SF Rotarians attended the presentation, and saw the delight in the children's eyes as they received the gift of mobility.

Rosey Wong

Roots of Peace

SF Rotary's international-service efforts received a real boost in 2006, when Heidi Kühn, a dedicated humanitarian, joined the club. Coming from the Rotary Club of San Rafael, Heidi already had ties to SF Rotary, as the granddaughter of the club's Past President William H. Thomas (1941–42).

In 1997, Heidi formed a humanitarian organization called Roots of Peace, whose mission was to rid the world of buried land mines, and to transform mine fields into productive farmlands. In addition to removing the daily threat of death to innocent children, Heidi's program enhances the local economies of mine-affected countries by reinstating the livelihoods of farmers where mines and unexploded ordnance have been removed. A key aspect of Heidi's vision of transforming "Mines to Vines," Roots of Peace works with other organizations to bring in crops such as grapes, cherries, and pomegranates, restoring the once-fertile lands to their earlier use. Roots of Peace has worked its miracle extensively in Afghanistan, where ten million land mines lie hidden, killing sixty people a month. Thanks to Roots of Peace, one hundred thousand land mines and unexploded ordnance have been removed, and ten thousand farmers have been retrained to grow new crops—often as an alternative to opium poppies. Fields have also been restored in Angola, Cambodia, Croatia, and Iraq.

In 2003, Heidi joined with her daughter Kyleigh and San Francisco television news anchor Cheryl Jennings to initiate the Roots of Peace Penny Campaign. The three women were inspired by visiting minefields in the Balkans. The Penny Campaign's initial purpose was to place penny-collection cans in schools, to collect pennies for Roots of Peace. In only four years, fifteen million pennies have been collected from schools across the United States.

Heidi Kühn and newscaster Cheryl Jennings launch SF Rotary Roots of Peace Penny Campaign, as President John Hoch looks on, 2007.
Photo by Steve Swaab

SF Rotary recently joined in the Penny Campaign, distributing penny-collection cans for Rotarians to take to their places of business. The club expanded its alliance with Roots of Peace during club President John Hoch's year (2007–08). Heidi, Committee Chair Jim Patrick, and International Service Committee Chair Jean Schore spearheaded the year's major international-service project of sponsoring a planting project on a demined field in Croatia. Grapes, peaches, and maraschino cherries will thrive in the temperate Adriatic climate. Later in 2008, Roots of Peace plans to build a sports field with money raised by SF Rotary. Club members and their families will travel to Croatia. They will take with them a team from the Hunters Point Boys & Girls Club to play with Croatian children—building a place of peace from a deadly place of war.

For her innovative and extensive humanitarian work with Roots of Peace, Heidi Kühn was awarded RI's highest individual honor, the Service Above Self Award, in 2006.

▪ ▪ ▪

The projects described reflect SF Rotarians' growing interest in international humanitarian service that began with wartime and emergency relief, then grew to include additional forms of assistance starting in the 1960s. Most represent individual actions of limited scope and duration, and mostly single-occurrence funding. Indeed, until a little over twenty years ago, SF Rotary's only substantial financial contribution to a continuing international-service program was to the RI Foundation in its capacity as the international Ambassadorial Scholarship fund. The club's own SFR Foundation was providing assistance on a continuing basis to a number of projects and organizations, such as the Boys' Club, but these were local to San Francisco. Then, in the mid-1980s, Rotary International issued a challenge to clubs everywhere. One million members strong, the world's oldest service organization inaugurated a twenty-year program of a kind and scope never seen before.

PolioPlus—What a World of People Can Do

> *What appeals to me is that as a group, you can accomplish something that as an individual you can't, and that's one of the great things about Rotary. This is a concerted effort—all the Rotarians around the world, putting in their money to stamp out polio. Just Marshall Blum, there's not a helluva lot I can do. . . . But as a group it's magnificent what Rotary has done, and can do.*

—Past President Marsh Blum

Nothing in Rotary's century-long history has electrified and united its members like its first world-wide humanitarian program. PolioPlus is Rotary's ambitious initiative to immunize all of the children in the world against the ravages of polio, and to eradicate the highly infectious but preventable disease from the earth. It reshaped Rotary's international role at the end of the twentieth century, and fashioned a new, broader understanding among Rotarians about their relationship with the people of the world.

An iron-lung ward for polio victims in Los Angeles, 1952.

An early case of Rotary involvement in vaccination for an underdeveloped country occurred in 1973, with a joint vaccination effort between a Pennsylvanian Rotary district and its Guatemalan counterparts. Then, for RI's seventy-fifth anniversary in 1980, RI searched for a project that could involve all clubs. The result was its five-year commitment to provide polio vaccine for children throughout the Philippines. This was RI's first endeavor in its new Health, Hunger, and Humanity (3-H) program. SF Rotary responded by contributing $1,500. Six million children were successfully vaccinated, and then the polio-vaccination program was introduced into five other nations.

Three years later, a committee created by RI's President Stanley McCaffrey surveyed Rotarians concerning a long-term direction for Rotary. One of the results of that committee's work was a program to immunize all of the children of the world by Rotary's one-hundredth anniversary in 2005. The program came to be known as PolioPlus, because it also supported a global health offensive against the five other major vaccine-preventable diseases—measles, diphtheria, pertussis, tetanus, and tuberculosis. At the fortieth anniversary of the United Nations in 1985, RI announced its pledge to raise $120 million to provide vaccine to all newborns for a five-year period, and to organize thousands of Rotary volunteers to help carry out the millions of vaccinations. To embark on such a massive project, Rotary joined forces with the World Health Organization (WHO) and the UN Children's Fund (UNICEF).[49]

When RI announced its ambitious public effort to raise $120 million, SF Rotary determined to give the program a high priority, by 1) asking each member to contribute specifically to PolioPlus; 2) organizing a community fund-raising; and 3) establishing a committee to coordinate support activities. The club took the challenge to heart, and looked to such novel fund-raising approaches as a PolioPlus biathlon. In November 1986, Past President Jim Patrick emceed a grand celebration of the district raising between $400,000 and $500,000 for the RI Foundation and PolioPlus. Marsh Blum's presidential year ended with the district leading the world and SF Rotary leading the district in contributions to the RI Foundation.

Incoming President Bill Sturgeon threw his support into PolioPlus. Through the efforts of Jim Patrick's committee, PolioPlus became the club's number-one fund-raising focus. When District Governor Aldo Simonetti announced in 1987 that the district goal for fund-raising was increased to $2,282,000, Jim addressed the club at lunch, calling for "total Rotary support" of PolioPlus, and the club announced a goal of $500 per member.

Jim was relentless, keeping PolioPlus in prominent view with his regular luncheon progress reports and PolioPlus ads in *Grindings*. He emphasized that each dollar would protect eight children from polio paralysis. Mary Huss of the *San Francisco Business Times* donated a full page of advertising space for contributions to the fund. Bill Sturgeon promoted the "PolioPlus" Paul Harris Fellow at a luncheon dubbed "PolioPlus Day," awarding the club's first such award to his mother. He tempted members with a PolioPlus tie for contributions of $1,000 or more. At the end of his year, SF Rotary was honored for its contributions to PolioPlus. In that year alone, the club's PolioPlus fund-raising amounted to $165,000.

During the two-year campaign push, SF Rotarians came to realize that their power to accomplish good was not limited to local service, or to specific individual projects overseas. To be sure, these were important, and would continue to constitute the daily and yearly works of the club's service work. But, by virtue of their membership in a worldwide organization of over a million people, SF Rotarians had become part of a force that could accomplish what would not have been imagined only a few decades earlier.

> "As Rotary International's first worldwide endeavor, the PolioPlus effort has given Rotarians the knowledge that they can become a factor on the world scene for peace, and the belief that Rotary has an international purpose different than that of the initial founders."
>
> —Past District Governor Bill Sturgeon

At the end of the campaign in May 1988, the Rotary world was astounded when the PolioPlus organizers announced that contributions amounted to $247 million—more than double the campaign's goal of $120 million. Rotarians everywhere realized that Rotary had exceeded its most optimistic expectations. The success of PolioPlus—the largest global health endeavor ever undertaken by

---

49. Occasionally, the RI Foundation has earmarked funds for children's programs other than immunization, such as a program in Malawi, Africa, to ease the plights of the country's "crawlers," by providing crutches, canes, and other devices.

a private entity—inspired the World Health Assembly to pass a resolution to eradicate polio, paving the way for the formation of the Global Polio Eradication Initiative. RI, WHO, UNICEF, and the US Centers for Disease Control and Prevention (CDC) agreed to expand the goal from control of polio to an ambitious new goal of polio's complete eradication in the world by the year 2000. This would require new commitments, fund-raising, and management of resources that would lead ultimately to more than $600 million in Rotary contributions and a massive volunteer dedication to immunize all the children of the world. Thus for SF Rotary, the call for funds was far from over. Jim Patrick and his committee continued their efforts and creative approaches to soliciting contributions. The following year, SF Rotary won the district's Bru Brunnier Award for Distinguished International Service.

After the initial fund-raising, RI volunteers worldwide began their massive contribution to the immunization effort. Wearing clothing marked to identify themselves as Rotary volunteers, they traveled by boat, Jeep, helicopter, and camel to administer the vaccine to children in remote areas. In another impressive accomplishment, volunteers helped maintain an unbroken "cold chain" necessary to retain the vaccine's effectiveness, through the use of Rotary-donated insulated vaccine carriers. In 1994—less than ten years after the start of the program—all of North, Central, and South America were certified polio-free, and PolioPlus was hailed in the scientific world. Soon after, the director general of WHO recognized the impressive benefits of its relationship with Rotary: "Without the contribution of Rotary International and many individual Rotarians, we would not now be predicting the eradication of polio."

In 1997, SF Rotary committed itself to "PolioPlus Partners," an RI Foundation program that offered a club (or district or individual) the opportunity to choose among a broad spectrum of specific PolioPlus needs, thus enabling the club to "adopt" a particular project and track its progress. For its project, SF Rotary chose to support a laboratory in Senegal that was used to monitor polio-fighting activity and to prevent or stop any new outbreak of the virus. Jim Patrick created an effective fund-raising device—a box to be hammered shut during luncheon meetings. He sold $100, $500, and $1,000 nails to those who contributed to "nail the lid shut on polio in Senegal." In total, Jim's high-spirited nail selling and hammering raised nearly $24,000 in contributions from 98 SF Rotarians.

In 2000, SF Rotarians joined members of other Rotary clubs from the Bay Area. They traveled to Accra, Ghana, to participate in a massive countrywide "National Immunization Day." They worked with local Rotarians to help at immunization posts, deliver polio vaccine, help parents get their children vaccinated, transport health workers, and recruit fellow volunteers to assist.

The PolioPlus program continued to perform its powerful mission. It mobilized sophisticated volunteer teams, who worked with health workers to immunize as many as 147 million children in India in a single National Immunization Day in 1997. The scourge of polio was eradicated in China and the Western Pacific by 2000, and in Europe with its former Soviet Bloc by 2002. The valiant effort to end polio in the world by Rotary's one-hundredth anniversary in 2005 was not fully

---

RAISING MONEY FOR
POLIOPLUS

"There was Jim Patrick standing up at a meeting with a box he'd built, and he had a hammer and he said, 'I want to nail this box shut. It costs $100 to buy one of these nails, who's gonna buy?'"

—Past District Governor Pete Lagarias

Jim Patrick on PolioPlus

Jim: Back in 1986 they said, "We're going to go after the polio problem." And we raised money for PolioPlus and it was eight cents a dose, so we could save a child for eight cents! So the goal was how many kids can we save! Our club raised $250,000 dollars—a lot, a lot, a lot, a lot, a lot of money! I couldn't believe it.

The important thing is that we took that $250,000, and money from all over the world went to RI, and RI said "You know, we're going to clear out polio." Well, that was in 1986, and now we're in 2001. Polio is almost gone from the world and it's thanks, in large measure, to Rotary. Someone had a vision to say, "Hey, we're going to wipe out polio!" I said, "No way, but I'll raise the money." We raised the money and I've watched this very carefully, and it's been a remarkable story.

Interviewer: So the historical success with polio gives you some optimism for the future?

Jim: We have the blueprint. We know what to do. And the strength of Rotary in PolioPlus is that we said, "We have the vaccine and we have to keep it cold." So we had a cold-chain. And we'd go to a place in Ghana and guess what's in Ghana? A Rotary club! And we said, "A Rotary Club in Ghana—we're going to do a great thing for the people. We all believe in the same thing." And the community representatives said, "Great! You bring us this; we'll bring the people to be vaccinated." And so they brought them in—all the young kids—and they were vaccinated. And voila! It's working. Everyplace!

Interviewer: How much difficulty has Rotary run into in dealing with the governments of these various countries?

Jim: But this is the good news. You know who's a member of the Rotary Club in Ghana? ...the Health Minister! So you have the connections. That's what makes it work. So, I believe— the exciting part about Rotary—we're going to re-exercise those connections in another manner. I just don't know how yet.

—an excerpt from an interview with Jim Patrick, 2001

successful, as new cases continue to appear in a few countries today, due in large part to factors such as geographical isolation, worker fatigue, armed conflict, and cultural barriers. But the cases are very few, and the end is in sight. During RI's one-hundredth anniversary month in February 2005, RI's General Secretary Ed Futa addressed SF Rotary. He declared the end of polio to be "near at hand." Rotary's present challenge is to complete total eradication by 2008.

Since the new millennium began, SF Rotary has continued to answer RI's calls for additional support, through contributions and efforts by individual members. In 2002 RI announced a new "Fulfilling Our Promise: Eradicate Polio" campaign. SF Rotary's board established a goal of $500 per member over three years, and established a "Committee of 100" for donors who would pledge $5,000 or more. The following year, PolioPlus announced that Rotarians had raised more than $118 million to support the final stages of polio eradication. At the time of this writing, RI has raised and contributed over $630 million for polio eradication, and there is more to come. In November 2007, RI announced a matching-funds partnership with the Bill and Melinda Gates Foundation that will raise another $200 million to complete the eradication effort. SF Rotarians have repeatedly stepped up to the challenge and will continue to do so—in part through sustained efforts with matching donations by members. Continuing acts of generosity such as these and many others, repeated for over twenty years, have given SF Rotary much reason to be enormously proud of its role in what has been called "Rotary's finest hour."

■ ■ ■

SF Rotary's enormous fund-raising effort on behalf of PolioPlus represented the largest single international-service objective in the club's history. As a counterpoint to this, the early-1980s movement of the club's members toward more hands-on acts of service began to influence some international-service projects as well as local community projects. Rather than fund-raising alone, SF Rotarians began to travel to other countries for humanitarian purposes.

One such member was Dr. Mike Sander. Mike traveled for weeks at a time with an RI dental program for indigent people in Jamaica and other countries. For his example of "Service Above Self," Mike was awarded the Rotary Foundation District Service Award and the Rotary Foundation Certificate for Meritorious Service, both in 1995.

SF Rotarians have revisited some projects several times. Project Amigo is an RI-designated district World Community Service site. It provides help to poor children in Colima, Mexico, in various ways, including work projects, field trips to broaden their horizons, and scholarships. Rotarians have worked with Project Amigo on a number of occasions. They have visited a Mexican orphanage, and have helped establish fruit and vegetable gardens using donated seeds from several seed companies. The club also brought twenty members of the San Francisco high-school Interact club to Colima to help build three low-cost shelters. Rotarians arranged transportation, conducted an orientation meeting, and supervised the construction team.

Beginning fifteen years ago, the club's participation in international-service projects underwent a significant shift to a focus on the homegrown. Moving beyond trips by individuals, several visionary SF Rotarians have conceived and developed three major hands-on, continuing international programs for children. With their wide-ranging goals and broad reach, Rotaplast, Rotavision, and Alliance for Smiles represent extraordinary accomplishments by members of a single Rotary club.

Rotaplast International

> *What in the world can be more satisfying than the experience felt when a child who wants to be like you and smile like you, can now say with a happy face, "Look, I am and smile just like you." It dramatically demonstrates the best way to promote peace and build bridges of understanding and goodwill.*

Only four months old, Felipe was born with a face disfigured by cleft lip and palate. More than his appearance was affected; the open channel through the roof of his mouth made eating difficult. His Chilean parents could not afford the three million pesos (about $8,100) for corrective surgery. Through Rotaplast, Felipe was given the chance for a full, normal life.

The cleft palate is much more than a surface facial deformity; it is a life-affecting birth defect. It occurs when the two parts that form the roof of the mouth fail to come together while the fetus is developing. Most afflicted children live through a lifetime of stares. Some cannot communicate because they cannot make themselves understood; as a result, they may be unable to go to school. Many face shunning and rejection, and will live much of their lives in seclusion. For some, their health is also affected, as they cannot swallow or breathe properly. Although cleft-palate surgery is common in the United States, there are few plastic surgeons in developing countries who perform the surgery, leaving tens of thousands of children untreated. The children helped by Rotaplast receive a gift far beyond the abilities of their families—many of whom live on less than $100 per year.

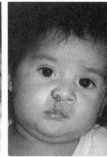

Juan Pablo, before and after cleft-lip surgery, during a Rotaplast mission to Bolivia, 2000. Photo by Berri Kramer; Courtesy of Rotaplast International

With its international scope, Rotaplast represents the most ambitious project for facial surgery in SF Rotary's history. However, it was not the first. In fact, the club has brought smiles to children's malformed faces in the past. Facial plastic surgery by SF Rotarian doctors began in the 1920s with the work of Dr. Alfred Davis. He was succeeded in the 1950s by Dr. Fred West. In addition, the club has supported the cleft-palate program of the Easter Seals Society, and has sent children to the Easter Seals cleft-palate speech camp.

Today, Rotaplast International is a nonprofit humanitarian organization, giving free reconstructive cleft-palate surgery and treatment to indigent children in developing countries worldwide. The organization's mission is to provide long-term solutions to cleft palate by funding and coordinating surgical missions, training and mentoring local physicians, launching public-education projects, and advancing research.

In 1992, however, it was but a vision in the minds of SF Rotarians Pete Lagarias and Dr. Angelo Capozzi. Pete's wife, Elaine Maurer, had visited Chile many times since the 1970s. Her love for the country led her to adopt a little Chilean girl, whom she named Kelly. After Elaine and Pete married,

*Peter C. Lagarias,
SF Rotary President
1992–93;
District Governor,
2001–02*

they decided to contribute something with a lasting impact in Chile. Rotary provided the way.

Through a connection with Hernan Reyes, a district governor in northern Chile, SF Rotary did a small project for developmentally disabled Chilean children. Rotarians also collected donated equipment and supplies from several Bay Area hospitals and other organizations. A Rotarian in Vallejo, California, arranged for the California Maritime Academy to transport several pallets of supplies on a ship's practice run to Valparaiso. Pete and Elaine followed the shipment to Chile, where they cemented their friendship with District Governor Reyes, whose Chilean Rotary connections would prove crucial to the project to come.

SF Rotarian Dr. Angelo Capozzi had made surgery trips to South America for fourteen years with Interplast, a humanitarian organization providing free reconstructive surgery in poor countries, sometimes with Rotary funding.

Dr. Angelo Capozzi

Pete approached Angelo about joining him in a Rotary project similar to Interplast. Unlike Interplast, however, Pete's idea was to add a traveling nonmedical support team, plus assistance from Chilean Rotarians. Angelo was ecstatic about the prospect of a large project with a volunteer support team, and the opportunity to work under the aegis of Rotary. The prestigious organization with worldwide connections would offer the potential to go anywhere that had a Rotary club, and to partner with local Rotarians in the countries visited. Messages were sent back and forth to Chile, and follow-up meetings were held at the next RI Convention in 1991. A few months later, President-Elect Pete outlined plans for a major medical trip to Chile, called "Rotaplast."

The first step was a site assessment trip. Angelo and Kay Clarke (an SF Rotarian and registered nurse) traveled with another RN to Chile to learn about the greatest needs for a medical project, and to select the locations where surgical skills could be best utilized. They chose two northern cities: La Serena on the coast, and Antofagasta, near open-pit copper mines in one of the driest deserts in

PETE LAGARIAS RECALLS

"I said, 'Angelo, I want this to be a World Community Service project that's hands-on for Rotarians who aren't in the medical field. We'll translate. We'll be the quartermaster. We'll organize the whole trip. We'll run the autoclave. You tell us—we'll be the record keepers. We're going to have people-to-people, between the United States and a developing country. That's an integral part of this—we're going to have the Rotarians down there working together with us. We're going to see their culture; they're going to see Americans. It's an international building of world understanding and goodwill, which is the point, as well as helping these kids.'"

the world. Neither town had a reconstructive surgeon. Resident pediatric surgeons in both places expressed eagerness to participate and learn from the methods the Rotary team could teach. Next, Hernan Reyes and the Rotary Club of Santiago arranged for Kay and Angelo to meet with Chile's minister of health, who approved the mission, and sent an official endorsement.

With the endorsement in hand, actual planning began. SF Rotarian Rosey Wong's travel agency negotiated discounted airfares and excess baggage allowances for the upcoming humanitarian journey. The head of the Chilean Air Force—a Rotarian in Santiago—arranged for flights for the team within the country.

As plans for the first surgical trip proceeded, SF Rotary worked with the Rotary clubs of Los Andes and Santiago on a hospital-equipment program. SF Rotarians obtained donated medical

Kay Clarke

equipment and supplies, and dozens of club members worked on collecting, planning, corresponding, and helping to warehouse and truck the donations to the shipping point. The thirty-five pallets of medical/surgical and computer equipment—9.6 tons—were worth $750,000. Once in Chile, the equipment and supplies were donated through Chilean Rotary clubs to charities, including an indigent children's nutritional center, a nonprofit burn clinic, several public hospitals, and a special school for handicapped children.

Funding for the first surgical trip in January 1993 came from SF Rotary Service donations, grant money, other Rotary clubs, and a matching grant from the RI Foundation. The donated surgeries were worth $500,000. Total donations for the mission, which included volunteer time of the medical staff and the equipment contributed by Bay Area hospitals, exceeded $2.5 million dollars.

Rotaplast's sixteen-day mission began in January 1993, with Angelo Capozzi as chief medical officer. Kay Clarke acted as project leader for the La Serena branch of the trip. She had worked with Interplast and served on its board. Pete Lagarias headed the smaller group to Antofagasta.

The thirty-one-member volunteer team included four plastic surgeons, four anesthesiologists, one pediatrician, eight nurses, one physical therapist, and thirteen nonmedical volunteers. Besides the eight SF Rotarians, two other Rotary clubs in Colorado and California each provided a member of the team. The nonmedical volunteers paid their own airfare, while the medical team members were sponsored with project funds. The team flew first to La Serena, bringing an additional three thousand pounds of equipment and supplies along with their minimal personal baggage.

The Chilean Air Force provided in-country flights from Santiago to La Serena and Antofagasta.

Felipe, a four-month-old. The staff nicknamed him "El Torito."

The first day, the team held open clinics, reviewing the patients who had come from a wide area around the two towns, after learning of the mission from the Chilean press and local television and radio. One village in the south had raised enough money to send a four-year-old child 2,500 miles to the clinic. Pete Lagarias recalls, "We weren't sure when we went down there whether there'd be five kids, or ten, or a hundred or what. Four hundred kids showed up. It was the biggest pandemonium you've ever seen! And before we did the first surgery, they were saying, 'Are you coming back next year?'"

After the preliminary clinic made its evaluation and selections, surgery began. As the doctors and nurses worked, the non-medical volunteers performed their support tasks. The youngest member of the team was Pete and Elaine's adopted daughter, Kelly, age ten. Returning to her country of birth, Kelly helped cheer the young Chilean patients by giving them colorful stickers that Kelly's school had collected. Like Kelly, relatives of Rotarians had pitched in before the mission. Jim Patrick's wife, Jo, collected Spanish-language books and a stuffed animal to give each child in the recovery room after surgery. Along with Kelly and Jo, the other nonmedical team members provided essential administrative, pre-op, and post-op support. They scheduled surgery and patient appointments, managed patients' charts, ran many errands, managed equipment and supplies, assisted pediatrician and surgeons in the pre-op clinic and surgery, carried babies to and from the operating theatre, worked in a supportive and compassionate role with the families in the hospital setting and recovery room, aided therapists in a children's rehabilitation institute, and helped document the mission with video and photography.

Fourteen Chilean Rotary clubs from the Antofagasta, La Serena, Los Andes, and Santiago areas took part. They were supported by fifty Las Damas Rotarias, women in a Rotary-affiliated women's auxiliary organization. Chilean doctors and nurses were part of the medical team, participating and learning. Local Rotarians obtained housing and local transportation for the medical team, and for patients and their families. They publicized the upcoming project with the local health authorities, and assisted the team wherever they were needed. Afterward, the Chilean Rotary clubs agreed to follow up on the patients. Many patients would require orthodontia or speech therapy.

The surgeries were marathon-like. The doctors operated from eight a.m. to eight p.m., without stopping. The team

One of the patients was a four-year-old boy, whose village raised enough money to send him 2,500 miles for the surgery. He was terrified before the operation. When he opened his eyes, the little boy looked at his mother and said, "Mommy, I didn't cry." As Kay Clarke recalled, "He didn't cry, but a whole lot of us did when he said that."

SF Rotarian Charlie Massen shows off the results of the surgery.

performed 159 free reconstructive surgeries on 111 children and young adults, most of them born with cleft lips and palates. They also operated on burns and facial scars. The surgery, hospital stay, and follow-up care were all provided free to the patients.

In an established procedure, the post-op staff erased emotional mothers' concerns by bringing them together with their children immediately after surgery. Nothing matched the experience of Rotaplast volunteers, who saw the parents' faces as their children were brought back to them. The faces and lives of the children were changed and their muffled voices brightened. Mothers who had blamed themselves for their babies' condition had the joy of knowing their children would lead normal lives.

In addition to the satisfaction of participating in the medical mission itself, the visiting Rotarians enjoyed hospitality and fellowship with their Chilean hosts. During the mission, several of the volunteers traveled three-and-a-half hours over a bumpy dirt road to visit a remote Andean village where some of the patients lived. They were greeted by the villagers with songs and a banquet. Members of the Rotaplast-Chile team attended ten different Chilean Rotary club meetings.

One of the project's goals was to record the mission and share the idea with other Rotary clubs. Well-known Bay Area television reporter Bob MacKenzie accompanied the team to Chile, and reported on the mission for two nightly documentary features. After the mission, newspapers and magazines in California and Chile reported on the team's success in prominent articles. For her part in the mission, and her earlier years of humanitarian service, Kay Clarke was awarded RI's prestigious Service Above Self Award in 1993.

After evaluating the mission's results, the SF Rotary board determined that the program would be an excellent international-service project for at least one more year. Under SF Rotary's sponsorship, Rotaplast returned to La Serena, and again in 1995. After the third visit to La Serena, network television reporter Connie Chung reported on Rotaplast in a fifteen-minute segment on CBS's *Eye to Eye*. That publicity, plus a four-page color spread in *The Rotarian*, generated interest in the program from a number of Rotary clubs.

In a few cases, the children's conditions required more surgical intervention than could be performed on-site. In 1995, a Chilean girl named Maribel was brought to the United States for pro-bono surgery by Angelo Capozzi. SF Rotarians housed her

"I felt like Albert Schweitzer," said SF Rotarian Charlie Massen, who traveled to Chile with his wife, Sandra. An architect at home, Charlie cut sutures in the operating room, freeing the surgeons up for more surgeries. Sandra did load after load of laundry at the Laundromat, exchanged money, and ran other errands for the surgeons, so they could concentrate on the task at hand.

family during their visit. Since then, almost a dozen children—which Rotaplast people refer to as "legacy kids"—have been brought to the United States for their surgeries.

By 1995, so many outside individuals and other Rotary clubs supported Rotaplast that two missions were planned for 1996—to Chile and Argentina. This tremendous success and growth in Rotaplast's first three years began to strain SF Rotary's capacity to remain the program's primary supporter. As a result, Rotaplast incorporated as Rotaplast International, Inc., in late 1996. The new nonprofit corporation was separate from SF Rotary. Since then, the club has continued to provide funding to the same extent that it contributes to other nonprofit organizations.

> "Nobody will make jokes about me now, and someday I will find someone who will love me."
>
> —A little girl in Chillan, Chile, 1999

Rotaplast's reorganization as a separate entity proved to be a good move, and the new organization thrived under the leadership of Anita Stangl. By the fifth Rotaplast trip in 1997, forty-seven Rotary clubs in the Bay Area, Oregon, Colorado, New York, and Florida lent their support to the project. Again, missions were sent to Chile and Argentina. That year, Rotaplast added a component for genetic research into cleft palate. SF Rotary funded $10,000 for one year of research for Rotaplast's geneticist, club member Dr. Marie Tolarova. Her hypothesis of a mutant gene in cleft families was verified, a significant development that indicated the need for nutritional education of pregnant mothers at risk. Such a measure could prevent 65 to 85 percent of cleft birth defects.

For his signature project in 2002–03, SF Rotary's incoming president Howard Waits designated a Rotaplast and Rotavision joint trip to China as a celebration of the tenth anniversary of the two successful international programs. SF Rotary's board approved funding for both segments of the joint mission.

Rotaplast has continued under essentially the same model as the initial mission. The teams have become more multidisciplinary, with the inclusion of dentists, orthodontists, and speech therapists. Rotaplast tries to develop good working relationships with the plastic-surgery societies in the visited countries. The missions emphasize training of local surgical professionals, with the aim of developing capabilities for year-round treatment and leaving local medical practices permanently improved after the visit.

Although Rotaplast sends missions by invitation from the distant country's ministry of health and Rotary clubs, Angelo Capozzi explains that in some cases, missions have encountered unforeseen difficulties with local politics. "Each mission has to be flexible," he says, "because we can't control the environment." Angelo also explains that the events of September 11, 2001, changed the logistics of missions con-

> "The thing that makes it all work is the Rotary connections. Because of District Governor Hernan Reyes's connections with Rotary leaders in Chile, the minister of health, and the Chilean Air-Force general, who was a Rotarian, we were able to complete a successful mission. We could never have done it without Rotary working the way it does."
>
> —Rotaplast founder Pete Lagarias

siderably. Boxed surgical supplies have sometimes been confiscated and returned home, and customs delays have increased. Some missions have had to avoid routing through certain localities altogether. Rotaplast tries to work through its connections with Rotarians in airlines, customs, and security organizations to smooth the way. Every mission presents different challenges.

SF Rotary provides substantial support for the Rotaplast organization, and club members continue to give generously of their time, energy, and other resources. Jim Patrick explained to SF Rotarians how one dollar contributed for the Rotaplast and Rotavision projects could be multiplied six times through district and RI matching funds. He immediately solicited $1,700, worth a net of $10,200 after matching. After noisily hammering away at nails for several meetings, Jim's hammer was retired with less than $800 remaining to raise to meet the Rotaplast goal. More recently, when club members were told that for $600 they could change the life of a child, Allan Herzog pledged to match fifteen Rotarians for $100 each. He doubled his gift when thirty Rotarians responded. Pete Lagarias offered his winnings from the club's weekly drawing for matching of donations by club members. SF Rotarian Evelyn Abad presently serves Rotaplast as its volunteer medical-team coordinator and board member, and Pete Lagarias and Angelo Capozzi still serve on Rotaplast's board.

Allan Herzog

Angelo Capozzi continues to work wonders through Rotaplast. He takes time from his position as chief plastic surgeon at Shrine Hospital in Sacramento to go on two or three missions per year. In 1996, Angelo was honored with Rotary International's Service Above Self Award. It is RI's highest award given to individuals.

Rotavision International

Rotavision International is an organization affiliated with SF Rotary's nonprofit Rotary Service, Inc. It is dedicated to improving children's eye health in developing countries by teaching local physicians techniques and providing them with equipment to do pediatric eye surgery. The program's emphasis is on children with strabismus—a condition where the eyes do not align symmetrically ("crossed eyes" or "lazy eye"). Rotavision was developed by ophthalmologist Otis Paul, who has been described as "a man who works quietly, diligently, and resourcefully to have a major impact on eye care in the developing world."

Dr. T. Otis Paul

Otis began making humanitarian trips to developing countries in 1974, during his earlier medical career in the U.S. Navy. The Navy sent doctors to Ethiopia and Egypt between 1974 and 1982, on cataract-surgery trips in conjunction with the International Eye Foundation. After Otis retired from the Navy, he set up his private practice in San Francisco, and began to establish himself as a teacher.

Otis's experience with Rotary began in 1993, when he learned of a trip—sponsored by the Rotary clubs of Alameda and Mount Shasta—to a remote village hospital in Binga, Zimbabwe. A plastic surgery and dental

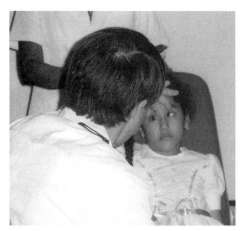

Dr. Otis Paul examines a young girl with strabismus.

team worked to restore the smiles of Zimbabwean wives, whose incisors had been removed to indicate their married status. Otis accompanied the team and performed cataract surgeries on several dozen patients. While he was there, a young missionary doctor—who was not an ophthalmologist by training—convinced Otis to teach him how to do cataract surgery from scratch.

Upon seeing the kind of humanitarian work done by Rotarians, Otis joined SF Rotary soon after his return. He immediately began his first of several trips to Zimbabwe and Nicaragua under Rotary sponsorship. Nonmedical volunteer Rotarians supported him with fund-raising and pretrip preparations, and accompanied him on the missions. SF Rotary funded donations of discounted supplies and surgical equipment, bought with RI and district matching-fund grants.

In 1995, something happened that transformed the nature of Otis's humanitarian work. During a trip to Harare, Zimbabwe, he was approached by a Zimbabwean doctor who suggested that Otis teach local doctors to do his surgical procedures. The same year, Otis was asked by doctors in Nicaragua to teach them pediatric eye surgery. With doctors from opposite sides of the world offering Otis a way to make better use of his time and skills, Otis decided that teaching, not surgery, would be the primary activity on his trips. Since that time, he has instead taught local physicians about the examination, diagnosis, treatment, and surgery of children's eye diseases. Most surgery he does while on humanitarian missions is for demonstration purposes in his teaching work.

When he was challenged to create a mission statement for his work, Otis described his "empowerment" model for a mission as based on three fundamental principles. First, it must utilize appropriate technology, geared to the specific needs of the local population (not just what American doctors might think they need). This principle has been shaped by several experiences, in which Otis found that not all equipment is usable in a specific location. For example, a water-cooled machine does not function in a location where water is purified by filtration through sand. Residual grit soon destroys some components and renders the machine useless. Air-cooled equipment is more appropriate to that location.

Second, the technology must provide empowerment. The local physicians must believe they have learned something they can continue to use, rather than a demonstration of something beyond their capability and that of their staffs. A mission will provide surgeries that improve and restore eyesight to only a few patients. But it will also transfer critical skills and knowledge to the local medical staff, who are then able to successfully complete the same surgical procedures themselves. The country benefits from a multiplication factor, as the local surgeons teach others the same skills. Otis has progressed to establishing residency programs, training local physicians to use appropriate technology, and doing demonstrative surgeries, thereby maximizing his surgical activities.

Third, the effects of the mission must be sustainable, providing a continuity to Rotavision's work. The mission's services must endure through future follow-up trips and with support from local organizations such as Rotary clubs. Otis makes this sustainability possible by repeat visits to the same location for advanced teaching, and through coordination with local Rotary clubs

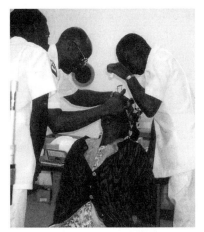

Doctors-in-training during a Rotavision mission.

for donations of greatly discounted surgical instruments and medical supplies. Physicians often lack the up-to-date equipment necessary to continue when he departs, unless he brings a full set of tools with him and leaves it in the place he visits. Anesthesia machines and eye-clinic equipment necessary for Otis's high-tech surgical procedures also do not leave the country at the end of the mission. Instead, they are donated to the local Rotary clubs, who "perpetually loan" them to doctors and hospitals.

These three principles—Appropriateness, Empowerment, and Sustainability—avoid the long-term negative effects of coming into a community as "heroes," doing the job, and disappearing just as quickly. An example of Otis's Empowerment model can be seen in what he has done in his Vietnam work. On Otis's first Vietnamese trip in 1997, Dr. Xuan Hong, a local physician, had never done any strabismus surgery. Otis taught her the basic surgical techniques that gave her the skills to do the most common forms of correction. He has returned three times, and has progressively taught her more complicated forms of "crossed eye" surgery, such as those seen after a stroke or head trauma. Dr. Hong now personally performs between five and six hundred surgeries annually and has taught these techniques to several other local ophthalmologists.

Within a few years of beginning with Rotary, Otis formalized the missions in an organization subsidiary to SF Rotary Service Inc., taking the name Rotavision International. Rotavision operates with funds raised by SF Rotary, plus matching district and RI grants.

In 2004, Dr. August Reader III joined Rotavision after traveling to Russia with Otis. August specializes in neuroophthalmology, in which neurological disease causes eye-alignment problems similar to those of genetic origin usually seen in children's strabismus. Thus, although August's surgical procedures are similar to those performed by Otis, August primarily

CURTIS BURR ON ROTAVISION'S COMMITMENT

"Otis Paul has gone back several times, and every time he goes back, the level of competence is higher and higher. The first time we went, he was doing basic teaching, and almost all of the surgeries. And the doctors were watching them, learning. Now their quality is so good, Dr. Paul just goes back and does the really unique ones. So it's been a very transformative process any place he goes. The goal is to help them elevate their skills, so it's not like just going in and doing something and leaving."

—Past President Curtis Burr

*Dr. August L.
Reader III*

focuses on adults rather than children. August had traveled in the 1980s with the International Eye Foundation on humanitarian trips overseas. Rotavision has given August the opportunity and framework in which to resume his humanitarian work. He is active on the Rotavision board, and is soon to become its medical director.

Each year, Otis and August take extensive time from their busy private practices for several Rotavision missions, and they plan to make more as retirement approaches. In 2006–07 alone, there were nine missions to countries in South and Central America, South and Southeast Asia, and Africa. Over 250 surgeries were demonstrated to more than twenty ophthalmologists. The doctors were accompanied on each mission by a number of Rotarians. Several, including Lisa Moscaret-Burr, Curtis Burr, Eric Schmautz, and Jean Schore, have found these missions so rewarding they have returned more than once.

Because Rotavision's activities consist primarily of teaching rather than extensive surgery sessions, Rotavision missions do not need the numbers of nonmedical support volunteers required by Rotaplast. Nevertheless, there is much to do. Cecile Chiquette is among the Rotary volunteers who prepare grant requests, and make predeparture plans and arrangements with the distant Rotary clubs. Other volunteers work on fund-raising activities and locating specific needed equipment. The volunteers who accompany the mission do much to smooth the way for the doctors' activities, such as setting up lecture rooms and working with the local press. They assist during the prescreening clinic by organizing the flow of examinations and comforting the frightened children. After surgery, they return the children to their parents and give each child a stuffed animal wearing a Rotavision T-shirt.

"I find it to be the most pleasant way for me to travel, as I get to see unusual places and work with colleagues and local businesspeople, rather than the tourist industry. I am shown parts of the country and culture that are not normally available when traveling as a tourist."

—Dr. Otis Paul

Rotavision works in the designated distant location with local Rotarians, who organize the visit and make arrangements for lectures and services. Otis enjoys working with the local Rotarians as businesspeople, because it affords him an escape from medicine and an insight into the local business world.

In addition to volunteer help, Rotavision relies on support from many sources. Much of the funding for the missions and equipment comes from SF Rotary and through matching RI and district grants. Rotavision receives significant discounts on first-rate new and rehabilitated medical equipment. Individual Rotarians have donated medical machines as well. Other funding comes through Rotarians' ideas and efforts. Jean Schore raised money from her Lithuanian relatives for a mission to Lithuania. While abroad, the traveling volunteers stuff their suitcases with local goods. These are brought back and sold at SF Rotary's annual Holiday Luncheon, to raise funds for Rotavision. Cashing in on the wild popularity of poker, August Reader has run an annual Rotavision "Texas Hold 'Em" Poker Tournament each year since 2004. Hosted by Steve Talmadge, the tournament raises several thousand dollars for Rotavision, and provides Rotarians with an evening of fun and fellowship. In 2007, the Jack Graf Memorial Rotavision Fund was established in memory of

Lester "Jack" Graf. At SF Rotary's Rotavision luncheon program, eight pecan pies (baked according to Jack's famous recipe) were raffled off, raising $1,000 for the Ghana mission.

Rotavision activities are not limited to SF Rotary. Rotavision receives substantial help from San Francisco's Greater Mission Rotary Club, which organizes and sponsors some missions.

In 2002, Otis joined with Rotaplast International in a dual-purpose trip to China. His teaching protocol was very different from Rotaplast's surgery orientation, in which a large team is normally involved. Nonetheless, he saw over sixty patients the first day. The second and third days, he operated on thirteen patients, and he lectured the last day. The techniques he taught and the instruments he donated would allow the local Chinese doctor to perform operations far more quickly than before. It would allow her to help more children, and would improve her status in the hospital.

Since 2002, Rotavision has partnered with Orbis, a twenty-five-year-old nonprofit humanitarian organization dedicated to blindness prevention and treatment in developing countries. The partnership is based on the two organizations' compatible mission statements and non-competing funding bases. Otis and August have made several joint trips with Orbis on missions to Bangladesh, Nepal, China, and India, with partial funding by Orbis. Otis was honored in Siddhartha-Nagar, Nepal, by being asked to cut the ribbon to open the Orbis-established Lumbini Eye Hospital for children.

Rotavision is not without its problems in a complex world. Rotavision doctors must make it a point to work with local physicians in a way that avoids any misperception of Rotavision's work as competitive. A second area of concern—wealthy patients crowding out the indigent—is avoided by having all patient screening done by the local doctors. Rotavision also ensures that the equipment donated—often rehabilitated used equipment—is clearly up-to-date, and not misperceived as outmoded castoffs from America. Otis explains that Rotavision is not always able to surmount local politics, and local doctors have been stigmatized after a Rotary trip—even to the point of a doctor who lost operating-room privileges in Zimbabwe. More than a decade after the USSR dissolved, Otis lamented to a Rotary audience that some of the old Communist-style politics remained in Lithuania. When a Lithuanian anesthesiologist lost his job because he wanted to help children instead of adults, Rotavision intervened. SF Rotarians donated an anesthesia machine for eye surgery, and sent it under the condition that it had to be operated by the professional who had lost his job. The maneuver worked, and the anesthesiologist regained his position. Otis says, "This was an example of Rotavision overcoming local resistance to help children get the eye care they need."

In 2000, Otis became one of the rare SF Rotarians whose self-imposed fine at luncheon was refused. In recognition of Otis's extensive humanitarian service, President Kathy Beavers declared that "his money is no good in this town."

Otis has won the San Francisco mayor's Humanitarian Service Award, and District 5150's Distinguished Individual Service Award. He is enormously respected in Rotary. Of him, SF Rotary Past President Curtis Burr said, "He is one of the finest, most humble people I have ever met. He continually goes out of his way to make things better for individuals specifically, and mankind in general."

Alliance for Smiles

Alliance for Smiles is the third major hands-on international organization created by SF Rotarians that assists indigent children in developing nations. It is an international-service organization dedicated to the treatment of cleft-lip and palate anomalies in underserved areas of China. The organization provides surgery, and fosters long-term care by establishing permanent treatment centers. It also works to provide education and research into treatment and prevention.

John Goings

Alliance for Smiles (AFS) was conceived and formed by five SF Rotarians—Jim Deitz, John Goings, Jim Patrick, Anita Stangl, and John Uth. Each had over ten years of Rotaplast experience; Jim Deitz, Anita Stangl, and John Uth each had served multiple years as Rotaplast mission directors. John Goings had been awarded the RI Humanitarian Award for his Rotaplast work.

These Rotarians envisioned an organization similar to Rotaplast, but with an important difference: a sustained concentration on a single country would enable the organization to build up a broad alliance with other humanitarian organizations. Working in concert with others would enable the alliance to create a long-term presence in the country, with the objective of permanently raising the quality of medical care.

In September 2004, the five Rotarians separated from Rotaplast International and formed Alliance for Smiles. Having visited China as directors of an earlier Rotaplast trip, John and Anita realized this country was ideal for Alliance to establish a long-term presence. China has an enormous number of cleft-lip and palate cases. Approximately 1 in 350 children born in China are afflicted, and to correct the anomaly costs roughly half of the average rural family's yearly income. Moreover, Anita and John had identified a suitable Chinese partner for a long-term China project. The China Population Welfare Foundation would arrange logistics with mission sites, find and house the children, and negotiate with customs and the government to smooth the way for Alliance missions.

*Anita T. Stangl,
SF Rotary President
2006–07*

Alliance's first operational trip was to Jiujiang in May 2005. John Uth served as mission director. While there, Alliance undertook its two-part mission. First, it brought help to Chinese children through cleft-lip and palate surgeries. Second, Alliance began exploring the possibility of establishing a permanent treatment center with the Jiujiang University Hospital. Back in San Francisco, Alliance formed a partnership with the director of the prestigious Craniofacial Treatment Center at the UC Medical Center. The director provided a four-month training course for Dr. Huang Xiaolin from Jiujiang, and Jim Deitz funded Dr. Huang's stay in San Francisco. Dr. Huang learned the team approach to a comprehensive methodology for cleft cases, and was able to take his knowledge back to his hospital in China.

In April 2007—only two-and-a-half years after its founding—Alliance for Smiles realized its founders' ambition, and opened its first permanent craniofacial treatment center, at the Jiujiang University Hospital. Partial funding for the center was provided by SF Rotary and the SFR Foundation.

The center will provide the necessary long-term treatment for children following surgery. Services will include dental treatment, speech therapy, psychological counseling, and parental counseling. Having successfully established Dr. Huang's hospital as a permanent center, Alliance will send small specialized teams two or three times a year, subsidize the cost for procedures, and cover the cost of patient travel from their rural homes to the center. The center's successful opening has provided the model for Alliance's creation of future permanent centers elsewhere in China. Since its initial trip, Alliance has returned to Jiujiang, and has also sent missions to Shenyang, Shantou, Harbin, and Huangshi.

Besides sending surgical missions and working to establish craniofacial treatment centers in China, Alliance will act as a long-term foundation. Its objective will be to raise funds for advanced training for Chinese medical professionals in the cleft-lip and palate field, and for ongoing research toward improving care and decreasing the incidence of cleft-lip or palate.

Like Rotaplast and Rotavision, Alliance for Smiles relies on volunteers. Each mission team consists of approximately twenty-five medical personnel—reconstructive plastic surgeons, anesthesiologists, pediatricians, dentists, nurses, and dental hygienists. They are accompanied by ten to twelve nonmedical volunteers, who act as mission director, logistical coordinators, quartermasters, translators, and assistants in the hospital. During a mission, 80 to 120 children receive surgery. The AFS team works side-by-side with local medical practitioners to exchange ideas on proper medical techniques and procedures, as well as to provide follow-up care.

True to its name, Alliance for Smiles has formed an impressive array of partnerships. Alliance's Chinese partners include the Jiujiang University

Volunteer Dr. Richard Siegal takes a child into the operating room during an Alliance for Smiles mission to Shenyang, China. Photo by Dave Fowler; Courtesy of Alliance for Smiles

"A seventy-two-year-old man with a classically chiseled face and a high fur-lined hat was waiting anxiously outside the recovery-room door. When he was allowed to come in, he beamed widely and gave the recovery-room staff two thumbs up. Then he wrapped his six-year-old grandson in his arms and soothed him as the boy revived comfortably. The man explained that he looked after his grandson every day because the boy's parents were working hundreds of miles away. I hope I never forget that grandfather's love and devotion."

—First-time Alliance volunteer Bob Warick

Hospital, the site of the first treatment center. The China Population Welfare Foundation will continue its logistical work, and the Red Cross will perform the same functions in other cities. The Craniofacial Treatment Center at the UC Medical Center in San Francisco will train Chinese doctors for future treatment centers. The Smile Train, another American humanitarian cleft-palate organization, provides grant funding for some AFS missions. AFS also relies on a number of individual donors for financial support.

A happy Chinese father and his child after cleft-palate surgery performed by Alliance for Smiles volunteers. Courtesy of Alliance for Smiles

Alliance for Smiles' primary relationship, however, is with Rotary and Rotarians. Although it is an independent organization and not an official RI project, AFS partners with Rotary clubs and districts. Alongside the Rotary Club of San Francisco and the Rotary Club of Wanchai in Hong Kong, AFS counts the Rotary Club of Chicago among its founders. The Chicago club and Chicago districts 6440 and 6450 have provided significant support to AFS. Nonmedical project directors must be Rotarians. AFS actively promotes Rotary while at a mission site. The mission's Rotarian volunteers are encouraged to seek additional ways to make an impact on the community through other Rotary-based service projects, such as eye care, orphanages, and educational projects. In San Francisco, Rotarians do their part, often raising money to help support Alliance missions. When Allan Herzog won $2,000 at the club's annual auction fund-raiser, he added $100 and proposed to give it in even parts to Rotavision, Rotaplast, and Alliance for Smiles, if it could be matched from the floor. He ended up leveraging his $2,100 to $6,000. Rotaract members help as well. They have sewn and presented blankets for the small Chinese patients.

Most importantly, Alliance for Smiles' philosophical base is the Rotary principle of "Service Above Self" as the path to international understanding and goodwill. This principle provides

Sheriff Jim Patrick arrests wanted criminal John Uth at an Alliance for Smiles fund-raiser.

a way for Rotarians to be involved in a hands-on World Community Service project, and a means of advancing Rotary's good work in the world.

The many humanitarian missions sent by Rotaplast, Rotavision, and Alliance for Smiles are the product of a special kind of vision. SF Rotarians used their medical skills and organizing talents to imagine and create lasting programs that will continue bringing a better life to less-fortunate children all over the world. Such programs are a demonstration of the power of Rotary, where an individual's idea can grow into an international force for good.

Taken in its entirety, SF Rotary's century of welcoming thousands of foreign visitors, sending ambassadors of goodwill, collaborating and cooperating with Rotary clubs around the world, providing wartime and emergency relief, protecting millions of children against the ravages of polio, and participating in uncounted other humanitarian projects is nothing short of remarkable.

"Alliance for Smiles will strive to give Rotary a 'face' in the world…. It is the goal of AFS to give an identity to the work of Rotarians in the world community so that when areas served look at the work of AFS, they will see Rotary at work."

—Alliance for Smiles

chapter seven

Always Taking Part:
100 Years of Women and Rotary

We went on record to allow women members. We were turned down by the International. . . . But women take part in all our programs.

—Bill Ecker, SF Rotary Executive Vice President, to *San Francisco Examiner*, November 9, 1983

When the eighteen members of the little Duarte Rotary Club near Los Angeles voted unanimously in 1977 to admit three women to full membership in their club, they knowingly violated the long-standing membership provision of the Rotary International constitution and bylaws. At their district governor's instruction, they recorded the new members using initials rather than first names. The ruse failed; RI dignitaries visiting the club's twenty-fifth-anniversary celebration later that year observed the women members, and notified the club to terminate the women's memberships. The club refused and RI revoked the club's charter, sparking a decade-long battle that ended only in 1987, when the U.S. Supreme Court ruled in favor of the Duarte club and its women Rotarians. The court's ruling transformed the landscape for men's clubs, for the men who belonged to them, and for the women who had remained outside.

Unlike most Rotary clubs, SF Rotary did not wait for the high court's 1987 decision. It admitted its first four women members in 1986. And as Bill Ecker's account to the *Examiner* three years earlier indicates, the change had been coming for some time. Most club officials and influential members understood that the club changes as society changes, and that the future admission of women was almost certain. Most regarded it as positive and beneficial. In admitting women, SF Rotary took a bold new direction after its seventy-eight-year tradition as a men-only club. SF Rotary was near the leading edge of a profound change that is still coming to fruition for Rotary worldwide.

Women in our era are very much a part of Rotary, just as they are in the mainstream of the American world of business, politics, and other cultural institutions long closed to them. But the story is not a new one. In hindsight, there truly is a century-long history of women and Rotary. In one way or another, women took part in various aspects of club life all along, despite their limited appearances in early club records. Their changing relationships to the club, and their long-awaited entry into it, have always been part of Rotary's story.

A Woman's Place

If a woman of 1908 had applied for membership to SF Rotary, she would have been promptly turned down. However, one of the club's earliest records—the club's constitution—did not actually exclude women. SF Rotary's first constitution adopted at its inception in 1908 was formulated without reference to gender or age, requiring only that a member be

> any person who is engaged as proprietor, partner, corporate officer, agent or manager in full charge in any legitimate business or professional undertaking in the City of San Francisco.

The qualification "any person" was unchanged through several amendments, at least through the constitution as of 1912. An amended constitution in 1914 states the membership qualification as "any adult, male person who is engaged as proprietor . . . "[50]

The changes in the constitution's language should not suggest that the issue of membership gender was ever in question at the club's beginnings, however. The Chicago club's founder Paul Harris invited only businessmen, and its first constitution and bylaws listed only members' business promotion and social fellowship as the club's objects. Homer Wood stated the same purpose for the new San Francisco club in his address to the initial meeting in November 1908:

> Composed as it is of one man from each line of business, it is safe to say that a more harmonious set of men could never be banded together. . . . A large acquaintanceship is a very valuable asset, the same as is a college education worth more than you can pay for it. And so to any man actively engaged in business, he has a very valuable asset when he knows a large number of influential men in other lines of trade.

These club limitations and purpose are entirely in keeping with turn-of-the-century gender roles. Very much a part of that era, the business-oriented Rotary Club of 1908 was, by its definition, a man's club. The businesswoman as we know her today was relatively uncommon, and the majority consensus dictated that the public arena of business was no place for a respectable woman. Some women—by choice or by financial necessity—moved into nursing, teaching, or the growing "pink collar" ranks of secretaries. But for the most part, the woman was expected to marry, and her proper domain was the home. If a wife chose other activities outside the home, it was to participate in cultural activities and groups that discussed subjects deemed suitable for proper women—literature, education, support of the local arts, and similar interests. In the turn-of-the-century Progressive era, many women also directed their efforts toward social improvement and civic reform, in the fast-growing cities that were rife with social ills.

---

50. The reason for SF Rotary's change to its bylaws is unclear. There are only a few known early cases where the issue of women's membership was raised. In 1912, for example, the Belfast, Ireland, club voted against admitting women. In 1916, the Dublin club asked RI for an opinion. RI's ruling was "unadvisable."

Grindings *advertisement for Rotarians' wives.* —Grindings, *October 26, 1915*

In this respect, women's voluntary interests were not entirely distinct from those of their civic-minded husbands at Rotary, but they were expected to pursue these separately and within the strict boundaries of ladies' etiquette and their lack of voting privileges. Just as business was not a part of the respectable woman's world, neither was the arena of civic betterment if it involved leadership and political office. Since the founding of the republic, politics was a male realm until women were granted the right to vote.[51] Without the vote, women's ability to effect civic change by improving government was limited to persuasion and grassroots activism. A number of middle-class women directed their efforts into women's suffrage rights, but the notion of women disowning the qualities of femininity to achieve political equality was uncomfortable for many women, as it was for most men.

This mainstream view of the proper and separate roles for men and women persisted until well into the second half of the twentieth century. It was not just the outlook of early Rotarians, but of American society in general, including a majority of women. The stories of women in the history of the Chicago and SF Rotary clubs are no different than the social history of middle-class women and men in America. The content of *Grindings* matched that of newspapers and magazines, in its articles and advertisements that credited women as the center and "heart" of the home.

Perhaps a good example of early SF Rotarians' (and society's) outlook on women can be seen in a 1921 announcement of the club's efforts to rid the city of salacious movies and reading matter. At an elaborate luncheon meeting program, in which three reports about the sorry state of the press, movies, and literature were presented, the club placed itself on record as "in favor of a clean, sane policy" for the reading and viewing material of San Franciscans. The luncheon program included a live tableau, depicting "the ideal woman, guarded and honored." The program's chairman told the assembled club members, "Socially we have had much to disturb us since the war, but we expect the year 1921 to usher in a new state of chivalry in which woman will be found standing forth resplendent in the fact of the dawn, honored and protected by American manhood."

---

51. California granted women the right to vote in state and local elections in 1911, nine years before the Nineteenth Amendment was ratified in 1920.

History today celebrates women who defied tradition and challenged limitations placed on their gender—such as Anna Bissell and Caroline Burnam Taylor in the world of business, Jane Addams and Margaret Sanger who labored to improve social conditions, and Susan B. Anthony and Elizabeth Cady Stanton in their campaign for suffrage. But crossing into that male world of leadership in business, civic, and political affairs was a tricky proposition, and most middle-class women didn't cross into it very far, if at all. The early-twentieth-century social norms governing male and female roles were more complex and varied than a simple rule of women at home or in charity work, in contrast to men in business and politics. But in the general sense, that rule was true for women throughout the first half of the twentieth century.

Thus the story of the majority of women in the early Rotary story is the story of the wife. Her part in the story was consistent with the roles and behavior appropriate to the wife (or wife-to-be) in the public lives of men of a certain status in this early San Francisco society. Her relationship to her husband's club was generally as a representative of the Rotarian's family life. The public roles for a Rotarian's wife were as a supportive social companion and in the helpful volunteer work suited to her feminine characteristics.

The Wife as Social Companion

The wife's role of social companion in her husband's public life has persisted throughout the century, changing as social customs have changed. Accordingly, the early Rotarian's wife (or the single member's respectable lady friend) accompanied her husband to certain functions. Rotary's rapid growth created a number of occasions for travel to other club locations, and events soon took members and their wives far out of town.

From Rotary's beginning, ladies were present at all the large gatherings. A number of the sixty members who attended the National Association's formative meeting in Chicago in 1910 were accompanied by their wives. Some wives attended the earliest district conferences. Distance (and expense) may have limited SF Rotary wives' attendance, however. But wives were always welcome at these events. After the chartered train to the 1914 Houston RI Convention returned home, *Grindings* reported that Ann Brunnier and a Los Angeles Rotarian's wife—the only women among the traveling group of ninety Rotarians—"were the angels of the crowd and will long be remembered by every member of the Pacific Coast Delegation."

Interesting women's activities became an essential part of conference planning. Visiting women to early

JEAN HARRIS REMEMBERS

Paul Harris's wife, Jean, accompanied him to California on their first Rotary trip together after they were married in 1910. She recalled her worries:

"How would the ladies of these Rotarians receive me?…But when such wonderful hosts as Harvey and Edna Johnson of Los Angeles took us to clubs up and down the coast and on all manner of sightseeing excursions, and when we found ourselves talking with wholly new acquaintances as if they were lifelong friends, I was seeing in a new way what a wonderfully friendly thing this was our men had started."

conventions were "gathered up," taken for auto rides, and treated to fashion shows, all-day shopping events, museum visits, and a shower of gifts. They were welcome at regular sessions at the RI conventions—and they attended, as can be seen in photographs of "Rotarians and their ladies" at the enormous opening meetings. A Ladies' Attendance Trophy was awarded to SF Rotary at the 1921 RI Convention in Edinburgh, after nine wives journeyed from San Francisco for a combined distance of nearly sixty thousand miles. Plans for the San Francisco RI Convention in 1947 stipulated that not less than three ladies' "retiring rooms" be furnished and staffed with maids to attend to the women. A doctor and nurse were to be on call for the ladies as well. During an era that emphasized middle-class respectability and expectations about the family lives of such men, the presence of women accompanying their husbands on out-of-town trips offered the opportunity for members to travel with their wives, to enjoy social events such as dinner and dancing, and to see themselves and fellow Rotarians as upstanding family men.

Closer to home, men's clubs often furnished the occasion for the wives of members to enter their husbands' club as honored guests at certain functions. These were frequently events of considerable significance in the annual social calendar. At the time of SF Rotary's founding, the occasional presence of wives as social companions was customary in the fellowship purpose of many men's clubs, such as the Brotherhood of Elks and the prestigious Bohemian Club.

The Rotary Club of Chicago held a "Ladies' Night" as early as 1908, and SF Rotary soon adopted the custom. In his semiannual report to the National Association in 1911, SF Rotary Secretary Rusty Rogers reported that for social affairs, "We have a blow-out once in every 3 or 4 months and about 2 ladies' nights per year." One such early event was the Ladies' Night Jinks in April 1910, a Wednesday evening dinner at the St. Francis Hotel. The elegant menu was tailored to a lady's sensibility, featuring extras that included Dainty Chips, High Teas, and Spiced Gum Drops. The formal menu did not, however, neglect the men's primary interest—business. It listed the members' firms that supplied the delicacies, table settings, gifts, and other offerings at the festivities.

Events such as these were largely honorary—to pay tribute to these women as Rotarian wives. SF Rotary established a tradition of annual events to welcome women on certain special

"Ladies' Night" at the St. Francis Hotel, 1910.

occasions. Most took place during the Tuesday luncheon hour, but some were held as dinners or Saturday luncheons. Beginning around 1915, the club started one of its most long-standing traditions, the annual gala Christmas party for ladies. It was the social highlight of the club year. A typical announcement promised "A Good Lunch, Beautiful Ladies, Clever Entertainment, Dozens of Prizes." In a custom apropos to an organization composed of business representatives, wives were presented with "splendidly equipped" baskets of gifts provided by members from various retail establishments. In time, the party came to be held at the elegant Palace Hotel Garden Court. The festivities included music and Christmas caroling. For many years beginning in the 1930s, local radio station KGO broadcasted the musical programs from the party, and the club sponsored a wartime broadcast in 1943 "over short wave to the entire world." Until mid-century, the Ladies' Christmas Luncheons were not the only holiday luncheon festivities. The week following the Ladies' Luncheon was a Christmas meeting for the men (although not as elegant), and a year-end day dedicated to boys.

SF Rotary also fêted women with a special Tuesday luncheon or dinner in May or June. As the club grew, these became significant events in the club's annual social life. For a Ladies' Luncheon on a Saturday in May 1913, members were encouraged to invite "two or more" ladies, and it was predicted to be "the big day of the year—300 are expected." Early dinners included the "May Mélange" dinner "for Rotarians, Rotarianettes, and friends."[52]

Gradually, the May event became an opportunity for Rotarians to introduce and praise the mothers in their lives. The widespread American movement to create a national day dedicated to mothers, living and deceased, emphasized the role of women in the home. The Mother's Day movement in the United States was only one year older than SF Rotary, and President Woodrow Wilson signed a proclamation in 1914 establishing Mother's Day as an official May holiday. Wives of members of SF Rotary and other clubs were credited with helping to make Mother's Day a national success. Although not as lavish as the Christmas luncheons, the SF Rotary Mother's Day events were quite sentimental, as was becoming the custom across America. A speaker at one Mothers' Day Luncheon described mothers as "the true Rotarians" of the world. Not surprisingly, Mother's Day commemorations at Rotary were particularly important at wartime, with poignant tributes such as those at the Mother's Day Luncheon following the World War I Armistice. Declaring that "every mother belongs to every man," a Red Cross nurse spoke to her appreciative luncheon audience of the heroic sacrifices and the "fortitude, unfailing devotion, and influence" of wartime mothers all over the world, who

ELABORATE PRIZES FOR THE LADIES
In addition to the usual lavish baskets of gifts, women attendees won over one hundred member-donated prizes, ranging from note-paper and soap to such items as six squab, a four-hour automobile "joy ride," a baseball season ticket, a wedding cake, a suckling pig, and an installation of wire-drawn tungsten lamps in a house of ten rooms or less.

—*Grindings*, May 27, 1913

---

52. Affairs such as these formed a long-standing tradition in much of Rotary's world. The commemorative book of RI's golden anniversary in 1955 features several historical pictures of "Ladies' Day luncheons" in countries all over the world.

prayed that their sons "be given strength and courage to do their duty." She also attributed the spirit of motherhood to officers who tended to wounded soldiers in their mothers' absence.

HER DAD

Beside his boy he swells with pride;

But put a daughter by his side,

And ere his lunch he will digest—

There'll be no buttons on his vest.

—*Grindings*, April 12, 1938

Another tradition that emerged at SF Rotary as a festivity for members' favorite females was the annual April "Daughter's Day." Club members showed off their cherished darlings, as fathers did everywhere. After one luncheon, a *Grindings* review assured readers that "smiles on members were just a bit broader than usual; and so they should be, for they had their daughter on review."

Some of the men's "fun" functions included women as well. In addition to festivities specifically intended for them, wives accompanied their husbands on other local outings, such as picnics and sports events. Only a few years after SF Rotary's big annual sports carnival at Del Monte was instituted in the 1920s, *Grindings* reported that the event "is the only sports outing at which our Rotary ladies participate—in fact, they dominate." Women competed for special prizes in several games, including golf, dice, and bridge. But wives were not invited to all of SF Rotary's party events, such as the 1950s annual stag dinners and entertainment to honor the club president.

·Over time, these club events reflected changes in social customs in several ways. Instead of instructing members to "tell the little woman," a *Grindings* cover in the 1970s announced "women welcome." The Christmas Luncheon became the more inclusive Holiday Luncheon in 1995. One constant for most of the century, however, was the luncheon's long-standing designation—official or not—as the annual "Ladies' Day," on which wives were not only accepted, but acclaimed as the honored guests. Club life was an indicator of status in the middle-class family, and members were encouraged to invite not only their wives and daughters, but their wives' friends and sisters as well. Rotary members took pride in their club, and these luncheons and dinners were a way to show off their club life to their families. As the luncheon announcement that "each Rotarian will bring the most beautiful lady Rotarian with him" indicates, the occasions were also a way for them to show off their charming wives and daughters to the club. Moreover, they were intended to show club members as good family men; the presence of his wife lent a moral dimension to a man's character, certifying him as a man to be trusted.

Ladies' Auxiliaries

In many cases, Rotarians' wives were not content to attend occasional Ladies' Day Luncheons and ceremonies at inter-city gatherings and conventions. They looked for greater participation and a sense of belonging.

Women already enjoyed a wide range of clubs. During the week of SF Rotary's founding meeting in 1908, San Francisco saw meetings of the Local Council of Women, the Outdoor Art League, the Equal Suffrage League, the Cap and Bella, the Clionian Club, the Council of Jewish Women, the Forum Club, the Pioneer Mothers Statue Committee, the Corona Club, the Laurel Hall Club, and the Papyrus Club. Most such women's clubs reflected three general interests: culture, charity, and civic service. By 1910 almost one million American women were members of clubs in a consolidation known as the General Federation of Women's Clubs. These clubs pursued an enormous number of objectives, engaging in all forms of charitable work, social reforms such as ending child labor, and work toward the goal of women's suffrage.

For some, however, these clubs lacked the unique appeal of Rotary. As they became aware of the strength of the Rotary ideal and the fellowship aspects of the club, many women wished to take part somehow—to enjoy Rotary's supportive friendship and community service that their men found in their weekly club meetings and civic activities.

In a very few cases, women tried to create affiliated versions of the club itself. Not surprisingly, the concept also held strong appeal for women in business. In 1911, the Minneapolis Women's Rotary Club advertised itself as "composed of business women, one woman from each line of business. . . . The object of the club is to promote sociability among the business women and to work for business advantages." The following year, a woman addressed the 1912 Rotary Convention about the Women's Rotary Club of Duluth. Although she asked for support in establishing similar clubs in other cities, the 598 convention delegates ignored her request.[53]

The Dangers of Clubism

In 1905, the *Ladies' Home Journal*, a champion of the principle of women's domestic role, ran a controversial opinion piece by former President Grover Cleveland. He warned of women's clubs as "harmful in a way that directly menaces the integrity of our homes and the benign disposition and character of our wifehood and motherhood." Cleveland worried that "the saving womanly traits that distinguish us above other nations" was in peril. Although his underlying concern was the threat of women's suffrage, the danger lay in "clubism," and the woman's attraction "to be and to do something not within the sphere of her appointed ministrations." He cautioned that "membership in one such organization is apt to create a club habit," and that "the best and safest club for a woman to patronize is her home." Much of American society took Cleveland's dire warning to heart.

—Grover Cleveland, in "Women's Mission and Women's Clubs," *Ladies Home Journal*, May 1905

Apart from a very few short-lived women's Rotary clubs that stressed a business purpose, however, wives of Rotarians sought various ways to become part of the life of the men's club itself. For some, that meant joining right in by attending club meetings. One of the first known instances of women regularly attending Rotary meetings is that of the Belfast club, founded in 1911. The club's history recounts that it was the early custom for members to bring their ladies to a monthly meeting. Within a year, however, members discussed the issue of women's participation, and decided it was undesirable to elect ladies to membership or have them at weekly luncheons.

Women's presence at SF Rotary's weekly meetings appears to have been the exception for its first several decades. Despite the occasional appearance by invitation, nothing suggests that women attended regular luncheon meetings, although they might have welcomed the idea. Unable to join

---

53. Denied access to the emerging men's business/service clubs such as Rotary, Lions, and Kiwanis, many women turned to similar women's service clubs—organized along the lines of the men's clubs—such as the National Association of Altrusa Clubs (formed in Indianapolis in 1918), Zonta International (Buffalo, 1919), and Soroptomist International (Oakland, 1921).

Ladies at the Luncheon

In 1914, *Grindings* announced that, due to low expected attendance in June because of vacations and the distant RI convention, a regular luncheon meeting at Techau Tavern would be opened up to "the feminine touch, the female heart, the slender form, the maiden's glance, the bewitching smile, the love-lit eye, the wavy tress, the 'created' dress, the velvet voice, and all the other virtues and wiles that make our wives, sweethearts, mothers, sisters and daughters. . . . Every man is entitled to bring one lady to lunch with him." The following week, *Grindings* reported that the ladies "joined in our Roll Call and had a very enjoyable time. They voted to be allowed to come often."

Rotary or to participate in its weekly meetings, Rotarians' wives turned to activities that were not only acceptable, but advantageous for their husbands. They extended their wifely roles as helpmates into Rotary activities.

One way was to participate in Rotary's emerging service role. Just as women played a major part in charitable work in American society, the same was true of Rotary's early division of labor in community service. In preparation for the annual Christmas charity giveaway, SF Rotary's Ways & Means Committee looked to "the services of Lady Rotarians who can drive automobiles, to help investigate each and every case" of destitute children unable to attend school because they lacked shoes and stockings. A subsequent committee reported that "Rotarianettes" had given up a great deal of their time locating and investigating 216 deserving families in need of assistance. The committee attributed this to the "sympathetic understanding" inherent in the "gentler sex." Responsibilities such as these suited charity-minded women, and they participated in many such activities.

Another way for women to engage in their husbands' Rotary lives was by assisting in club functions. Rotarians' wives worked tirelessly behind the scenes from the earliest years, helping to ensure the success of club events. They planned luncheon festivities, staffed reception tables, hosted parties for their husbands' club friends, and organized ancillary functions.

Hospitality to visiting Rotarians was usually left in the capable hands of the lady of the house, and she was often able to enjoy the company of the accompanying wives. From the beginning, when women traveled with their Rotarian husbands to distant conventions and conferences, wives in the hosting cities took responsibility for the entertainment of the visiting spouses. Groups of Rotary women gave elaborate teas for wives of out-of-town Rotary dignitaries.

Women continued serving in Rotary as community volunteers and providing support for club functions through the decades.

Registering for the 1943 RI Convention.

A telling indicator of the extent to which women filled a designated role as the Rotarian's helpmate over the years is the case of district governor training at the International Assembly. While governors-elect attended training sessions, their wives were instructed on their own roles, with special sessions to teach them how best to help the district governor fulfill his duties.

From their very early efforts to take part in their husbands' clubs, many Rotarians' wives began to view the possibility of extending this participation to their lives as club women. They formed themselves into auxiliary groups, to support their husbands' clubs as charity volunteers and assistants in club functions, and to enjoy socializing with women like themselves.

The issue of women's auxiliary clubs in Rotary was disputed from the start. The topic was addressed in 1910, at Rotary's first national convention in Chicago. The president of the Los Angeles club emphatically objected to the notion of a ladies' auxiliary, then or in the future. He was seconded by a Rotarian from Kansas City. (The following day, three Chicago newspapers poked fun at the Rotary men's view of women as "unmanageable.")

Not all Rotary men were critical of the idea. Some local clubs, such as San Francisco, thought the auxiliary might prove to be a beneficial resource for the club. When the club investigated poor families, a number of the ladies thought the Rotary Club should appoint a ladies' auxiliary to carry on the splendid work done by the club on Thanksgiving and Christmas. The *Grindings* editor suggested that "our ladies, owing to their knowledge and experience, could put this over," and would become better acquainted with Rotary. In addition, an auxiliary would further the club's interest by eliminating a great amount of nonleadership work for the Ways & Means Committee. With the ladies' assistance, SF Rotary would soon become "a power in the vast field of charity." In 1924, *Grindings* proposed "the formation of a chapter of 'Rotarianettes,' composed of wives, sisters, or mothers of our club members." The editor noted that Portland "has a flourishing 'Ladies' Chapter' up there—and if in Portland, why not here?"

But although many local clubs viewed the formation of a ladies' auxiliary as beneficial in many respects, RI envisioned trouble, and consistently objected on various grounds. In large part, the reason was that Rotary found itself constantly guarding against the use of its name and its emblem by imposter clubs seeking to benefit from Rotary's growing importance. During the first decade of RI's existence, its executive committee and board of directors went on record with a number of attempts to arrive at a viable policy by discouraging the formation of "Women's Rotary Clubs," or "Women's Auxiliary Rotary or Women's Independent Rotary Clubs and the use of the Rotary name." It added that it had no objection to "the spirit of our organization

PAUL HARRIS'S VIEW

"It is heartening also to know that the wives, daughters, and mothers of Rotarians in many cities, impressed with the value of Rotary, have organized clubs of their own and are doing effective service in charitable enterprises....While the business and professional women have been unsuccessful in their efforts to gain admission to Rotary, they have not been unsuccessful in their efforts to embrace Rotary principles. They now have several strong and growing organizations of their own."

—Paul Harris, *This Rotarian Age*, 1935

being carried out under some other name." The issue came up repeatedly over the next few years, and RI repeatedly objected. In response to the incorporation of the Women of Rotary in Chicago in 1921, RI cited the history of its objections in a special section of the annual convention proceedings entitled "Membership for Women Impossible."

"Women through the ages have always practiced 'Service Above Self.' Now we have the opportunity to put the slogan into practice in serving our community."

—Mrs. Alwilda F. Harvey, wife of Chicago Rotary's president, who formed Women of Rotary in 1921, even as RI was objecting to women using the Rotary name

Despite RI's objections and the fact that there were other large women's services organizations such as Soroptomists, Rotary wives wanted to work with their husbands' clubs. They continued to frustrate RI's efforts by forming clubs that included the Rotary name, and the issue continued to surface at the annual RI Convention in several guises. One year, for instance, the issue centered on discussion of whether members of these women's groups should be permitted to wear the Rotary pin.

Some clubs avoided the naming issue by adopting names that did not mention Rotary. The longest-lived of these is the Inner Wheel, formed in Britain in 1923 at the behest of an RI official who had witnessed the good works performed by the women during World War I. Inner Wheel has grown into one of the world's largest women's organizations, having its own service projects outside of the scope of the Rotary organization. The Inner Wheel organization never gained a large foothold in the United States, but the name did provide an alternative for some clubs, which renamed themselves "Inner Wheel" under pressure from RI. In time, however, a name for Rotary women emerged that overshadowed the rest, and became a source of great pride for San Francisco Rotarians, and for Bru Brunnier in particular. That name was "Rotary Ann."

Rotary Ann and Other Names

After SF Rotary's formidable task of hosting the district conference in 1982 was accomplished, President Bob Lee (1981–82) marveled that "it was very humbling to watch how hard the wives of San Francisco Rotarians worked to make the conference Rotary wheels spin." After giving credit by name, he observed that "there was not a single wife named Ann!" Bob was, of course, referring to "Rotary Ann"—the affectionate term then used worldwide to acknowledge wives of Rotarians, after it was first given to SF Rotary's own Ann Brunnier in 1914.

The name "Rotary Ann" was one of many terms for Rotarians' wives used over the years. The club's 1912 roster began including the term "Lady of the Household." Alternately, members often feminized the club's name in reference to their wives. An early advertisement for dry-goods purveyor O'Conner, Moffatt & Company instructed Rotarian readers to "tell Mrs. Rotarian this is Home Sewing Week." Not long after, *Grindings* featured a notice inviting Rotarians and "Rotarianettes" to take the train to the district conference in Los Angeles. Other lesser-used titles included "Rotarianess" and "Lady Rotarian." Sometimes these names were taken with tongue-in-cheek; after one Ladies' Dinner, *Grindings* reported that a lady guest "very justly complains about the similarity of Rotarianette,

Suffragette and Vinaigrette." On the more formal side, the annual *RI Convention Proceedings* referred to "Rotarians and their ladies" for decades. These diminutives and titles were common usage in speech and in publications such as *The Rotarian* and *Grindings*. Over time, they generally gave way to "Rotary Ann."

According to an oft-told tale in Rotary historical lore, Bru Brunnier was on a train with other delegates to the Houston Rotary Convention in 1914. One of two wives aboard was Bru's wife, Ann, and she was introduced as "the Rotarian's Ann," which then became shortened to "Rotary Ann." Someone aboard made up a little chant about Rotary Ann to sing at the convention. Upon arrival in Houston, they were introduced to Philadelphia Rotarian Guy Gundaker and his wife, Ann. As frivolity ensued, the two Anns were carried about on the shoulders of Rotarians, who sang, "Our Ro-tary Ann, Ro-tary Ann!" and the new name was given to all of the wives at the convention. The name remained very much in use, particularly as Guy and Bru both eventually served as RI Presidents (in 1923–24 and 1952–53, respectively)—each of the original Rotary Anns becoming "first ladies" of Rotary International in the process.

"*Rotarianette*" *in* Grindings *advertisement.* —Grindings, *May 25, 1920*

Thereafter, the original "Rotary Ann" Brunnier became a celebrity in the world of Rotary wives. Over the years, Bru Brunnier and SF Rotary took a great deal of pleasure in the source of this international term of endearment. In a special brochure—"For our Rotary Anns"—distributed at a San Francisco district conference in 1965, women were invited to all meetings, sessions, and events of the conference. They were assured that the San Francisco Rotary Anns "will do their best to please and serve you," with a full schedule of special events, and promised an opportunity to greet Rotary Ann Brunnier.

As "Rotary Ann" grew in popularity as a name for Rotarians' wives, it also came to represent their contributions as helping participants in their men's club life. It gradually earned a place as the name most used by women organizing Rotary auxiliary organizations. The first Rotary Ann Club was formed in Oklahoma City in 1928. The purpose of the club was to assist Rotarians in various club and community projects, to extend fellowship to the families of Rotarians, and to uphold the purposes and aims of Rotary. The idea caught on in the United States and abroad.

BRU BRUNNIER RECALLS

"We were trying to get the Convention in 1915, so all sorts of stunts were planned and someone wrote a 'Rotary Ann' chant. When we arrived in Houston, some Rotarians grabbed Ann, put her on their shoulders, and marched around the depot singing this chant. We were all kids then, remember."

—Bru Brunnier, in *The Rotarian*, 1951

"Rotary Ann" Brunnier, 1916

The RI board of directors never granted the name "Rotary Ann" official status, nor was it ever listed in the "Glossary" of the *Manual of Procedure of RI*. The board addressed the issue occasionally. The *1934–35 Convention Proceedings* noted that the Board took no action regarding the formation of clubs of women relatives of Rotarians, but stated its belief that "the best interests of all concerned will be better served if they would refrain from using the word 'Rotary.'" Fifteen years later, the board concluded that "there shall be no legal recognition of women's clubs auxiliary to Rotary Clubs."

Nonetheless, the name "Rotary Ann" gradually defused the long-standing issue concerning the use of Rotary's name and its limitation to the men's club. It already enjoyed popularity as a nickname for Rotarians' ladies. The term was clearly feminine, and its origins lay in a well-known story that charmed men and women alike. It did not engender the same degree of RI opposition as the other names that included "Rotary," and it was sanctioned in local clubs and districts by virtue of its longtime use. Finally, in 1984, the RI board recognized the excellent service and sociability of the groups of women relatives of Rotarians, and encouraged all Rotary clubs to sponsor such informal organizations.[54]

There is no record of an official ladies' auxiliary in the history of SF Rotary. However, the club considered such an auxiliary. In 1923, SF Rotary President Paul Rieger inquired about the existence of organizations called "Women in Rotary." An RI official responded by referring to the previous year's convention proceedings, and cited the "policy to discourage the formation of women's auxiliary units or other organizations using the word 'Rotary.'" Nevertheless, there was a great deal of work to do, and SF Rotarians' wives continued to do it. Through the Depression and two World Wars, they worked in the unique circumstances of the times. Over the decades, they planned and carried out club functions, performed all manner of volunteer work on behalf of Rotary, and supported their husbands' club work. The same is true of Rotary Anns everywhere.

Through the years, SF Rotary encouraged members to inform their wives about Rotary. One way was to take *Grindings* home to "Rotary Ann," so she would become interested in the club and its activities and speakers.

■ ■ ■

As the twentieth century progressed, certain aspects of American society's viewpoint of women changed—the predominant change, of course, being women gaining the right to vote in 1920. But many underlying notions remained the same. Women were accorded that special position of respect reserved for them. They were to be treated with impeccable courtesy, but not as equals.

---

54. Other service clubs grappled with the same issue. The Lions Club International sanctioned a large affiliated network of women's auxiliaries called "Lioness Clubs."

Men-only clubs, such as SF Rotary, embodied a distinctly male viewpoint. Luncheon programs reflected that view in various ways. A 1916 luncheon talk—"The Two Greatest Sources of Trouble: Blondes and Brunettes"—promised a fellow member's scientific explanation of the notion that "one lady is dark and mysterious, and another lady is mysterious and light." Later, in the *Playboy* magazine era of the 1950s, the prevailing view was sometimes reflected in unabashed admiration of feminine attributes at club functions. After a luncheon fashion show presented by the downtown I. Magnin department store, the *Grindings* editor noted that "the male species predominates among the readers of this publication" and opined to his fellow readers concerning the negligee and lounging pajamas that they were indeed "marvelous creations, but wasn't that brunette in the two-piece bathing suit just out of this world?"[55]

At the same time, women were often seen in a different light. From its early years, SF Rotary welcomed women as luncheon speakers on various topics, and accorded their positions due respect. In 1922, for instance, the club welcomed the first woman on the San Francisco Board of Supervisors. When a visiting woman industrialist spoke after World War II on the evils of the federal income tax, she was accompanied by twenty businesswomen at the head table. Despite social expectations for women in general, not all women limited themselves to conventional pursuits, and some negotiated the fine line in a way that brought forth praise. In 1917, *Grindings* commented favorably on a woman speaker who "would certainly make a good Rotarian—she can say a lot in a short space of time, and she can say it with a punch."

While intended as sincere compliments, comments such as this also served to underscore the fact that women were not Rotarians in the dues-paying sense. Although they were welcomed as respected guests, women remained apart. Rotary clubs continued as men's clubs, and only occasionally did a serious effort to admit women to membership arise.[56] The men's world of business, politics, and the clubs—where they enjoyed fellowship, shared common interests, and met business acquaintances—were effectively unchallenged for more than a half century.

Changing Times

Throughout this period, middle-class women who chose to work had for the most part been limited in their options. In normal times, teaching, nursing, and secretarial/clerical occupations were generally the only options open to them. The two World Wars thrust women into men's jobs, but only temporarily.[57] Men returned home after the wars, taking back their jobs, and the traditional notions of women in the workplace resumed.

The turbulent 1960s and '70s drastically changed the landscape, as women's rights became a significant aspect of the social movements that swept the two decades. Women's entry into the

---

55. The annual spring fashion show (to which ladies were invited), lasted from the postwar 1940s well into the 1960s. It featured models from I. Magnin, showing off the latest negligees, swimsuits, and Paris fashions.

56. In 1950 and 1964, for example, proposals to delete the word male from the Standard Club Constitution made at the RI Conventions were withdrawn or rejected.

57. Bru Brunnier employed a draftswoman in his firm during World War I.

THE DECLINE OF "ROTARY ANN"

Noting that it "expressed what several of our local ladies have been telling us," The Rotarian published a letter in 1981 from a woman in Oregon: "As a wife who loves and respects her Rotarian husband very much, I feel I must share the put-down connotation I feel every time I see or hear the term 'Rotary Ann.'" She observed that the term had lost its usefulness for "lumping together all wives of Rotarians," and that in the present day, "not all Rotarians even have an 'Ann' (if that is synonymous with 'wife') anymore, and even for them the term must be hollow. Can't people simply say, 'Rotarians and guests,' and let the choice be up to the member?" Voicing a real-life difficulty with the ubiquitous "Rotary Ann," she pointed out that "I belong to the American Association of University Women, and we frequently have bring-a-guest functions. Think of the howls which would arise if we were expected to bring our 'AAUW John'! Please, everyone, drop the term 'Ann'!"

That year, SF Rotary President-Elect Bob Lee made it known that he did not intend to use the term "Rotary Ann" in *Grindings* or other publications during his upcoming year in office (1981–82).

workplace increased when women sought to expand their lives outside the home or took jobs to help sustain their families' expanding lifestyles. As they made inroads into occupations and professions previously closed to them, women looked for a means of access to these new opportunities, and found themselves on the outside looking in.

One such means of access for women was the club—the large business/service clubs such as Rotary, Kiwanis, Lions, and Jaycees; and the country/golf clubs such as the Bay Area's Olympic and Peninsula clubs. All were places where small signals were given, where business acquaintances became friendships, where deals were started. Without access to the advantages provided by these opportunities for business acquaintanceship and leadership experience, many women faced additional difficulties reaching above the lower levels of business or corporate management. A woman might be welcome to attend as many social functions with her husband as she liked, but as an adjunct to the voting membership, Mrs. John Clubmember was not to be taken seriously as Ms. Jane Businesswoman. Nor was she able to demonstrate her skills at a board meeting or chairing a policy-making committee.[58] From the mid-1970s on, women increasingly sought to gain entry to the closed world of the club. Increasingly they found it necessary to pursue their goals through court challenges based on discrimination.

Although women's attempts to gain entry to these venues of opportunity were met with widespread resistance, there were expanding pockets of support. Nationally known speakers had chided Rotary clubs from the rostrum, or refused to speak at Rotary events. Many companies stopped subsidizing their employees' memberships in discriminating clubs. Kiwanis reported clubs losing membership because of the organization's men-only policy, with the result that a few clubs breached Kiwanis rules and allowed women to become members beginning in 1975.

---

58. Interestingly, Rotaract, with its vocational aspect for young adults, was open to women from its inception in 1968.

> "My father, my uncle, my grandfather, were all members of Rotary, and I could never understand why I couldn't be a member."
>
> —Leni Miller, one of the first four women members of SF Rotary, 1986

The male members of most clubs, on the other hand, quite understandably resisted an intrusion into the enjoyable world of their men's club. Without doubt, the admission of women would change the atmosphere of camaraderie they found pleasant and comfortable, as had their fathers and grandfathers before them. For the many clubs to which women were not invited on a regular basis, the very presence of women could disrupt the convivial male atmosphere and would introduce different behavior. For SF Rotary and other clubs where women were frequently present, the ambiance would nonetheless be different—altered by the fact of women on an equal-status basis. For most members of these clubs, there could be no good reason to change something that had existed comfortably for generations, unless one appreciated the unfairness of the inequality inherent in the men-only club and its privileged place in the business network.

Not all women felt the men's clubs should admit women as members, either. Many women remained traditionalists. Some wives expressed concern that professional women would participate in their husbands' clubs, and their husbands would attend club functions in and out of town with these female members.

Although SF Rotary increasingly welcomed women to its meetings, its membership was not yet in favor of admitting them as full members. In 1972, the club resolved to reject an RI Council on Legislation move to allow admission of women. But the club began to feel the pressure. In one instance, a 1976 female student of the month from the University of San Francisco sounded the call to admit women into Rotary at the club's weekly luncheon. In the following year, the Rotary Club of Duarte would change it all.

> Upon hearing of a new Senior Active member's association with the Western Women's Bank, SF Rotary President Bob Tuck (1975–76) inquired whether this might be a precursor to "Women in Rotary." The resounding reply was, "We hope not."

Duarte—"The Mouse That Roared"

In 1977, California led the nation in the growth of female-owned businesses. Duarte, a city of fifteen thousand near Pasadena, was typical of dozens of fast-growing Los Angeles suburbs. It was in California cities such as Duarte that American women were making the greatest gains in business. And as in other such California cities, Duarte's clubs and other bastions of male privilege were under pressure to add women to their ranks. Three of the Rotary Club of Duarte's members resigned because their corporate employers stopped reimbursing employees for dues paid to clubs that discriminated against women. Faced with possible extinction, the eighteen male members of the dwindling club voted unanimously to admit three women, knowing their actions were in conflict with the bylaws of Rotary International. When the club's transgression was discovered by RI, the three women members offered to resign so the club would not lose its charter. However, the club's other members twice voted unanimously to retain them. The club was officially expelled from Rotary early the following year, after an unsuccessful hearing with the RI board of directors.

The Duarte club raised funds from the community and sent a member to the RI Tokyo Convention, to plead with RI convention delegates to reinstate the club. The convention made its position clear, voting 1060 to 34 against Duarte's reinstatement. With their RI charter revoked and the Tokyo trip unsuccessful, the Duarte members determined to continue as a club. They placed an "X" over the Rotary emblem, made new pins and banners, and renamed the club the "Ex-Rotary Club of Duarte." The club continued to meet in its accustomed spot each week, and followed its customary routine, operating as an independent service organization.

A month after the Tokyo Convention, the Duarte club and two of its female members filed suit for reinstatement in the California Superior Court in Los Angeles, under California's Unruh Civil Rights Act, which prohibits organizations that conduct business activities from discriminating based on sex, race, color, religion, ancestry, or national origin.

The lawsuit engendered by the actions of Duarte and RI sent ripples out across Rotary clubs in the United States. SF Rotary *Grindings* editor Bob Rockwell remarked that "the issue may come to us all," as he began his occasional columns about the situation shortly after RI told Duarte to remove its female members.

Women's involvement would not be a new thing for SF Rotary. Women had been regular visitors at the weekly luncheons for some time. Upon hearing from the wife of a Rotarian that she would like to attend many Tuesday meetings to hear the outstanding speakers, SF Rotary President Bob Lee (1981–82) reminded the membership that visitors, especially Rotarian wives, were "always welcome at Rotary." He noted that "apparently this is not generally known to our own membership, so please advise your spouses that they are always our honored guests." Women were also free to participate in most club events. Wives were invited to attend the annual Rotary/Boys' Club Camp Mendocino weekend with their husbands, and women joined men in the Rotarian "Centipede" at the annual Bay-to-Breakers footrace.

The club continued its longtime practice of including serious and interesting women speakers at its luncheon meetings. Many during this period were "firsts": one of the first female FBI agents, the first woman president of a Chamber of Commerce chapter in the United States, and the first woman in a leadership post in the California Assembly. A number of speakers were active in women's organizations, including the president of the ten-million-member General Federation of Women's Clubs. In her 1980 address to the club about the state of the city, Mayor Dianne Feinstein pointedly opened her talk by remarking, "I wish I could say ladies and gentlemen." In 1984 and 1985, the club held joint luncheon meetings with the Soroptomist Club of San Francisco, and wives were emphatically invited.

After Duarte inducted its women members, SF Rotary began to seriously address the idea that the admission of women to Rotary was simply a matter of time. But in 1980, as Duarte's lawsuit wound its way toward trial, RI's triennial Council on Legislation voted for the third time since 1972 to retain male-only membership—despite the fact that RI President James Bomar Jr.'s board brought to the Council a strong recommendation favoring admission. At SF Rotary's next board meeting, the directors expressed favor toward the proposal to delete club references to male persons.

Two years later, RI delegates at the Dallas Convention voted to remove all "unacceptable" vestiges of racism, and banned the use of race, color, creed, or national origin to restrict membership. But the RI Council retained its ban on women as members.

Not all RI officials opposed the admission of women. Many knew Rotary had to progress in a changing society for its own survival. But from the time of Duarte's initial admission of women, RI found itself on the horns of a dilemma. What made the issue sticky for American Rotarians was that it juxtaposed two of Americans' most precious rights—the constitutional right to freedom of association versus increasing rights to equal opportunity under American laws. At first, the prevailing attitude among a majority of Rotary members in America was against the admission of women to the traditionally men-only association. But after Duarte's action in 1977 and into the 1980s, many members and officials gradually changed their thinking. For some, it was the sense of an inherent unfairness in the denial of opportunity for business and professional women in a place of obvious business advantage. For others, the reasons were more pragmatic: 1) membership numbers were stagnant or declining (as Duarte's had been); 2) many companies refused to subsidize memberships for an organization with discriminatory policies; and 3) new equal-rights laws in several states conflicted with RI's policy on women members. But only one-third of all Rotary clubs were in the United States. And as an international organization, Rotary was not free to dictate the obligatory admission of women worldwide, when such a mandate would conflict with the laws and customs of other countries. Thus far, each time RI's Council on Legislation had voted to strike the word *male* from the membership qualifications, it had not achieved the two-thirds majority vote necessary to change the bylaws, although those voting in favor increased each time the Council met.

In 1983, the Council again voted against women in Rotary. With the unanimous backing of the board, SF Rotary had issued a recommendation to RI in support of the admission of women as members. SF Rotary acknowledged RI's international dilemma, believing that a policy admitting women might have to be on a country-by-country or a locally optional basis. The club declared that "it must be done to preserve Rotary in our country." In a subsequent newspaper interview during the club's seventy-fifth-anniversary week later that year, club Secretary Bill Ecker explained SF Rotary's position, and remarked on RI's action:

> SF Rotary and District 513 acknowledged that a growing number of wives were joining the ranks of businesswomen. Announcing a special program for the wives, a district assembly brochure promised "a select panel of professional business consultants will be presenting them with an invaluable array of information that will be beneficial throughout their lives."
>
> —*Grindings*, 1982

> "Rotarians around the world are not as quick to recognize the woman in business as we are, so as an international issue, it has a close-to-zero chance."
>
> —Bob Rockwell, SF Rotarian, 1980

"We went on record to allow women members. We were turned down by the International. . . . But," he proudly noted, "women take part in all our programs." Referring to the women's inability to obtain full membership, he said, "The only thing they don't do is to pay dues."

During the same month (February 1983) that the RI Council had voted against admission, the California Superior Court sanctioned Rotary's male-only membership and refused to reinstate the Duarte club, ruling that Rotary is "not a business establishment." The Ex-Rotary Club immediately appealed the decision, and the case began its slow path to the appellate court.

Meanwhile, SF Rotary's leadership continued its steady support for women in Rotary. By 1985, many club leaders were beginning to anticipate the movement's eventual success. Al Feder was pleased to report from the Presidents-Elect Training Seminar that RI President-Elect Ed Cadman had voiced "positive views" on women in Rotary. As Jim Patrick neared the end of his 1984–85 presidential year, his board decided to ascertain the club members' wishes, and continue to do what it could do to influence the adoption of new Rotary rules. It also determined to establish groundwork among leading San Francisco businesswomen. Past President Bob Lee's Long-Range Planning Committee recommended approval of women's membership in SF Rotary and RI as a long-term goal. The board moved to again petition the triennial RI Council on Legislation to resolve the issue of women's admission. The entire club membership was polled by mail with a resulting two-thirds vote. The board submitted the proposal to the district's Council delegate. Despite SF Rotary's effort, the 1986 RI Council again lacked a two-thirds majority to strike the "male" membership requirement—for the fifth time in fourteen years. It was, however, moving in that direction. In 1977, only 30 percent of Council delegates had voted to admit. By 1980, fully one-half voted in favor, and in 1983, the percentage increased to 60 percent. When the vote was taken in 1986, 65 percent voted in favor, barely short of the required votes.

> "In a big club like ours, we could assimilate quite a few and only look like visitors' day. They probably would be obvious because their attendance would be better than the men."
>
> —Bob Rockwell, 1980

SF Rotary petitions the Council on Legislation

> "Don't you agree that Paul Harris would certainly have included women in Rotary had they enjoyed the same status in 1905 that they do today? If our charter is truly 'World Service,' how can we continue to deny the assistance of women in our projects to further health and humanity and to eradicate hunger throughout the world?"
>
> —SF Rotary petition to Council on Legislation, 1985

1986: A Year of Action

Despite the RI Council's insufficient vote, women seeking entry into clubs such as Rotary made progress. Only one month after the RI Council ruled against women members, the California State Appeals Court reversed the California Superior Court's 1983 ruling. It found that

Rotary clubs were indeed business clubs, subject to California's Unruh Civil Rights Act, and it affirmed that business concerns were a motivating factor in joining local clubs. In celebration of its victory, the Ex-Rotary Club of Duarte inducted two more women members.

For SF Rotary, the California Appeals Court's decision opened up the real possibility of the club taking action on its intention to admit women. The topic was a major item of the board's agenda throughout 1986, during the presidencies of Al Feder (1985–86) and Marsh Blum (1986–87). Bill Ecker later recalled that, although the California law certainly made the process of admitting women "less rocky," the real reason for the strong support in SF Rotary was an issue of fairness.

In light of the favorable outcome of the California court case, the club was legally free—perhaps obligated—to admit women, at least for the time being. Uncertain about RI's appeal to the California Supreme Court, however, the board decided not to take action immediately, and to have member attorneys study the judgment. Other clubs in the area were hesitant to act as well. They contacted SF Rotary, the district's largest club, as to how it intended to proceed. Secretary Bill Ecker replied to one inquiry that at least two-thirds of the club membership agreed that women belong in Rotary. He also explained that the board had discussed establishing a list of prospective women executives, and inviting them to attend regularly and perhaps to serve on committees until "the bars come down," when they would be brought in as full-fledged members. SF Rotary's board also studied legal developments involving the Lions and Kiwanis organizations.

At Al Feder's final board meeting as club president, three SF Rotarian attorneys—Pete Lagarias, Bill Sturgeon, and Hank Todd—presented their evaluation. They recommended waiting to see if the California Supreme Court would hear the case. At the same time, Al Feder outlined the club's position in writing to the district governor: the board unanimously conveyed its "continued strong support for the prompt admission of women into Rotary." SF Rotary stated that as the premier service organization in the world, Rotary must not let discrimination penalize its humanitarian and educational programs by denying women the right to participate. SF Rotary understood why RI must comply with membership wishes to pursue all legal measures to overturn the Duarte decision, but urged RI to deal with the issue and admit women in the United States, allowing each country outside the United States to exercise "national options."

Outside developments in the summer and early fall of 1986 indicated that the battle to open the doors of men-only clubs to women might be nearing its end. The California Judges Association voted 194 to 192 to ban judges from belonging to discriminatory clubs. A federal judge upheld a New Jersey Kiwanis chapter's right to admit women, and several other Kiwanis chapters across the country welcomed women as members. The Lions Club International's board of directors voted unanimously in favor of the admission of women, although the convention vote to admit failed to pass. The Lions had experienced a situation very much like Duarte.

> "If the board of Rotary International could imagine the Rotary world as being a tall building with 22,000 rooms in it and the foundation of the building being, historically, the American clubs, they must realize that the foundation is at great risk and, therefore, the whole structure eventually."
>
> —Al Feder, SF Rotary President, 1986

In July 1986, SF Rotarian Marsh Blum took the reins as club president. A longtime advocate of women's admission, he was determined to bring women into the club as soon as possible. He did not have to wait for long. Later that month, the U. S. Supreme Court refused RI's request for a temporary injunction against readmitting the Duarte club.

Surprisingly, however, the first Rotary club after Duarte to induct women was not in California. The Seattle-International District Club (Seattle-ID) voted unanimously in July to admit fifteen women, and won a federal-court injunction to prevent RI from terminating their memberships.

In September, the California Supreme Court refused to hear RI's case, and permitted the Appeals Court's decision in favor of Duarte to stand. RI wrote to California clubs throughout the state, stating that they were permitted to admit women, in accordance with the lower court's ruling, and the state Supreme Court's refusal in July to review the ruling. RI also announced its intent to immediately appeal to the U.S. Supreme Court.

> "We were free. We looked at all this and thought it was pretty clear. I mean, you can't guarantee things as a lawyer, but it's the same set of issues and every step of the way Rotary International lost. So we said that it looks pretty clear that Rotary International is going to lose, and that clubs that have women cannot be expelled. And that was it. We were off to the races before the Supreme Court issued the final finding."
>
> —SF Rotary Past District Governor Pete Lagarias, 2006

SF Rotary's member attorneys reevaluated the situation. All of the California court obstacles had been removed. But what would happen if the Supreme Court were to find in favor of RI? It seemed unlikely. In previous years, state courts had steadily ruled against organizations conducting business, finding that the constitutional right to freedom of association did not entitle these types of organizations to deprive an individual of business opportunity through discrimination. Most tellingly, the U.S. Supreme Court had already ruled in 1984 against the 300,000-member Jaycees, after two Minnesota chapters' charters were revoked when they admitted women. The case had hinged on the same issue—whether the Jaycees was a business or a purely social organization. Thus if the U.S. Supreme Court were to decide to hear the case, it seemed likely it would rule in favor of Duarte. If not, the California Appeals Court's decision in favor of Duarte would stand.

Energized with the California's Supreme Court's action, and the belief that the U.S. Supreme Court would uphold the California ruling against RI should it decide to hear the case, SF Rotary President Marsh Blum and his board moved quickly to induct women. That October, Marsh brought Mayor Dianne Feinstein into the club as an Honorary Member. As Marsh "pinned" her, Mayor Feinstein called the move "one small step for womankind," and the club rose in a standing ovation.[59] At the same time, in accordance with the club's bylaws concerning admission procedure, the board approved four

Dianne Feinstein

---

59. At the same luncheon, Police Chief Frank Jordan spoke of his department's ten-year effort to balance the number of women in the department.

> "The minute it was announced out of Rotary International that it was legal, I got a hold of Dianne Feinstein's office and got her in....I brought the first one into San Francisco."
>
> —Marsh Blum, 2000

sponsored women and published notification of their approval in *Grindings*. The attorneys also began to draft a bylaws revision to eliminate the "male-only" requirement. The revision was subsequently approved by the club's membership.

At the Palace Hotel on November 25, 1986, with the press in attendance, four smiling new Rotarians were introduced to the Rotary Club of San Francisco by their sponsors: Laura Bernabei by Les Andersen, Cleo Donovan by Marsh Blum, Mary Hillabrand by Ken Miller, and Leni Miller by Bill Ecker. Laura was a director of the San Francisco Boys & Girls Club; Cleo, a senior vice president of Blue Shield; Mary, president of her own legal services company; and Leni, owner of an employment agency. Club member Dick Saxton went to congratulate Laura, and she offered her cheek, prompting Dick to remark that this was the first time he "kissed a Rotarian." Nine years after Duarte's bold action, SF Rotary became the first Rotary club in the district (and the largest club to that point) to welcome women into its ranks and to make women Rotarians in name as well as in spirit.[60]

That month, the U.S. Supreme Court agreed to hear RI's case. RI asked to be permitted to delay admitting women until the case was decided by the high court. When the Supreme Court refused to stay the appeals court's order, RI instructed clubs to begin complying with California's law—but suggested that members restrain themselves from nominating women.

Two months later, SF Rotary joined the Seattle-ID Rotary Club in an *amicus curiae* brief to the Supreme Court on behalf of the Duarte club. When the case was argued before the U.S. Supreme Court in March 1987, the RI attorney argued for the right of association, declaring that the move to

The first four women admitted to SF Rotary (left to right: Mary Hillabrand, Laura Bernabei, Leni Miller, Cleo Donovan), 1986. Courtesy of Leni Miller

admit women "threatens to force us to take in everyone, like a motel." The Duarte club was assisted in its response by an attorney from a neighboring Rotary club and an attorney from the American

---

60. SF Rotary was almost not the first. The Foster City Rotary Club had scheduled an induction ceremony for two women several days earlier, but a last-minute objection by a member scuttled the plan.

Civil Liberties Union. Duarte's argument countered that exclusion from organizations where business decisions were made would harm women's careers.

Six months after SF Rotary brought in the four new women members, its confidence in the court case's outcome was justified. On May 4, 1987, the U.S. Supreme Court ruled 7 to 0 that Rotary was, in fact, a business organization, subject to California and other states' antidiscrimination laws.

Cleo Donovan Recalls

Cleo: Our chairman and CEO became president of Rotary [Tom Paton, 1982–83]....He asked me if I'd like to work with him on the Program Committee and it seemed like an interesting thing to do, so I did. And that was really my introduction to Rotary. He was very good about giving me all kinds of responsibilities and letting me go to meetings. I used to go to the luncheon meetings quite often and knew quite a few Rotarians before they ever decided to open their doors to women....

Interviewer: Were you the only woman at the club?

Cleo: Sometimes if there was a very special speaker, the Rotarians would bring their spouses. Usually I was the only woman....

Interviewer: Was that uncomfortable at times?

Cleo: ...I used to think, What will they think of him bringing me along? But because he had me making phone calls and working with Rotarians—he had a fairly large Program Committee of about ten people and I worked with them—they all got used to me. I was never made to feel unwelcome....

Interviewer: Now it was Mr. Paton who asked you?

Cleo: Yes, he came back from Rotary one day—the day they announced the results of their vote. And he came into my office and he asked, "How would you like to be one of the first women to join Rotary?" And I said, "You're kidding!" He said they'd been talking about it and they'd voted to bring women in, and "I think you should join. Marshall Blum is going to sponsor you."... It was just a very pleasant surprise when we were told women would be joining. And of course I was delighted....

We got a ton of publicity....I walked in that day, and there were so many photographers and newspaper people, and they were always putting microphones in front of you! It really got a lot of publicity!

Although Rotary members' right of association might be "slightly infringed," the Court said, "that infringement is justified because it serves the state's compelling interest in eliminating discrimination against women." The Court also noted that RI's argument was "undermined by the fact that women already attend the Rotary clubs' meetings and participate in many of their activities." The following day, RI issued a letter to all Rotary clubs in California, declaring that all female members of California Rotary clubs were officially recognized as members by RI.

> "The tide of social change in this arena is clear, and the Court's unanimous opinion gives it resounding support. The days of discrimination against women and minorities are numbered, and all those who still engage in this practice should step aside before they are brushed aside."
>
> —*Los Angeles Times*, May 5, 1987

The Duarte Ex-Rotary Club had continued to admit women since its expulsion from Rotary ten years earlier. By the time of the Supreme Court's ruling, ten of the club's nineteen members were women. One of them, Sylvia Whitlock, had already been elected president of the club for the following year. Sylvia had been invited to attend the California PETS (Presidents-Elect Training Seminar), where she was the only woman among 311 attendees. In July 1987, she became the first woman Rotary club president in the world, even though RI had not yet changed its constitution and bylaws.[61] The tiny Duarte Ex-Rotary Club's ten-year banishment was over. It had prevailed against an eighty-two-year-old institution with more than a million members.

After Duarte

News editorials across the country praised the Supreme Court's decision, and the aftermath was swift and dramatic. The next day, Lions Clubs International sent letters to U.S. clubs encouraging them to admit women, and a San Francisco woman joined the Lions' South of Market Club within a week—becoming the first official Lion woman worldwide. The dominos continued to fall one by one. The board of Optimist International voted to permit Optimist clubs to add women to their rosters

PEANUTS: © United Feature Syndicate, Inc.

61. She went on to serve again as club president for 2001–02, the second woman in Rotary to serve twice as club president.

retroactive to the date of the Supreme Court's Rotary decision. Two-thirds of the delegates from 8,200 Kiwanis clubs voted to admit women. In a period of less than two months, the doors of the world's four largest men's service organizations no longer said "Men Only." The American Association of University Women (AAUW) voted to admit men to the organization by a near-unanimous vote.

It would be two years until the RI Council on Legislation was scheduled to meet again. In the meantime, the doors to Rotary clubs in the United States, Canada, and several other countries were opened. Lawyers, bankers, managers, small-business owners, and other professionals who happened to be women joined, and became productive and respected members of the Rotary family.

As in hundreds of Rotary clubs, the SF Rotary board voted unanimously to cosponsor legislation to strike the word *male* from the RI constitution. This time, the legislation—voted on by delegates from all over the world—was adopted by the Council at its next meeting in 1989. Clubs worldwide were free to follow the laws and customs of their countries. Once again Rotary reflected the society of the era.[62]

> "We most definitely welcome this change—and remind you that among the large Rotary Clubs, Past President Marshall Rotary Blum led the way!"
>
> —*Grindings*, February 14, 1989

During the course of women rapidly joining Rotary clubs in the United States, news reports indicated difficulties in a few clubs. But SF Rotary did not suffer from the transformation for several reasons. Women had attended luncheon meetings for years before they were admitted in 1986, and they had already participated in a wide variety of Rotary activities and programs. The club's proactive leadership admitted the first four women members well ahead of the Supreme Court's decision without being pressured to do so, and the move engendered considerable pride and support among the membership. Club members stepped up to sponsor more women for Rotary membership.

> "The fact is that when women did come in, they made such a memorable contribution to the activity level. They were so positive in their activities that it very soon became a general feeling that it was very good to have women in Rotary. No reason not to."
>
> —Past President Al Feder, 2006

The first four women and those who followed soon became integrated into the club. Once they were in, these new Rotarians brought ideas and a willingness to give their time and energy to the club's programs. They immediately began work on committees. The next roster showed ten of the club's fifteen new women members serving in thirty-two committee positions. Five women served on four or more committees. In 1988, Past President Tom Paton commended the women members for bringing "a wonderful fresh flow of talent and participation to our club." He added, "We have always made women guests welcome to our club and we're delighted that they are now full members." Because of SF Rotary's successful transition to a men's-and-women's club, the Business and Professional Women's Club of San Francisco invited the club to join in on its seventy-fifth anniversary in 1991.

---

62. Given the close vote in 1986, it is highly likely that the Council would have voted in favor of admitting women in 1989, even without the US Supreme Court decision.

Outside SF Rotary, women progressed as well. District 513 sent its first all-women Group Study Exchange team to New Zealand in 1988, and another to Sweden the following year. In 1995, the Rotary world welcomed eight women district governors. Three years later, Mary Janney became the first woman district governor in SF Rotary's new District 5150. The same year, Past District Governor Virginia B. Nordby was sent as the first woman delegate to the RI Council on Legislation—only nine years after its vote to admit women.

SF Rotarian Kay Clarke (center) leads an all-women Group Study Exchange team to Sweden. The group is given a tour of a mining operation, 1989. Courtesy of Bill Sturgeon

The past decade has seen further advances by women SF Rotarians. In 1997, President John Uth reported to the membership that although women had been members of SF Rotary for eleven years, there were no women eligible to serve on the Nominating Committee—which the club's bylaws limited to the president and past presidents. Because there were no women past presidents, there could be no women on the committee. John commented that women actively participating in club activities and serving on important chairs should be represented in choosing club officers. The club membership voted to change the bylaws to add five members-at-large to the Nominating Committee, thus enabling women to serve on the committee. A nominating member-at-large was required to have been a director, a chair of a committee, or a five-year member.[63]

With their energy and eagerness to serve in leadership positions, women did progress in the club. Three years after she became one of the original four women admitted, Cleo Donovan was elected as the first woman on SF Rotary's board of directors in 1989. Nine years later, women Rotarians outnumbered men on the board—despite the fact that fewer than 25 percent of the club's members were women.

The club's highest leadership position remained unfilled by women while they gained club experience and met the bylaws' requirement that a club president be a member for five or more years. After a time, a number of women were qualified to fill the position. For several years, the club's leadership searched among its qualified women for consideration by the Nominating Committee for the office of club president. Kathy Beavers recalled that "there were several women asked, who were not in a position to serve. I wasn't the first woman asked by any means. A number of women had a blend of experience in the club, knowledge of the club, experience in leadership of larger groups of people, and would have the ability to step in and be able to keep all the various balls we have up in the air. But to serve as president you have to be at a position in your

---

63. At the same time, SF Rotary's bylaws were also revised to add a nondiscrimination clause.

Kathy Beavers, SF Rotary's first woman president (2000–01).

life, in your work, where you can dedicate that amount of time and energy for a three-year period.[64] I had been asked for several years before I could finally say yes." As a result, President Jim Bradley stepped up to the podium in early 1999, and proudly announced Kathy Beavers's election as first vice president (president-elect), putting her in line for the club presidency for the year 2000–01.

Gradually, women's roles in the club's leadership have become commonplace. Many have chaired committees and headed large projects. In 2006, Anita Stangl followed Kathy Beavers as the club's second woman president. Beginning in 2005, Lisa Moscaret-Burr served two years as president of the San Francisco Rotary Foundation board of directors.

The addition of women to Rotary has brought changes to many traditions.

Lisa Moscaret-Burr

With the court decisions in the 1980s, and with more women in the professions than ever before, the term "Rotary Ann" fell out of favor. While the name "Rotary Ann" has not disappeared entirely, wives and husbands of Rotarians are more commonly known as "Rotary spouses," or "partners." Most Rotary Ann clubs disappeared in the United States in the late 1980s, although not entirely. With the admission of women to Rotary, some Rotary Ann clubs became "partner" clubs. These Rotary auxiliaries welcome male and female relatives of Rotarians. "Ladies" events at conventions and meetings, and district governor training for wives, have become "spousal" events. SF Rotary underwent changes as well. The 1986 "Stag Night" was the last one so named. Afterward, the annual game night—still "spouse-less"—was humorously renamed the "Bucks and Does Night." The annual holiday party raffle drawings, formerly open only to Rotarians' wives, were changed to include everyone at the party.

Elsewhere in the world, women have gradually been welcomed into the Rotary family. By the early 1990s, traveling SF Rotarians reported women joining in some European countries and elsewhere. SF Rotary member Gene Edwards attended a makeup meeting in Hong Kong in 1991. When he was introduced as a member of SF Rotary, a number of women rose and bowed. It turned out that the Hong Kong club had agreed to admit women only if Rotary #2 did, and SF Rotary's action opened the door.

Rotary International has recognized the valuable role female Rotarians played during the first years of their membership. The 2001 Council on Legislation and the RI Board of Directors encouraged the promotion of dual-gender clubs. Subsequently, RI President Jonathan Magiyagbe (2003–04) applauded the contributions of women in Rotary. He also declared that, despite the

---

64. The position of club president involves certain responsibilities in each succeeding year as president-elect, president, and immediate past president.

rapid increase in female business owners and leaders, "women remain woefully underrepresented in Rotary," forming less than 10 percent of the total membership worldwide. He encouraged local clubs to actively seek out and invite qualified women to become members.

As their numbers have increased, SF Rotary's female members have distinguished themselves in their service to the club and to the wider community. The club boasts four recipients of the Rotary International Service Above Self Award, Rotary's highest honor for an individual Rotarian. Of the four—Kay Clarke (1993), Dr. Angelo Capozzi (1996), Dr. Scharleen Colant (2006), and Heidi Kühn (2006)—three are women. For over two decades, many women have contributed to SF Rotary's success. Some are among the earliest to enter the club. Women such as Anita Stangl, Kathy Beavers, Laura Bernabei, Marie Brooks, Kay Clarke, Cleo Donovan, Susan Goldstein, Mary Hillabrand, Dana Gribben, Joanne Ireland, Leni Miller, and Lisa Moscaret-Burr—all broke new ground and showed that women truly belonged in Rotary. Other talented women followed. Cecile Chiquette, Carol Christie, Dr. Scharleen Colant, Jacqueline Drum, Stephanie Hanebutt, Christina Harbridge-Law, Shawn O'Hara, Jane Riley, Jean Schore, Lillian Tsi-Stielstra, and Rosey Wong came later, but have nonetheless taken on central roles in the club's operations and major activities. SF Rotarian women such as these have fulfilled the hopes of club leaders like Marsh Blum, who called three decades ago for women to be permitted to step up and take their progressive parts in the world's most exciting service organization.

Marshall Rotary Blum, SF Rotary President 1986–87

chapter eight

Perspectives

Rotary's been a way of life with me. My father was a member of the club. At one point, my brother was a member of the club. My sister-in-law was a member of the club. My son was a member of the club, so I've tried to keep it going.

—Marshall Rotary Blum, 2000

As its first century draws to a close, SF Rotary has much to look back on—and much to look forward to. Challenges have presented themselves. And as with any group of individuals, there have always been difficult times as well as good. But throughout the century, SF Rotarians have remained bonded in service and a tradition of fellowship that has sustained Homer Wood's club for one hundred years. Members from around the Bay Area meet once a week in the city they are pledged to help. Supporting it all are dedicated members and office staff. Working together, they have contributed to a record of accomplishment any Rotary club would be proud to call its own. And—working together—they will face the future of the club, its challenges, and their continuing commitment to serve their community and the world.

Three Challenges

In its one hundred years, SF Rotary has faced many challenges. Three in particular stand out because they represent long-standing issues that club presidents, boards, and committees have grappled with for decades.

Membership

As SF Rotary approaches its Centennial in 2008, it confronts an intractable problem—a decline in membership, from a high of 604 in 1967—to 550 in 1978—to 548 in 1988—to 375 in 1998—to 241 today. How the club addresses the issue of membership will determine much of SF Rotary's future in its second two hundred years.

For most of its early years, SF Rotary was pleased with its continuing rise in membership. There was a single exception. The club's year 1915–16 ended with 271 members, making SF Rotary the largest Rotary club on the West Coast. So many names were proposed for some classifications that the Membership Committee found it difficult to decide whom to accept. The incoming president chose to limit the growth of the club so it could assimilate its new members over the next year.

Otherwise, SF Rotary has always endeavored to increase its membership. Slowly but steadily, the club climbed to 300 members in the 1920s, then to 400, and at 416 members in 1939. *Grindings* proudly reported that SF Rotary was the fourth largest Rotary club in the world (out of 4,713 clubs). Membership topped 500 by 1950, and in 1967, SF Rotary membership reached its all-time year-end high of 604. The club then ranked as the second-largest western club in the United States after Houston (at 816).

Thereafter, membership started to weaken. It alternately dipped and rose within the 500s, but dropped below 500 in the early 1990s. At that point, SF Rotary membership began a serious decline, and became a constant subject of discussion at club board meetings. In 1991, the board confronted an unexpected reality: it had projected that a membership level below 500 would create a financial deficit for the club. The actual loss of members in 1990–91 resulted in a far greater shortfall than expected. In just a few more years, membership dropped below 400.

New members continued to join throughout this period. During Bob Lee's presidency in 1981–82, Kline Wilson's Membership Committee brought in a record 97 members with an additional ten-in-waiting, winning a district award for the club with the greatest number of new members. Kline also celebrated setting a record himself by bringing in three new members in one month. In 1985–86, Hank Todd's Membership Committee topped that record, with 102 new members. Hank was awarded the unofficial title of "Ambassador of Membership Development." Nine years later, John Uth chaired a Membership Committee that brought in 74 new members.

Hank Todd

These gains, however, were insufficient to offset the losses. Each year in the early 1990s, 13 to 18 percent of members left the club (not counting new members added), with a particularly severe loss of 22 percent in 1995–96.[65] That year, President Andy Kirmse made membership development his major project. For a time, Past President Dick Volberg was assigned as assistant to the president for membership development. As the president's assistant, raising membership was Dick's sole responsibility. But with few exceptions, membership continued its overall decline each year, and it dropped below 300 in the early 2000s.

What are the reasons for this steep decline? Many factors have been suggested—some beyond the control of the club itself. No single factor alone can be blamed entirely, but together, they overwhelmed SF Rotary's ability to attract and retain members.

The 1970s witnessed a national exodus of millions of middle-class Americans to the suburbs. In 1981, only 20 percent of the club's members resided in San Francisco. It became more difficult to inspire out-of-town prospects to join a club dedicated to community-service activities in San Francisco.

---

65. Other Rotary clubs suffered as well. In 1994–95, District 5150 lost 250 members.

Concurrently in the late 1970s, many of San Francisco's largest corporations began to move their headquarters out of San Francisco to less-expensive "business parks" in suburban areas. These moves were accelerated by a general hardening of attitude toward business by San Francisco city officials and many city residents. SF Rotary's membership suffered as the large corporations' chief executives moved and dropped out of the club.

SF Rotary also underwent a loss of prestige as a result of losing its office and luncheon location in the Palace Hotel when the hotel closed for remodeling in 1988. As membership seriously declined in the 1990s, many members believed the club should relocate back to the Palace or another first-class hotel. However, club finances made such a move impossible at the time.

By the 1990s, SF Rotary's membership had become considerably less corporate. It was increasingly drawn from small businesses, which were less likely than corporations to pay their employees' membership dues for a relatively expensive club. A 1997 survey of the club's membership showed a significant increase in the percentage of members who were self-employed. These members tended to be busier and often worked away from downtown, making it more difficult to attend a downtown luncheon.

SF Rotary was by no means alone in its dilemma. Most clubs of all kinds, including Rotary, have experienced substantial declines in membership within the United States. In 2000, author Robert Putnam (*Bowling Alone: The Collapse and Revival of American Community*) described a general lessening of Americans' participation in all sorts of social organizations, from bowling leagues to civic organizations. The same year, SF Rotary President Kathy Beavers studied large Rotary clubs and learned that almost none were increasing their membership. As a result of this general loss of social-organization membership, SF Rotary faces competition from other San Francisco organizations such as the Commonwealth Club, whose membership has also suffered losses.

The general problem of membership development is two-pronged—attracting new members and retaining existing ones. For most of its history, SF Rotary has worked to attract members through publicity and word of mouth, as well as relying on the club's prestige. The club's Membership Committees have used various methods. In 1959, for example, a Rotary Information Committee was formed to give an educational program and instruction to several prospective members at the weekly meeting.

The club has always relied on a limited segment of its membership to bring in new members. Fewer than 10 percent of the members in most large Rotary clubs ever propose a new member. During the withering 1990s, board officers and directors were specifically charged with recruiting new members themselves, and the club tried various incentives, such as recognition for bringing in a member.

From SF Rotary's first meeting in 1908, it has endeavored to attract members at the top levels in their firms. Facing the serious decline in corporate membership in the early 1990s, the club's board appointed a "Blue Ribbon Committee" of past presidents for long-range planning "to improve the club's vitality and visibility as a major club player." The committee reported that Rotary's PolioPlus campaign should help attract new high-level members. The board also asked Marie Brooks and other women members to try to recruit top women in San Francisco.

As it lost large-club membership in big cities across the nation, RI took measures to stem the flow. In 1994, Bill Ecker conferred with RI President Bill Huntley and Past RI President Cliff Dochterman in a newly formed "Urban Concerns and Opportunities Committee" that sought ways to overcome large-clubs' membership problems. RI commissioned a Gallup poll in several large cities to determine how to encourage top-community leaders to be members. A two-hour session with non-Rotarians was held in San Francisco, and observed by Cliff Dochterman, Bill Ecker, and club President Bill Koefoed. The poll reported a strong finding to the RI Urban Concerns and Opportunities Committee that Rotary was in need of an effort to help public relations at the local, national, and international levels. RI recognized that large clubs needed assistance with video and printed materials to help develop and retain members.

Another enduring problem in membership development has been that of attracting younger members, to whom the club looks for its future leadership. A SF Rotary survey in the 1990s found that of 360 members, only four members were under thirty, and forty-six were between the ages of thirty and thirty-nine. The largest group was between the ages of sixty to seventy. In 1999, the board agreed on a new membership plan to attract new members under thirty. There would be no initiation fee, but each member would be required to sign up for a meal plan for the first quarter of their membership (to foster a good attendance habit), and encouraged to continue on the meal plan thereafter. Today, individuals under thirty-five can join for a half-price initiation fee.

Attracting new members has been only half the battle. They must also be retained. The challenge is to keep members interested and engaged. In 1997, a club Task Force on Membership Development reported that "most members join Rotary for three reasons: fellowship, community involvement, and business contacts. When members don't find these three, they drop out. If people give up two-and-a-half hours a week and spend about $2,000 a year to belong to an organization, they expect more than a lunch and a speaker." One problem has been keeping members informed and enthusiastic about opportunities for involvement in service. At one point, several members indicated they might resign because "there was nothing for them to do on projects." They were not being kept aware of opportunities for service. In fact, the club generally found itself with more openings for service volunteers than it could fill. In addition to making service opportunities known, several club administrations have placed a special emphasis on spotlighting work done by committees and hardworking committee members.

Retaining the new member has posed its own problems. One way has been to encourage early participation. In 1928, for example, a special luncheon "Freshman Program" consisted of hilarious entertainment by the year's new members, who portrayed schoolboys. On the more serious side, the Acquaintance Committee's purpose was to introduce new members to the club, and urge new members to give one-minute talks about themselves and their businesses. Known by various names (acquaintance,

"What the indoctrination does is give a person a chance to see everything and then say, 'Where do I fit in?' And if they had that for me, I would have heard about Camp Enterprise and gotten into it sooner, I think."

—Past President Jim Bradley

assimilation, and indoctrination), committees have worked to familiarize new members with the workings of the club, to be sure they are given opportunities to meet their fellow SF Rotarians, and to assign them to committees right away. Indoctrination has been especially important. For the past fifteen years, the committee responsible for indoctrination is always chaired by a club past president.

Efforts have also been made to continue the process of keeping new members. In an old SF Rotary tradition, members are recognized on their first anniversary with the club. They exchange their "rookie" blue badges for regular member badges, announcing their new status.

A committee for new members, called the "49ers," was introduced in President Jim Huckins's year (1970–71). Consisting of the newest forty-nine members of the club, its purpose was to assimilate new members and ensure they were not left out—a real concern for a club of nearly six hundred members.

The 49ers concept grew dormant for a while, but was revitalized by President Pete Lagarias and cochairs Tom Parry and Jim Patrick in 1992. Over time, the committee tried out new ideas. Joanne Ireland and Jack Selway prepared a video presentation for use at orientation meetings, 49er meetings, and by the membership development committee. Pete Lagarias also recalls that the 49ers Committee decided to try what Rotary's founders did originally—rotating from person to person's place of business. He explains that "we looked around, and our members had interesting businesses." After touring a member's business, the group would adjourn to a social hour or dinner at a restaurant. Since then the 49ers Committee underwent a few name changes: Rotablasters and, more recently, the COG Club.

Retaining SF Rotary's youngest members presents a special challenge, primarily because they have always been relatively few in number. Most efforts have provided fellowship opportunities appropriate to younger members. Some club administrations have reserved tables at weekly luncheons for members under thirty-five or forty.

When Pete Lagarias joined SF Rotary in 1983, he realized there were only four young members including himself. With Executive Vice President Bill Ecker's help, Pete formed the "Under 35 Club." Together, the club enjoyed van trips to wineries, or football and baseball games. As young businesspeople joined over time, the group increased to more than sixty members. In 2003, the idea was carried forward to a new group for members under forty, called the "Whippersnappers." The name proved unpopular, and was changed in 2006 to the Young Rotarians. The club's average age has lowered over time, and the number and kinds of fellowship activities were changed accordingly. Younger members benefit from the fellowship offered by Birthday Division activities such as dinners, cocktail parties, and museum tours.

Today, SF Rotary remains strongly challenged to raise its membership levels by attracting new members and retaining existing ones. The problem is still not limited to SF Rotary alone. In early 2006, District 5150 announced that district membership had dropped below 2000, whereas RI has defined a "vital district" as one with at least 2,500 membership. However, prospects may be improving somewhat as this is written. Club President Anita Stangl's year of 2006–07 closed with 241 members, a net gain in membership of 26—the first increase in several years.

Public Recognition

The issue of public recognition has posed a dilemma for SF Rotary time and time again. How can a club attract new members without making itself known? Yet how should a club make itself known, without appearing to unduly toot its own horn?

From its founding, the club had a Publicity Committee. Other than to keep local reporters informed, the unique new club had little to worry about, as it generally drew favorable responses from the press.

Then, as public opinion began to turn against Rotary in its "back-scratching" and boosting years, the Committee encouraged club members not "to hide their work and light under a bushel, . . . and if the public does not know what Rotary means, they will probably form their own opinion." RI notified Rotary clubs that information of public interest about a club should be sent to newspapers, and newspaper representatives should always be welcomed at meetings.

Still, SF Rotarians were generally uneasy about what might appear to be pompous bombast about their accomplishments, or choosing projects solely for their visibility. A 1923 RI policy suggested a moderate approach. It stated that publicity should not be the primary goal of a Rotary club in selecting a community-service activity. However, rather than eschewing publicity, the policy went on to say that "as a means of extending Rotary's influence, proper publicity should be given to a worthwhile project well-carried out."

The question of how Rotary clubs should achieve public recognition remained a matter of discussion for decades. In 1966, RI urged clubs to create and promote a positive image of Rotary as an international-service organization, and to give the public an accurate and up-to-date picture of Rotary and its activities worldwide. RI stressed that a public-relations committee was the best way to accomplish this. "The days are past," RI President C. P. H. Teenstra said, "when Rotary could afford to be passive in this field and thus be misunderstood as a secret organization or luncheon club."

As its membership declined sharply in the early 1990s, SF Rotary emphasized the importance of favorable publicity in attracting new members. In 1991, the club's good works were showcased in *San Francisco Rotary Today*, a half-hour, biweekly local television program. One episode, "Service Above Self," was created by the Vocational Service Committee. Club volunteers taped meetings and community-service events. Another episode described the club's efforts toward San Francisco's AIDS epidemic. Later that year, RI President Rajendra K. Saboo advised Rotarians to declare a major project. SF Rotary President Pete Taylor called for the club to identify and publicize projects that would enhance Rotary's image in the community.

Peter V. Taylor,
SF Rotary President
1991–92

SF Rotarians have been critical of the tendency of the press to report heavily on negative events, and to give little or no emphasis to positive topics such as Rotarians' good works. When the *San Francisco Chronicle* ran a reader's op-ed piece criticizing Rotary, Past President Chet MacPhee and President-Elect Bill Sturgeon wrote responses to the *Chronicle* (also published), pointing out SF Rotary's early admission of women members, its numerous good works for

San Francisco, and the 1.1 million Rotary members worldwide dedicated to service. After a number of Bay Area newspapers praised SF Rotary's Rotaplast missions, Rotaplast still had not been covered in either the *San Francisco Chronicle* or the *San Francisco Examiner*. Rotaplast founder Pete Lagarias wrote to the editors of both newspapers, urging them to give positive coverage to such a worthy endeavor, and inviting them to attend the club's Rotaplast luncheon. Rotarians strove for as much public visibility as possible. During Bill Koefoed's year (1994–95), SF Rotary's child-immunization project was featured in a two-minute segment on KTVU television in 1994. However, a number of SF Rotarians expressed concern that the broadcast did not sufficiently spotlight Rotary. The club's board encouraged volunteers to wear Rotary T-shirts at immunization events. On a number of occasions, SF Rotarian and public-relations professional Pete Taylor created newspaper supplement inserts for local newspapers such as the *San Francisco Business Times*. The inserts were designed as a membership-recruiting tool, and to enhance the image of Rotary and the club by publicizing Rotary's projects. Club members and their businesses, as well as *Business Times* publisher Mary Huss, contributed space for the inserts. In his report on his official visit to SF Rotary, District Governor David Cresson (1997–98) praised the club's Academic Decathlon, its Boeddeker Park improvements, and its international work with Rotavision "flagship projects," which could be strongly emphasized in general media publicity and membership promotion. He added that they could generate favorable community attitude, and bring service-minded leaders of business and professions to consider joining the ranks of the club.

C. John Hoch,
SF Rotary President
2007–08

In recent years, SF Rotary has continued its efforts to generate and receive favorable publicity. The Academic Decathlon awards ceremony was broadcast on public-access television. So was a segment about the Organ and Tissue Donor Registration program, featuring a transplant surgeon and transplant patients. Past President Jim Bradley has appeared on public-access television's *Headline News*, explaining Rotary and what it does. SF Rotarians staff a booth at San Francisco's annual Dragon Boat Races to raise public awareness of Rotary and its programs. Steve Talmadge places magnetic placards advertising Rotary's humanitarian programs on his messenger company's fleet of vehicles. President John Hoch (2007–08) defined his primary goal of increasing SF Rotary's public exposure as an active community-service organization. To this end, the club emphasized its most visible hands-on projects, including monthly work days at the Rotary Meadow, a Rotary day for Habitat for Humanity, and its ambitious Centennial project—sponsorship of the rebuilding of the Boys & Girls Club Mission Branch clubhouse.

A Question of Territory

Throughout much of its history, the Rotary movement was represented in each city by one club. SF Rotary drew its membership from San Francisco's entire business population, most of it centered downtown. From the club's earliest days, however, this arrangement periodically came under challenge, and was one of the most contentious issues to confront the club.

Returning from Rotary's 1913 International Convention in Buffalo, SF Rotary's delegate reported on the proposed admittance of four distinct clubs in New York City. He predicted that the notion would attract a great deal of attention from the International Association in the future. Subsequent conventions debated the issue, and in 1922, RI legislation made it possible to form additional clubs in large cities. By 1934, New York City had admitted additional clubs, and Los Angeles had more than one as a result of city annexation of surrounding areas. In a city of smaller geographical area, SF Rotary was on record as opposing the idea.

Over succeeding decades, business grew less centralized, and a large business community had emerged in the western part of the city. The question of allowing another Rotary club in San Francisco came under earnest consideration and debate beginning in 1953. Most of the club's past presidents were against such a move. The idea surfaced again in 1970, when club President Syd Worthington requested a survey of the business and professional community in San Francisco's Stonestown area to determine whether there was sufficient interest to encourage the establishment of a Rotary club in that area. Later that year, the district governor criticized SF Rotary for its reluctance to sponsor additional clubs in San Francisco. The club took no concrete action, however, and for the remainder of the 1970s, successive presidents and boards alternated—some in favor of and others opposed to—extension within San Francisco. The question continued to be viewed quite unfavorably by many club members.

In 1982, President-Elect Tom Paton came out in favor of a "chance to share Rotary," and announced that one of his goals for 1982–83 would be to accomplish the organization and establishment of a new Rotary club in Stonestown. Later that year, the district governor asked SF Rotary's board to sponsor and support an all new Stonestown club. SF Rotary's board authorized SF Rotarian and Past District Governor Bob Rockwell to determine if enough interest existed among Stonestown businesses to justify a Rotary club. Several SF Rotarians furnished names of potential members from Stonestown firms, including a number of large corporations with offices in that area. Bob held several meetings with Stonestown businessmen, and reported considerable enthusiasm among them. By the following year, over twenty businessmen were meeting provisionally every week, and announced that they were ready to apply for a charter, needing SF Rotary's sponsorship and support. Following SF Rotary board approval in 1984, the club membership voted to cede territory for the new Stonestown club. The new club was launched in May, under the stewardship of Bob Rockwell, with the proviso that the name of the club would not include "San Francisco," but would be "Rotary Club of Stonestown." SF Rotarians encouraged and supported the fledgling club, and the charter night for the new Rotary Club of Stonestown was held in January 1985. SF Rotary presented the club with its new bell, and SF Rotarian and RI Past President Stan McCaffrey gave the keynote address.[66]

In 1988, the district governor announced his goal to encourage the formation of a new club in the noncompeting business area of San Francisco's Outer Mission district. SF Rotary formed a committee to cooperate, and club members helped collect names of potential members. In 1989,

66. The club is now called the Rotary Club of San Francisco West.

Pete Lagarias (front right) attends a meeting of the San Francisco Greater Mission Rotary Club, 2006.

SF Rotary ceded territory for the new club, and the new San Francisco Greater Mission Rotary Club was founded under SF Rotary's sponsorship.

During Bill Sturgeon's district governorship the following year, SF Rotary again agreed to sponsor and cede territory for a new club, this time in the Fisherman's Wharf area. The club was formed in short order, and SF Rotary proudly presented a bell to the Rotary Club of Fisherman's Wharf.

In 1995, the district governor set a goal of establishing two new Rotary clubs in San Francisco, one in Chinatown and one in Hunters Point. At the district governor's request, Pete Lagarias took the lead in forming a new club in Bayview near Hunters Point, noting that there were no residents of the area among the SF Rotary membership. SF Rotary began its sponsorship of a provisional new club, this time sharing its territory. The Rotary Club of San Francisco Bayview held its Charter Night in 2000, and the club has prospered.

Pete's next effort to form new clubs took place the following year during his district governorship (2001–02). Under Pete's leadership, the San Francisco Golden Gate Rotary Club was formed in San Francisco's Presidio area. Pete recently helped District Governor Holly Axtel with the formation of the new Rotary Club of Chinatown, which is presently in provisional status.

SF Rotary has taken its sponsorship of new clubs seriously. As area representative for the district governor in 1994, Bob Wilhelm worked with understrength clubs to build up their membership, programs, and projects. In 2000, SF Rotarians conducted a joint fundraiser for the San Francisco West and Greater Mission clubs.

The club has collaborated with its fellow San Francisco clubs on dozens of projects throughout the city. Rotarians from across San Francisco have worked together on Career Day, jointly raised funds to restore the Third Street Gym (a health club for at-risk youth), and upgraded the Rhododendron Dell in Golden Gate Park (returning on several more occasions for tree plantings and cleanup).

Rotarians from San Francisco clubs participate in an interclub cleanup and redwood tree-planting party at Golden Gate Park, 2001.

Fellowship—A Bedrock Tradition

The first steps in Rotary are to be found in the fields of acquaintanceship—
where the flowers of friendship and the fruits of service are to be gathered.

—SF Rotary President Paul Rieger, 1923

In the early twentieth century, the fellowship that a man found in his clubs, including Rotary, played a large role in his life. Absent the many means of communication we have today—long-distance telephone, rapid mail delivery, e-mail, and the Internet—a man looked to his local environment for fellowship and a sense of belonging.

For one hundred years, Rotary has provided unparalleled opportunities for this kind of fellowship. Some are found in the local club, and others through national and worldwide Rotary connections. Some arise through service, some through business acquaintance, and many through just having fun. SF Rotary has a rich history of all of these—filled with traditions from the past, but changing with the passage of time.

The Weekly Luncheon

One of the keystones of Rotary fellowship is the institution of the club's weekly luncheon and the sense of continuity conveyed by its many long-standing traditions. Throughout its history, members have been warmly welcomed upon their arrival at the weekly meeting. From the earliest days, SF Rotarians and luncheon visitors were met in greeting lines before the meeting. A Reception and Hospitality Committee was explicitly formed in 1923, and has existed ever since. (It is known today as the Greetings & Reception Committee.) At times, the committee has been huge—with well over eighty members in the 1960s, it was the largest committee in the club.

The present-day "hospitality hour" is held before each meeting. One thing has changed over time, however. Whereas in the club's earliest years members were encouraged to use the hospitality hour (and the luncheon meeting itself) as a means to specifically promote one's business, the practice is frowned upon today.

SF Rotarians have not always addressed each other by first name, although the practice was encouraged at the Rotary Club of Chicago from its very beginning. In 1916, incoming SF Rotary President Jim Lynch dubbed his first meeting "An Assimilation Party," and requested that members drop "Mister" and greet each other with first names only. He created an Assimilation Committee, charged with seeing that none who came to Rotary meetings would leave as strangers, but would instead have met every member present. The Assimilation Committee urged that each member "do try and be similar." Greeting one's fellow Rotarian with his first name was considered a large step in that direction. The same year, the club roster was changed to include members' first names.

"Do you really appreciate what a valuable asset you have in 250 Rotarians who stand ready to be your friends?"

—President Charles Victor, 1915

From the opening sentence of the luncheon, tradition plays a part. Rotary #2 is especially proud of its one-hundred-year history of meetings, and many recent presidents have announced the meeting by its historical number. (The luncheon in the week of the club's one hundredth anniversary on November 12, 2008, will be SF Rotary's 5,058th meeting.)

A tribute to America has endured as a club tradition ever since SF Rotarians first joined in singing "My Own United States" at the club's third meeting in February 1909. Club members have always displayed their patriotism at the luncheon's beginning by reciting the Pledge of Allegiance, or—more frequently—singing the National Anthem or other patriotic songs.[67]

Singing was a favorite meeting activity from the very start. The first club singing included the members enthusiastically accompanying the Golden Gate Quartet in choruses of old familiar songs in early 1909. After that, singing and music was the rule at club meetings and other SF Rotary functions. By 1923, President Paul Rieger announced his desire to make the club "a real singing club," and formed a Music Committee. Songbooks were provided at the meetings, and the Rotary Male Quartet made its debut.

The club's golden years of music and singing were unquestionably from the 1920s through the 1940s, when the new Music Committee was guided by Uda Waldrop, Charlie Bulotti, and Austin Sperry. The three sang beautifully together, and were invited by club Past President Charles Wheeler to sing at the 1932 RI Convention in Seattle. The trio's leader was Uda Waldrop, a profes-

sional composer, pianist, and singer. Uda also led a group of male choristers, and played weekly at the Palace of the Legion of Honor and on radio broadcasts. From his first year in the club, Uda brought singing and music to his fellow members for more than twenty-five years. His annual highlight was the spectacular Christmas luncheon program, which was broadcast on local radio.

Uda, Austin, and Charlie were SF Rotary's music makers for many years.

For several decades, it was also commonplace for the club to enjoy entire musical programs at the weekly luncheon, such as the annual visit of the A Cappella Choir of SF State College in the 1950s.

Public singing as a popular pastime has lessened over the years. A notable exception at SF Rotary is the singing of carols at the annual Holiday Party. And club members still appreciate good music. For a number of years, member Jack Selway entertained Rotarians with his beautiful tenor voice.[68] Now the club takes pleasure in serenades by the Rotary Singers, an informal, unrehearsed group of club members. Several club members, including Matthias Kuntzsch and Jim Emerson, bring in musicians and singers for Rotarians' enjoyment.

The origin of the Thought of the Day (formerly an Invocation) is unclear, although an Invocation Committee consisting of fourteen invocators appeared in the club roster during Marv

---

67. For a number of years in the 1940s, the singing was accompanied with a spotlit flag waving in the breeze of a fan.

68. Jack was the city of San Francisco's "official singer."

Cardoza's year of 1978–79. Chaired for many years by Rev. David Stechholz, it provides a moment of reflection before the busy agenda takes over.

As with other Rotary clubs, an important tradition has been the introduction and greeting of visiting Rotarians and other guests at the luncheon meeting. Earlier meetings received more visitors than today, routinely numbering in the dozens. Guests numbered an average of eighty per week (sometimes over one hundred) in the mid-1950s—more than four thousand in one year alone. Most surprisingly given these large numbers, the club office sent out Season's Greetings to the year's long list of visitors in the 1940s and 1950s. Guests from abroad have received special treatment. Club President Francis Whitmer (1955–56) customarily honored foreign visitors by greeting them in their native tongues, and President Bob Lee (1981–82) initiated the flag program to honor visiting Rotarians from outside the United States.

In earlier years, looking to the visitors' comfort while they were in San Francisco was a significant club activity. In a city that is a world-class tourist destination, club members graciously provided hospitality and sightseeing arrangements. For a period of time in the 1920s, SF Rotarians informed luncheon visitors that automobiles would be waiting outside after the meeting, to take them and their families on business or pleasure trips throughout the city. During the 1940s, the club secretary provided each visitor with a printed memo, acquainting him with the club's office facilities and inviting him to use them.

Announcements come next, and the introduction of the Birthday Division of the month is a long-standing practice dating back to the divisions' inception in 1910. Another tradition for over twenty years was the weekly "news." Initiated in 1971–72, five minutes were delivered by well-known newscasters, including Herb Caen, and club members Wayne Jordan and Jane Riley.

Very few of SF Rotary's luncheon traditions have lasted for the entire century and done as much good as the good-natured "fining" of members. Fining began early in the club's history. President Homer Wood levied the first known fine when he collected $5 from founding member Jim Patrick, for opening a new store on Market Street. (Decades later, Jim's boisterous son, Past President Howard Patrick, paid a $4.99 fine with a sack of 499 pennies, which—as *Grindings* reports—"he unceremoniously dumped in the general direction of the Charity Box.") Ever since Homer fined Jim, SF Rotarians have continued to hand over their fines in the spirit of fun, and to raise money for good causes. Casting a wide net, fines have been levied for becoming a father or grandfather, having one's business promoted in the press, baldness, sitting at a noisy table at lunch, failing to wear the Rotary pin, attending the Bohemian Grove Outing, and more (including a twenty-first-century custom of exacting a fine on any member

Shortly after SF Rotary moved its headquarters to the Palace Hotel in 1916, it told *The Rotarian*:"We believe that our headquarters are as fine as those of any club in Rotary. There is a spacious lunch room, a directors' room, and a secretary's office, and visiting Rotarians will be welcome at all times. A stenographer will be available for the visitors who may desire to have work of this kind done. We are going to emulate New York's example and make Rotary headquarters 'the best information bureau' in San Francisco."

When President Marv Cardoza accidentally addressed Mayor Dianne Feinstein as "Supervisor Feinstein" in 1979, he offered to "show proper penance for such a slip" and ring the bell for $100, if ten others would ring it as well. Instead, fourteen fellow Rotarians stood up and rang the bell to "right" the club and honor the mayor and her proper title.

whose cell phone rings during the luncheon). Over the years, fines became such an intrinsic part of the luncheon that a high-school student visiting in 1962 summed up his impression of the Rotary luncheon experience as "Friendship, Food, and Fines." Some club presidents have invented euphemisms for the traditional fine. Despite President Jim Emerson's declaration of a year of "free-will offerings" to replace the fine system, he continued to extract weekly contributions to Rotary Service. The following year, President Pete Taylor changed it to "Rotary Service Charges."

"Bell ringing" began in 1968, when payment of a $100 fine initiated the member into the "Bell Ringers of San Francisco Rotary," and exempted the ringer from further fines that year. In its early years, bell

ringing was a real wallop of a fine—$639 in today's dollars for the privilege of ringing the bell! Yet in the tradition's first year, there were always at least one or two members eager to benefit Rotary Service, and bell ringing became a regular feature at every meeting. Bell ringing reached its peak in the mid-1980s, with several years of at least three ringers per meeting. At the end of Bob Lee's presidency,

Marvin E. Cardoza, SF Rotary President 1978–79

the club held a reception to honor the club's 147 bellringers during his term. The record of 184 bell-ringing members was reached in Harold Gray's year in 1983–84. There have

been some memorable moments. Bighearted club member Ed Thompson performed a "symphony on the bell" with his contribution of $10,000 to the San Francisco Boys' Club in 1981. He followed up by ringing the bell ten times again less than a month later, and again the next year. In 1984, President Jim Patrick introduced the "Zinger"—a contribution of $250 or more to Rotary Service, which he announced with a noisy siren. Jim charged the first Zinger to his father, Past President Howard Patrick. Howard then turned the tables and sounded the second Zinger on Jim.

Comedian Carol Channing attends SF Rotary luncheon with Boys' Club members, 1965. President Edward Sequeira presides. Courtesy of Moulin Studios Archives

Throughout the club's history, SF Rotarians have been fortunate to hear an extraordinary range of important and interesting speakers. The earliest speaches were often instructional. *Grindings* reprinted the entire text of talks on matters of civic operations and finance, such as "Municipal Finance and Civic Improvements" and "The Depositor and His Banker." During the "boosting" days, club members spoke about their businesses. Over time, the club gained more outside speakers. Many have been national celebrities, including Ann Landers and Abigail Van Buren ("Dear Abby"), nuclear physicist Edward Teller, and 1986 America's Cup skipper Tom Blackaller.

During the 1970s and 1980s, the heads of several of America's largest corporations, such as the president of the Ford Motor Company and the CEO of Chevron Oil, addressed the club. In 1970, Ross Perot spoke about his goal to obtain humane treatment and early release for prisoners of war. Subsequently, SF Rotarians heard from two

President Anita Stangl presents a club banner to San Francisco Mayor Gavin Newsom, 2007. Photo by Steve Swaab.

well-known former POWs—Captain John McCain and the Navy's most decorated officer, James Stockdale. Many important political leaders have addressed the club. They include: former President Richard M. Nixon; California Governors Ronald Reagan, Pete Wilson, and George Deukmejian; Secretary of Defense Casper Weinberger; Arizona Governor Barry Goldwater and Texas Governor John Connally; and California Senator Alan Cranston. An annual tradition is the appearance of the mayor of San Francisco. Dianne Feinstein spoke on a number of occasions, and Willie Brown was always an entertaining favorite.

In 1923, "the most distinguished Rotarian in all the world"—President Warren G. Harding—was staying at the Palace Hotel, where SF Rotary had its office and luncheon location. The club issued an invitation for the president to attend the weekly luncheon as a "make-up" meeting, but *Grindings* noted that "the demands of his classification—that of President of the United States—make it hardly likely." President Harding passed away at the Palace, two days after the invitation.

SF Rotarians have been kept up-to-date on current topics, domestic and international, with timely talks by experts in their fields. Knowledgeable individuals have given club members very early information on topics such as illegal immigration (in 1955) and the "coming crisis in medical services" in the early 1980s. One area in which the club has enjoyed a wealth of speakers has been in new developments and technology. In the club's first decade, members heard about the new "Auto Truck," as an alternative to horse-drawn drays for transportation, and a recent addition to cars—the tail lamp. Rotarians learned about the invention of television in 1931, and plastics and the lightning-fast microwave cooking in 1956. Cell phones are

RI President Frank Devlyn visits SF Rotary (left to right: Past President John Uth, Frank Devlyn, Anita Stangl, President Kathy Beavers, District Governor Erich Zorr). Courtesy of Kathy Beavers

James Getty as Abraham Lincoln speaks to high-school students. Photo by Bill Sturgeon

nothing new—with the help of a telephone-company speaker in 1947, club members were thrilled to hear the voice of a fellow member over a mobile telephone from Coit Tower. Rotarians also kept up with the space race. An expert explained Sputnik three months after its launch in 1957. NASA experts delivered talks on Project Mercury and the Apollo program, and the club has met three astronauts.

Several crowd pleasers have made multiple appearances. In 1972, Jill Knight—member of the British Parliament—spoke on the British parliamentary system, in what began a long-term relationship with SF Rotary. Now a member of the House of Lords, Baroness Knight has continued to fascinate and charm club members. She was made a Paul Harris Fellow of SF Rotary in 1997. Frank Devlyn and Cliff Dochterman, two RI past presidents and accomplished speakers, have made repeat visits to the club.

One of the most unusual speakers among the club's array of interesting visitors was the sixteenth president of the United States. Abraham Lincoln was portrayed by James Getty, who has depicted Lincoln for thirty years. On several occasions, Mr. Getty impressed luncheon-goers with his convincing rendition, packed with tailored remarks that included aspects of California history. For several years, Bill Sturgeon introduced Mr. Getty to SF Rotary and other Bay-Area Rotary clubs. President Lincoln also appeared before thousands of students at many schools in the area. His fee for the school appearances was underwritten by SF Rotary.

In addition to outstanding speakers, the club has a long tradition of special annual events. By far the longest is the annual Holiday Luncheon. Begun in 1915, the luncheon was originally a Christmas program to celebrate the ladies—Rotarians' wives, sweethearts, and sisters. The attendees enjoyed music, Christmas festivities, fine food, and gifts. It soon took its annual place at the Palace Hotel Garden Court, where it remained for decades. In 1995, the luncheon became the Holiday Luncheon, and continues as SF Rotary's most festive event of the year.

As post-World-War-I boys' work began, the yearly Fathers and Sons Christmas Luncheon was instituted in 1920. Fathers proudly introduced their young men to fellow members. Boys' Club members were "loaned" to "sonless fathers" for the day, a practice that continued until the late 1960s. Shortly after the beginning of the Fathers and Sons Luncheon, the Boys' Work Committee issued a call for a Daughters' Day, noting that daughters "will be the wives of the Rotarians of tomorrow." The luncheon was eventually moved to Easter time, allowing for the girls to display their Easter finery. In 1971, Fathers and Sons Day was discontinued in favor of a party where fathers showed off their sons and daughters together. Gradually the post-Christmas party was extended to include members' grandchildren. Children were entertained with balloons, noisemakers, and a clown. The Children's Holiday Party continued through the 1980s.

James G. Emerson Jr.,
SF Rotary President
1990–91

Celebrations of the holidays have included a Thanksgiving program. For almost ten years, member Jim Emerson led the Thanksgiving program with character reenactments of historic characters. And barely a month after the Loma Prieta earthquake in October 1989, President-Elect Jim brought a Thanksgiving theme of "Let's give thanks at a moment like this."

Following the annual Holiday Luncheon in December, SF Rotarians are given the opportunity to rearrange their financial affairs after the new year, with the expert predictions of the financial speaker. Club member Sid Schwartz (president of the San Francisco Stock Exchange) gave his first occasional financial addresses about the economy of World War I in 1918. His popular financial forecasts became a regular annual affair in 1949. Sid was followed by Ken Smith, then by Al Barnston. For thirty-seven years, Al's annual program was one of the club's biggest luncheon draws. Gary Wollin followed Al in 1997. Since then, the annual predictions have been delivered by several fine financial prognosticators including Sam Yates, Burt Berry, Ben Atkinson, Allan Herzog, and Everett Price.

Every year, SF Rotarians thank members of the city's emergency services on Emergency Services Recognition Day. A vocational-service program since 1987, the club honors the police officer, firefighter, deputy sheriff, and Coast Guard seaman whose superb performance, extraordinary dedication, and achievement on the job protect the community. SF Rotary's Emergency Services Committee evaluates the nominations of individuals from each of the four agencies represented. The committee considers the individual from each agency who most meets the criteria for acts of bravery and heroism. Each winning recipient's family and top chain-of-command are hosted at

President Curtis Burr honors San Francisco's emergency-services personnel, 1997.

Outgoing President Kathy Beavers is "roasted" by SF Rotarian Joe Raffetto, at her last meeting as club president. Her husband, Lynn, looks on, 2001.

a well-attended luncheon meeting. The chain-of-command's report is read, describing the recipient's action(s) that contributed to the award. The recipient is presented with a commemorative plaque and a night on the town, complete with a hotel reservation and spending money.

At the end of every Rotary year, the club holds its annual "de-throning" of the outgoing club president. As early as the 1940s, the ceremony took the form of a "roast," when club members recounted the celebrant's funnier moments, as well as the year's high points.

Another traditional luncheon program from the 1950s until the early 2000s was the annual Big-Game Day. SF Rotary is fortunate to count many UC Berkeley alumni among its membership. With a comparable representation of Stanford alumni, a good-natured rivalry between them is a club tradition. Held the week before the "Big Game" between Cal and Stanford, the celebration has featured "Calford" and "Stanifornia" banners at the head table, a luncheon rally with cheerleaders and head football coaches from both schools, and enthusiastic renditions of school fight songs by SF Rotarians of both stripes.

One of the club's earliest regulations prohibited political activity at meetings. Members were cautioned that "Rotary principles do not permit political or religious discussions," and that "great care should be exercised that neither one of these subjects be brought up in Rotary meetings." The board was instructed to ensure that no candidate for any office be introduced at Rotary luncheons. This prohibition continued for many years, although speakers were permitted to debate the pros and cons of ballot issues. In more recent years, this prohibition no longer exists. Since at least 1963, the club has occasionally held political luncheon programs on an "equal time" basis, such as debates between the city's mayoral candidates. In 1974, Democrat Jerry Brown officially announced his candidacy for governor of California, in a luncheon overflowing with members, reporters, and city dignitaries.

> One year, club President Jack Ingold fined each Stanford alumnus $1, then allowed each Cal alumnus to dip into the pot for $1—quite a way to "give away" Rotary Service money!

Many luncheon programs have adopted patriotic themes. SF Rotary has periodically held a flag pageant on Independence Day or on Flag Day in June. Sometimes the theme is military, as befits SF Rotary's longtime connections with the military, and the Presidio in particular. In the club luncheons that celebrated Armed Forces Day, the Sixth Army often participated by presenting the Colors.

The giving of a gift to the day's speaker is a long tradition in the club. Gifts have ranged from the ordinary to the unusual—such as a slice of cable from the Golden Gate Bridge mounted on a plaque, or a small section of cable-car track removed during the city's cable-car replacement project in the 1980s. Some presidents have made donations in the speakers' names. In John Uth's year (1997–98), the club donated a book in the name of the speaker to a school library. The speaker signed the book and "gave" it to the school in lieu of the standard speaker's gift. Howard Waits (2002–03) presented speakers with a photo and a certificate showing the donation of a wheelchair through the Wheelchair Foundation. The donation was made in the speaker's name, and would be given to a specified recipient.

SF Rotary has a number of closing traditions. Since Burr's Bogus Bucks made its debut in the 1990s, recent years have featured a bit of fun and fund-raising with the weekly drawing. Ever since Herb Taylor set the Golden Rule to four questions, the Four-Way Test has endured as a strong Rotary tradition. The Test has had a prominent presence for SF Rotary, in the large gold and blue banner that hangs on the front of the podium. The banner was presented to the club in 1962, by the Vocational Service Committee. A number of SF Rotary presidents have chosen a recitation of the Four-Way Test as an appropriate and inspiring way to bring the luncheon meeting to a close.

Since early in 1909, SF Rotary has remained a downtown luncheon club. When the club grew too large that year to meet at members' places of business, it began to hold its luncheons at the Techau Tavern at 1 Powell Street. The Techau was known for its excellent food and gracious surroundings.

In 1916, SF Rotary outgrew Techau Tavern, and moved its luncheon to the elegant Palace Hotel, at the same time the club moved its office there. For seventy-two years, the Palace was home to SF Rotary—a tradition in itself. The club was extremely proud of its location at the Palace, and featured it in two long-running versions of the *Grindings* masthead. Particularly enjoyable were the special luncheons and events held in the Palace's gorgeous Garden Court, with its soaring golden stained-glass ceiling.[69]

SF Rotary also enjoys a tradition of holding occasional luncheons elsewhere. One popular location was the Bal Tabarin club (later known as

The splendid Garden Court in the Palace Hotel.

---

69. For a time, the Garden Court was known as the Palm Court.

Bimbo's 365 Club). SF Rotary has also met for lunch at the sites of many of its community-service beneficiaries. In four months alone in 1975, the club held three outside luncheon meetings at locations of club service beneficiaries: the Recreation Center for the Handicapped, the Salvation Army Senior Citizens' Complex, and the University of San Francisco (of which nine club members were regents, trustees, or advisers). On many occasions, the club has held luncheon meetings at the Boys & Girls Club.

In 1988, the Palace Hotel closed for remodeling. SF Rotary's last luncheon at the Palace was its Christmas luncheon in December. The club moved its luncheon location to the Kensington Park Hotel on Post Street. Nine years later, SF Rotary moved its office and meeting place to the Marines' Memorial Club on Sutter Street, and changed to a buffet luncheon. The first meeting there celebrated Oktoberfest. Today, the club meets at the Kensington Park Hotel.

Rotary Fellowship Connections Worldwide

When several SF Rotarians journeyed to Oakland for a meeting with the new Tri-City Rotary Club in January 1909, they began a tradition of inter-city meetings. The Oakland and San Francisco Rotary clubs enjoy the oldest inter-city pairing in the Rotary world. Early in their existence, the two clubs met frequently. Then for decades, dozens of members traveled annually to enjoy transbay fun and fellowship. The visiting club customarily took charge of the program for the day. Some were informative, others packed with frolic.

At a San Francisco-Oakland inter-city meeting in 2002, the Oakland club conducted an elaborate trial— complete with judge, jury, attorneys, and witnesses—contesting SF Rotary's claim as Club #2. After disproving Oakland's claim that notes in bottles washed up on the beach showed that Oakland was Club #2, SF Rotary retained its status, and a good time was had by all.

SF Rotary began another early inter-city pairing with the Rotary Club of Los Angeles in 1913. Although these longer-distance meetings were not as frequent as the meetings with Oakland, they were well-attended affairs. In a typical meeting with Los Angeles in the 1930s, eighty-five members of the Los Angeles club chartered a special train for the journey north to visit SF Rotary. It was "a purely stag affair." The travelers were joined in Burlingame by a delegation of SF Rotarians, who continued for the short remainder of the ride. The luncheon program, staged by the Los Angeles visitors, featured a discussion of the history, the beauty, and the progress of San Francisco and Northern California. In addition to the luncheon, the visit concluded with a traditional golfing contest between Club #2 and Club #5.

Surprisingly, the heyday of the inter-city meeting was in the earlier days of Rotary. Some meetings were enormous affairs, rivaling the attendance at district conferences. Members numbering in the hundreds arrived from clubs as far away as Bakersfield for an evening dinner hosted by SF Rotary in 1920. In the days when transportation was more difficult, getting there was half the fun. Rotary clubs chartered buses or railroad cars, so that all members could travel together and enjoy the journey itself.

Visiting Rotarians arriving in San Francisco by train were met by a delegation of Rotarians to drive them to the luncheon at the Palace Hotel, often escorted by a motorcycle police corps led by the Rotarian chief of police. After World War II, as commercial flying became more commonplace, members began flying to distant inter-city meetings. In 1951, fifty-two SF Rotarians chartered a plane to a meeting in Salt Lake City, and club members flew to Honolulu in 1953.

In addition to the inter-city meetings, SF Rotarians have always traveled—sometimes considerable distances—to attend official RI functions. The district conference, district assembly, and RI convention have drawn SF Rotarians since they were first instituted, and gave club members the opportunity to participate in the workings of Rotary. Even before flying, SF Rotarians traveled to faraway conventions on specially chartered trains or ships with Rotarians from all over the continent. The

SF Rotarians arrive at an inter-city meet in Los Angeles, 1927. The Los Angeles chief of police came out to meet the train. —Grindings, *January, 25, 1927*

SF club President Bru Brunnier (center) arriving by train with 110 SF Rotarians on a visit to Burlingame, 1914. The banner on the train is campaigning to hold the next year's 1915 RI Convention in San Francisco. —Grindings, *May 12, 1914. Photo by Arthur J. Brunner*

journey itself offered an unparalleled opportunity for inter-club fellowship. Many took longer than the convention itself, such as the five-day trip from the West Coast to Atlantic City in 1920. There were stops at several places across the continent for celebratory dinners, city tours, and to take aboard more Rotarians.

Any travel can open doors for SF Rotarians. They have long recognized there is no passport in the world equal to Rotary membership. For one hundred years, SF Rotarians and their families have been welcome in any city with a Rotary club. A club

SF Rotarians travel to an inter-city meeting in Honolulu, 1953. Courtesy of United Airlines

Bru Brunnier and others at a party in San Francisco after the International Convention in Salt Lake City, 1919. Bru Brunnier is at left bottom with hat, Ann Brunnier is 3rd from bottom right, SF Rotary club Secretary Ervin Feighner is at top left.
Courtesy RI Archive

member can have lunch with fellow Rotarians and enjoy their hospitality nearly anywhere in the world. In turn, *Grindings* has routinely posted notices from Rotarians worldwide, seeking accommodations for them and their families.

One special aspect of Rotary life is the opportunity to participate in the almost one hundred RI recreational and vocational fellowships, called Global Networking Groups. Starting with a Yachting Fellowship in England in 1947 which was taken up officially by RI, recreational fellowships have offered club members the opportunity to pursue their interests with like-minded Rotarians in their club, outside their club, and around the world. RI has approved more than fifty recreational fellowships, ranging from motorcycling to magic. Several have over a thousand members worldwide. SF Rotarian Carroll Tornroth has been a member of the RI Yachting Fellowship for many years, and knows that reaching out can take many forms. Once he answered a ship-to-shore telephone call in the middle of the night. An Australian Rotarian was out at sea in the Farallone Islands, looking for a place to berth his boat. Carroll found a berth for him. Vocational fellowships welcome Rotarians sharing a business or profession. SF Rotarian Pete Lagarias is chair of the Vocational Fellowship of Law. The group promotes the rule of law, and is developing a Web site of important cases around the world.

"Rotary membership makes every city your own home town."

—*Grindings*, May 24, 1927

Having Fun

The fellowship and fun at this club is obvious at every level—from the board meeting to the weekly gathering. Guests are greeted and appear to be included. Members enjoy each other and create a great atmosphere for meetings. Obviously, the extra parties and get-togethers during the year that include families have made the club a part of members' lives. A nice balance of serious business and frolic."

—District 5150 Governor David Cresson, 1997

SF Rotary's history is replete with fellowship activities to please the fun lover in everyone. One of the club's earliest enjoyable pastimes outside the luncheon was the "Outing," made possible by a new way to get where one wanted to go—the automobile. The first recorded automobile outings were "grape crushers," hosted by Clarence Wetmore at his winery in Livermore. During the overnight trip, the Rotarians were wined and dined, engaged in silly hijinks, and slept on a straw-covered floor in a barn. In 1913, SF Rotary's Outing Committee held an "Auto Run" to Walnut Creek—a family picnic outing, to which members were encouraged to "bring your auto or your friend and his auto," and enjoy fun, food, fresh air, sunshine, good company, prizes, and contests. An early annual outing down the Peninsula promised bowling, swimming, racing, games, music by the Stanford Jazz Orchestra, and dancing. Members and their families would be driven there by a "cavalcade of automobiles." Racing was a popular sport at these events. There were races for men, women, boys, girls—and this was supplemented by a "Ladies' Nail-Driving Contest." By the 1920s, these events had grown into elaborate annual auto trips and family picnics away from San Francisco. One year, 610 SF Rotarians and family members were kept entertained with dozens of prizes, a circus, an orchestra, a chauffeur, nurses, and two maids for the ladies.

Outings have continued through the decades, although transportation advances have made more distant travel possible. SF Rotarians and their families have traveled as groups to Brazil and South America, Alaska, and Germany. The 1980s were the years of club cruises. Groups of SF Rotarians cruised—for as long as two weeks—through the Panama Canal, to Alaska, the Vancouver Expo in 1986, Southeast Asia, Egypt, and down the Blue Danube.

The centerpiece of SF Rotary fun has always been sports. *Grindings* reported on "Rotary Recreation" in 1913, when "the boys meet each Thursday, play ball, and have a little recreation." That year, SF Rotary issued its first of many challenges to the Oakland club. Accepting the invitation for a five-game baseball tournament, Oakland replied, "Come on over." Confident in their club team's ringer (former semiprofessional player Bru Brunnier), SF Rotarians crossed the Bay to Oakland—whereupon they lost the first game. In fact, they went on to lose all five games. Nonetheless, baseball continued as a popular pastime for SF Rotarians. A more recent event, perhaps reminiscent of the Oakland debacle, occurred in 1991, when SF Rotary President Pete Taylor's team suffered a spectacular loss (7-24) to Mayor Art Agnos's All-Stars softball team.

The first annual SF Rotary Sports Chapter dinner, 1920.
Courtesy of Moulin Studios Archives

"Our early sports activities included grape crushes, picnics, baseball, bowling, and subsequently golf and horseshoes."

—Past President Bru Brunnier, 1959

SF Rotarians also took up bowling around 1916, and played several inter-city games with Oakland and other clubs during the next few years. But SF Rotary's most robust and long-standing sports tradition lies not in baseball or bowling, but in golf. In January 1920, around a dozen club members arranged to play golf. There were an estimated one million golfers in the United States that year, and the sport immediately overtook SF Rotary's other outdoor activities. The club held a second tournament later that month, then another and another. After the third successful monthly tournament, it was clear that monthly golf meetings were going to be permanent. Soon, the "Monthly Outing Day," as it came to be called, included a dinner after the tournament, followed by bridge, mahjong, and dominoes. Later that year, SF Rotary issued its first inter-city golf challenge to the Oakland club. SF Rotary won the first tournament, and Oakland returned the favor a few weeks later.

It was the club's golfing craze that prompted the formation of the Sports Chapter soon after the monthly tournaments began. The Sports Chapter has continued as a SF Rotary committee to the present day. (It is now called the Recreational Activities Committee.) The chapter held its first annual dinner in August 1920.

That same month, the Sports Chapter arranged the club's first annual golf tournament, to be held at Del Monte on the Monterey Peninsula in September. It was a three-day gathering, with a revolving trophy cup, ladies' golf, and a formal banquet on Saturday night. The annual "Del Monte Sports Carnival" became one of the club's favorite events. In addition to golf, it included tennis, swimming, horseback riding, badminton, bridge, and dancing. The tradition was not abandoned even when the government took over the Hotel Del Monte for wartime use in 1943, but was moved to the California Golf Club instead. After the war, the event was moved to the Sonoma Mission Inn. It subsequently returned to Pebble Beach, near the Del Monte Hotel, where it remained from the 1950s until it was discontinued in the 1970s. One of the most popular events of the annual weekend was the Golden Buck Party on Sunday morning. It was hosted for many years by Past President Jim Patrick, then by his son, Past President Howard. Also popular were the morning

Robert M. Lee,
SF Rotary President
1981–82

breakfast shows. SF Rotarians performed song and dance routines from popular musicals, and the men dressed up as glamorous models in a "women's fashion show."

Besides golf, the early Sports Chapter organized other events. "Barnyard golf," or horseshoes, became popular in the 1920s as well, and the chapter held well-attended horseshoe tournaments.

As sports events became the most popular extra-luncheon activities in the club, the Sports Chapter grew in importance. During the 1940s, the committee had as many as fifty-nine members, the second largest committee in the club (after the Inter-City Relations Committee). It was divided into subcommittees for sports other than golf, as well as entertainment and special events.

SF Rotarian Joe Thieben, champion horseshoe thrower in the 1930s.

The club's enthusiasm for sports continued in full force into the 1990s, with golf at Bay Area courses, trips to Hawaii and Central America, and a new emphasis on tennis. Skippering his boat "The Office," Jim Patrick organized an annual sail, usually to Half Moon Bay, in the 1980s and 1990s. Winter sports also became popular with an annual family "Winter Sports Outing"—also hosted for several years by Jim Patrick.

Golf, however, reigned supreme, and still does. An occasional tradition, the "grudge match" Club #2–Club #5 Rotary Golf Tourney between San Francisco and Los Angeles, has continued with a perpetual trophy into the 2000s. Nowadays, the club's Twilight League provides late-afternoon golfing. Members compete for the Don Bering Perpetual Trophy, named in memory of one of the club's most avid and well-liked golfers.

In addition to playing at sports, SF Rotarians have enjoyed gathering to root for professional teams as well. Beginning in the 1960s, Family Day provided the opportunity to meet for a day or evening at the baseball park to enjoy a game and good company.

SF Rotarians at the Club #2–Club #5 Golf Challenge.

President John Uth celebrates Oktoberfest, 1997. Courtesy of John Uth

Harold Hoogasian's annual Giants "tailgate party" met at his floral warehouse before the game for a number of years, and Steve Talmadge enjoys barbequing for his fellow Rotarians in the parking lot before 49ers football games.

Not all of the club's fellowship activities revolve around sports. SF Rotarians have enjoyed Valentine's Day dinner-dances, Oktoberfest (with Past President John Uth in lederhosen), and dinners to experience various international cuisines.

President Pete Taylor (1991–92) brought fun into the club with his Norwegian chili cook-off. As president in 1996–97, Curtis Burr encouraged his fellow Rotarians to "Live, Laugh, Love, Leave a Legacy." With the emphasis on "Laugh," Curtis improved fellowship within the club by having more fun. During his presidential year, the club held three major fellowship events—a Road Rally and Barbeque, a Monte Carlo Night, and a springtime Napa Valley excursion.

> "My first priority was to increase opportunity for Rotary fellowship. I looked for as many ways as I could for Rotarians to have fun with other Rotarians."
>
> —Past President Curtis Burr, 2006

Besides ad hoc organizing of fun events, SF Rotary relies on a long-standing structure to promote fellowship among its members—the Birthday Divisions. Since 1910, the club has divided its membership into smaller sections. In 1925, President Walter Marwedel instructed that each section "constitute itself as a little Rotary Club, with genuine leadership from the section officers and great activity from the sections." As the club grew larger, the sections were looked to as a way to make it easier for a member to feel welcome and among friends—something many find difficult in a group of several hundred. The present-day system of Birthday Divisions was put in place in 1927.

Curtis A. Burr,
SF Rotary President
1996–97

> "The success of the club depends on all members feeling a sense of relationship with others. The success of developing that sense of relationship depends on small groups. The heart of the small group opportunity in our club is the Division."
>
> —Past President Jim Emerson, 1993

Over the years, the Birthday Divisions have taken on responsibilities such as presenting luncheon programs. During a few brief periods, they have been called on to conduct their own service projects, sometimes with Rotary Service funding. Throughout their entire history, however, they have served two important purposes: they function as a training ground for prospective leaders, and they encourage fellowship and communication among a large and diverse group. In the interest of fostering fellowship, the Birthday Divisions organize a wide variety of social functions. Monthly dinners and cocktail parties enable SF Rotarians—particularly the younger ones—to mix and meet without the constraints of the brief weekly luncheons. One example of the elaborate functions that have been created by the Divisions was the annual Mystery Trip, sponsored by the December Division in the 1980s. Attendees did not know what the evening had in store. On one such occasion, SF Rotarians and their wives were transported by bus to Jim Patrick's office for cocktails and hors d'oeuvres, then to the Wax Museum, followed by a dinner-dance.

For over three decades, some club members enjoyed the extracurricular fellowship of Rotary Club #2½. In the 1950s, a group of SF Rotarians began a custom of meeting on Tuesdays at Shield's, a tavern across the street from the Palace Hotel on New Montgomery Street. There they partook of a beverage or two before attending the club's weekly luncheon. The gathering came to be known as Rotary Club #2½. They were ribbed whenever they walked into the regular meeting late. On one occasion, the group fined themselves, buying a Paul Harris Fellowship in the process. Club 2½ continued to meet until SF Rotary moved its luncheon from the Palace in 1988. In 2001, many club members mourned the closing of Shield's, with its memories as the pre-Rotary-meeting libation spot for Club 2½.

Pete Taylor leads a Centipede in the Bay-to-Breakers footrace, 1992. Courtesy of Pete Taylor

In the club's many fund-raising activities, SF Rotarians often combine fun and fellowship with service. In so doing, they experience the best of both worlds. Charlie Massen's nine-member Centipede running in the annual San Francisco Bay-to-Breakers footrace took on the challenging Rotary Club of Richmond in 1982, raising over $1,175 in pledges for Rotary Service. The following year, Les Andersen and Boys' Club members formed the refreshment crew for Captain Charlie's crew, and the club's Centipede entry became an annual event. Ten years later, a Centipede headed by Pete Lagarias finished 34,673rd out of 80,000.

Since 1976, the annual Rotary Ski Challenge has mixed fun with fundraising. Along with hundreds of skiers from Northern California, Nevada, and

SF Rotarians participate in the Rotary Ski Challenge.

Oregon, SF Rotarians ski in what is billed as "the world's largest gathering of skiing Rotarians." Proceeds from the Challenge benefit the Rotary Club of Tahoe City's community-service activities, raising thousands of dollars and garnering recognition for Rotary.

Fun fund-raising takes many forms. Started in 1981, "Game Night" grew into an annual event held at the Boys & Girls Club, featuring cocktails, hors d'oeuvres, and all kinds of games. SF Rotarians occasionally enjoy a "Monte Carlo Night" or "Casino Night," featuring games of chance. The event has been used variably as a fund-raiser, sometimes for the club's main annual auction, and at other times for specific service purposes such as the Boys & Girls Club. SF Rotary's "Texas Hold 'Em" Poker Tournament benefits Rotavision International.

Fellowship Leads to Business

SF Rotary's tradition of fellowship reaches back to its first meeting, where forty-five businessmen gathered to inaugurate a new kind of club. These men intended to meet regularly and learn about each other, in the hope of furthering one of Paul Harris's primary objectives for Rotary: "a club where businessmen could openly talk about business." We've seen how the objectives of Rotary evolved to reflect a collective desire to provide service to the community and the world. But throughout SF Rotary's history, club members have never stopped talking about business. They have instead developed a number of creative ways to facilitate business promotion in the spirit of fellowship.

Even as SF Rotarians began their extraordinary expansion of work with youth in the 1920s, treating crippled children and taking over sponsorship of the Boys' Club, they also met to gain better business acquaintances. In 1923, several dozen members began gathering on Thursday for lunch at a "round table." They met primarily to invite and welcome the club's new incoming members. The meetings were so successful that the group decided to hold the lunches on a regular basis. They were open to any SF Rotarian who had no luncheon engagement that day. Later, the group also began to meet Tuesday evenings at a reserved table in the Palace Garden Court for dinner. SF Rotarians attended the meetings to foster acquaintance and to discuss issues in greater depth than the brief weekly club

James E. Deitz,
SF Rotary President
1979–80

luncheon permitted. Business was among the most common topics of interest. As it gained in popularity, the gathering came to be called the "Round Table." It started meeting five days per week, at member Charlie Hellwig's restaurant. The Birthday Divisions began a custom whereby two Divisions would hold a joint meeting at the Round Table. In the 1930s, SF Rotary also instituted an extension of the daily Round Table, in a monthly evening of supper and bridge, and many members sponsored a monthly breakfast meeting. The Round Table's meetings continued into the early 1950s.

Another focus on business emerged during the presidency of Jim Huckins in 1970–71. Through the efforts of Jim Deitz and the Vocational Service Committee, SF Rotary devoted a weekly meeting to a special Business Associates Luncheon program. This annual program furnished an opportunity for SF Rotarians to bring bosses, friends, and associates to a club meeting, and to hear a featured speaker. Some members even invited their competitors and employees. The annual Business Associates Luncheon continued for nearly twenty years.

The 1990s brought two new ways for SF Rotarians to exercise vocational service and advance their business objectives. In 1996, John Uth and Jean Schore conceived of a new venue for members to promote their businesses. That year, SF Rotary organized a "Rotafair." Created as a "District 5150 Trade Show," the fair was intended to continue the early tradition of Rotarians doing business with Rotarians, to share their business opportunities, and to foster a greater bond among Rotarians in District 5150. Over 150 Rotarians from the district showcased their businesses in dozens of booths. Several additional booths were donated for use by community and nonprofit organizations (as varied as the Boys & Girls Club and the San Francisco Zoo). The fair attracted three hundred attendees. Its net profit of $4,000 was donated to SF Rotary Service. District Governor Tony DeAngelis called the Rotafair "more vocational involvement than this district has ever seen," and SF Rotary won the 1995–96 District Award for Vocational Service. Rotafair was repeated in 1997 and 1998.

Meanwhile in 1997, President John Uth formed a new committee called Business Partners, to "help business in Rotary and add value to your membership." Chaired by Jean Schore, Business Partners met before the luncheon meeting each week. Any club member interested in sharing business ideas was invited to attend. The committee also encouraged SF Rotarians to advertise in *Grindings*, in the club's roster, and eventually on the club Web site. Other business promotion activities have included members' sponsorship of the pre-luncheon social hour and the luncheon's "news" item.

After Business Partners underwent a period of inactivity, Jean Shore revived it in 2004. Members of SF Rotary and the Rotary Club of San Francisco Golden Gate formed Rotary Means Business. With contemporary business etiquette discouraging active business promotion discussions in social settings, such as the greeting period before the weekly meeting, Rotary Means Business would provide a venue where discussion of business was encouraged. Its intent was to create a spirit of cooperation and education, to help Rotarians grow their businesses and in turn to provide growth within Rotary. The formal meeting was held as a cocktail party, and included an introduction of each member and their business. In return for providing a supportive networking environment, the committee encouraged Rotarians to voluntarily return 10 percent of the proceeds earned from the opportunity and to make larger contributions of time to their Rotary club.

Jean Schore

Good ideas grow. District 5150 announced that the Peninsula Rotary clubs were also forming Rotary Means Business, and the idea spread to Monterey as well. In 2007, Rotary Means Business became the Rotary Business Roundtable. The change came about because the committee wanted not so much a "networking group," as a venue for vocational service and the exchange of ideas. Today, the Rotary Business Roundtable serves two purposes: older members mentor younger members about business practices; and the gatherings include an educational component, such as a discussion about conducting business according to the Four-Way Test.

■ ■ ■

Sometimes the fellowship offered by Rotary is more important to people than they realize. While district governor in 2001, Pete Lagarias decided to make the district's annual benefit for The Rotary Foundation a real fellowship activity, where the district's Rotarians could mingle and talk and have fun. He arranged for a Greek-themed event at a winery in Sonoma, with catered food and Greek dancers. The benefit was scheduled for September 16, but the tragic attacks on September 11 intervened. As Pete recalls, only two people suggested the event should be cancelled. Pete replied, "We're going forward, because people want to talk." He judged correctly—"We wound up having over 900 people show up. We had told the caterer to expect 750. And our district has never had more than 300 at one of those events."

A Club for San Francisco

In a town where service clubs meet, the Lions enjoy it, the Kiwanians run it, and the Rotarians own it.

—SF Rotary President Francis Whitmer, 1956

In many respects, SF Rotary is an intrinsic part of San Francisco. Throughout its history, the club has enjoyed a tradition of close ties to its community. Most evident is SF Rotary's extensive record of service to San Francisco's residents. But there are other ties as well.

"Rotary Grove": A planting of eighty trees at Golden Gate Park, by President Lloyd Pflueger and Past President Jim Deitz, 1980. Courtesy of RI Archive.

The club has never stopped boosting for San Francisco or performing valuable acts of civic service. After World War I, the club contributed to the success of the construction of a new War Memorial Building on Van Ness Avenue. In 1936, SF Rotary was appointed as one of the publicity committees for the upcoming 1939 Golden Gate International Exposition. That same year, SF Rotary joined the city's other service clubs and civic organizations to host a joint luncheon for 1,500 to 2,000 businessmen, as part of the city's enormous celebration of its two bridges nearing completion. SF Rotary supported the campaign to "Save the Cable Cars" in the 1980s. After crisscrossing the city's hills for over a century, San Francisco's little traveling icons required a complete rebuilding.

SF Rotary's hand of service has touched many areas of the city, bringing improvements and beautification wherever it passes. A wide-ranging number of civic-service projects have included the refurbishment of the Fort Mason Museum kitchen in authentic period equipment, and a grant to San Francisco's antigraffiti office to produce an educational video for showing in public schools.

One of the club's earliest hands-on city beautification projects was its 1980 creation of a "Rotary Grove" in Golden Gate

Park. During Lloyd Pflueger's presidential year, club members planted eighty trees in the park, creating a reminder of Rotary's good work to all those who would welcome a moment of rest in the trees' shade. Since then, SF Rotarians have returned many times to the Park, planting and cleaning up.

More recently, SF Rotary embarked on a multi-year program to create a place of beauty where a NIKE missile-tracking station once stood. At one of the highest topographical points in the city on the very summit of San Francisco's Mount Sutro, a three-acre clearing in the Sutro Forest offers breathtaking views of the city, bay, and ocean.

In 2001, the University of California at San Francisco (UCSF) undertook a long-term program to restore this urban open space and make way for hikers and native plants once again. SF Rotary President Harold Hoogasian proposed a partnership between UCSF and SF Rotary to create a Rotary park on the site. To be called the "San Francisco Rotary Meadow," the project presented a "naming opportunity" and a visible presence for Rotary in San Francisco. It would also offer ongoing opportunities for hands-on service by San Francisco's Rotarians.

Harold M. Hoogasian,
SF Rotary President
2001–02

SF Rotary funded a $100,000 grant to UCSF, to help clear the overgrown former NIKE site and plant the meadow as a first step in the Mount Sutro Open Space Management Plan. The club pledged ongoing, multi-club support for the project with other Rotary clubs in San Francisco and San Mateo counties. The initial phase of the project took place over the next few years. It included trail rehabilitation and planting native trees and more than 1,500 native perennial flowers and other plants grown at the Presidio Nursery from local seeds. SF Rotarians participated in work days with other Rotary clubs. They weeded, prepared and planted hundreds of plants, and carted tons of gravel for paths. In the course of the restoration, some plants thought to have become extinct in San Francisco were rediscovered.

"I envision the meadow being enjoyed by the medical students at the nearby UC medical school. Perhaps in their later professional lives, some of them might recall San Francisco Rotary's good work—maybe even join and participate as Rotarians in a Rotaplast or Rotavision mission."

—Past President Harold Hoogasian, 2007

On June 25, 2005, Rotarians gathered to dedicate the San Francisco Rotary Meadow. They placed a permanent plaque, signifying Rotary's contribution to the meadow, and commemorating the founding of the United Nations in San Francisco sixty years before on that date.

The initial phases of SF Rotary's work are completed, and the San Francisco Rotary Meadow is open to the public. It provides a first-class demonstration area for a coastal-plant setting—a key part of the long-term UCSF project to rehabilitate the entire area. UCSF has created a wide-ranging volunteer base called the Mount Sutro Stewards, which oversees the ongoing work days once a month.

SF Rotary continues its support of the Rotary Meadow, with a monthly Rotary work day. Rotarians and members of

SF Rotarians participate in the first work party at the San Francisco Rotary Meadow on Mount Sutro, 2002.

the Rotaract Club of San Francisco enjoy a day outdoors, as they clear and restore overgrown trails, tend plants, and add signage. The work days enable SF Rotarians to enjoy hands-on service and fellowship in a beautiful outdoor setting. They continue to contribute to their city, while seeing first-hand the fruits of their Rotary service. The San Francisco Rotary Meadow will serve as a permanent public reminder of Rotary to all who visit, walk its trails, and enjoy a place of beauty in San Francisco's urban setting.

Some of SF Rotary's visible works are reflections of their time. At the end of the twentieth century, children have grown up in a society filled with guns. In 1999, SF Rotary supported a program called Peaceful Streets, which provided classes at the Boys & Girls Club that gave practical, potentially life-saving information for children about what to do when a gun is present. In addition, Peaceful Streets also works with schools, parks, or individuals to install park benches or bicycle racks made from melted-down weapons. At SF Rotarian Christina Harbridge-Law's suggestion, the club sponsored a children's

Christina Harbridge-Law

contest to design a pattern for a bicycle rack. The police department donated turned-in guns, and SF Rotary took school children to the foundry to watch the guns being melted down and cast into a bike rack—an instance of Peaceful Streets' "Guns Into Art."

SF Rotary's markers are evident throughout the city. The most visible and wellknown is the Four-Way Test plaque, placed during the club presidency of Chet MacPhee. In July 1974, Mayor Joseph Alioto signed the board of supervisors' request to designate the prominent intersection of Post, Montgomery, Market, and New Montgomery streets as the "Four-Way Corner," in honor of Rotary's Four-Way Test. The following February, Chet led the unveiling and dedication of an imposing bronze plaque, located on the outdoor wall of the Palace Hotel at the corner of the four-way street intersection. A quarter-century later, SF Rotarian Lillian Tsi-Stielstra shared a poignant story with club members. She told them how she saw the Four-Way Test plaque, "while meandering through the streets of San Francisco," shortly after she immigrated

A bicycle rack made with seventy-five semiautomatic pistols and installed in front of the San Francisco City Hall through a generous donation from SF Rotary.
Courtesy of Peaceful Streets

to this country. Lillian said she knew then that she would become a member of the Rotary Club.

Homer Wood envisioned Rotary as an important addition to San Francisco's most prestigious clubs. Within only a few years, the club was indeed a notable part of San Francisco's social fabric. A telling indication of the club's importance in San Francisco civic life dates from 1914. The Chamber of Commerce notified SF Rotary of its directors' vote to change the chamber's weekly luncheon meeting day from Tuesday to Friday. The chamber did not want its luncheon to conflict with Rotary's Tuesday meeting and create difficulty for the many SF Rotarians who would attend. After that, nearly

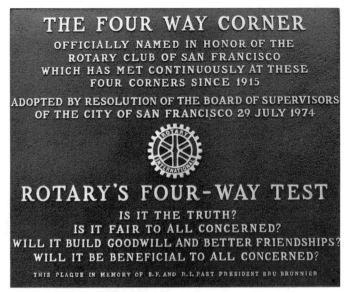

The Four-Way Test bronze plaque, placed on the wall of the Palace Hotel during the club presidency of Chet MacPhee, 1975.

seventy SF Rotarians attended the chamber's luncheon on Friday. In 1916, more than 50 of 275 SF Rotarians worked on the chamber's committee to recruit new chamber members. The efforts of the campaign gave San Francisco the largest Chamber of Commerce in the country.[70] SF Rotary continued its commitment to the chamber. In 1943, SF Rotarians were serving in the positions of president, general manager, and nine directorships.

The same year, club members also occupied the top spots of the Convention and Tourist Bureau. The club has also had a large presence in the Better Business Bureau as well. By 1956, nine of the previous ten presidents of the bureau had been SF Rotarians. At the time, three Rotarians were on the bureau's executive committee and fourteen Rotarians were directors. Historically, SF Rotary has also been well represented in the prestigious Bohemian Club. In 1953 alone, eighty-five members attended the club's annual Grove Encampment. (Members who attended the encampment were invariably "fined" each year when they returned.)

Barely into its first decade, SF Rotary was regarded by the city of San Francisco as an important city representative and a participant in city protocol. When U.S. President Woodrow Wilson visited San Francisco in 1919, Mayor James Rolph appointed club President Rusty Rogers and other Rotarians to serve on the Reception Committee for President Wilson. *Grindings* asked the club's 190 automobile owners to hold their cars for use in the festivities. SF Rotary held a joint luncheon in the president's honor at the Palace, along with the San Francisco Advertising Club, the Downtown Association, the Home Industry League, and the Commonwealth Club. The same year, King Albert I

---

70. At the 1928 district conference, one speaker offered the recommendation that membership in the chamber should be a prerequisite to joining Rotary.

"Rotarians hold key positions of leadership in our city, and they have shared their inside knowledge to give our members an advance look into the workings of our City."

—President Jim Bradley, 1999

of Belgium honored SF Rotary with his presence as a luncheon guest. The club in turn named King Albert an Honorary Member. King Albert subsequently invited SF Rotary President Paul Rieger to sit next to him at the main banquet's head table during RI's 1927 Convention in Ostend, Belgium. SF Rotary has a long-standing tie to the city's mayoralty. Most mayors of San Francisco have been members of the club—some Active, others as Honorary Members. Many mayors speak at club luncheons, and follow in a San Francisco tradition of proclaiming a special day to honor the outgoing SF Rotary president. SF Rotary honors the members of the San Francisco Consular Corps on World Wide Rotary Day, and "the city's finest" on Emergency Services Recognition Day.

Making It All Happen

SF Rotary's fellowship has come as a result of hard work by an office staff and thousands of club members serving on committees.

The Office

SF Rotary has maintained an office since 1910, when the club rented space in the Humboldt Savings Bank Building. Prior to that date, President Homer Wood had conducted club business from his law office in the First National Bank Building.

An early SF Rotary office.

The club remained at the Humboldt building until 1916, when it took up its longtime occupancy at the Palace Hotel. It encouraged members to make use of the large headquarters for business appointments and meetings.

In 1980, after sixty-four years at the Palace, the club relocated its office across the street to 55 New Montgomery (the building designed and occupied by Bru Brunnier's firm). In 1997, the office was moved again, this time to the Marines' Memorial Club on Sutter Street, where it also began to hold its luncheon meetings. When the club relocated its luncheons to the Kensington Park Hotel in 2004, the club moved its office back to 55 New Montgomery Street, where it remains today.

Since SF Rotary's founding, the club's affairs have been managed by a succession of outstanding secretaries and assistants. Although the club's first elected secretary, A. S. Darrow, served for only two months, SF Rotary has been fortunate. Most secretaries have served for extended periods, providing the continuity necessary for a club that changes administrations yearly. Darrow was succeeded in 1909 by club member "Rusty" Rogers, who served until 1914. The club hired its next secretary, Howard Feighner, as an employee, who served until 1917. His brother, Ervin Feighner, took charge and remained until 1937. Ervin's successor, Ed Whitney, served as secretary for twenty-seven years, until 1964. He was so popular he became the first employed secretary asked to join the club. Bud Park held the position for the next two years.

Brad Swope became the next to fill the position. He was a regular club member, and was hired as executive secretary in 1966. Brad was greatly respected in the club. He had occupied high-level administration positions

> "Stop talking business on street corners, and in hotel lobbies. Use that which is yours—the Rotary Offices."
>
> —*Grindings*, November 7, 1916

Executive Secretary Brad Swope

before coming to the club, and he brought his administrative skills with him. Brad passed away shortly after his retirement in 1980. The Bradford Swope Rotary Memorial Scholarship Fund was formed in his memory. He was also awarded one of the club's first Bru Brunnier Fellows. Several years later, his widow, Libby, became the only non-Rotarian Homer Wood Fellow.

Brad was succeeded in 1980 by Bill Ecker, hired as executive vice president and secretary. Bill, a retired army major general and corporate executive, also came to the club with administrative credentials. With his outstanding organizational skills, Bill helped guide club presidents gracefully through their presidential years. Bill was named a Bru Brunnier Fellow in 1992. Amid concern over declining membership in 1995, Bill proposed that his position be split, and Past President Dick Volberg be hired part-time to concentrate on membership development and retention. Bill remained executive vice president, while Executive Assistant Tessie Reyes became executive secretary. The year before Bill retired in 1997, District 5150 Governor Tony DeAngelis initiated a new award to be given to Rotarians within the district for lifetime achievement. He announced that the first award was presented to and named thereafter for Bill Ecker. Upon Bill's retirement, Mayor Willie Brown declared a "Bill Ecker Day" in San Francisco. Bill continued his membership in SF Rotary, and served as club president in 1999–2000. During his presidency, SF Rotary was awarded

William H. Ecker, Executive Vice President, 1980-1997; SF Rotary President 1999-2000

"Best Club" in the district, and received an Outstanding Club citation from RI.

Tessie Reyes, SF Rotary's present executive vice president, came to the position well-prepared with sixteen years of service. She was hired by the club as an assistant in 1981, and was promoted to executive assistant in 1993–94. Since becoming EVP in 1997, Tessie has run an office that serves the club well. Tessie has worked for periods without an assistant (at times the club has had as many as three), and she has taken over a number of tasks previously handled by club committees, including the demanding job of publishing the *Grindings* newsletter every week.

Executive Vice President Tessie Reyes

Honorary Member Helen Daugherty works regularly at the luncheon reception table.

Running SF Rotary efficiently is not a simple task. Over the years, a number of assistants have worked diligently, often behind the scene. Several have remained with the club for many years, helping to make the annual administrative changes happen more smoothly. Hired as assistant secretary in 1917, Adeline Worrell worked for the club for twenty-two years before her retirement in 1939. In 1967, assistant Barbara Shokal received a standing ovation for her thirty years of service.

Most recently, Administrative Assistant Shoko Valle worked ably and conscientiously, all the while maintaining a sunny disposition. Shoko left in December 2007 to become a mother.

Few have served SF Rotary as faithfully for as long as Helen Daugherty. Helen Chipian was hired as a clerk in 1959.[71] She retired in 1992, after thirty-three years. Upon her retirement, the club named Helen an Honorary Member. Helen continues with several long-time volunteer duties. Since her retirement, she has chaired the Sunshine Committee. She frequently helps out during busy periods in the office, and is most visible while staffing the reception table before the weekly luncheon. She still holds her Honorary Membership, a tribute to her nearly fifty years of dedicated service to SF Rotary.

Keeping Members Informed—Grindings *and www.sfrotary.org*

Since Homer Wood published his first bulletin barely two weeks after the club's founding banquet in 1908, SF Rotary has worked to keep its members informed of happenings within their club. After Homer left SF Rotary in 1911, the club introduced a short-lived new form of newsletter publication. *Spokes* appeared as a set of pages, interspersed in a complete club roster. The first issue of today's newsletter, *Grindings*, made its debut on April 8, 1913, as a pocket-sized eight pages. It reprinted the weekly speaker's text in full, sold advertising, and announced the "Boost Week" special.

Grindings has undergone a number of format changes in its ninety-five-year lifetime. In its first major format change in 1917, it became four full-size, densely packed pages. It claimed that its profuse advertising space was more than 70 percent subscribed for the full year, to help make the publication self-sustaining. The newsletter remained at four pages until 1931, full of writing about news, essays, poems (and a good deal of member advertising), all well presented and professionally printed. As the Great Depression struck America, *Grindings* was suddenly and drastically cut to one page, without advertising. Even that was perhaps too expensive, because the club's board considered eliminating it entirely in favor of a mailed notice of events. The club's members did not favor the change, and its size was temporarily reinstated to four pages. As the Depression continued, economic conditions forced a cut to one cheaply reproduced page in 1933. During World War II, the paper shortage forced *Grindings* to include the membership bulletin on its reverse side, rather than as a

---

71. Helen subsequently married Joe Daugherty, executive director of the Boys' Club.

separate page. *Grindings* remained at one typed page until a printed four-page format was introduced in 1964–65. Since then, its size and shape have undergone several more changes. *Grindings'* design was revised to the two-sided, one-page color format of today in 2001. In 2000, delivery of *Grindings* via e-mail was offered as an option to members, and it is also available on the club's Web site.

Grindings' masthead has undergone many changes over the years. During most of its history, it has in one way or another depicted some aspect of SF Rotary's city, San Francisco. The 1920s featured the Palace Hotel. At various times, sketches or photographs of the city's skyline have adorned the front page. In 1938, the masthead adopted the recently completed San Francisco–Oakland Bay Bridge. The Golden Gate Bridge has made an appearance as well. Today's familiar masthead features a sketch of San Francisco's most familiar sights by member and artist Al Tolf. His amusing drawings were first seen in the early 1980s. Although they changed periodically, they always included the city's best-loved icon, the cable

SF Rotarian Al Tolf's sketch appears on the Grindings *masthead each week.*

car. For a brief time, the masthead sported a little "Save the Cable Cars" sign, during the city's fund-raising campaign to rebuild the cable-car system. Al's cable cars have continued to enhance the masthead since his death in 1997.[72]

Grindings' content has varied considerably in ninety-five years. Descriptions of members' businesses have ranged from a weekly full-page spotlight on a single business as recently as the 1960s, to today's long-standing tradition of including the business name alongside the member's name. (The name in capital letters is another old tradition.) It is indicative of San Francisco's manufacturing past that issues of the 1920s contained extensive articles about the nature and manufacturing process of various kinds of products. Several forms of member biographies have come and gone, and some years' issues have included extensive obituaries of recently deceased members. Several club presidents have made it their practice to address the membership periodically on matters of club interest.

Humor occasionally takes over *Grindings'* back page. The "Roving Reporter" gossiped his way through most of the 1940s. He bore a striking resemblance to today's "Phantom," whose exposés of SF Rotarians' escapades and foibles (particularly Scott Hildula's) leave no stone unthrown.

Grindings has a history of commendable editorship. Although editors have not always been identified, Rusty Rogers probably served the longest as one of the newsletter's first editors. During SF Rotary's peak levels of membership in the 1960s, the newsletter was published by an editorial

---

72. Artist Al Tolf also contributed the beautiful painting of the Golden Gate Bridge and San Francisco that hangs in SF Rotary's office.

staff and a five-person committee. Another longtime and prolific editor was Bob Rockwell, who performed the task from the 1970s to 1981, at which time he left to serve as district governor. Bob's eloquent back-page essays about issues facing the club were always concise and thought-provoking. In recognition of his editorship, Bob was named an "ex-officio" board member. Today, Executive Vice President Tessie Reyes continues to publish the club's weekly newsletter with the help of rotating weekly "editors of the day."

Mike Tarantola

Grindings has frequently been recognized as the "Best Club Bulletin" in the district. It is remarkable that SF Rotary—through good times and bad—has an unbroken ninety-five-year record of publishing its weekly message to SF Rotary's members.

SF Rotary has been on the Internet for the past decade. Member Mike Tarantola brought the club's first Web site online in the 1990s. It welcomed SF Rotarians and visitors, and offered information about upcoming events. Each issue of *Grindings* was available on the site weekly, as well as an archive of several previous months' issues.

Scott Plakun

In 2000, the Technology Committee was formed, with Scott Plakun as chair. A new website was developed to bring up-to-date capabilities to the office and club members.

Scott and committee member Vikki Cooper introduced a redesigned Web site—www.sfrotary.org—in mid-2006. The new site has been greatly expanded, with information about the club's history, and descriptions of SF Rotary's many projects and alliances. The site's pages can be individually updated by the corresponding club committee chair. Members can access and update their profiles in the member directory. Several SF Rotarians and their businesses support the site through sponsorships. The Technology Committee is continuing development work to expand the site and add new capabilities for the future.

Points of Pride

SF Rotary's rich history is a source of great pride for the club's members. Among the club's impressive accomplishments, certain points stand out as worthy of note.

Conventions

SF Rotary has had the pleasure of hosting four Rotary International conventions. From the time of Rotary's first convention in 1910, SF Rotary sought to bring a convention to San Francisco. In 1911, when the city was awarded the privilege of holding the 1915 Panama-Pacific International Exposition, SF Rotarians recognized that 1915 would be the ideal year to welcome Rotarians from all over the world. Hosting an international RI Convention is always regarded as an honor, and San Francisco was competing with several clubs in the eastern United States. The decision for the 1915 convention would be made in 1914.

As the 1914 RI Houston Convention approached, SF Rotary and other California Rotary clubs spared no expense or effort as they planned a full-out campaign to win the prize for San Francisco.

They determined to create a big splash by entering Houston in a special train chartered by all of the clubs on the West Coast.[73] Along with the traveling Rotarians, the Exposition Company sent delegates on the special Rotary train, bringing motion pictures of San Francisco and the growing Exposition grounds, to promote the Exposition to all of the Houston Convention attendees. Knowing that creating interest in the Exposition would tilt the convention decision toward San Francisco, SF Rotary President Charles Victor boosted for the Exposition while in Houston. He pointed out that Rotary would undoubtedly extend around the world someday. What better way to expose people from all over the world to Rotary than during a major international world's fair?[74] Another popular SF Rotarian who worked the crowd was Charles A. Woodward—at age ninety-one, well-known as the oldest Rotarian in the world.

SF Rotary's "Uncle Charlie" Woodward, the oldest Rotarian in the world in 1915. —Grindings, August 31, 1915

Three months later, the decision was made. SF Rotary secured the convention unanimously, when the other five contending clubs withdrew their proposals. Instead, they pledged their backing to SF Rotary as a way to support the Panama-Pacific International Exposition, which they feared might suffer from European countries' withdrawals because of the recent outbreak of war in Europe. As *Grindings* reported, they "stepped aside in order that Rotary contribute her share to the success of the great Exposition, thus showing the world an exemplification of the Rotary spirit."

Held in the city's new Exposition Auditorium, the 1915 RI Convention in San Francisco was a huge success. The 1,988 attendees (the largest RI convention to that date) basked in the city's pleasant weather, and packed the Exposition. During "International Rotary Day" at the Exposition, a large Rotary flag flew high above the buildings. It was attached to a huge kite, and at night a fifty thousand candle-power searchlight played on it, making the flag plainly visible from all parts of the grounds and from many points in the city. In appreciation

Participants at the 1915 RI Convention in San Francisco enjoy the Panama-Pacific International Exposition.

73. This was the train journey that created "Rotary Ann."

74. Unhappily, while in Houston, the entire SF Rotary delegation was stricken with ptomaine poisoning. They fortunately recovered in time to return as planned to San Francisco.

Grand March in the Civic Auditorium at the 1938 RI Convention in San Francisco.

to the Rotary Club of Oakland for its support in bringing the convention to San Francisco, SF Rotary extended a courtesy to the Oakland club by inviting it to host a day of the convention. The 1915 Convention is memorable in Rotary history, for the adoption of the Rotary Code of Ethics and the division of Rotary clubs into the new system of districts under the direction of Bru Brunnier.

In 1938, SF Rotary again had the privilege of playing host to the Rotary world, during the club presidency of Johnny Crowe. Early that year, the RI committee set up its convention headquarters at offices in the Palace Hotel. Bru Brunnier was chosen to head the Host Club Convention Committee. Bru requested hosting and transportation help and assistance with foreign languages. Members' sons and daughters were asked to help a "Youth Committee" plan events for the convention's young visitors. Paul Harris accepted an invitation to stay at the home of a SF Rotarian—an honor indeed.

Spread between the Civic Auditorium, the Opera House, the Veterans Building, and the Fox Theater, the convention was a grand affair. The 10,481 attendees marveled at the beauty of the gardenlike House of Friendship, designed by SF Rotary Past President Al Roller. The room had been ingeniously transformed from the elegant site of the formal Grand March at the convention's opening to a relaxing oasis of garden furniture, colorful parasols, and hundreds of trees and flowers.

Market Street was ablaze with illuminated signs welcoming Rotarians from all over the world. Eight ferryboats transported Rotarians around the bay for a glimpse of San Francisco's two new bridges.

Bru Brunnier takes 1938 Convention-goers on a ferry tour to view the new San Francisco–Oakland Bay Bridge.

The Civic Auditorium during RI's San Francisco Convention, 1947.

Again in 1947, Rotarians came from the world over to enjoy the famed sights and lovely weather of San Francisco. SF Rotary President Earl Lee Kelly's committees were well-prepared for the largest convention attendance ever, and nearly fifteen thousand visiting Rotarians and families took advantage of the eased travel restrictions following the war.

Thirty years later, SF Rotary and other Bay Area host clubs welcomed 14,168 attendees to the 1977 RI Convention in San Francisco. Although RI's convention committee and SF Rotary President Arch Monson had been assured that the city's new Convention Center under construction would be ready to house the convention, it was not, so the convention was held for the fourth time in the Civic Auditorium. One of the key happenings of the convention was the traditional Tuesday Home Hospitality, when 3,000 Bay Area Rotarians opened their homes to 6,300 visiting Rotarians. Thousands of convention attendees cheered the rechartered Rotary Club of Madrid, which had met secretly for almost forty years since the Fascist takeover of Spain.

Anniversaries

Throughout SF Rotary's history, club members have paused to celebrate milestones, to recognize their accomplishments, and to look ahead to the future. On the club's thirtieth anniversary in 1938, President Harry Mitchell initiated the research and writing of the club's history. The two-year effort produced William Mountin's fine *History of the Rotary Club of San Francisco*, published in 1940.

A San Francisco icon decorates the poster for RI's 1977 Convention in San Francisco.

Ten years later, SF Rotary celebrated its fortieth anniversary—a span of two generations. Club founder Homer Wood was honored with a commemorative plaque, and Past RI President Tom Davis spoke on "The Inspiration of Rotary."

In 1958, SF Rotary gave itself a big fiftieth-anniversary party. The festivities included a Tuesday luncheon meeting, led by club Past President Lloyd E. Wilson. A record 750 Rotarians attended from SF Rotary and other clubs. RI President Clifford A. Randall predicted that in another fifty years, the international organization would grow to 1.25 million members in 27,500 clubs. Homer Wood and SF Rotary's three former RI Presidents were each presented with a nugget of

Homer Wood and three RI Presidents from SF Rotary meet at the club's fiftieth anniversary, 1958 (left to right: Charlie Wheeler, Homer Wood, Bru Brunnier, Almon Roth). Courtesy of Moulin Studios Archives

SF Rotarians and wives fill the Palace Hotel Garden Court for a dinner and pageant celebrating the club's fiftieth anniversary, 1958. Courtesy of Moulin Studios Archives

gold in a redwood jewel box. The following evening, 532 Rotarians and their ladies attended a formal dinner and pageant. They filled the Palace Garden Court, which was decorated with magnificent floral arrangements, and blew out the candles on fifty years of service to youth, community, and business. A SF Rotarian read greetings from other Rotary clubs in thirty-three countries. Homer Wood confidently predicted fifty more purposeful years for Rotary in San Francisco, "for its very nature calls out the best from our top leaders."

For SF Rotary's sixtieth anniversary in 1968, Bru and Ann Brunnier were honored at the club's luncheon meeting. Bru was recognized as the longest serving Rotarian in the world.

The club celebrated its seventy-fifth anniversary during Hal Gray's year in 1983, with a number of events and projects. Two years earlier, the board had decided to update the club's history in another book. Mitch Postel's *Seventy-Five Years in San Francisco* was published in the anniversary year. The centerpiece for the anniversary celebration was "Up with People"—an internationally famous education group, who presented their widely acclaimed musical show. SF Rotary provided housing for the 110-member group. *Grindings* announced that SF Rotary's club flag would fly over Union Square for one week, and the Union Square stage was reserved each lunchtime for Up with People performances.

Up with People also performed at Civic Center

Harold W. Gray Jr., SF Rotary President 1983–84

Plaza, where Mayor Dianne Feinstein presented Hal Gray with a proclamation acknowledging the community-service work done by the club.

While in San Francisco, the group also performed for many charities, including hospitals, clubs and institutions such as the Boys' Club, Laguna Honda Hospital, and Letterman Hospital. They entertained SF Rotarians at the weekly luncheon, and at the black-tie gala at the St. Francis Hotel.

As its major project for the anniversary year, SF Rotary raised $100,000 dollars to provide computers to the San Francisco Unified School District. Chet ("Soak") MacPhee Jr. arranged a private foundation

San Francisco Mayor Dianne Feinstein presents a Proclamation to SF Rotary President Hal Gray (left), on the club's seventy-fifth anniversary. The chairman of the City and County Employees for the United Way looks on, 1983.

Presentation of $100,000 of computers to San Francisco schools (left to right: Jim Patrick, Schools Superintendent Dr. Robert Alioto, SF Rotary President Hal Gray, Chet MacPhee, Jr., Dr. Gene Hopp), 1983.

gift of $25,000 for Rotary Service, if SF Rotarians would match the amount. A computer company in turn agreed to match the $50,000 and install the computers. In another anniversary-year act of community service, SF Rotary committed to building the bridge at the Boys' Club Camp Mendocino. SF Rotary presented a ceremonial model of the bridge to Les Andersen.

Kline A. Wilson Jr., SF Rotary President 1988–89

Club President Kline Wilson presided over SF Rotary's eightieth anniversary in 1988. Mayor Art Agnos declared a "Rotary Club Day" in honor of the club's eighty years of service. The celebration event was a Monte Carlo Casino Night. Each attendee received $100 in play money, and enjoyed games of chance. With the "funny money" winnings, the player could buy gifts donated by San Francisco retailers. After hors d'oeuvres, there was a prize drawing, and an auction conducted by Butterfield & Butterfield.

President Jim Bradley presided over the club's ninetieth anniversary in 1998. Sporting special ties and scarves designed by Past President Bob Wilhelm's wife, Irene, SF Rotarians and members of other District 5150 clubs attended an anniversary dinner at the Palace Hotel. They were in the company of three RI Presidents: James L. Lacy, Past RI President Cliff Dochterman (1992–93), and Past RI President Stan McCaffrey (1981–82). James Lacy addressed the gathering. To honor visiting RI President James Lacy, SF Rotary donated money to build five new cinder-block houses for Nicaraguan families left homeless in a hurricane. The evening concluded with a presentation, in which Paul Harris "conversed" from the past with Homer Wood about the founding of Rotary #2.

This year, SF Rotary will again celebrate its history, traditions, and achievements. Rotarians will enjoy a gala dinner at the St. Francis Hotel—the site of SF Rotary's founding banquet one hundred

SF Rotary Presidents at SF Rotary's ninetieth-anniversary celebration, 1998. Front row left to right: Bob Wilhelm, Marsh Blum, Pete Lagarias, John Uth; Middle row left to right: Dick Volberg, Allen Feder, Stuart Menist, Bill Koefoed; Back row left to right: Curtis Burr, President-Elect Bill Ecker, President Jim Bradley, Jim Patrick, Pete Taylor, Bill Sturgeon, Jim Deitz, Arch Monson.

years ago. There will be a parade down Market Street, tours and entertainment for visiting Rotarians, scarves and ties by Irene Wilhelm, and a special ceremonial Tuesday luncheon the week of the anniversary.

Awards

Each year, District 5150 rewards one club for its outstanding overall programs and projects during the year. SF Rotary has been awarded "Best Club" or "Best Large Club" during the club presidencies of: Pete Lagarias (1992–93), Bill Koefoed (1994–95), Curtis Burr (1996–97), Jim Bradley (1998-99), Bill Ecker (1999–2000), Howard Waits (2002–03), and Anita Stangl (2006–07).

While Bru Brunnier was still alive, District 513 created a Bru Brunnier Award for Distinguished International Service, to be awarded to the club submitting a project that most effectively encourages and fosters the advancement of international understanding through world fellowship. Bru himself presented the first award to SF Rotary President Ed McLellan in 1969. Since then, the district has recognized SF Rotary during the presidencies of Kline Wilson in 1989 and Pete Lagarias in 1993.

Rotary International presents its Significant Achievement Award to a club for an outstanding service project that addresses a community problem or need. During President Bill Koefoed's year (1994–95), SF Rotary received the prestigious Significant Achievement Award for the club's child-immunization project.

The club has been recognized with other awards. The Rotary International Presidential Citation is designed to motivate clubs to actively participate in service. Presented on an annual basis, the award traditionally highlights the RI president's emphases. President Dick Volberg accepted a Presidential Citation in 1990, as did President Howard Waits in 2003.

Individual SF Rotarians have been honored for their outstanding Rotary service. The Rotary Foundation District Service Award is given for a Rotarian's service on a broad basis

Bru Brunnier (right) presenting the district's Bru Brunnier Award for Distinguished International Service to SF Rotary President Ed McLellan, 1969. Courtesy of Moulin Studios Archives

over an extended period of time. SF Rotarians so honored are Dick Buxton, Kay Clarke, Bill Ecker, Joanne Ireland, Bill Koefoed, Pete Lagarias, Dr. Michael Sander, Bill Sturgeon, and Dick Volberg.

The Rotary Foundation awards the Citation for Meritorious Service for demonstrated active service to The Rotary Foundation over a period of more than one year. One Rotarian from each district may be recognized with the Citation by the Trustees each year. The citation has been awarded to Dr. Michael Sander and Dr. Scharleen Colant.

Rotary International's highest award for an individual Rotarian is its Service Above Self Award. It recognizes Rotarians who have demonstrated exemplary humanitarian service, with an emphasis on personal volunteer efforts and active involvement in helping others through Rotary. A maximum of 150 recipients may be selected each year. Four SF Rotarians are recipients of the prestigious award: Kay Clarke (1993), Dr. Angelo Capozzi (1996), Dr. Scharleen Colant (2006), and Heidi Kühn (2006).

SF Rotary honors individual members as well. Several presidents have awarded "Rotarian of the Month" to recognize specific accomplishments. Special appreciation has been given to members by some presidents, who present a "Rotarian of the Year" award. Such a member is Cecile Chiquette, who was recognized by President Anita Stangl in 2007 for her "years of consistent service" to the club, hard work on many committees, and readiness to serve whenever she is called upon.

Cecile Chiquette

Rotary International Presidents

SF Rotary claims four presidents of Rotary International among its membership.

Almon Roth, RI President, 1930–31

Almon Roth rose quickly through the ranks of Rotary. He was one of the organizers of the Rotary Club of Palo Alto in 1922. He served as its third president in 1925–26, then as district governor of District 2 in 1927–28. The next year, he served as RI director and second vice president. Two years later, he became RI's twentieth president—the first from District 2.

Al joined SF Rotary later, in 1937. As a shipping executive, president of a number of national ship owners organizations, and an expert in employment issues, Al spoke out throughout his Rotary career for fair and mutually beneficial labor-management relations.

Charles L. Wheeler—RI President 1943–44

Charlie Wheeler served as SF Rotary president in 1929–30. He went on to become district governor in 1938–39, then RI third vice president, and to head the Rotary world as RI president in 1943–44. As a shipping and lumber executive, Charlie was well prepared for the extensive world travel required of an RI president. His wartime presidential year is described in chapter 4.

Charlie continued to attend SF Rotary weekly meetings into an advanced age. In 1981, at age ninety-four, he accepted a certificate of appreciation from the club, and attended the Past Presidents' luncheon the following year. He was RI's oldest living past president. Upon his death in 1982, his tribute in *The Rotarian* was written by another Past RI President from SF Rotary, Stan McCaffrey.

Bru Brunnier—RI President 1952–53

Bru Brunnier became a member of SF Rotary in 1909. He served as RI President in 1952-53. Bru remained an active member of SF Rotary throughout his lifetime. At the time of his death in 1971, Bru was the longest-serving Rotarian in the world. Chapter 3 tells the story of Bru's illustrious life and career.

Photo courtesy of Moulin Studios Archives

Stanley E. McCaffrey—RI President 1981–82

Stanley McCaffrey was a member of SF Rotary from 1961 to 1971. He served as district governor of District 513 in 1964–65, during which time the district celebrated its fiftieth anniversary. He moved to Stockton in 1971.

Ten years later, Stan served as RI President. In his presidential year, he traveled 250,000 miles and visited seventy-five countries. He adopted "World Understanding and Peace Through Rotary" as his RI presidential theme, and later as the title of his book about his life. Many of his speeches during and after his presidency reflected his thoughts on this theme, which laid the visionary groundwork for several of RI's programs. During his year, Stan established the New Horizons Committee, chaired by Cliff Dochterman. The committee's task was to develop a long-term direction for Rotary. The efforts of the committee resulted in the initiation of the PolioPlus campaign.

Have We Made a Difference?

*Superficially, Rotary is seen as a federation of local groups of men who eat
together once a week. Actually, it is a reservoir of manpower, energized by common ideals and purposes, capable of doing great and good works.*

—SF Rotarian and RI President Charles Wheeler, 1943

As the Rotary Club of San Francisco looks back over the past century, an accounting is worthwhile.
What has been accomplished in these one hundred years? Have we made a difference? Where and
how? Some of SF Rotary's efforts are easy to assess; many are more difficult to quantify. All deserve
recognition.

SF Rotarians have given unstintingly of their time, effort, and money, as they have performed real civic and community service to the city and people of San Francisco. Since the founding of the club, they have worked to bring prosperity to San Francisco by "boosting" and striving
to attract business and tourists. They have sponsored useful civic projects, including beautification
efforts in Golden Gate Park and the Rotary Meadow.

Far more important than their civic work, however, is the genuine help SF Rotarians have
brought to the lives of uncounted San Franciscans, through humanitarian work for the poor, hungry, homeless, aged, sick, and disabled. SF Rotarians' broadest and most long-standing community service is their work with young people. This is the club's overarching legacy in its history
as a service organization. The treatment and care of handicapped children and the creation of the
Sunshine School eased the painful lives of many of these most unfortunate souls. SF Rotarians took
a leading role in the creation of a major organization that would become the Easter Seals, assisting
hundreds of thousands of disabled children and adults through services and advocacy.

Thanks to SF Rotarians' continuing commitment to the Boys & Girls Clubs of San Francisco,
this remarkable institution has flourished—bringing help and hope to tens of thousands of San
Francisco boys and girls, while guiding them to a better life. The club serves 1,200 children per
day in its nine branches, where they play and learn in a wholesome, safe environment. More than
1,400 kids attend camp per year. And because of the Rotary Bridge of Friendship, many can attend
"mini-camps" in the winter.

SF Rotarians' work with San Francisco's school-age children is exemplary. Club members
have mentored thousands of high-school students in programs such as Camp Enterprise, Academic
Decathlon, and Career Day. Donations of computers and books have brought knowledge to school
children. Thousands of dollars in scholarships have helped promising young people gain an education. Interact sponsorship has helped create service-minded young adults, and possible Rotarians
in the future.

SF Rotarians have reached out to the community in other ways, through assistance and
fund-raising for people with AIDS, advocating for organ/tissue donation registration, and bringing

shelter and services to the homeless. Thousands of children have been immunized against child-hood diseases. City facilities to serve young people have been upgraded.

Through Rotaract, SF Rotarians have helped young adults as they enter the business world. With guidance from SF Rotarians, Rotaractors have created their own community and international-service programs.

In times of city, national, and international crisis, SF Rotarians have stepped in. They have helped provide relief after earthquakes and floods throughout the world, and have raised money that built homes for Sri Lankans left homeless after an devastating tsunami. They have helped re-build a small Mississippi town's library in the wake of Hurricane Katrina, and provided emergency services to New York City residents following September 11, 2001.

As Rotary has opened its heart to the world, SF Rotarians have opened theirs. After two catastrophic world wars, they brought emergency relief to war-torn countries. For decades, they have extended the hand of friendship, welcoming thousands of visitors to their great city. Club events such as World Wide Rotary Day have strengthened the bonds between SF Rotarians and their guests from foreign lands.

SF Rotarians have given generously of themselves by participating in Rotary's work to bring about world peace and understanding. Club members' contributions of time and funding for pro-grams such as Ambassadorial Scholarships, Group Study Exchange, and Rotary World Peace Scholars have enriched the lives of hundreds of young adults around the world. Through their broadened out-look, many more people in distant lands have been touched indirectly by the friendship of Rotary.

The past twenty-five years have witnessed explosive growth in SF Rotarians' humanitarian efforts on large and small projects, each bringing much-needed assistance to the less fortunate in all corners of the world.

In the most successful humanitarian project ever adopted by any government, service club, or religious body in the world, Rotary International's extraordinary PolioPlus campaign has brought polio to the brink of eradication. Because of the hundreds of thousands of dollars raised and contributed by SF Rotarians, millions of children have been spared this crippling disease. Club members have traveled great distances to take an active part in immunization efforts.

Through their unbounded creativity and energy, SF Rotarians have introduced three extraor-dinary international programs that bring medical services to children in undeveloped countries. Rotaplast International has grown into an independent organization that sends an average of fif-teen cleft-lip/palate surgery missions per year. Since its first mission to South America in 1993, Rotaplast has sent 116 teams to forty-six sites in sixteen countries all over the world. It receives support and sponsorship of missions from more than fifty Rotary districts in the United States and Canada. Rotaplast has brought smiles and a normal life to over 10,500 children and young adults. It has also helped make local surgeons and nurses in each country self-sustaining givers of the Rotaplast gift to children of the region.

Rotavision International has sent more than fifty missions to seventeen countries across the globe. More than 1,800 children have been examined for pediatric eye disease, and over 1,200 surgeries have been demonstrated to more than 100 local physicians in seventeen developing countries. These physicians, in turn, have performed several thousand independent surgeries, using techniques and equipment provided by Rotavision. Best of all, they have trained other surgeons to take these skills back to their rural areas. This has greatly magnified the initial efforts of the Rotavision doctors and volunteers.

Since its founding in 2004, Alliance for Smiles has sent ten missions to five locations in China, bringing smiles to nearly 1,000 children suffering from cleft-lip/palate deformities. The first craniofacial treatment center has opened, and Alliance's long-term concentration of effort and alliance building has permanently improved the well-being of people in the Chinese regions it serves.

Most recently, SF Rotarians have undertaken a new partnership with another Rotarian-founded organization, Roots of Peace. The club will raise funding for demining efforts and re-planting projects to reestablish productive agriculture in areas overtaken by the deadly weapons of war.

Rotaplast, Rotavision, Alliance for Smiles, and Roots of Peace—in addition to serving their primary purposes, they advance international goodwill by enabling SF Rotarians to carry the message of Rotary throughout the world.

SF Rotarians' support and sponsorship of community and international programs and projects would not be possible were it not for their openhanded generosity. They have contributed substantially to The Rotary Foundation of Rotary International. Their contributions help make possible the worldwide miracle of Rotary's educational and humanitarian work. In addition, much of the money is returned as District Designated Funds for SF Rotary's local and international projects.

SF Rotarians have also contributed generously to the San Francisco Rotary Foundation. In each decade since its founding by forward-thinking club members in 1959, the Foundation has donated hundreds of thousands of dollars for educational and humanitarian purposes in the community and abroad. Under outstanding stewardship, it has grown to become one of the largest local Rotary club foundations in the United States.

SF Rotarians' enduring tradition of fellowship and service has brought benefits to San Franciscans, citizens of our nation, and people of the world. It has also brought abundant rewards to the club's members, whose lives have been enriched through their membership. They have experienced the incomparable satisfaction that comes from hands-on work to improve people's lives. Many, such as Les Andersen, have a lifetime of memories of children they've helped, one by one.

SF Rotarians' horizons have been vastly broadened through contact with other cultures. Humanitarian travel with Rotaplast, Rotavision, and Alliance for Smiles offers Rotarians unequalled travel experiences and the opportunity to bring a message of goodwill from America.

SF Rotarians have made close friendships. A Rotarian can have lifelong friends all over the world. Moreover, the fellowship found in Rotary is magnified a hundredfold when Rotarians are bonded in service. What can compare to working side-by-side with fellow club members for hours, then sharing in the sight of a grateful mother's joy?

SF Rotarians are continually able to bring their vocational skills to bear in helping their fellow members and others. Whether mentoring children, using their medical skills, or sharing business experience with other Rotarians, they are putting the spirit of Vocational Service into practice.

SF Rotarians have received the benefits of their club's weekly meetings, that provide a spirit of camaraderie and the opportunity to hear experts speak on a wide range of topics. Through their club activities, they increase their leadership, organizational, and public-speaking skills.

SF Rotarians have profited fairly through their contact with businesspeople of high integrity. Rotary's tradition of ethical conduct touches all aspects of their lives. They have found they cannot constantly apply the Four-Way Test to all their business relations eight hours each day without getting into the habit of doing it in their home, social, and community lives. They thus become better parents, better friends, and better citizens.

In the balance of all they have done to make a difference, a case can be made that SF Rotarians' greatest achievement came within the club's first year. By spreading the word of Rotary first on the West Coast, then to the East Coast, then to the British Isles, SF Rotarians introduced Rotary to the world. In the years that followed, SF Rotarians followed in Homer Wood's missionary footsteps and started Rotary clubs in California, New Mexico, Nevada, and Hawaii. Most recently, SF Rotarians have continued in this tradition. Their sponsorship and support of new clubs in San Francisco have brought new members into Rotary, and provided a diversity of programs in non-downtown parts of the city. Homer would be proud.

At the founding banquet of the Rotary Club of San Francisco on November 12, 1908, Homer Wood stood before a gathering of businessmen. He addressed them in a spirit of optimistic pride, as he declared, "I am glad to be a charter member of the Rotary Club because it is a civic organization which is going to accomplish more for the common good of San Francisco than any organization which is called a club." One hundred years have proved Homer was right. But in his optimism, Homer could scarcely have imagined what over four thousand men and women would go on to accomplish—a century of making a real difference for the people of San Francisco and the world.

▪ ▪ ▪

The Rotary Club of San Francisco has been fortunate to have among its members three men whose lineage is traced back to the club's beginnings. James M. Patrick was present at the club's founding banquet, and went on to serve as club president in 1933–34. His son, J. Howard Patrick served as president in 1959–60. Howard was followed by James M. Patrick II, who served the club as president in 1984–85. Boldly creative, gently irreverent, and unfailingly generous, these three men have moved forward with the progress of the club. As the living representative of this distinguished lineage, Jim Patrick offers a challenge:

The curtain is coming down on our first one hundred years, and we can
  hear the applause from behind the dense fabric.
We also hear through a break in the curtain
  many people still crying out for help.
The sounds of the poor and the needy seem to be greater than
  the applause.
Rotary's shout of "Service above Self" will continue to be needed,
  who knows, even after the curtain falls on the second one hundred years.

1908–10	Homer Wood		1959–60	J. Howard Patrick
1910–11	Arthur S. Holman		1960–61	George O. Bahrs
1911–12	M. Louis Wooley		1961–62	Alvin F. Derre
1912–13	Harold R. Basford		1962–63	Ernest Ingold II
1913–14	Henry J. Brunnier		1963–64	Harry H. Smith
1914–15	Charles H. Victor		1964–65	David N. Plant
1915–16	Constant J. Auger		1965–66	Edward C. Sequeira
1916–17	James Lynch		1966–67	Clarence C. Walker
1917–18	Harry G. McKannay		1967–68	Harold D. Bostock
1918–19	Roy R. Rogers		1968–69	Edgar G. McLellan
1919–20	Thomas Doane		1969–70	Sydney G. Worthington
1920–21	Roscoe F. Haegelin		1970–71	James C. Huckins
1921–22	Perry T. Cumberson		1971–72	Norman J. Corlett
1922–23	Paul Rieger		1972–73	Edwin S. Moore
1923–24	Howell H. Ware		1973–74	Raymond W. Hackett
1924–25	C. Walter Marwedel		1974–75	Chester R. MacPhee
1925–26	Matthew A. Harris		1975–76	Robert G. Tuck
1926–27	Henry Bostwick		1976–77	Arch Monson, Jr.
1927–28	Ben F. Blair		1977–78	Stuart D. Menist
1928–29	James A. Johnston		1978–79	Marvin E. Cardoza
1929–30	Charles L. Wheeler		1979–80	James E. Deitz
1930–31	Raymond M. Alvord		1980–81	Lloyd A. Pflueger
1931–32	G. Harold Porter		1981–82	Robert M. Lee
1932–33	Albert F. Roller		1982–83	Thomas C. Paton
1933–34	James M. Patrick		1983–84	Harold W. Gray, Jr.
1934–35	Austin W. Sperry		1984–85	James M. Patrick, II
1935–36	Alfred J. Gock		1985–86	Allen S. Feder
1936–37	Hubert M. Walker		1986–87	Marshall R. Blum
1937–38	M. H. "Johnny" Crowe		1987–88	William B. Sturgeon
1938–39	Harry A. Mitchell		1988–89	Kline A. Wilson, Jr.
1939–40	Thomas Rolph		1989–90	Richard C. Volberg
1940–41	Edward B. Ward		1990–91	James G. Emerson, Jr.
1941–42	William H. Thomas		1991–92	Peter V. Taylor
1942–43	Prentiss A. Rowe		1992–93	Peter C. Lagarias
1943–44	Herbert S. Shuey		1993–94	Robert B. Wilhelm
1944–45	Weller Noble		1994–95	William A. Koefoed
1945–46	E. W. Stephens		1995–96	W. Andrews Kirmse
1946–47	Earl Lee Kelly		1996–97	Curtis A. Burr
1947–48	H. C. "Deac" Hendee		1997–98	John Uth
1948–49	Ernest Ingold		1998–99	James W. Bradley
1949–50	Warren E. Griffith		1999–2000	William H. Ecker
1950–51	Lloyd E. Wilson		2000–01	Kathleen L. Beavers
1951–52	James E. Holbrook		2001–02	Harold M. Hoogasian
1952–53	James M. Tuttle		2002–03	Howard R. Waits
1953–54	Reginald L. Vaughan		2003–04	Richard B. Rosen
1954–55	Clyde L. Chamblin		2004–05	Grant E. Hundley
1955–56	Francis E. Whitmer		2005–06	Joseph S. Talmadge
1956–57	Ansel W. Robison		2006–07	Anita T. Stangl
1957–58	Eric M. Stanford		2007–08	John C. Hoch
1958–59	Russell J. Bowell		2008–09	Eric E. Schmautz

District Governors

1915–16	Henry J. "Bru" Brunnier
1923–24	Paul Rieger
1927–28	Almon E. Roth
1937–38	Charles L. Wheeler
1941–42	Roy N. Dreiman
1944–45	Prentiss A. Rowe
1949–50	Herbert S. Shuey
1955–56	E. Wick Stephens
1960–61	Francis E. Whitmer
1964–65	Stanley E. McCaffrey
1981–82	Robert R. Rockwell
1989–90	William B. Sturgeon
2001–02	Peter C. Lagarias

Rotary International Board of Directors

1910–11	Arthur S. Holman—Director
1912–13	M. Louis Wooley—Director
1917–18	Henry J. "Bru" Brunnier—Second Vice President
1928–29	Almon E. Roth—Second Vice President
1931–32	Almon E. Roth—Director
1935–36	Charles L. Wheeler—Third Vice President
1944–45	Charles L. Wheeler—Director
1953–54	Henry J. "Bru" Brunnier—Director
1953–54	Prentis A. Rowe—Director
1954–55	Prentis A. Rowe—Director
1969–70	Stanley E. McCaffrey—Director
1970–71	Stanley E. McCaffrey—First Vice President
1980–81	Stanley E. McCaffrey—President-Elect

Rotary International Presidents

1930–31	Almon E. Roth
1943–44	Charles L. Wheeler
1952–53	Henry J. "Bru" Brunnier
1981–82	Stanley E. McCaffrey

MEMBERS OF THE ROTARY CLUB OF SAN FRANCISCO, 1908–2008

This list was compiled by members of the Rotaract Club of San Francisco.

Evelyn Abad
George W. Abbett
Gregory W. Abbett
J. Conrad Abbett
Richard L. Abbott
Kyutaro Abiko
Richard W. Achuck
Fred W. Ackerman
Samuel P. Ackley
Alfred A. Acquaye
Wade Acton
Henry A. Adams
James L. Adams
Leland D. Adams, Jr.
Raymond C. Adams, Jr.
Roy D. Adams
Stuart R. R. Adams
Kristin J. Adryan
Harold P. Agmar
Francis J. Ahern
Tina M. Ahn
Gilbert S. Ahrens
King Albert I of Belgium *
Verna G. Aldous
Sophie Lei Aldrich
Alfred P. Alessandri
R. Michael Alexander
Robert F. Alioto
Henry A. Alker
Lewis Allbee
Caroline G. Allen
Chauncey D. Allen
Cleo D. Allen
Clifford R. Allen
Leighton Allen
Robert F. Allen
Kenneth W. Allen II
C. Donald Allen, Jr.
Dr. Robert E. Allen, Jr.
William B. Allender
John W. Allison
Robert W. Alspaugh
Oscar C. Alverson
J. Robert Alves
Raymond M. Alvord
Alan H. Ames
Joseph L. Amwake
Matthew P. Anagnostou
Charles L. Andersen
Christopher Andersen
Walter H. Andersen
Alan G. Anderson
David Anderson
Donald E. Anderson
Edward E. Anderson
Elmer E. Anderson
Frank J. Anderson
Howard F. Anderson

J. Milo Anderson
Marvin J. Anderson
Mike Anderson
Milton W. Anderson
P. Arnold Anderson
Ronald R. Anderson
Romano S. Andreini
F. O. Andres
Paul B. Andrew
Thomas P. Andrews
H. P. Anewalt
Lt. Col. Robert J. Angel
Cheryl G. Angelo
W. P. Angelo
Gregory L. Angermeier
Harry G. Annan
D. L. Anthony
Le Roy W. Anthony
N. John Anton
Frank J. Antony
Robert L. Appleby
William T. Archer
Stanley E. Arden
Robert L. Appleby
Bartley H. Arbing
Stanley E. Arden
Katsuhiro Arimatsu
Robert H. Armsby
C. F. Armstrong
George Armstrong
Msgr. Rev. Peter G. Armstrong
Michael Arndt
Albert Arnold
Laban A. Arnold
Lou Aronian
Dave L. Aronson
Joseph Arrigo
Lt. Gen. Robert Arter
Noel L. Arthur
T. S. Ary
Dr. Joseph Asher
Dr. R. Kirklin Ashley
Dr. Rea E. Ashley
Wallace I. Atherton
Benjamin C. Atkinson
Louis E. Aubrey
Constant J. Auger
Robert Auger
Frank W. Aust
Arthur Austin
Harry E. Austin
Edgar N. Ayers
John R. Ayers
James W. Azeltine
Robin Azevedo
Raymond E. Baarts
Willis W. Babb
Charles B. Babcock

Bradley S. Bach
Carl Bach
Paul Eric Bach
R. W. Bachrach
Edward R. Bacon
Paul B. Bacon
Hon. Alfred U. Baehler
H. Baerman
Henry B. Baerman
Colleen Bagan-McGill
Arthur J. Baggenstos
Kenneth B. Baggott
Ned D. Baglion
George O. Bahrs
Arthur Bailey
Emerson R. Bailey
George H. Bailey
Harry C. Bailey
Robert J. Bailey
Arthur L. Bailhache
John N. Baird
Walter M. Baird
Albert H. Baker
E. Harold Baker
Edward J. Baker
Geoffrey B. Baker
Gerald R. Baker
Herbert C. Baker
Joseph M. Baker
Lawrence C. Baker
S. A. Baker
W. R. Baker
Frank C. Balbo, Jr.
George E. Baldi
Joseph A. Baldi
Edward L. Baldwin
Curtis P. Balko
Eric S. Ball
F. W. Ball
Townley Ball
Willis E. Ball
Douglas P. Balluff
Robert A. Balzari
Polly M. Baney
B. A. Banker
William H. Banker
Charles F. Bannan
Philip L. Bannan
George W. Bannzhaf
John Banta
Dr. J. Henry Barbat
Renolds J. Barbieri
Mark C. Barden
D. R. Bardue
Edgar M. Barker
Arthur F. Barnard
Stephen E. Barnes
Wilbur L. Barnes

Wendell B. Barnes
Ray G. Barnett
Christopher H. Barnish
Alfred J. Barnston
Charles Barr
Robert H. Barr
William J. Barrett
Dr. Xavier O. Barrios
Victor S. Barrios
Jeffrey H. Barron
Raymond H. Barrows
Daniel D. Barry
Robert J. Barry
W. H. Barry
Frank A. Barsocchini
Dougald F. Barthelmess
Very Rev. C. Julian
  Bartlett, D.D.
Laurence Barton
Philip E. Barton
Harold R. Basford
L. Christon Basham
Cecil J. Bastedo
Claude E. Bates
Dr. Ernest A. Bates
Dudley S. Bates
Sylvania K. Bates
Louis F. Batmale
Adolph Battaini
Guy E. Baty
Edwin B. Bauer
Ernest S. Bauer
G. W. Bauer
Herman K. Bauer
D. F. Baxter
Howard W. Baxter
Kenneth S. Baxter
Paul N. Baxter
Lloyd F. Bayer
Fay C. Beal
Ralph R. Beal
Albert H. Bean
Elwin C. Beane
John Beater
Robert T. Beattie
David E. Beatty
David F. Beatty
Charles A. Beauchamp
Kathleen L. Beavers
J.C. Bebb
William R. Beck
John J. Becker
Scott F. Becker
Valerie L. Becker
Prof. Ernest G. Becker-
  Colonna
E. Hale Beckmann
Louis S. Beedy

* Honorary Member

Albert C. Beeson
Robert E. Begley
Robert F. Begley
Thomas R. Behrens
Rev. Joseph A. Belgum
J. Craig Bell
Nathan L. Bell
C.L. Bell, Jr.
C.L. Bell, Jr.
Jack Bellingham
Laurence D. Benamati
Harry R. Benjamin
George E. Bennett
H. C. Bennett
Helmer G. Benson
Marvin T. Benson
Jess E. Benton III
William F. Bentz
John Bentzen
Luther Bergdall
Herbert E. Bergren
Donald A. Bering
Charles T. Beringer
Douglas A. Berl
Laura E. Bernabei
Byrne Bernhard
Chris Bernhard
George M. Bernhard
H. Bruce Bernhard
Howard F. Bernhard
J. Alvin Bernhard
Robert Bernheim
William M. Bernheim
Burton Berry
Kenneth B. Berry
James G. Berryhill
Dr. Melvyn D. Bert
G. Joseph Bertain, Jr.
Andrew S. Berwick, Jr.
Dmitry Beskurnikov
Christoph Besmer
Joseph H. Best
Percy G. Betts
Josef Betz
Ralph J. Bidwell
Jack R. Bierma
David M. Bigeleisen
Russell T. Bigelow
Eugene K. Biggerstaff
Tiffany Birch
Myron Bird
Scott S. Bird
A. F. Bishop
George F. Bishop
L. Roy Bishop
Ralph R. Bishop
Roy N. Bishop
H. H. Bishopric
Paul A. Bissinger
Earl S. Bjonerud
Dr. James A. Black
John H. Black
Campbell W. Black
John R. Blackinger

Ben F. Blair
Robert S. Blake
William Ford Blake, MD
Curtis P. Blako
Harry B. Blatchly
Charles B. Blessing
Donald L. Blinco
Robert E. Blinn
A. Lee Blitch
Fernand Bloch
Jerry G. Blodgett
Marsden S. Blois
Henry J. Blommer, Jr.
Warren J. Blomseth
Roger G. Bloom
Alvin H. Blount
Robert T. Blowney
George P. Bloxham
Jean Blum
Joan K. Blum
Mark A. Blum
Marshall R. Blum
Robert C. Blum
Sello J. Blumenthal
T. Danforth Boardman
Fred J. Bobby
George U. Bocarde
J. B. Bocarde
Paul C. Boettcher
Harry R. Bogart
Johnson S. Bogart
Adolph C. Boldemann
Gerald M. Boldemann
Oscar Boldemann
Oscar Boldemann, Jr.
David C. Bole
Bradley S. Bolsinger
Carol R. Boman
Louis C. Boone
Norman M. Boone
Frank E. Booth
Norman T. Booth
F. Edward Borchers
Edwin A. Borden
John B. Bordi
Paul H. Bordwell, Jr.
David D. Borgonovo
George C. Bornemann
Angelo J. Boschetto
Dan Bosschart
William Bosschart
Dr. Frederic C. Bost
Harold D. Bostock
Harry Bostwick
Henry Bostwick
Nicholas D. Botaitis
David M. Botsford
John R. Botsford
David Botsford, Jr.
Harrison C. Bottorff
Vanessa A. Boulous
Pierre G. Bouret
Norman H. Bouton
William E. Bouton

Norman H. Bouton, Jr.
Hon. Henry E. Bovay
Clayton C. Bovyer
Russell J. Bowell
Charles C. Bowen
George T. Bowen
Harold G. Bowen
Kenneth B. Bowerman
William P. Bowersock
Peter J. Bowes
Philbrick Bowhay
Alpheus A. Bowman
George H. Bowman
Wentworth A. Bowman
Ralph S. M. Boyce
Harold J. Boyd
William B. Boyd
William J. Boyd
Henry F. Boyen
Ronald G. Boyer
Jarvis G. Boykin
Harry J. Boyle
Albert E. Boynton
H. Rollin Boynton
Nicholas J. Bracco
Harry R. Bracken
James M. Braden
James R. Bradford
Frank F. Bradley
Jack W. Bradley
James W. Bradley
Elizabeth R. Brady
Fred J. Brand
Charles A. Brandenburg
Charles Brandenstein
F. T. Brandenstein
J. H. Brandlund
Ivan Branson
Charles Bransten
Joseph A. Braun
Samuel B. Breck
William R. Bremner
Charles J. Brennan
John J. Brennan
Stephen F. Brennan
William A. Brennan
Arthur R. Breuer
William A. Brewer
Bradley M. Breyman
Dr. Elmer C. Bricca
John L. Bricker
Charles A. Brigham
Dennis Brimhall
Tobias S. Brink
J. C. Brittain
Hugh B. Brittan
John A. Britton
William H. Broadbent
John K. Brocklehurst
David H. Brodie
Major Harold Brodin
William F. Broll
Stuart A. Bronstein
Eugene H. Brooks

Marie K. Brooks
Nigel A.L. Brooks
Thomas A. Brooks
George W. Brouillet
Alvin W. Brown, Jr.
Ben C. Brown
C. O. Brown
Caspar M. Brown
Dr. Amos Brown
Dr. E. C. Brown
Geoffrey Brown
Geoffrey P. Brown
Henry S. Brown
James A. Brown, Jr.
James D. Brown
Lloyd F. Brown
Lyle M. Brown
Mark E. Brown
Philip F. Brown, Jr.
Steven D. Brown
Stephen F.M. Brown
William Brown
Hon. Willie L. Brown, Jr. *
Harry L. Browne
R. A. Brownlee
Stewart Brownstein
Dean Brubaker
Jack W. Bruce
William T. Bruce
Edward H. Brumfield
William C. Brumfield
Arthur J. Brunner
Thomas M. Brunner
Henry J. Brunnier
Walter Neat Brunt
Ralph H. Brunton
Gerald F. Brush
Spencer Brush
Dr. John R. Bryan
John E. Bryan
William Bryan
William V. Bryan
Thomas J. Buckholtz
Charlton H. Buckley
Henry M. Buckley
Richard M. Budd
Roy N. Buell
Fernando Buesa
George C. Bukowsky
Robert L. Bullard
Simpson A. Bullerwell
August F. Bulotti
Charles F. Bulotti
Charles F. Bulotti, Jr.
Lynn B. Bunim
Thomas E. Bunker
Dr. George E. Bunnell
Brig. Gen. Leslie M. Burger
Irvin L. Burke
Warren Burke
Richard M. Burkett
William A. Burkett
Victor L. Burner
Victor L. Burner, Jr.

* Honorary Member

Robert F. Burnett
Dr. Stanley Burnham
Edward M. Burnham
Edw. F. Burns
Guy W. Burns
Curtis A. Burr
M. J. Burress
G. Steven Burrill
Charles E. Burt
Clarence S. Burtchaell
Samuel W. Burtchaell
Dodge Burtt
Millard S. Bury
Brig. Gen. Fred N. Bussey
Frank I. Butler
John L. Butler
L. Francena Butler
Peter R. Butler
T. C. Butler
Fred R. Butterfield
John A. Butters
Dr. Otto Butz
Dickson C. Buxton
Julienne Buxton
Richard O. Buxton
Matthew J. Buzzell
Raymond E. Byler
Dr. Richard C. Caesar
Thomas J. Cahill
Richard S. Cahn
Charles P. Cain
Charles P. Cain, Jr.
Edward T. Cairns
Keith P. Calden
Marcus L. Caldwell
Mark Calender
Alexander D. Calhoun, Jr.
W. P. Calkins
Guyon L. Call
Charles G. Callaghan
W. C. Callaghan
John G. Callagy
James A. Callahan
Richard E. Callahan
Robert R. Callan
Hugo Callenberg, Jr.
John O. Camden
Gerald Campbell
J. Alan Campbell
James T. Campbell
L. Neil Campbell
M. Campbell
George Campe
Louis R. Campiglia
Carney J. Campion
James R. Campodonico
Carroll M. Cannoles
John F. Cannon
Charles Cantu
Angelo Capozzi, MD
Bal Raj Capur
Dr. Gregg J. Carb
Marvin E. Cardoza
Leo V. Carew

Rev. Harry V. Carlin, S.J.
Dudley N. Carlsen
Bonnie L. Carlson
Todd R. Carlson
D. Edward Carmichael
J. Halford Carmona
Julian S. Carnes
J. Michael Carney
George A. Carpenter
Russell D. Carpenter
Wm. Herbert Carr
Arthur P. Carroll
Dr. Howard F. Carroll
F. H. Carroll
Paul T. Carroll
Roy Carruthers
J. Philip Carson
Richard G. Carson
Dr. Leland E. Carter
Joan C. Cartwright, PhD
James Carver
Charles P. Cary
Donna M. Casey
Daniel J. Casey, Jr.
Armand Casini
Elmer G. Casperson
Lester O. Casperson
John R. Cassidy
Peter J. Caswell
Robert F. Cathcart
Robert F. Cathcart, Jr.
Glenn R. Caudell
Robert G. Caughey
C. Harold Caulfield
Joseph L. Cauthorn
John B. Cella II
Mayra Centeno-St. Andrew
Raymond N. Cerles
Charles A. Chaban
Michele L. Chaboudy
H. F. Chadburne
George Chalmers
Albert G. Chamberland
Clyde L. Chamblin
Garth A. Chamblin
Robert Louis Champion
Archie Chandler
Alex S. Chang
Andrew N. Chang
Walter R. Chao
Charles S. Chapman
Donald J. Chapman
George E. Chaquet
C. L. Chase
Julian D. Chase
Thoms H. Chatham
Louis C. Chausse
Claudine H. Y. Cheng
Guy Cherney
N. Ralph Cherrigan
Hsin-Pao Chia
Lauren Chiang
William K. Chiang
Neal T. Childs

Daniel K. Chinlund
Harold E. Chipman
Cecile Chiquette
Alexis S.M. Chiu
George Chow
Glenn L. Chrisman
Keith F. Christensen
Nancy B. Christenson
Carol Christie
Dr. Werner H. Christie
Lloyd F. Christie
Lloyd M. Christie
Robert M. Christie
Hon. George Christopher *
Philip D. Christopher
Myron M. Christy
Edward K. Chu
Steven D. Chung
Dr. Caesar A. Churchwell
Alex Chuzhoy
Sal Cisneros
Eugene W. Clapp
Addison L. Clark
Alexander T. Clark
Charles R. Clark
Donald P. Clark
Donald W. Clark
E. C. Clark
Michael C. Clark
Richard W. Clark
Ross M. Clark
Walter C. Clark
Gary R. Clarke
James T. Clarke
Kay P. Clarke
Peter A. Clarke
George Clarkson
Ervin H. Clausen
Tom F. Clausen
William H. Clawson
M. Colebrook Clayton
Alfred J. Cleary
John P. Cleese
Robert E. Clement
Sydney Clements
Horace B. Cleveland
Bertram J. Clifford
Charles H. Clifford
Curtis T. Clifford
Eugene S. Clifford
Mr. Cline
Edmond J. Clinton
Hon. Elias Clis
Herbert C. Clish
Michael Clothier
John U. Clowdsley, Jr.
Joseph A. Clyde
George S. Cobb
Russell H. Cobb
R. E. Cochran
Stanley L. Cocks
Stanley L. Cocks, Jr.
D. Coffin
Edward A. Cohen

Ernest J. Colant
Scharleen H. Colant, PhD
Gene D. Coldiron
Frank G. Cole
John R. Cole
Kelly Smith Cole
L. Charles Cole
Wallis W. Cole
Basil A. Coleman
William S. Coleman
Edward B. Collins
George C. Collins
George F. Collins
James R. Collins
John J. Collins
John T. Collins
Joseph J. Collins
R. M. Collins
Arthur M. Colomb
Rodney F. Coltart
C. C. Combellack
Emmet D. Condon
Edwin J. Conn
Brig. Gen. Richard M. Connell
Richard M. Connell
George C. Conner
George W. Conner
Leland S. Connick
Damon M. Connolly
Frank B. Connolly
Rob Connolly
Rt. Rev. Msgr. Matthew F.
Connolly
Hon. Donald B. Constine
Manuel C. Conte
John F. Conway, Jr.
Gil M. Coogler
Jesse B. Cook
Lew Cook
Milton H. Cook
Walter G. Cook, Jr.
Frederick O. Cooke
Leslie W. Cooley
Terence Coonan
C. E. Cooney
Paul H. Coop
Capt. Martin K. Cooper
Frank E. Cooper
Montague E. Cooper
Tim P. Cooper
Todd B. Cooper
Verner S. Cooper
Victoria A. Cooper
Walter F. Cooper
Jack D. Coplen
Almon L. Copley
James P. Copolla
Edward F. Corbett
Sam E. Corbin
Charles W. Corbitt
Norman J. Corlett
Rhes. H. Cornelius
Harold R. Cossitt
Joseph V. Costello

Richard W. Costello
Ronald E. Costello
Lorenz Costello III
Lorenz Costello, Jr.
F. E. Cotharin
E. B. Courvoisier
Clarence A. Cowan
Max A. Cowan
William Cowden
Coleman Cox
Gerald F. Cox
William G. Coxon
Robert C. Crampton
Guy W. Crane
Arden A. Crawford
Dr. David J. Crawford
Hubert M. Crawford
Robert F. Crawford
Paul J. Creasey
Leonard E. Creed
Leonard F. Creed
Fred J. Crisp
Walter G. Criswell
J. S. Critchlow
Eugene O. Crocker
Robert M. Crocker
L. Gordon Crocket
Pierce E. Cromwell
Elizabeth Cronin
Marshall F. Cropley
David E. Crosby
C. V. Cross
Charles V. Cross, MD
I. O. Crosscup
R. V. Crowder
Johnny W. Crowe
Milton H. Crowe
Robert M. Crum
Allan T. Crutcher
George Thomas Cullen
Terrence P. Cullen
Charles M. Culver
Irving S. Culver
W. E. Cumback
Perry T. Cumberson
Harold W. Cummings
John L. Cummings
James Cummins
Arthur F. Cunningham
Neil P. Cunningham
Richard C. Cunningham
Robert B. Cunningham
Herberet C. Cupit
John S. Curran
Dean A. Curtin
Aaron I. Curtis
Albert G. Curtis
Claudia Curtis
Ralph G. Curtis
Ray H. Curtiss
Frankland L. Cutshall
E. F. Cykler
Ronald C. Cynor
Robert R. Dable

A. K. Daggett
John P. Dahl
John Dahlinger
Richard Dahut
Robert W. Dailey
Charles M. Dale
James R. Daley
Irving R. Daly
F. A. DaMert
Charles H. Dana
Anjelo J. Daneri
Ernest A. Daniels
Thomas M. Daniels
Joseph N. Daniszewski
John Danli
William E. Danver
A. S. Darrow
Dr. Rose Dastmalchi
William L. D'Atri
Helen C. Daugherty *
Joe B. Daugherty
Wade Davenport
Scott A. Davey
Paul David
A. L. B. Davies
P. Michael Davies
A. B. Davis
Dr. Albert David Davis
George R. Davis
George T. Davis
Harrison H. Davis
Joseph J. Davis
Julian R. Davis
Owen H. Davis
Paul Davis
R. J. Davis
Sylvan D. Davis
Christopher M.
Dawson-Roberts
Osborne H. Day
Thomas E. Day
William A. Day
Philip S. Day, Jr.
Alfred B. Dayton
Frank J. De Benedetti
P. Leroy De Bevoise
Pio V. De Feo
Dr. Albert P. de Ferrari
James E. De Franco
Harold G. De Golia
David De Haven
Edward V. De La Torre
Francois De Lajugie
Rev. James W. De Lange
Elie F. R. De Lanoy
John D. De Leeuw
Stephen L. De Maria
Robert De Martini
James G. De Martini IV
C. Vincent De Nevers
Donald J. De Porter
Dudley Deane
Dr. Martin W. Debenham
James G. Decatur

Joseph A. Dee
Thomas J. Dee, Jr.
Frank Degen
Walter Degen
James E. Deitz
Filippo Del Favero
Gina Del Vecchio
Bert L. Delaney
L. E. Delano
Thomas A. DeLay
Ana Maria Delgado
Thomas F. Delury
Joseph A. DeMaria
Willis M. Deming
C. E. Dempsey
Howard E. Denbo, MD
Wilbert W. Dennis
M. R. Denton
Paul E. Derby
A. T. DeRome
Alvin F. Derre
David C. Detrick
Edward W. Detrick
John R. Dettner
Diana W. Detwiler
Ralph B. Dewey
Ranjan K. Dey
Massimo Di Giulio
Owen S. Dibbern
Leland C. Dibble
James S. Dielschneider
John M. Diggs
Dr. Howard H. Dignan
Philip J. Dillon
Bruce A. Dingwall
H. Dinslage
John H. Dissmeyer III
Frank L. Ditzler
Hugh W. Ditzler
Ben D. Dixon
Jay R. Dixon
R. T. Dixon
William R. Dixon
Leland A. Doan
Osborne C. Doane
Thomas H. Doane
Evan S. Dobelle
Michael L. Dobrov
Douglas W. Dodge
H. C. Dodge
Neil F. Dodge
Elena Dokuchayeva
Lee S. Dolson, Jr., PhD
Catherine E. Dombrowski
Bob Donahue
Thomas E. Donahue
John R. Donlan
Joseph P. Donnelly
William F. Donnelly
Paul D. Donohue
Cleo P. Donovan
David M. Dooley
Thomas H. Dooling
Detlev Doring

Milton E. Dorman
Dr. Nazila Doroodian
Reece H. Dorr
Richard E. Dotts
H. E. Doty
James T. Doty
Arthur H. Dougall, Jr.
Michael J. Dougherty
Calvin H. Douglas
Robert M. Douglas
George A. Dow
Henry Dowden
John J. Downey
Donald D. Doyle
James F. Doyle
John F. Doyle
Roy N. Dreiman
Jesper Drejet
Luigi Dreon
Forrest H. Dresslar
Donald W. Dreusike
John S. Drew
Pierce A. Drew
Dan A. Driscoll
Charles F. Drocco
Clarence A. Drucker
Jacqueline H. Drum
E. L. Drury
Richard C. Drury
Sherman P. Duckel
Louis M. DuCommun
Robert L. Duerson
A. Blair Duffy, Jr.
J. Glen Duke
Charles W. Dullea
Robert L. Dumas
Robert F. Dumesnil
Glenn S. Dumke
Charles L. Duncan
Jules Dundes
Howard E. Dunlap
Ritchie L. Dunn
T. J. Dunn
Thomas C. Dunworth
Milton J. Durand
Morris D. Durham
Lavell S. Durrell
Grayson Dutton
John J. Dwyer
Michael B. Dybeck
David A. Dye
H. D. Dye
Roland E. Dye
Ezra Hunt Dyer
Maj. Gregory W. Dyson
James M. Eaneman
George H. Earhart
Robert J. Easterlin
Harvey V. Eastling
C. A. Eastman
Hart Eastman
Dianne M. Easton
Henry J. Eavey
George H. Eberhard

---

* Honorary Member

Harry E. Echols, Jr.
Maj. Gen. William H. Ecker
E. T. M. Eckert
Robert H. Eckhoff
Roberta Economidis
Robert L. Eddy
R. Carl Eddy, Jr.
Mary Edington
John W. Edminson
Thomas R. Edmiston
Douglas L. Edmonds
William R. Edmonson
Frank Edwards
Frederick R. Edwards
Gene M. Edwards
George P. Edwards
Harry Edwards
Norman W. Edwards
Raymond A. Edwards
Robert F. Edwards
Robert W. Edwards
Thomas R. Edwards
Clarence E. Edwords *
Warren C. Eggert
Henry R. Ehlers
Albert Ehrgott
Erich A. Eisenegger
P.J. Eisenmann
Dalhart R. Eklund
Paul Elder
Paul Elder, Jr.
Richard M. Elefant
David F. Elgart
Hon. Siri Marie Eliason
Paul Eliel
Tom H. Elkington
Albert D. Elledge
Charles M. Elliot
David H. Elliot
Stewart P. Elliot
Charles V. Elliott
Johnston Elliott
Robert S. Elliott
Thomas E. Elliott
Jack M. Ellis
Raymond L. Ellis
James O. Ellison
Dr.Ranveig Elvebakk
Merton E. Elwess
John W. Elwood
Joseph L. Emanuel
Walter A. Emerick
E. A. Emerson
Dr. James G. Emerson, Jr.
G. W. Emmons
Jerome J. Engel
Edward E. Engelhardt
David M. Engelman
Elizabeth A. England
Erick A. Engman
Erick R. Engman
Leif T. Engman
Edward W. Engs, Jr.
Hilton F. Ennis

Frank Enos
James M. Ensign
Clarence Eppstein
George C. Erb
Phillip A. Erbes
James B. Erickson
John V. Erickson
George E. Erlin
J. Theo. Erlin
Eugene E. Ernst
Robbi G. W. Ernst III
William W. Erskine
Robert H. Erwin III
Robert H. Escher
E. E. Esdon
Douglas O. Esposito
Harold P. Etter
M. Sherman Eubanks
Charles H. Evans
Charles S. Evans
Del Evans
Dr. John C. Evans
Gerald Evans
John C. Evans
Robert J. Evans
Marvin P. Evenson
Donald L. Everingham
Frank H. Evers
David G. Ewing
J. C. Ewing
J. Cal Ewing
Ralph S. Exley
Robert J. Exley
George P. Fackt
Arthur Faget
Kenneth M. Fahy
R. Thomas Fair
John A. Fairchild
Joseph S. Fairchild
Donald P. Falconer
Hon. John H. Faltz
Louis E. Fambrini
Stanley R. Farber
Hala Farid
Mandana Y. Farmaian
Dr. Daniel C. Farnham
Bruce C. Farnow
Frederick W. Farnow
Stephen R. Farrand
Lawrence N. Farrell
Jane E. Fassett
Claude T. Faw
Norvin A. Fay
Don Fazackerley
Louis J. Fazackerly
A. T. Feaster III
Allen S. Feder
John M. Feder
Dr. William A. Federal
Alfred F. Federico
Claudine Feibusch
Howard H. Feighner
Hon. Dianne Feinstein *
Morris Feintuch

Jesse Feldman
Walter Feldmann
Douglas J. Fellom
Arthur R. Fennimore
John D. Fenstermacher
Roger H. Ferger
Thomas E. Fergoda
W. K. Allen Ferguson
Milton W. Ferrari
John D. Ferris
Paul J. Ferroggiaro
Roy J. Feuchter
Harry A. Fialer
William H. Field
Paula C. Fillari
William M. Fine
James A. Finklenstein
Raymond A. Finn
Herbert E. Fischbeck
C. Alan Fischer
Emil A. Fischer
Sam A. Fischer
Sophian E. Fischer
Glenn H. Fisher
Herbert T. Fisher
Charles C. Fiske
Marjorie F. Fitterer
Kristen Fitzgerald
Terence S. Fitzgerald
Harry F. Flachs
Clifford J. Flack
John W. Flanagan
Patrick J. Flanagan
Thomas J. Flanagan
Charles Fleischman
Edward C. Fleischman
Martin R. Fleischmann
Dr. Carol A. Fleming
Eugene D. Fletchall
Steven R. Fletcher
David B. Flinn
Lawrence Flores, Jr.
James L. Flournoy
Kenneth M. Flower
Marybeth Flower
Robley E. Flynn
Harry B. Fogerson
Lisa Fong
Thomas L. Fong
William Fong
Tracy M. Fontana
Willis M. Forbes
Joseph A. Forbush
Arthur E. Forderer
George S. Forderer
Arthur E. Forderer, Jr.
Ed. H. Forestier
Leonard J. Fortun
David C. Forward *
Donald F. Foster
W. Blair Foster
Dirks B. Foster
Lori Foster
Frederick O. Foster, Jr.

Dr. Dudley J. Fournier
James R. Fowler
W. H. B. Fowler
Wilson S. Fowler
G. L. Fox
Charles W. Foy
Keith Fraizer
Anthony M. Frank
James E. Frank
C. Dean Franklin
David G. Franzblau
Jack S. Fraser
James E. Fraser
John P. Fraser
I. Benjamin Frasse
Homer B. Frazier
A. R. Fredericks
Max Fredrick
David I. Freed
Barry L. Freedman
Murray H. Freedman
Gilbert Freeman
Thelma-Jeanne Freeman
Timothy F. Freeman
Todd L. Freeman
Harold J. Freemon
Harold R. Freemon
B. Thomas French
Holland French
Tab S. French
Leon N. Fricke
Robert Fried
Dr. Meyer Friedman
K. Bruce Friedman
Duane L. Frisbie
Karen Frishman
Ralph D. Frisselle
John E. Fritz
Lynn C. Fritz
James R. Frolick
Elizabeth Frome
Koji Fujii
William S. Fulwider
B. Reed Funsten
Horace R. Furnas
Harry Gabriel
Sharon L. Gadberry
Eugene M. Gaetano
Michael A. Gaffey
Frank S. Gaines
Clement E. Galante
Donald M. Galbraith
Fred B. Galbreath
J. W. Gale
Gary M. Gallagher
Raymond J. Gallagher
Robert F. Gallagher
Edward R. Galland
Melissa Galliani
Clark Galloway
Michael Ganahl
William Ganey
Thomas M. Gannon
Bud Gansel

---

* Honorary Member

John O. Gantner
Fiore Garbarino
Robert F. Gardiner
Verne E. Garehime
Dr. L. Henry Garland
Joseph F. Garriott
John Garth
Judith M. Garvey
Noah C. Gause
George D. Gavin
George R. Gay
Henry M. Gay
Robert H. Gay
Bert A. Gayman
Herbert E. Gearon
M. B. Geary
Philip E. Geauque
Donald M. Geesey
Robert L. Geiger
Harold H. Geissenheimer
Dennis P. Gemberling
Edward D. Gendason
Clare R. Gennaro
Raymond D. Gennette
John R. Gentry
Pam Gentry
Charles E. George
Martha Geraty
Peter C. Gerhardt
Peter W. Gerhardt
William S. Gerrard
Carl H. Gertridge
Ben C. Gerwick, Jr.
Joseph B. Ghirardo
Roberto Giannicola
Dr. Morton R. Gibbons
Dr. John O. Gibbs
Clifford E. Giesseman
Joseph G. Giesting
Alva H. Giffin
Ranson D. Gifford
C. Robert Gilberg
Frank L. Gilbert
Hinda S. Gilbert
John B. Gilbert
John P. Gilbert
E. Archie Gilbert, Jr.
William E. Giles
William E. Gillaspy
James E. Gilleran
Robert G. Gillespie
James R. Gillette
Vern C. Gillmore
Don E. Gilman
Floyd R. Gilman
James N. Gilman
Glenn A. Gilmore
Robert M. Gilmore
Robert M. Gilmore, Jr.
J. H. Gingg
Barrett L. Giorgis
Carol Rae Giovannini
Victoria Ann Girard
Andrew P. Girerd

Augustus L. Gladding
Kenneth M. Glaser, Jr.
William E. Gleason
John O. Glover
Alfred J. Gock
Edward Goeppner
Charles W. Goetting
Edward H. Goetze
John William Goetze
Bruce R. Goff
William F. Goines, Jr.
John W. Goings
Benned M. Golcher
W. J. Golcher
D. Daniel Golden
Dr. Albert C. Goldenberg
Dr. Morris Goldstein
Henry Goldstein
Susan N. Goldstein
Rex M. Golobic
Richard O. Gomez
Douglas M. Good
James C. Good
Will B. Goode
Harry Goodfriend
Orton E. Goodwin
Charles W. Goodwin, Jr.
Danilo C. Goquingco
De Voy E. Gordon
Linda S. Gordon
Roger L. Gordon
William M. Gordon
Phil E. Goss
Andrew Gotelli
Sophus C. Goth
Jos. A. Gottlieb
Harry P. Gough
Charles L. Gould
Lewis A. Gould
Russell Gowans
Janet Goy
George S. Goyer
Daniele F. Gozzi
Lester B. Graf
Lester G. Graf
Wilson C. Graff
Charles H. Graham
Coleman J. Graham
Evelyn J. Graham
Leo E. Grandi
Irving H. Granicher
Roland K. Grannis
Donald Grant
Dr. Jon B. Grant
Wallace A. Grant
Alfred E. Grantham
Peter T. Grassi
Robert C. Grassi
F. Warren Grawemeyer
John G. Gray
Peter J. Gray
Harold W. Gray, Jr.
Barry A. Graynor
E.C. Grayson

Eugene J. Grealish
George Greaves
Dr. Vincent H. Greco
Bartley C. Green
Edwin A. Green
Fred H. Green
George R. Green
J. Charles Green
Philip N. Greenaway
Stuart L. Greenberg
Stuart N. Greenberg
Brydon S. Greene
H. W. Greenfield
Will S. Greenfield
Louis H. Greenhood
Ronald Greenspane
Jonathan Greenstein
George E. Greenwood
Michael C. Greenwood
H. G. Gregory
William R. Greig
Mark A. Grenadier
Raymond C. Grialou
Rene C. Grialou
Norman L. Grib
Dana J. Gribben
Carlos P. Griffin
Herbert K. Griffin
W. J. Griffin
Walter C. Griffin
Gerald R. Griffith
H. Dennis Griffith
Warren E. Griffith
Roscoe W. Griggs
Dr. Frank P. Grimaldi
William D. Grimmer
Ole Grini
William E. Grohe
Charles E. Grosjean
Leon E. Grosjean
Olaf J. Groth
Edward T. Grove
Roul J. Gruenberg
Willard W. Grundel
James A. Gruner
Alfred W. Gruss
Francisco J. Guedez
Richard J. Guggenhime
Gil M. Guglielmi
John A. Guilfoy
Dr. John Gullett
Alfred S. Gump
Richard B. Gump
William E. Gump
Roger W. Gunder
Charles M. Gunn
George A. Gunn
Harry W. Guppy
Leland M. Gustafson
Rev. William Kirk Guthrie
H. W. Gutte
Gregory J. Gutting
Edward D. Haas
George Haas

Lewis E. Haas
Reuben C. Haas
George Habenicht
Rudie Habenicht
Rudolph Habenicht
Raymond W. Hackett
William D. Hadeler
Peter Haeberlin
Roscoe F. Haegelin
Russell C. Haehl
Harold F. Haener
C. Craig Hagerman
J. Milton Hagler
William E. Hagler
Max W. Hahn
Dr.David W. Haines
James C. Hale
Otis R. Hale
Lloyd A. Hales
Harry S. Haley
John G. Halkett
A. Leonard Hall
Col. F. Whitney Hall
George G. Hall
Norman W. Hall
Mons Hallberg
James M. Halligan
C. Wiles Hallock, Jr.
Samuel L. Halsey, Jr.
W. A. Halsted
Jay P. Hamerslag
Julian L. Hamerslag
Earl Hamilton
Lawrence A. Hamilton
Rear Adm. Thomas J. Hamilton
Robert J. Hamilton
Noble Hamilton, Jr.
Col. John D. Hamilton, Sr.
Ruskin B. Hamlin
Edwin C. Hammer
F. Albert Hammergren
Julian L. Hammerschlag
F. Arthur Hammersmith
John A. Hammersmith
William C. Hammersmith
Alfred P. Hammond
Fred W. Hammond
James E. Hammond
Stefanie Hanebutt
William J. Hanley
Frank S. Hanlon
Charles C. Hannah
A. Hanselman
Adolf L. Hansen
Bernhard A. Hansen
Dr. Warren K. Hansen
Eleanor S. Hansen
George F. Hansen
Edward B. Hanson
George B. Hanson
Ralph Happer
J. Harry Harbour
Christina A. Harbridge-Law

Stanley R. Harding
Harold L. Hardwick
Charles C. Hardy
Elizabeth Hardy
Henry C. Hargis
Frank R. Harlocker
A. L. Harlow
Max W. Harman
Richard H. Harms
Winslow K. Harnden
Michael L. Harp
Logan Harrell
William H. Harrelson
J. L. Harrington
Patricia M. Harrington
Robert W. Harrington
Clark H. Harris
Dave E. Harris
David W. Harris
Granville L. Harris
Gregory Harris
Matthew A. Harris
Milton M. Harris
Ward Harris
J. Stewart Harrison
Lt. Gen. William H. Harrison
Alan S. Hart
George D. Hart
George H. Hart
James J. Hartigan
Alfred A. Hartley
Hugh V. Hartley
Fred Hartsook
Dennis J. Hartzell
Dr. Robert A. Harvey
Edward Hase
William Hasenberg
Elmer G. Haskin, Jr.
S. Montgomery Haslett
S. M. Haslett, Jr.
Howard Hassard
Wallace F. Hastie
Earle R. Hatch
Scott B. Hauge
Carl W. Hauser
William D. Hautt
L. Q. Haven
David H. Havice
Byron L. Haviside
C. A. Hawkins
Col. Eugene D. Hawkins
James S. Hawkins
Ernest R. Hawkinson
W. A. Hawley
Anthony Hay
Douglas Hay
James C. Hayden
Arthur H. Hayes
David A. Hayes
Dr. Phil B. Hayes
Philip L. Hayes
Richard B. Hayes
Webb W. Hayes, Jr.
William E. Haynes

T. A. Hays
Paul E. Hazelrig
Harold L. Heakin
E. C. Healy
James P. Healy
Richard R. Heath
Jonas Heaton
Norris J. Heckel
Arthur E. Hedges
S. Ralph Heger
Adam J. Heidenreich
Erwin A. Heieck
Erwin N. Heieck
Paul J. Heieck
Kurt W. Heinrichson
Richard W. Heintz
Henry D. Heitmuller
Thomas P. Helch
Leslie A. Helgesson
Charles A. Hellwig
W. L. Helvey
C. C. Hemler
Harold C. Hendee
Clark T. Henderson
John Henderson
T. Stephen Henderson
W. H. Hendricks
Larry G. Hengl
Joe J. Henkel
H. H. Henrici
Robert S. Henry
Thomas G. Henry
William E. Henry
David H. Hepburn
James C. Hepburn
John Hepburn
Alfred E. Herer
Edward N. Hermsen
Warren Hernand
Robert I. Herndon
George V. Herrero
J. Willis Hershey
Joseph Herstam, Jr.
Allan L. Herzog
Boris A. Hesser, PhD
George W, Heuermann
William A. Hewitt
Capt. I. N. Hibberd
Raymond D. Hickey
Richard C. Hickman
Louis A. Hicks
Douglas M. Hiemstra
John M. Higgins
John F. Higgins, Jr.
Richard J. Hightower
John L. Higley
Scott A. Hildula
Arthur B. Hill
Donald P. Hill
Dr. S. Anson Hill
Mallory P. Hill
Thomas L. Hill
Mary Hillabrand
Stanley V. W. Hiller

Herbert G. Hills
Ira L. Hillyer
Fred L. Hilmer
Wray F. Hiltabrand
Alfred W. Hincks
Robert R. Hind
Omar E. Hines
Henry M. Hink
Dr. Allen T. Hinman
Alphonse Hirsh
Richard A. Hiscox
Heather Hitchcook
Harold H. Hixson
C. John Hoch
Fred C. Hock
Harold H. Hoeber
Charles P. Hoehn
Dan E. Hoffman
Ralph M. Hoffman
Robert J. Hoffman
Wayne W. Hoffman
Zachary Hoffman
Harry Hofius
John M. Hofmann
William J. Hogan
William H. Hogue
William L. Hoisington
George C. Holberton
James E. Holbrook *
Walter E. Holcomb
H. E. Holladay
C. Wendell Holland
Robert P. Holland
Robert B. Hollenbach
Robert P. Holliday
Earl W. Hollingsworth
Charles B. Hollywood
William Hollzer
Arthur S. Holman
Charles Devens Holman
Burdette J. Holmes
Charles M. Holmes
Gene E. Holmes
Hans Holmes
Henry E. Holmes
Lt. Col. Robert S. Holmes
Oren A. Holmes
Perry Holmes
Jeanine B. Holmlund
Robert W.P. Holstrom
Edgar Holton
A. Gerlof Homan
Soon-Kyung Hong
George E. Honn
Harold M. Hoogasian
Frank W. Hook
Keith W. Hooks
Joseph Hoomany
Barney W. Hoon
Alfred S. Hooper
Winston P. Hoose
John F. Hoover
Dr. Eugene S. Hopp
Robert E. Hopper

H. R. Hopps
Timothy P. Hornbecker
Dr. Warren D. Horner
C. W. Hornick
A. E. Hornlein
Ellett W. Horsman
Jack K. Horton
Thomas A. Horvath
Larry L. Hostetler
Joseph Hotchner
A. J. Houston
Dean W. Hovencamp
Jack H. How
Edward R. Howard
Harmon K. Howard
Harry W. Howard
Thomas J. Howard
Thomas M. Howard
Charles K. Howe
Colby Howe
Felton W. Howe
Lewis B. Howe
Albert J. Howell
Dr. Edgar H. Howell
Edward B. Howell
John L. Howell
Dr. Carl G. Howie
Greg B. Howie
Frank B. Hoyt
John W. Hoyt
Thomas Hsieh
Fred W. D. Hu
Elmer R. Hubacher
C. B. Hubbard
Adolph Huber
Dr. Wolfgang K. Huber
Robert E. Huber
James C. Huckins
Howard W. Hudgins
Hillman Hudson
Leo C, Hudson
James R. Hughes
James S. Hughes
Julie T. Hughes
Randolph B. Hughes
Walter N. Hughes
William L. Hughes
W. L. Hughson
Fred G.E. Huleen
Stanley W. Hulett
Eugene E. Hundley
Grant E. Hundley
Charles P. Hunt
Phelps S. Hunter
Robert C. Hunter
Richard J. Huntington
Lu Hurley
Leslie E. Hurst
Jack A. Hurt
C. Susan Huskisson
Mary Huss
E. Elmore Hutchison
Stan Hutton
Carlton E. Hyde

* Honorary Member

Walter G. Hyman
William L. Hyman
Alton P. Hynes
John D. Hynes
Laurence B. Icely
Sam Ickelheimer
Carl Ilg
Marta E. Illescas
Conrad E. Imhaus
Edwin G. Imhaus
Ronald E. Imhaus
David D. Imrie
Herbert D. Imrie
Michael M. Inan
Theodore A. Ingham
Ernest Ingold
Ernest Ingold II
Edward Injayan
Steven A. Injayan
Dr. T. Christie Innes
Joanne K. Ireland
B. Clifford Irelend
Fred A. Irvin
Myford P. Irvine
Jacques L. Iselin
William Isler
Edmund Ivani
Harold H. Iwamasa
Mike K. Iwasaki
Harry Jackson
Harry W. Jackson
Wilbert H. Jackson
Godfrey F. Jacobs
H. Earle Jacobs
J. Dean Jacobs
E. Edwin Jacobson
Fred Jacobson
William H. Jaenicke
Richard S. Jamar, Jr.
Allan P. James
Harry T. James
Thomas N. Jamieson
Donald F. Javete
Louis A. Jeanpierre
J. Arnell Jeffery
Wesley E. Jenkins
Edward B. Jennings
Joseph J. Jeno
James E. Jensen
John D. Jessup
Kevin P. Jewell
Robert M. Jochner
Hermann-Victor Johnen, PhD
A. S. Johnson
Alan C. Johnson
Augustus Johnson
Douglas M. Johnson
Edwin A. Johnson
Edwin A. Johnson, Jr.
Elmer B. Johnson
Elmer E. Johnson
Frank Johnson
Leland H. Johnson
M. Marvin Johnson

Lt. Col. Robert G. Johnson
Stephen W. Johnson
Stephen W. Johnson, Jr.
Thomas P. Johnson
Vernon Johnson
Walter B. Johnson
Wilber R. Johnson
Ivar Johnsson
Jack H. Johnston
James A. Johnston
Samuel P. Johnston
Brig. Gen. Homer Johnstone
Ernest S. Jones
Gretchen T. Jones
H. A. Jones
Harry T. Jones
Hon. Proctor P. Jones
Howard P. Jones
J. Carl Jones
Lorna D. Jones
O. T. Jones
Owen T. Jones
Paul M. Jones
Randall L. Jones
Robert E. Jones
Beverly-Charlotte Jones
Rev. Albert R. Jonsen
Daniel Joraanstad
Allan R. Jordan
Harry C. Jordan
Hon. Frank M. Jordan
Hon. Pierre Jordan
Wayne G. Jordan
Clarence C. Jorgensen
Richard F. Jose
Robert D. Joyce
Leon B. Jpnes
Jerry J. Judd
F. W. Judson
James B. Judy
Felix Kahn
Paul S. Kaiser
Oleg A. Kaluzhny
Steven D. Kam
Robert H. Kammer
Pius Kampfen
Donald M. Kantola
Arthur Kanzee
Arthur Kanzel
Yezdar S. Kaoosji
Arlene J. Kaplan
Gwendolyn Kaplan
Murray J. Kaplan
Emil Kardos
Clas G. Karlberg
Louise Karu
Dr. Arthur J. Katz
Jon R. Katzenbach
Harold Kaufman
Hiroshi Kawabuchi
James Kay
Roland T. Kay
Robert Keagy
Jeannette Kearney

Daniel F. Keefe
Jack M. Keeney
James C. Keesling
James B. Keister
Arthur R. Keith
Angel S. Kelchev
Richard G. Kellenbach
D. Susan Keller
Walter N. Kelley
William H. Kelley
Shirley Kellicutt
Fred W. Kellogg
Brig.Gen. Patrick J. Kelly
Earl Lee Kelly
Walter E. Kelly
Louis O. Kelso
John H. Kemp, Jr.
Marron Kendrick
David D. Kennedy
George W. Kennedy
James H. Kennedy
John F. Kennedy
John M. Kennedy
Richard R. Kennedy
John M. Kennedy, Jr.
Joseph L. Kenrick
Harold W. Kephart
James H. Kepler
John F. Kerbleski
Robert B. Kern
Douglas A. Keyston
Frederick B. Keyston
William C. Kiefer
T. C. Kierulff
Charles S. Kilcourse
Dr. Eugene S. Kilgore, Jr.
Hugh W. Killebrew, Jr.
David C. Killingsworth
Harold W. Kilpatrick
Frank F. Kilsby
William R. Kilty
Kun Sam Kim
J. V. Kimball
William R. Kimball
Roy W. Kimberlin
Joseph K. Kimes
Arthur F. King
Claude R. King
James A. King
James D. King
Lloyd J. Kingsley
William A. Kingwell
William G. Kinsey
Charles H. Kinsley
Jerome W. Kintner
Ronald F. Kinton
William T Kirk, Jr.
George D. Kirkland
W. Andrews Kirmse
Ernest L. Kirschner
Graham T. Kislingbury
Howard D. Kisner
John Kitchen, Jr.
Williams S. Kiyasu, MD

Andrew F. Klase
Addison Klays
A. J. Kleinke
J. G. Klemm
Fred M. Kleppe
Henry C. Klevesahl
Frank J. Klimm
Christopher C Knapp
William D. Knick
T. Max Kniesche, Jr.
Arthur W. Knight
Ralph D. Knight
W. Arthur Knuckey
Elizabeth H. Koefoed
William A. Koefoed
William A. Koefoed, Jr.
John F. Koehnel
Forrest Koenig
Frank Koenig
L. C. Koesel
Fred S. Kohlruss
Michael L. Kokesh
John F. Kooistra
Henry R. Kopcial
Andreas Korbes
C. L. Koster
Frederick J. Koster
Leo Paul Koulos
A. G. Kraus
Ellen D. Krengel
Franklin E. Kriebel
L. B. Krieger
Naresh Kripalani
Robert W. Krobitzsch
Harry Kroft
Barry E. Kroll
Dr. Oscar J. Kron
Victor A. Kropff
Laurence Krueger
K. Marissa Krupa
Dorothy S. Krzyzanoski
Keith F. Kube
F. Robert Kuchem
Henry N. Kuechler, Jr.
Leonard V. Kuhi
Heidi T. Kühn
Dr. Roger C. Kühn
Tucker Kühn
Matthias A. Kuntzsch
Isamu Kurokawa
Courtney H. Kurtz
M. Kuttner
David Kweder
Bartholomew M. H. Kwok
W. D. Kyle
Fred La Cosse
La Verne A. La Counte
Ernest A. La Fleur
Frank P. La Rose
Herbert H. La Vigne
Emile L. Labadie
Mary C. LaBriola
Louis Lacaze
Arthur G. Lachman

* Honorary Member

Gustave Lachman
Robert D. Ladley
William A. Ladley
Nina LaDow
Peter C. Lagarias
Harold J. Laipply
Richard Lakers
Shivraj Lalchandani
H. T. Lally
Benjamin Y. Lam
Ngam Lam
Joseph P. Lamberson
Alfred E. Lampe
Paul L. Lamson
Edmund S. Lancaster
William J. Lancaster
Eric J. Landtbom
Richard F. Landy
Alfred W. Lane
Herbert J. Lane
Carl E. Lang
Wendy Lang
Laurence Lange
Arlington Langley
Ellis B. Langley, Jr.
Robert Langseth
Frank P. Lansing
Edward Lanz
Henri Lapuyade
Kenneth V. Larkin
Richard J. Larkin, Jr.
William B. Larkins
Emile Laroulandie
Niels Larsen
Ralph N. Larson
L. R. Larzelere
William E. Lashbrook
Philip G. Lasky
Carlos B. Lastreto
Edward T. Lau
Fred H. Lau
Fred Laubscher
C. S. Laumeister, Jr.
Deborah J. Lauricella
Charles J. Lawlor
Leslie M. Lawrence
Ernest G. Lawson
Harry M. Lawson
James L. Lazarus
William Lazorchick
Orville L. Le Noue
William M. Le Roy
William D. Leahy
Chester Leatham
George H. Leathurby
Leo Lebenbaum
Brig. Gen. Frank F. Ledford
Alfred S. Lee
Edwin A. Lee
Eugene W. Lee
Frank E. Lee
Frederic M. Lee
Harry A. Lee
Joseph E. Lee

Robert M. Lee
Theodore B. Lee
Russ B. Leech
Robert L. Lefebvre
Louis A. Lefevre
Charles Legalos
J. George Leibold
Walter S. Leland
William E. Leland
Warren M. Lemmon
William R. Lenderking
Edmund B. Lennig
Gus A. Lenoir
Pascal J. Lenoir
Wilbur N. Lenz
J. Paul Leonard
James H. Leonhard
Ben K. Lerer
Hector Leslie, Jr.
Albert L. Lesseman
Sol L. Lesser
Joseph S. Lester
M. S. Lester
Emil J. Leuenberger, Jr.
Elizabeth K. S. Leung
Kai Leung
Samuel Leung
Louis F. Leurey
William M. Levensaler
Sam M. Levenson
Paul J. Levey
Louis Levin
Mitchell S. Levine
Robin B. Levine
David J. Levinson
M. Levinson
John G. Levison
Sidney T. Levy
S. Rutherford Levy, MD
Dr. John C. Lewin
Werner Lewin
Philips F. Lewis
Thomas A. Lewis
William J. Lewis
Vernon A. Libby
M. George Lickteig
Lloyd H. Liebman
Bruce W. Liedstrand
Joseph H. Light
Keith A. Ligons
Ira S. Lillick
Raymond C. Lillie
Marc C. Limacher
David Yintso Lin
Anthony Lincoln
Carl E. Lind
Robert T. Lindemann
Alfred Lindenbaum
Arne C. Lindholm
Clarence R. Lindner
Dr. Gary Lindsay
Brendan M. Linn
John H. Linneman, Jr.
George H. Linsley, Jr.

George J. Linsley, Jr.
Jesse O. Linzer
Edgar H. Lion, Jr.
Douglas M. Lipinski
Alfred Lipman
Michael Lipman
Robert L. Lippert, Jr.
Thomas S. Liston
John A. Lithgow
I. F. Littlefield
Archie E. Littler
Lifong Liu
Robert L. Liu
William J. Livermore
Benjamin J. Y. Lo
Lester F. Lobe
Bruce L. Locken
Charles Loesch
John C. Logan
Ralph E. Logan
Clarence J. Loges
Robert R. M. Logie
E. L. Lomax
John A. Lombard
Lawrence J. Lombard
Daniel E. London
Dr. Ward W. Long
Herbert L. Long
Jeffrey G. Long
Stanley B. Long
John R. Longmore
Harry E. Loomis
Loren Lopin
J. N. Lopstad
David A. Lord
Jean-Baptiste Lorda
Scott R. Loring
William H. Losee, Jr.
Xiangjie Lou
Joe D. Loughrey
Jason Louie
Lt. Col. Richard Love
Ernest C. Low
Peter C. Low
James F. Lowrie
James W. Lowrie
Kathleen M. Lucas
Raymond F. Luce
George H. Luchsinger
Dr. Lloyd D. Luckman
David R. Luddy
C. W. Ludwick
Carl A. Luhrs
Edward R. Lund
Louis B. Lundborg
James M. Lundy
Theodore Lunstedt
Harry Lutgens
Harold J. Lyman
James Lynch
Joseph M. Lynch
Malcolm A. Lynch
John P. Lynn
Wallace R. Lynn

Anthony K. Lynott
John G. Lyons
Fred C. Lyser
Frank G. Mac Ilroy
Donald A. MacArthur
John J. Macauley
William E. MacBeath
Emmett W. MacCorkle, Jr.
Iain A. MacDonald
Wallace MacFarlane
Lynn M. MacFayden
R. J. Machen
Albert E. Macino
J. D. MacKenzie
J Gazzam MacKenzie, Jr.
Martin Mackey
Albert C. MacMahon
Chester R. MacPhee
Chester R. MacPhee, Jr.
J. Kenneth MacPherson
Richard G. Maddox
Jon C. Madonna
J. Harold Magee
Albert E. Maggio
Henry C. Maginn
S. D. Magnes
Patrick Maguire
Frederick Mahan
Geralyne Mahoney
James W. Mahoney
John F. Maillard
Charlotte Mailliard-Shultz
Emilio J. Maionchi
Dr. Daniel H. Mairani
Alexander M. Maisin
William A. Majors
George Makins
Walter J. Malberg
Phillip A. Mallet
Lt. Gen. Glynn C. Mallory, Jr.
Arthur H. Malm
William D. Manca
J. Chester Manchester
Brooks T. Mancini
Jay C. Mancini
Joseph A. Mancini
Robert T. Mann
John L. Manning
Halsey E. Manwaring
Eligio Maoli
Giuseppe Maoli
Jerry W. Mapp
Darlene V. Mar
Howard Marans
Philip J. March
George M. Mardikian
Haig G. Mardikian
Herbert S. Margetts
Howard H. Markell, MD
William M. Markell
George A. Markey
Jon C. Markoulis
Willard G. Marks
Thomas D. Marquoit

Frederic R. Marschner
Anne Marselis
H. T. Marsh
Harry C. Marsh
Robert B. Marsh
Henry A. Marshall
Richard F. Marshall
Richard H. Marshall
Susan C. Marshall
Michael E. Martello
Bernard L. Martin
C. U. Martin
Dennis T. Martin
Donald J. Martin
J. P. Martin
Jerry D. Martin
John Martin
Terry P. Martin
Jerry D. Martin
Frank L. Martinelli
Remo A. Martinelli
Marc F. Martini
C. Walter Marwedel
C. Arthur Marwedel, Jr.
Thomas F. Maschler
Donald B. Maskell
Angela Y. Mason
Joseph G. Mason
Roy T. Mason
John L. Mason
Charles Massen
Dr. Judith L. Mates
Chris S. Mathieson
Chris S. Mathieson
John H. Matkin
F. L. Matthes
Albert Matthews
C. E. Matthewson
Robert H. Matthey
Lawrence C. Mattison
Louis G. Mauer
Charles D. Maurer, Jr.
Charles H. Mauvais
Byron Mauzy
Charles S. Mauzy
Harry U. Maxfield
Jack Maxfield
Charles H. Mayer
Herbert J. Mayer
Herbert J. Maynard
Richard P. Mazurek
Lloyd L. Mazzera
Judith E. McAbee
William A. McAfee
Frank McArthur
W. D. McArthur
Warren H. McBryde
John C. McCabe
Stanley E. McCaffrey
John D. McCamish
Melnotte McCants
Charles L. McCarthy
E. Walter McCarthy
George J. McCarthy

John J. McCarthy
Robert M. McCarthy
William H. McCarthy
Alex D. McCarty
Harry McClelland
Vice-Adm. Joseph J.
  McClelland
Barney H. McClure
Marshall D. McClure
Marshall F. McComb
Dr. Joseph L. McCool
Ferd S. McCord
Ferdinand S. McCord
John W. McCorkle
Michael F. McCormac
Ernest O. McCormick
James A. McCormick
Paul J. McCormick
H. D. McCoy
Peter M. McCoy
Edward D. McCrary
Dorothy McCrea
Thomas E. McCullough
Harry S. McCurdy
William H. McDaniel
George G. McDonald
J. M. McDonald
Miles V. McDonald
William V. McDonald
Phillip A. McDonnell
Brian McDonough
James H. McDonough
Clyde S. McDowell
Harry H. McElroy
Lloyd H. McFadden, Jr.
Charles L. McFarland
John W. McFarland
Dr. William K. McGarvey
Donald J. McGee
F. L. McGillion
John D. McGilvray
Jerry L. McGinnis
Dale McGlauflin
Hugh McGlynn
Joseph P. McGuinness
Frank X. McGuire
Robert J. McGuire
William J. McHarg
F. J. McHenry
John J. McHugh
Rev. William C. McInnes, S.J.
Gary P. McKae
Kelly K. McKae
Harry G. McKannay
Audrey O. McKeague
Frank McKee
Richard L. McKee
James I. McKeown
Harlow E. McKinney
Ron McKinney
Lachlin C. McKinnon
Rae C. McLaren
A. Cyrus McLaughlin
Robert McLean

Ron McLean
Edgar G. McLellan
Wakeman G. McLellan
William McLeod
Donald McMillan
John A. McMillan
Patrick D. McMillan
Patrick J. McMillan
A. Ward McMullen
Andrew W. McMullen
K. David McNamara
D. Roy McNeill, Jr.
B. Harding McPhun
Ben H. McPhun
R. Bruce McQuarrie, Jr.
Robert L. McRoskey
George E. McShea
L. Roy McWethy
Wallace McWhirter
William B. McWhirter
R. P. Meehan
Donald Meek
Constant Meese
Robert A. Mehaffey
Ellison L. Meier
John Carl Meinbress
G. Harold Melander
Frank Melcher
Hon. A. John Melhuish
Robert A. Mellin
Thomas J. Mellon
Charles K. Melrose
Robert J. Mengarelli
Stuart D. Menist
David R. Mercer
Sam N. Mercer
James P. Mergens
Pierre F. V. Merle
Pierre F.V. Merle
Dr. Pierre V. Merle, Jr.
Jon Merrell
Charles H. Merrill
John O. Merrill
Charles H. Merrill, Jr.
Will L. Merryman
Massimo Messina
Melly Metcalf
Alan E. Metheny
Mary A. Mettler
Grant W. Metzger
Arthur H. Meussdorffer
Fred H. Meyer
Fred R. Meyer
Harold A. Meyer
John P. Meyer
Milton S. Meyer
Wilson Meyer
Theodore J. Meyers
Douglas Michael
Henry R. Michael
Joan Michlin
Howard Middleton
Krishan Miglani
Axel Mikkelsen

Jeffrey L. Milde
E. C. Miles
William H. Miles
A. Bruce Miller
Barton C. Miller
Elmer L. Miller
Garth H. Miller
J. Winthrop Miller
John B. Miller
John D. Miller
John N. Miller
Kendrick W. Miller
Leni H. Miller
Louis A. Miller
Richard K. Miller
Thomas A. Miller
Washington J. Miller
Winthrop A. Miller
T. Wainwright Miller III
H. Fraser Mills
Carl W. Millsom
Bill K. Milner
Richard P.N. Milner
Nat F. Milnor
Steven Minchen
Nagel T. Miner
Richard R. Miranda
Zina E. Mirsky
Donald W. Mitchell
Dr. James G. Mitchell
Harry A. Mitchell
James H. Mitchell
John S. Mitchell
Donald H. Mix
Willard H. Mixter
David W. Moar
Edward J. Moe
Ralph R. Moe
James O. Moen
James K. Moffitt
James P. Molinelli
Jurgen Mollers
Ernest L. Molloy
William W. Monahan
Eugene R. Monceau
Mark B. Mondry
Henri P. Monjauze
Philip F. Monohan
Alfred Monotti
N. S. Monsarrat
Arch Monson, Jr.
Dr. Algerd S. Monstavicius
Dani Montague
Jack F. Montaldo
Herbert C. Montgomery
Edwin S. Moore
George E. Moore
George P. Moore
J. Max Moore
Lt. Gen. James E. Moore, Jr.
James T. Moore, Jr.
James W. Moore
Lois Moore
Michael W. Moore

Nina Moore
Robert B. Moore
Scott M. Moore
T. W. Moore
Timothy O. Moore
William W. Moore
Victor P. Morabito
Charles A. Moraghan
Ernst C. Morck
C. C. Morehouse
Steven P. Morena
Geroge U. Morf
Cynthia A. Morff
A. Dale Morgan
Dr. James W. Morgan
Dr. Richard K. Morgan
Frederick A. Morgan
Horace W. Morgan
Horace Wilcox Morgan
Stephen C. Morgan
William P. Morgan
H. E. Morley
Henry C. Morris
Henry R. Morris
Howard H. Morris
Sage L. Morris
John Morrisey
John F. Morrisey
Charles J. Morrison
Harry F. Morrison
Albert C. Morrisson
John F. Morrissy
W. S. Morrow
Charles P. Morse
John J. Morse
Lester L. Morse
Robert H. Morton
Thomas J. Morton
Thos. G. Morton
William F. Morton
E. Mosbacher
Lisa Moscaret-Burr
Austin W. Mosher
James E. Moss
Ygnacio L. Mott
Donald J. Moulin
Gabriel Moulin
Irving V. Moulin
Raymond M. Moulin
John Mount
William J. Mountin
George J. Mountz
Mary Louise Muckler
Maj. Gen. Gilman C. Mudgett
Frank Mueller
Martin Mueller
Hansrudi Muggli
Stefan Muhle
Fred R. Mühs
P. H. Mulcahy
Bernard H. Muldary
Frank Mulks
Harry Mullen
Timothy J. Mullen

Harry Muller
James J. Mulpeters
Fenina Mundisugih
Anne C. Munson
Richard L. Muratet
Bernard A. Murith
Marvin A. Murphey
Clarence E. Murphy
Daniel J. Murphy
Frank S. Murphy
James K. Murphy
Kevin E. Murphy
James C. Murphy
Peter J. Murphy
Walter F. Murphy
James D. Murray
James W. Murray
Stanley B. Murray
William F. Murray
Richard C. Murray, Jr.
Eugene J. Muscat
W.Maye Musk
J. Michael Myatt
Kitty Myers
Lawrence P. Myers
Mary K. Myers
Warren F. Myers
William R. Myers
Timothy L. Naehring
Richard S. Nakano
Sean P. Nalty
Gerald E. Napier
Ralph J. Nartzik
Eric W. Nath
Marvin N. Nathan
Kenneth F. Nattress
Clarence C. Nauman
G. F. Neal
Percy H. Nealy
Anne M. Neeley
Anne M. Neely
Fred M. Neely
Robert W. Neighbor
Alvin E. Nelson
Calvin H. Nelson
Frederic S. Nelson
Richard D. Nelson
Joan C. Nemeth
John A. Nerland
Jim Nesbit
John C. Neubauer
John G. Neukom
Per B. Nevard
Ernest H. Newall
H. R. Newbauer
Lt. Col. Victor L. Newbould
Richard W. Newburgh
Ralph A. Newell
Gerald E. Newfarmer
Kenneth L. Newkirk
Edwin S. Newman
George H. Newman
S. Walter Newman
Sterling R. Newman

Walter S. Newman
Hon. Gavin C. Newsom *
Robert G. Newsom
George F. Newton
J. William Newton
Leonard V. Newton
Marion P. Newton
Dr. Michael W. Niccole
William A. Niccolls
Charles L. Nichols
James G. Nichols
Wendel K. Nicolaus
Alfred H. Nicoll
Hans Niebergall
Hans J. Niebergall
Brandom K. Nielsen
Devan T. Nielsen
Paul M. Nippert
R. E. Noble
Weller Noble
Jared Robert Nodelman
Arthur C. Nodine
James B. Noel, Jr.
John D. Nolan
Henry A. Nordquist
Eric L. Nordskog
Ralph L. Norling
Patrick W. Norman
Robert F. Northfield
H. C. Norton
Joseph P. Nourse
James P. Nuss
Phyllis Nusz
Chung D. Ny Tihon
Hans W. Nykamp
R. F. Oakes
Alexander G. Oakley
W. H. Obear
Col. Charles J. O'Brien
Daniel J. O'Brien
Dr. Noel S. O'Brien
Richard O'Brien
Robert J. O'Conner
Charles L. O'Connor
John C. O'Connor
Leslie V. O'Connor
Hugh O'Donnell
James E. O'Donnell
Mark S. Oei
Kevin F. O'Gara, Jr.
Vernon V. Ogburn
Shawn E. O'Hara
Robert H. O'Hea
John A. O'Kane
Neil O'Keeffe
Hugh E. Oliphant
George F. Oliva
Paul L. Oliver
E. H. Olney
William V. Olney
Richard A. Olrich
Dr. Erik D. Olsen
George H. Olsen
George H. Olsen, Jr.

Raymond D. Olson
Quentin M. Olwell
Robert E. O'Meara
C. L. O'Neal
Donald G. O'Neill
Francis J. O'Neill
John T. O'Neill
Patricia O'Neill
Roark O'Neill
Donald F. Onken
Jan Oostermeyer
Ramsey Oppenheim
Peter K. B. Or
Benjamin Orames
Harry Orbelian
Harry J. Orchard
Herbert J. Orchison
Horace Orear
Elliott F. O'Rourke
J. Clinton O'Rourke
Chester W. Ort
Lawrence M. Osborn
Bill F. Osborne
Robert F. Osborne
Peter M. Oser
John W. Otterson
James B. Outsen
Eugenio J. Ovalle
Ed Overmyer
Clinton G. Owen
Fred W. Pabst
Casey F. Pacheco
Roger J. Pacheco
Dr. Seaver T. Page
Richard J. Palenchar
Brig. Gen. Donald J. Palladino
Kimball S. Palm
Ernest H. Palmer
Eugene F. Palmer
Kimball S. Palmer
Victor F. Palmer
Wharton B. Palmore
John R. Pangrazio
Gilbert Papazian
Alex W. Pape
Ronan Papillaud
Donald G. Parachini
David A. Paradine
Arthur Park
Ernest S. Park
Alison Parker
Frederick C. Parker
Gus H. Parker
J. Ralph Parker
Murray T. Parker
Neel D. Parker
Sabrina E. Parker
Todd R. Parker
William J. Parkins
Thomas J. Parry
Richard G. Parsons
Stanley T. Pasternak
Thomas C. Paton
Thomas C. Paton, Jr.

A. R. Patrick
J. Howard Patrick
James M. Patrick
James M. Patrick II
Bluce L. Patte
James L. Patten
Doug Patterson
Leo R. Patterson
Lloyd H. Patterson
Morrie L. Patterson
William L. Pattiani
Lyle E. Patton
Richard V. Patton
Richard Patzold
Dr. S. Barre Paul
T. Otis Paul, MD
Varnum Paul
Ray E. Paulson
Linda S. Pavia
Stephen C. Paxton
Dr. Clyde Payne
George R. Payne
Silas O. Payne
Eugene C. Payne III
Sterling E. Peacock
Stephen S. Pearce
Beverly J. Pearson
Mark W. Pearson
Marshall S. Pease
Carson C. Peck
Rear Adm. Paul A. Peck
Bernhard S. Pedersen
R. C. Pell
Nancy Corinne Pelosi
Isaac Penny
Morris A. Penter
Richard R. Peppin
George S. Perham
Dudley B. Perkins
Dudley B. Perkins, Jr.
Edward Perkins
John S. Perkins
Rev. William B. Perkins, S.J.
Victor A. Perrella
Lance E. Perrin
Glenn L. Perry
Harry L. Perry
John M. Perry
K. L. Perry
Raymond O. Perry
V. S. Persons
Jack M. Perz
Frank W. Peters
Frederick W. Peters
Myrl Ross Peters
Jesper E. Petersen
T. C. Petersen
Warren T. Petersen
William H. Petersen
Ben A. Peterson
Clarence E. Peterson
Claude E. Peterson
Edward H. Peterson
H. W. Peterson

Melvin T. Peterson
Seth Peterson
Stig O. Peterson
John N. Petosis
James P. Petray
Albert Petri
Albert Petrini
Dr. John J. Petrini
Richard R. Pettingill
Garry W. Pettis
John Pfeiffer
Lloyd A. Pflueger
Ralph L. Phelps
Clarence A. Phillips
Gary O. Phillips
Herbert A. Phillips
John B. Phillips
Edward J. Phipps
Alain Piallat
Joseph N. Picetti
Daniel J. Pickrell
Lyman L. Pierce
S. W. Piercy
Richard A. Pimentel
John S. Pinney
Alfred Pinther
Col. George H. Pippy
Manon E. Pischel
E. C. Pitcher
W. E. Pitcher
Allan L. Pither
Harold P. Pitts
Robert B. Pitts
Bernard R. Pizzoli
Scott Plakun
David N. Plant
Ernest A. Plattner
Dr. Lionel P. Player
Charles M. Plum
Charles A. Pohley
Charles H. Pohlman
William D. Poil
William F. Poland
Dr. Percy P. Poliak
Betty G. Pollack
Owen W. Polousky
Deanna L. Ponting
Stacey Poole
Thomas M. Poole
W. Douglas Poole
Bruno Porrati
Edward C. Porter
G. Harold Porter
Warren W. Porter
William T. Porter, Jr.
Melvin Posada
Frederick F. Postel
David S. Pottack
Robert K. Potter
Joseph L. Powell
St. Elmo M. Powell
Barry D. Powers
Henry C. Powers
Joseph P. Powers

Roy C. Powers
Christopher R. Powis
William F. Poynter
Clarence F. Pratt
Ransom Pratt
Roy L. Pratt
Charles Pratt, Jr.
George P. Prechtel *
E. H. Prentice
E. Whitman Prentice
George J. Presley
Archibald H. Price
Dr. Merton Price
E. C. D. Price
Everett L. Price
Harvey L. Price
John B. Price
Patrick Price
Patrick H. Price
Sandra Price
William Price
Alvin L. Prichard, Jr.
H. F. Prien
Stanley Prior
Michael Pritchard *
Martin J. Procaccio
Owen W. Proctor
Conrad E. Prusak
Fred Pruter
John G. Pugh
William J. Pugh
Arlyn Purcell
Charles H. Purcell
Thomas J. Purcell
Paul V. Pusateri
Frederick A. Quigley
Gregory Quilici
Richard D. Quinlan
Richard D. Quinlan, Jr.
William G. Quinn
William J. Quinn
Ernest G. Raas
Joseph C. Raas
Edward W. Rabin, Jr.
Michael Raddie
Edward J. Rafferty
Joseph V. Rafferty
Joseph A. Raffetto
Peter E. Ragsdale
Richard S. Railton
William A. Rainey, Jr.
John T. Raisin
John T. Raisin, Jr.
W. C. Ralston
Bipin M. Ramaiya
Charles Ramorino
William J. Rand, Jr.
Richard W. Randall
Janeane M. Randolph
Dr. Frank L. Raney, Jr.
Donald L. Ranis
Dr. Robert L. Raphael
Sidney C. Rasmussen
G. L. Rathbone

Robert R. Rathborne
Cecil Raymond
John F. Raymond
Adrienne M. Reader
August L. Reader III, MD
Doyle L. Reed
E. L. Reese
James S. Reese
Richard L. Reeves
Andrew M. Regalia
William V. Regan
William V. Regan III
Irving H. Reichert
William H. Reid
Diane L. Reifenstahl
Frank Reilly
Robert S. Reis
Harry L. Reiter
Philip D. Reitz
Victor J. Reizman
William A. Remensperger
John A. Remick
Louise H. Renne
Glenn M. Reno
William H. Rentschler
Charles Renwick
Jacob P. Rettenmayer
Emmett L. Rettig
Ronald T. Reuther
R. E. Revalk
Stephen Revetria
Alexander J. Reyes
Rev. Francisco G. Reyes
Teresita T. Reyes
Clark E. Reynolds
H. M. Reynolds
Quentin Reynolds
William B. Reynolds
Pierre S. Rhein
Robert F. Rhoades
W. H. Rhodes
Luciano C. Ricci
John B. Rice
Adelbert H. Richards
Ford A. Richards
Joyce A. Richards
Dale Richardson
R. R. Richardson
Rear Adm. Gill Richardson
Charles S. Richman
Dr. William L. Ridgway
Robert T. Riding
Bernard F. Rieber
Warren H. Rieders
Paul Rieger
William J. Riegger
Harvey Rifkin
George A. Rigg
Louis W. Riggs
Perseo Righetti
James G. Riley
Jane Riley
Patrick G. Riley
Bernard Ringer

John H. Ringgenberg
Howard G. Riper
Wilton P. Risenhoover
J. Stanley Rising
Chester H. Ristenpart, Jr.
H. P. Roach
Frank Robb
Grant A. Robbins
John Robbins
John R. Robbins
Craig A. Roberts
Daniel D. Roberts
David A. Roberts
Dr. Alexander C. Roberts
Lt. Gen. Elvy B. Roberts
John H. Robertson
Kenneth D. Robertson
Victor J. Robertson
A. James Robertson II
Beverly N. Robinson
E. J. Robinson
Francis H. Robinson
Frank W. Robinson
Joseph A. Robinson
Joseph A. Robinson, Ph.D.
Lt. Col. Raymond Robinson
Oscar M. Robinson
William B. Robinson
William S. Robinson
Ansel W. Robison
William D. Robison
Delbert V. Robson
Peter A. Roche
Quentin M. Rochefort
Jeanne Rockwell *
Robert R. Rockwell
Lewis H. Rodebaugh
Rosa Maria N. Rodriguez
George H. Roe
G. Adolfo Roensch
Ralph J. Roesling
Ian A. P. Roger
Harry E. Rogers
Robert S. Rogers
Roy R. Rogers
W. A. Rogers
Deborah R. Rohrer
Harry L. Rohrer
Waldemar Rojas
Albert F. Roller
Henry R. Rolph
Thomas Rolph
William N. Rolph
Benjamin B. Ron
Harold F. Ronan
A. F. Rooker
George H. Roos
Michael A. Roosevelt
Robert B. Rorick
Ed R. Rorke
Hon. Marzita S. Rosales
Richard B. Rosen
Louis F. Rosenaur
Richard M. Rosenberg

David M. Rosenberg-Wohl
Daniel Rosenblum
Max L. Rosenfeld
Ian H. Rosenfield
Nils C. Rosenquest
Ernest R. Rosentrater
Beth Ross
Dr. Harold L. Ross
Dr. John A. T. Ross
Wendy A. Ross
William A. Ross
William W. Ross
Alfred N. Rossi
Angelo J. Rossi
Clyde H. Rossi
Craig C. Rossi
Bruce E. Rossman
Isaiah B. Roter
Almon E. Roth
John Rothschild
W. Lansing Rothschild
Ronald H. Rouda
Giovanna Rovetti
Vincent J. Rovetti
Brian D. Rowbotham
Arthur E. Rowe
John S. Rowe
Prentiss A. Rowe
George T. Rowse
Frank M. Roy
Jerome A. Roy
Stephen B. Ruben
Stuart Rudick
A. C. Rulofson
Frank K. Runyan
George S. Runyan
Charles B. Rupert
Allen S. Rupley
Robert H. Rusch
Kenneth M. Ryals
Glenn Ryan
Patricia Ryan
Dan H. Ryder
Robert E. Ryker
Benjamin G. Sabraw
H. P. Sackett
Paul S. Sackett
Leslie Sage
Takayuki Sakamoto
Walter Saling
Sidney Sall
Arthur M. Sammis
Judith Samson
Maurice I. Samter
Albert S. Samuels, Jr.
Arthur P. Samuelson
Dr. Michael H. Sander
Charles V. Sandford
William Sanford
Frank G. Sankey
A. Wayne Sarchett
K. William Sasagawa
Louis E. Saubolle
Clovis P. Saunders

Edward E. Saunders
Arlene Sauser
Granville L. Savage
Robert M. Savage
Melvin D. Savage
Melvin D. Savage, Jr.
Mike Savannah
Samuel Savannah
Richard E. Saxton
Elizabeth K. Sayler
Robert H. Scanlon
James A. Scatena
James A. Scatena Jr.
John W. Schacht
Klaus H. Schaefer
Dr. Dagmar Schaefer-Gehrau
Alfred L. Schafer
N. Fred Schafer
H. Schaff
Dr. Ralph W. Schaffarzick
Randall Schai
Dr. Lee W. Schaller
Fred W. Schell
Eugene F. Schenk
Barry Schenker
John C. Schiek
James H. Schilt
David M. Schindler
Rev. John P. Schlegel
Eric E. Schmautz
Carsten E. Schmidt
Ian Schmidt
Lorenz L. Schmidt
Max H. Schmidt, Jr.
Hon. Horst Schmidt-
   Dornedden
Fred W. Schmitz
Robert J. Schmitz
James T. Schmuck
Wendy Schnee
C. H. Schneider
I. Frank Schnier
Kenneth S. Scholl
Jean E. Schore
J. W. M. Schorer
Charles R. Schreck
Kenneth B. Schreiner
Donald W. Schroeder
James B. Schryver
Theodore E. Schucking
Rolf Schuette
William A. Schulte
L. A. Schultz
Lawrence A. Schultz
A. Robert Schulze
John R. Schumacher
Ronald W. Schumacher
Karl F. Schuster
Roland Schuster
Donald W. Schwartz
Sidney L. Schwartz
Michael M. Schweiger
Roy J. Scola
Charles J. Scollin

Hal W. Sconyers
Frederick E. Scotford
Albert W. Scott, Jr.
Bert C. Scott
Duncan A. Scott
Merle Scott
Sarah E. Scott
Thomas R. Scott
William P. Scott, Jr.
George S. Scovell
John E. Scoville
O. Scribner
Mailler Searles
H. J. Sears
William M. Secor
Frank Seed
M. Harvey Segall
Dr. George A. Selleck
Kenneth W. Sells
Eugene S. Selvage
Jack M. B. Selway
John G. Selway
Thomas E. Senf
Edward C. Sequeira
Judson T. Sergeant
R. L. Sergeant
Rudolf H. Severin
Douglas J. Shackley
Dr. Robert N. Shaffer
Jas. P. Shaffer
Sherman S. Shaffer
Robert Shannon
Claudine Shapiro
Sergey Sharapov
Dr. Arun B. Sharma
William W. Sharon
William C. Sharp
Russell T. Sharpe
Albert W. Shaw
C. E. Loomis Shaw
Percy J. Shaw
William D. Shaw
Con T. Shea
Joseph W. Shea
Robert L. Shearn
Vernon C. Sheehan
John F. Sheehan, Jr.
Vernon C. Sheehan, Jr.
Hayne Sheerin
David T. Shen, DDS
John V. Shepard
William A. Sherman
H. T. Sherriff
Vincent P. Sherry
L. Allen W. Sherwood
Leo N. Sherwood
Col. Paul L. Shetler
Shuichi Shigaki
Tatemasa K. Shimizu
Max L. Shirpser
Daniel R. Shoemaker
Joseph Shoemaker
Deane S. Shokes
John E. Sholl III

C. Patrick Shook
Paul Shoupe
Barbara A. Shreve
Theodore E. Shucking
Hayden Shuey
Herbert S. Shuey
T. E. Shumate
F. Shurtleff
Roane T. Sias
Rev. Josiah Sibley
George E. Sibthorp
Lloyd W. Sichel
William H. Sickinger
Lester Siebert
Wilmer Sieg
Gene A. Siekert
Edward H. Siems
William H. Sievert
Edward L. Siller
Seth Silverman
F. J. Sime
William A. Simkins
Frank P. Simmen
Arthur W. Simmons
Sherry Simmons
Irwin B. Simon
Jerome Simon
Louis S. Simon
Charles C. Simons
George L. Simpson
Fred I. Sims
Kent O. Sims
L. Ross Sine
J. Francis Sinnot
Richard A. Sinnott
Raymond P. Siotto
Edward W. Sipe
Angelo J. Siracusa
Darrell E. Sisson
Richard H. Sites
John H. Skeggs
Alva E. Skerritt
Elmer F. Skinner
William S. Skowronski
Gregory D. Slapak
William P. Sloan
R. Tad Slocum
Alford R. Smith
Arthur O. Smith
Bashford Smith
Charles F. Smith
Clarence Smith
Curtis E. Smith
Curtis E. Smith, Jr.
Doyle E. Smith
Easdon K. Smith
Eugene Wood Smith
Floyd F. Smith, Jr.
Francis Smith
Francis W. Smith
Frank A. Smith
Grant W. Smith
Gregory A. Smith
Harry H. Smith

Harry S. Smith
J. J. Smith
James F. Smith
John J. Smith
Kelly A. Smith
Kenneth Smith
Laurence C. Smith
Leon C. Smith
Lisa L. Smith
Morgan J. Smith
Paul S. Smith
Pello Smith
Philip C. Smith
Capt. Philip L. Smith
Rae T. Smith
Ray W. Smith
Richard A. Smith
Roderick N. Smith
T. Harry Smith
W. Bashford Smith
W. H. Smith
W. M. Smith
Walter Z. Smith
Wesley J. Smith
Wilbert B. Smith
William G. Smith
Wilton F. Smith
Paul Smolinski
Charles E. Snell
Maj. Gen. Charles R. Sniffin
James A. Snook
Roger Snow
C. A. Snyder
Brig. Gen. John F. Sobke
Gerardo Socco
Dr. Susan E. Soderstrom
Walter J. Sohlinger
Lynn M. Solberg
Henry C. Solomon
Robert M. Solovieff
Maure Solt
Laszlo Somi
Herbert L. Sommer
Max Sommer
Dr. Myung S. Son
Leo Soong
Darrell C. Sooy
Robert L. Soper
Dr. Hans W. Sorensen
Roy Sorensen
Stanley E. Soule
E. B. Spalding
William H. Spalding
Edgar P. Sparks
John Speck
John C. Speh
Mary Z. Spellman
Paul J. Spengler
Peter J. Speros
Austin W. Sperry
William Sperry
Kevin G. Spier
Edward R. Spies
Isaac H. Spiro

John H. Spohn
Bradley W. Sprague
Edmund B. Spread
Edgar L. Springer
Robert L. St. John
Valerian E. St. Regis
Leonard B. Stafford
Charles Stallman
Nick W. Stamos
John W. Standen
Eric M. Stanford
Anita T. Stangl
Sandor J. Stangl
Roy Staniford
Herbert E. Stansbury, Jr.
Robert Stanton
Bradley Stark
Robert E. Starr
James A. Stasek
Charles F. Stauffacher, Jr.
Dr. Thomas M. Stauffer
William G. Stead
Robert B. Stechert
Rev. David P. Stechholz
Donald D. Steele
William H. Steele, Jr.
Reginald C. Steeple
Frank M. Steers
Jeffery D. Stein
Thomas J. Stein
Victor E. Stein
Mark Steinberg
Mervin L. Steinberg
Kurt Steindorff
Philip Steiner
Roger C. Steiner
James Steinhauer
H. G. Stenersen
Alfred B. Stephens
Carroll Stephens
Carroll H. Stephens
Edwin W. Stephens
Elisa Stephens
Eugene G. Stephens
James K. Stephens
Thomas J. Stephens
F.W. Stephens
Dr. Cynthia Stephenson
Ferdinand W. Stephenson
Konstantinos Stergioulis
Jamie Stern
Fred L. Stettner
Ludwig G. Stettner
Chris Steuri
Gloria A. Stevens
Harry O. Stevens
Jay M. Stevens
Walter F. Stevens
George H. Stevenson
Mark L. Stevenson
Robert C. Stevenson
William M. Stevenson
Paul C. Steward
Charles A. Stewart

Jay G. Stewart
John L. Stewart
Kenneth A. Stewart
W. Foster Stewart
B. J. Stiles
Stephen A. Stimpson
Elgin Stoddard
Louis F. Stoddard III
John E. Stolz
Sherilyn Stolz
Carol H. Stone
Jonathan Stone
Keith A. Stonefelt
Ellis L. Stoneson
Marshall D. Storz
W. Robert Stover
Harry P. Stow
Joseph W. Stretch
John Strishak
Harry A. Strong
William H. Struckman
John L. Stuart
Percy R. Stuart
Charles H. Stuckey
Paul H. Sturdivant
Sandra Sturgeon *
William B. Sturgeon
Armond E. Suacci
Arthur E. Sugden
Abdul M. Suleman
Dennis M. Sullivan
Donald W. Sullivan
Edward G. Sullivan
J. Frank Sullivan
J. J. Sullivan
Margaret A. Sullivan
Robert J. Sullivan
Thomas X. Sullivan
Vincent J. Sullivan
Narasimhan Sunderaj
Steven J. Susoeff
Herbert M. Sussman
D. Clair Sutherland
H. Lloyd Sutherland
Norman R. Sutherland
Joseph D. Sutton
Steve G. Swaab
Eliot J. Swan
C. O. Swanberg
Sally A. Swanson
Walter G. Swanson
Lloyd Swayne, Jr.
Ray W. Sweazy
Ernest J. Sweetland
Harry G. Swift
Darian W. Swig
David B. Swoap
Bradford Swope
Sebastian Tabarsi
John Tait
William J. Talbot
Allen I. Tallman
Joseph S. Talmadge
Joseph S. Talmadge, Jr.

---

* Honorary Member

Peter Tamaras
Gloria Tan
Dean Tanaka
Dawson Tang
Joseph C. Tarantino
Michael R. Tarantola
Nick G. Tarlson
Nadia Tarzi
Fred C. Tatton
Howard M. Tayler
James D. Tayler
James H. Tayler
Edmund Leslie Taylor
F. L. Taylor
Henry Taylor
Howard H. Taylor
J. Curtiss Taylor
James I. Taylor
James W. Taylor
Michael E. Taylor
Peter V. Taylor
Ronald D. Taylor
Samuel H. Taylor
Thelma-Jeanne Taylor
Wyman Taylor
William P. Taylor II
D. Rae Te Roller
Barbara H. Teaford
Frederick A. Tegeler, Jr.
Stanley E. Teixeira
Harvey E. Teller
Malcom S. Teller
John C. Temple-Raston
F. Whitney Tenney
George C. Tenney
Sharon Tennison
Bruce R. Tepper
James D. Terrell
Pauline Terrelonge
Lee D. Terreo
Walter F. Terry, Sr.
Robert C. Thackara
Donald E. Thal
Charles E. Thatcher
Wallace R. Thaxter
David B. Theobald
Joseph Thieben
Harold V. Thies
Angy B. Thomas
Edwin W. Thomas
John D. Thomas
John M. Thomas
Joseph D. Thomas
Ralph E. Thomas
Robert L. Thomas
Robert T. Thomas
Robert W. Thomas
William H. Thomas
Willis H. Thomas
Daryl G. Thomas
George H. Thomas, Jr.
Andrew L. Thompson
Edward A. Thompson
Evertt G. Thompson

F. Thompson
Henry A. Thompson
L. H. Thompson
M.E. Thompson
Robert F. Thompson
Robert J. Thompson
Susan A. Thompson
Harry S. Thomson
Harold W. Thorne, Jr.
Mary C. Thorsby
Paul J. Thurau
Charles R. Thurber
G.J. Ticoulat
John Tiedemann
Floyd Tiemann
Justin N. Tierney
John L. Tilden
Albert S. Tiley
Frank F. Tippett
Dr. Dale L. Tipton
Patrick D. Tisdale
Henry C. Todd
Dr. Marie M. Tolarova
Burl A. Toler
Albert B. Tolf
Robert Tolifson
Edward A. Tolley
Dr. R. Eugene Tolls
William E. Tolson
James Tom
George C. Tom
Vincent E. Tomera
Kenneth C. Tomlinson
George E. Tooker
Conrado Topacio
John J. Tornes
W. Carroll Tornroth
Saundra Totty
Christine Tour-Sarkissian
James W. Towne
Edward S. Townsend
James A. Townsend
Lawrence G. Townsend
Louis E. Townsend
Grover S. Tracy
Philip R. Trapp
Elmer A. Trask
Richard H. Travers
Marcia Traversaro
Donald M. Travis
Ernest W. Travis
Thomas P. Treichler
F. George Trescher
William D. Trewartha
Joseph M. Trickett
Charles S. Tripler
Arlin Trocme
George S. Trotter
H. C. Truchs
Michael R. Truesdell
E. H. Tryon
Lilian Tsi-Stielstra
Robert G. Tuck
Howard J. Tuckett

William M. Tudor
Arturo F. Tudury
Ture S. Tulien
C. B. Tull
Ray W. Turnbull
Albert W. Turner
Frank I. Turner
Fred E. Turner
George M. Turner
William B. Turner
Wilbur H. Tusler, Jr.
James M. Tuttle
Dr. Herbert S. Twede
Joseph J. Tynan
Joseph J. Jr. Tynan
Bernard J. Tyson
Michael Tzorbatzakis
George Uhl
Michael D. Uhlig
John L. Ulrich
Henry Untermeyer
Clarence M. Updegraff, Sr.
Kenneth S. Uston
John Uth
Stanley M. Vail
Carmen L.B. Valdes
Joseph W. Valentine
Omar Valle
Shoko Valle
Andrea M. Valo-Espina
Marcel P. Van Aelst
W. F. Van Cott
Charles L. Van Horne
Dr. Ezra A. Van Nuys
Howard L. Van Orden
William O. Van Wyck, Jr.
Murray F. Vandall
Gerrit Vander Ende
Andrew A. Vandeveld
Jefferey V. Varacalli
Robert B. Varner
Yuliya Vasileva
Hon. Adamantios T. Vassilakis
H. G. Vaughan
Reginald L. Vaughan
Harry D. Vaughn
René A. Vayssie
Kathie S. Velazquez
John E. Venter
Carl A. Verhagen
Richard B. Vertrees
Charles H. Victor
Shirley A. Victor
George B. Viets
Ralph V. Vincent
George M. Vlazakis
Philip O. Vogel
Les Vogel, Jr.
Paul C. Vogelheim
Richard C. Volberg
Dale Vollrath
Dieter Von Breymann
Julian H. Voorsanger
Leon M. Voorsanger

Robert C. Voss
John F. Vyverberg
Myron Wacholder
George Wagner
Harold A. Wagner
Henry F. Wagner
Vice-Adm. Austin C. Wagner
Howard R. Waits
Bethel W. Wakeley
Kevin E. Waldeck
Gary A. Walden
Uda Waldrop
Bethel W. Walker
Clarence C. Walker
Hubert M. Walker
Lawrence Walker
Lawrence F. Walker
P. J. Walker
Robert C. Walker
Robert L. Walker
Robert W. Walker
George A. Wallace
George J. Wallace
Donald R. Wallen
Charles W. Wallen, Jr.
Horace H. Walling
Edward P. Walsh
Richard J. Walsh
Thomas A. Walsh
Thomas J. Walsh
Vincent S. Walsh
Carl R. Walston
Dale E. Walter
J. F. Walters
Lawrence F. Walters
Robert C. Walther
James E. Walz
John W. Walz
Julia Wan
Phil M. Wand
Phil W. Wand
Linchi Wang
Edward B. Ward
John W. Ward
Michael J. Ward
Charles A. Warden
Emily Warden
Howell H. Ware
Donald L. Warmby
Curtis E. Warren
Nigel C. Warshaw
Fred L. Washburn
Edwin A. Wasserman
Channell M. Wasson
Hiroshi Watanabe
E. W. A. Waterhouse
G. B. Waterman
Cyrus B. Waters
David E. Watkins
Gwendolyn Watkins
Fred E. Watson
Harley J. Watson
J. Michael Watson
W. J. Watson

* Honorary Member

James E. Watt
Richard N. Waugh
Dr. Stuart C. Way
Clarke E. Wayland
Thomas J. Webb
Warren C. Webb
Donald R. Weber
Robert W. Weber
Maurie Webster
W. B. Webster
Robert W. Weed
H. A. Weichhart
Charles B. Weil
Julius C. Weil
Vicki Weiland
William A. Weiler
Robert L. Weinberg, PhD
Martin S. Weiner
Louis Weinman
Teller Weinman
Sanford L. Weintraub
John R. Weiss
John W. Weitzel
R. John Wekselblatt
Chester B. Welch
Edward G. Welch
Rosemary Welde
Nils Welin
Ralph A. Weller
Donald A. Wells
Robert E. Welsh
Darian Weltman
Maximilian C. Wendt
Lee Wenger
Carl F. Wente
A. Wenzelburger
Carl F. Werner
Richard J. Werner
Worron E. Wert
Peter K. Wertheimer
David H. West
Dr. Frederick T. West
Ernest L. West
Jack C. West
Kirby P. West
Ross R. West
Kirby P. West, Jr.
Dr. Philip R. Westdahl
Russell C. Westover, Jr.
Dr. Otto F. Westphal
Volker Westphal
Debra L. Wetherby
Clarence J. Wetmore
R. Kevin Wewerka
E. A. Weymouth
Lawrence V. Wheat
Harold W. Wheatley
Charles L. Wheeler
Franklin C. Wheeler
Scott D. Whipple
C. Harry White
Daniel P. White
Don F. White
Donald L. White

Donald W. White
Edward A. White
George A. White
Jerome B. White
John J. White, Jr.
Lynn A. White
Mark K. White
Rev. Victor V. White
Roxane White
Theodore A. White
Zaccheus W. White
Robert B. Whitehill, Jr.
James A. Whiting
Frederic B. Whitman
Francis E. Whitmer
Ralph H. Whitmore
Edwin L. Whitney
George K. Whitney
L. Leland Whitney
Leo C. Whitney
George K. Whitney, Jr.
James H. Whitworth
Barbara Wichmann
Rolland E. Wick
Jane S. Wiegand
Barry A. Wiegler
Jay Wiener
James M. Wiggins
Ronald R. Wiggins
Lawrence Wilbur
D. Linn Wiley
G. Russell Wiley
August C. Wilhelm
Robert B. Wilhelm
Robert F. Wilk
Thomas H. Wilkinson
C. J. William
Charles G. Williams
Charles H. Williams
Charles W. Williams
Cheryl S. Williams
Dameron H. Williams, Jr.
Edward G. Williams
F. W. Williams
George E. Williams
J. B. Williams
James F. Williams
John B. Williams
R. Douglas Williams
Richard T. Williams
Fred B. Williamson
Charles J. Willin
Howard Willoughby
Walter J. Willoughby
A. B. Wilson
Clare W. Wilson, Jr.
George W. Wilson
Henry R. Wilson
J. R. Wilson
Kline A. Wilson, Jr.
Lloyd E. Wilson
Lloyd L. Wilson
T. Carroll Wilson
Thomas B. Wilson

William W. Wilson
Henry Windt
Joseph N. Wineroth III
Joseph N. Wineroth, Jr.
Harold E. Winey
Chester L. Wingham
Dart Winship
Sumner R. Winship
Ray H. Winther
Ray H. Winther
James P. Winzler
Park Wisdom
David Wisnom, Jr.
Frank E. Witte
Albert W. Wold
Michael S. Wolfe
Albert C. Wollenberg
Charles M. Wollenberg
Gary A. Wollin
Gerald D. Wolsborn
Brad A. Wong
Edward L. Wong
Jason Wong
John B. Wong
Rosey Wong
Samson Wong
Donald J. Wood
Homer W. Wood
Victoria Wood *
Martin L. Woodard
Robert K. Woodcock
William Woodhead
Keith S. Woodland
James Woods
Kaye M. Woods
Charles A. Woodward
George H. Woodward
John R. Woodward
Lt. Cmdr. Tommy G.
    Woodworth
P. David Wool
M. Louis Wooley
Dr. Chester H. Woolsey
Dr. Mark H. Woolsey
William C. Woolston
C. M. Wooster
M. E. Wooster
Philip A. Wooster
William H. Worden
Dr. Walter P. Work
Charles H. Workman
Samuel F. Worswick
Sydney G. Worthington
William F. Worthington, Jr.
Thomas D. Wosser
C. A. Wright
F.J. Wright
Harvey R. Wright
Jonathan G. Wright
Joseph J. Wright
Randall F. Wright
Walter R. Wright
William J. Wright
Bo Wunsch

Dr. Paul S. Wyne
David J. Yang
Dr. Benjamin C. Yang
Mimi H. Yang
Jack H. Yates
Samuel M. Yates
H. A. Yeazell
Bernadette Yee
Leonard A. Yerkes
David B. Yeske
Kenneth Y. Yeung
Frank Yih *
Lloyd E. Yoder
Kunio Yoshioka
Charles S. Young
Dr. Robert M. Young
Millard W. Young
Robert L. Young
Rosilyn B. Young
Susan Young
J. Arthur Younger
Jesse M. Yount
Victor Yu
Wai Kwok Yu
Jason G. Yuen
Magdalen Yum
Victor N. Zachariah
Kesa Zagar
Omar Zaher
R. R. Zane
Jerome M. Zavagno
George J. Zeagas
Joseph L. Zem
Samuel L. Ziegler
Joseph Zimmerman
Joseph C. Zimmerman
Donald P. Zingale
Paul Zuest
Lee Zusman
Carvel G. Zwingle
Earl H. Zwingle

* Honorary Member

ABBREVIATIONS USED

AFS	Alliance for Smiles
BdMin	Board Minutes
DG	District Governor
PDG	Past District Governor
RGHF	Rotary Global History Fellowship
RI	Rotary International
SFBC	San Francisco Boys' Club
SFBGC	San Francisco Boys & Girls Club
SFR	SF Rotary
SFRF	San Francisco Rotary Foundation
TRF	The Rotary Foundation

SOURCE NOTES

I have tried to recount the history of the Rotary Club of San Francisco in the most accessible way possible—by telling stories based on the best facts I could find. These stories are derived from an extensive array of sources that were made available to me by the SF Rotary office and club members, as well as from several outside sources.

The club has maintained a full set of its weekly newsletter, *Grindings*, for the entire ninety-five-year duration of publication from 1913 to the present. It has also retained many years of minutes from meetings of the board of directors and the San Francisco Rotary Foundation Board of Directors. Also available in its entirety was the full set of club Rosters, dating from January 1909 onward, from which I learned of the club administrations and their committees. In addition, the SF Rotary office made available a wide range of documents, including correspondence, club members' folders, Rotary International matters, and files concerning programs, projects, and other activities.

I interviewed several dozen club members and spoke briefly to many others. Several past presidents and other members lent me their records, which were invaluable. I had access to PDG Bill Sturgeon's extensive set of RI's monthly newsletter, *The Rotarian*, and *RI Convention Proceedings*, plus his interview and correspondence with Homer Wood's son, Homer Jesse, and other memorabilia Bill has collected over the years.

Although I relied mainly on original primary sources, the two previous histories of SF Rotary, William J. Mountin's *History of the Rotary Club of San Francisco* (San Francisco: Rotary Club of San Francisco, 1940), and Mitchell Postel's *Seventy-Five Years in San Francisco: A History of Rotary Club Number 2* (San Francisco: Rotary Club of San Francisco, 1983), contain facts from documents that are no longer available. The histories of Rotary clubs #3, 4, and 5—*Rotarily Yours: A History of the Rotary Club of Oakland* (Oakland, CA: Rotary Club of Oakland, 1969), *Seattle Rotary, the First Eighty Years 1909–1989* (Seattle: Rotary Club of Seattle, c. 1989), and *History of the Rotary Club of Los Angeles: Organized June 25, 1909, Club no. 5, Rotary International*, Golden Anniversary ed. (Los Angeles: Rotary Club of Los Angeles, 1955) add to the story of early Rotary extension on the West Coast. Rotary International has published a number of useful books over the years, including *Adventure in Service* (Evanston, IL: Rotary International, [1949] 1967), *Rotary: Fifty Years of Service, 1905–1955* (Chicago: Lakeside Press, 1955), Cliff Dochterman's *The ABCs of Rotary* (Chicago: Rotary International, 2003), and, of course, David Forward's *A Century of Service: The Story of Rotary International* (Evanston, IL: Rotary International, 2003). Two outside studies—Charles F. Marden's *Rotary and Its Brothers: An Analysis and Interpretation of the Men's Service Club* (Princeton: Princeton University Press, 1935) and Jeffrey A. Charles's more recent *Service Clubs in American Society: Rotary, Kiwanis, and Lions* (Urbana: University of Illinois Press, c. 1993)—offer analyses of the still broader context of service clubs in general.

Notes by Chapter

This is by no means a complete list of every source I used in the writing of this book. Instead, I've included the most important and descriptive among them.

Chapter One—A New Club for San Francisco: Rotary's Beginnings

Homer Wood told the story of his meeting with Manuel Muñoz on many occasions—see for example letters to Robert Dorsett (RI), Oct. 29, 1954; to Paul Harris, Aug. 9, 1930; and *Rotary Club Early History*, [1923], Apr. 1955.

Beginnings in Chicago

Paul Harris described the founding and early days of the Rotary Club of Chicago in his books *My Road to Rotary: The Story of a Boy, a Vermont Community, and Rotary* (Chicago: A. Kroch & Sons, 1948), chapter 33; *The Founder of Rotary* (1928: n.p.); and *This Rotarian Age* (Chicago: Rotary International, 1935); see also Harry Ruggles, "Paul Harris As I Knew Him," *The Rotarian*, Mar. 1952; and Forward, *Century of Service*, 28–32, 138–139.

Paul's relationship with Manuel Muñoz is explained in Paul Harris to R. R. Rogers and Homer Wood, Mar. 16, 1928; Manuel Muñoz to Chesley Perry (RI), Jul. 25, 1930; and Mountin, *History of the Rotary Club of San Francisco*, 23. Note that 1928 correspondence from Paul Harris to R. R. Rogers and Homer Wood and his request for Manuel to send a photograph for the Chicago club's new roster (to Manuel Muñoz, Oct. 5, 1908) indicate that Manuel was a member of the Chicago club during his time in San Francisco, despite an erroneous statement to the contrary in a document from Ches Perry in 1959 (to Harry Ruggles, Jul. 7, 1959).

Paul described his vision of an international organization in Harris, *This Rotarian Age*, 72–73.

Rotary Number Two Is Born

Homer Wood's accounts of his earliest planning are in letters to Robert Dorsett (RI), Oct. 29, 1954; to Paul Harris, Aug. 9, 1930; and "Rotary Club Early History," [1923], Apr. 1955. There are no surviving letters from June 1908, but later accounts of the first planning meetings are in Homer Wood, *Rotary Club Early History*, [1923], Apr. 1955; R. R. Rogers to Chesley Perry, Mar. 28, 1928; and Frank Turner to R. R. Rogers, Mar. 15, 1928. The only known accounts of the initial attendees in June are from recollections decades later and in William Mountin's club history. Memories cloud, as can be seen in various accounts of the June meetings: Rusty Rogers recalls three meetings as follows: (first meeting) Woolsey, Rogers, Fraser, Turner, Patrick; (second meeting) Woolsey, Rogers, Fraser, Turner, Patrick, Webster, and Reese; (third meeting) Woolsey, Rogers, Fraser, Turner, Patrick, Webster (R. R. Rogers to Chesley Perry, Mar. 8, 1928). Rusty's 1929 article in *The Rotarian* names Woolsey, Rogers, Fraser, Turner, Patrick, and Webster (R. R. Rogers, "A Footnote to Rotary History," *The Rotarian*, Apr. 1929, 44). In a letter to Paul Harris 1930, Homer Wood described the first meeting as consisting of Woolsey, Rogers, Fraser, Turner, and Arthur Holman (Homer Wood to Paul Harris, Aug. 9, 1930). In his club history written in 1940, William Mountin names Wood, Woolsey, Rogers, Fraser, Turner, Patrick, Webster, Col. George Pippy, and H. C. Norton as attendees of a meeting in the latter part of June at Homer's office (Mountin, 24).

The earliest contemporary letters are between Paul Harris, Homer Wood, and Manuel Muñoz. They include: Paul Harris to Manuel Muñoz, Oct. 2, 1908; Paul Harris to Manuel Muñoz, Oct. 5, 1908; Manuel Muñoz to Paul Harris, Oct. 9, 1908; Homer Wood to Paul Harris, Oct. 12, 1908; Paul Harris to Homer Wood, Oct. 15, 1908; Homer Wood to Paul Harris, Oct. 18, 1908. In their letters to Paul Harris in October, Homer and Manuel each began a claim as the founder of Rotary in San Francisco. Manuel referred to himself as "an organizer by trade" (Manuel Muñoz to Paul Harris, Oct. 9, 1908), and Homer asserted that he had "taken it solely upon myself to start the club here" (Homer Wood to Paul Harris, Oct. 18, 1908). The debate as to who founded SF Rotary is discussed further in chapter 3.

As to the October meetings, the exact number of organizing meetings, their dates, locations, and attendees are unknown. Chester Woolsey later recalled a meeting at the Union Club of about ten men where things "crystallized," but such a meeting is not mentioned in other extant sources. It may have occurred earlier in the summer (Chester H. Woolsey, MD, to Chesley R. Perry (RI) March 17, 1928). Homer Wood later recalled "several committee meetings" in Homer Wood to Chesley H. Perry, RI, c. March 1928.

The founding banquet on November 12, 1908 was reported in the newspapers *San Francisco Chronicle*, Nov. 13, 1908, 1, 3, and *The Call*, Nov. 13, 1908, 1, 2. Homer Wood also described the banquet in a letter to Paul Harris, Aug. 9, 1930, and the minutes of this first meeting have survived. Homer's address to the club was reprinted as "Address of Homer W. Wood," Nov. 12, 1908.

The Earliest Days

Information about the club's first few monthly meetings is from the "Club Bulletins" and meeting minutes from this period.

San Francisco Extends Rotary

Paul Harris's earliest efforts to extend Rotary are described mostly in correspondence: Harry Ruggles to Manuel Muñoz, Oct. 3, 1908; Chesley R. Perry to Harry Ruggles, Jul. 7, 1959; Paul Harris to Manuel Muñoz, Oct. 2, 1908; Paul Harris to Homer Wood, Oct. 22, 1908, cited in Mountin, *History*, 120; Paul Harris to Manuel Muñoz, Oct. 2, 1908; Paul Harris to Manuel Muñoz, Oct. 13, 1908; Paul Harris to Homer Wood, Oct. 15, 1908; Paul Harris to Manuel Muñoz, Oct. 5, 1908; Paul Harris to Homer Wood, Jan. 27, 1909; and Paul Harris to Homer Wood, May 24, 1909. See also Harry Ruggles, "Paul Harris As I Knew Him," *The Rotarian*, Mar 1952.

Homer Wood described the founding of the Tri-City Club in Homer Wood to Edmund Horwinski, Mar. 25, 1954; Homer Wood, "Club Bulletin," Dec. 1908; Homer Wood, "Club Bulletin," Jan. 1909; and Homer Wood, "Rotary Club Early History," [1923], Apr. 1955. See also Mountin, 115–116. Homer wrote of the Seattle club in Homer Wood to Paul Harris, May 18, 1909. Mountin, 116–118, describes the formation of the Los Angeles club. He told of Herbert Quick's dealings in Homer Wood to Paul Harris, Aug. 9, 1930. Paul Harris's version of the origins of the New York club differs from the New York club's attribution to a San Francisco Rotarian: Harris, *This Rotarian Age*, 52, and Rotary Club of New York, "History," http://www.newyorkcityrotary.org/History/history.html [Aug 23 2004]; see also Forward, 41.

Forward, 41–49, describes the subsequent spread of Rotary and the formation of the national and international organizations, and see Harris, *This Rotarian Age*, 79. Paul Harris reported on Stuart Morrow's extension success in *My Road to Rotary*, chapter 34. Mountin, 119–120, addresses subsequent extension by SF Rotary in the western states.

Chapter 2—From Back-Scratching to Service: The Question of Purpose

The Rise and Decline of Boosting

Mountin, 26–27, 32–33, 56 describes SF Rotary's earliest civic service and the subsequent shift to "back-scratching." Contemporary club bulletins and meeting minutes exhibit the emphasis on business advantage, especially SFR BdMin, Oct. 1, 1909 and Homer Wood's remarks in *Rotary Bulletin*, June 1909. However, in later recollections, Homer said that he did not approach prospective members with the "trade with each other" practice of Chicago Rotary because he did not believe in it (Homer Wood to Chesley Perry, Jun. 4, 1930). Instead, he described Rotary as a booster club with discussion of public questions and civic betterment (Homer Wood to Paul Harris, Aug. 9, 1930). It seems more likely, however, that although he was a strong believer in civic boosting and later recalled it as his main focus, he did emphasize the business advantage route. A copy of "The Other Ticket" and Mountin, 34, show the extent of members' desire for a shift in purpose. Note: In a letter to SF Rotary's President Edward Ward after reading William Mountin's *History of the Rotary Club of San Francisco* in 1940, Homer Wood made an oblique reference to "some of the dark and difficult days of holding the club together and carrying on." Homer Wood to Edward Ward (SFR president), Nov. 22, 1940. This is likely the period he had in mind. Mountin, 35–36, describes early back-scratching practices. *Grindings* made its debut in 1913, and is full of examples of boosting for members throughout 1915. For the early seeds of Rotary's service and ethics philosophy, see Forward, 61–63, 150. *Grindings'* subsequent disavowal of early business-advantage practices appears in "Rotary and Business," *Grindings*, Jan. 16, 1923, 4; and *Grindings*, Feb. 27, 1923, 1.

A New Outlook—Service for San Francisco

Mountin, 36–37, and Postel, 39–40, outline SF Rotary's early connection with the bringing of the Panama-Pacific International Exposition to San Francisco. Rotary's subsequent boosting for the Exposition is clear throughout *Grindings* in 1914–15. The Golden Wheel is described in *Grindings* May 5, 1914, 2; *Grindings*, Apr. 28, 1914, 7; and *San Diego Union*, Apr. 10, 1914, 4:10. Details of the long-distance telephone call with Albany during the Exposition appeared in the *New York Times*, Jan. 26, 1915; *Grindings*, Sep. 28, 1915, 2; and *Grindings*, Oct. 12, 1915, 2.

Grindings in 1920 details several examples of the club's civic-service efforts in the postboosting years. The club reported on its early community service for the destitute in "Report of the Ways and Means Committee, 1920–21 and 1921–22. Mountin, 85, 150, 153, 156, and *Grindings* are the best sources for the beginnings of service to the young.

Starting in 1917, the *RI Convention Proceedings* addressed the issue of work for handicapped children. See also Forward, 170–171. For the club's work with handicapped children, refer to Mountin, 86–92, and *Grindings* from 1916 onward. The Sunshine School is documented in "Reports and Recommendations of 1923–24 Committees" and *Grindings* in the fall of 1924. It also received national mention in *The Rotarian*, Jan. 1925, 47; and *RI Convention 1926 Proceedings*, 447–449. For the story of "Daddy" Allen, see "So We Call Him 'Daddy' Allen," *The Rotarian*, Nov. 1940, 15. A history of Easter Seals can be found on http://www.rotaryfirst100.org/foundation/grants/easterseals/. Various *Grindings* in 1926–27, as well as Postel, 78–80, describe SF Rotary's role in founding the California Society for Crippled Children. Mountin, 91–92, is the best source for the Spastic Clinic and School.

Building Better Boys—Boys' Work, The First 50 Years

Boys' work entered as a Rotary interest starting in 1916, as seen in that year's RI Convention Proceedings, 44–45. Subsequent years' Proceedings show the expanding importance of boys' work for Rotary. Mountin, 92–93, discusses SF Rotary's initial work with boys. From that point forward, *Grindings* frequently reported on the club's work. Also see Mountin, 147–150.

The earliest days of the San Francisco Boys' Club have been documented in San Francisco Boys & Girls Club, "Background Information" 1991; "History of the SFBC," Jan. 10, 1951; and a book by Don Shoecraft, *Purple Cow to Purple Kumquat: Centennial History of the San Francisco Boys and Girls Club* (San Francisco: San Francisco Boys and Girls Club, 1991). *Grindings* reported regularly on the club starting in 1923, and see Mountin, 93–101. For the Depression years, see *Grindings* and Mountin, 100–102. Shoecraft, *Purple Cow to Purple Kumquat*, 30–31, 56–57, discusses the pre-Camp Marwedel camping experience, as well as the opening of Camp Marwedel (see also Mountin, 98–100). The camp was later featured in *The Rotarian*, Jun. 1949. For the purchase of the camp, see "San Francisco Boys & Girls Club, Inc., Historical Background," Jan. 16, 1986. Shoecraft, *Purple Cow to Purple Kumquat* and *Grindings* continue the story of the Boys' Club into the 1950s.

The Four Avenues of Service

Mountin, 80–81, and club rosters explain the origins of the Birthday Divisions. The club's prohibition on dual-membership in other service organizations was expressed in *Grindings*, Jan. 2, 1923, 1, and Jun. 6, 1920, 1. Mountin, 44–45, 63–64, 66–67 discusses the beginnings of Rotary's philosophy on business ethics. For the history of the Four-Way Test, see Forward, 153–154. *Grindings* in 1920 and Jan. 12, 1926 explains the establishment of SF Rotary's Business Counsel Committee.

Chapter 3—Three Men of Rotary

Vision of a World of Friends—The Story of Paul Harris (1868–1947)

Paul Harris wrote of his life in his three books *My Road to Rotary*, *The Founder of Rotary*, and *This Rotarian Age*. See also Forward, *Century of Service*, 10–21, 52, 192; Chesley Perry, "Foreword" to *The Founder of Rotary*; RGHF, "What Paul Harris Wrote," http://www.whatpaulharriswrote. org/ [5-2-2007]; RGHF, "Presidents and Conventions," http://www.rotaryfirst100.org/presidents/ 1910harris/paulharris; and Harry Ruggles, "Paul Harris as I Knew Him," *The Rotarian*, Mar. 1952.

Rotary's Missionary—The Story of Homer Wood (1880–1976)

Homer's children, Homer Jesse Wood and Peggy Wood Penton, wrote a brief history of Homer Wood's life, at the request of the California Press Association. Much of this biography is taken from that history: Homer J. Wood, "Biography/History of Homer Winfrey Wood" [Sturgeon papers]. Homer Jesse wrote again of his father in H. J. Wood, "Homer Wood History" [Sturgeon papers]; Homer J. Wood to Amador County Museum, May 26, 1991 [Sturgeon papers]; and in a letter to Warren Deveral, Feb. 15, 1999 [Sturgeon papers]. Homer's life was also described in an article in *The Rotarian*, Mar. 1972, 47; and his obituary in the *Porterville Recorder*, Jul. 19, 1976. Homer Jesse gave a number of his father's papers to PDG Bill Sturgeon, including Homer's "Fourth of July Oration," 1902; Senate Resolution, Mar. 22, 1961; and undated news clippings from the *Bodie Miner* and the *Sacramento Bee*. In addition, Bill Sturgeon interviewed Homer Jesse. Homer's resignation from SF Rotary is in Homer Wood to SF Rotary Board of Directors, Jan. 6, 1911. Two years before his death in 1976, Homer's Rotary life was featured in "The Man Who Seconded the Motion," *The Rotarian*, Feb. 1974, 48. The Rotary Club of Petaluma has a brief story of Homer's founding of the Petaluma club in "A Brief History," http://www.petalumarotary.org/history.htm [5-24-07]. Homer's later visits to SF Rotary and the Chicago club are reported in Homer Wood to Paul Harris, c. Mar. 13, 1928; Chesley Perry to Manuel Muñoz, Oct. 18, 1933; SF Program, fortieth anniversary of RI 1945, *Grindings*, Feb. 26, 1935, 1; Edwin Whitney to Homer Wood, Sep. 19, 1952; and Homer Wood to SF Rotary, Mar. 4, 1965. A. W. Agnew to Bill Sturgeon, Aug. 16, 1995 [Sturgeon papers] describes the dedication of the Homer Wood Grove and Bench in Golden Gate Park.

Homer wrote many letters attempting to set the record straight about his founding of SF Rotary. See, for example, Homer Wood to Paul Harris, c. Mar. 13, 1928; and Homer Wood to Chesley Perry c. Mar. 13, 1928. Ches Perry commented on the origins of the idea that Manuel Muñoz started the club in Chesley Perry to Harry Ruggles, Jul. 7, 1959. Efforts to correct the record are seen in Bradford Swope to Phillip Talmantes and Tom Van Groningen, Sep. 17, 1973; and Art Agnew to Bradford Swope, Sep. 21, 1973.

Integrity and Leadership—The Story of Bru Brunnier (1882–1971)

At the age of seventy-seven in 1959, Bru Brunnier was interviewed by his friend Frank Killinger. Most of this story of Bru is from that interview, which was published in Gail H. Shea, ed., *Connections: The EERI Oral History Series: Henry J. Brunnier* (Frank Killinger, interviewer) *and Charles De Maria*

(Stanley Scott, interviewer) (Oakland: Earthquake Engineering Research Institute and Regents of the University of California, 2001). Bru's life was also briefly recounted in "And Now . . . A Word About 'Bru,'" *The Rotarian*, Jul. 1952, 92; and [cover story] *Consulting Engineer*, Feb. 1962. Additional details are from *San Francisco Examiner* and *San Francisco Chronicle*, Dec. 12, 1971; "He Helped Create the City's Skyline," *San Francisco News*, Jun. 11, 1958; and *The Rotarian*, Feb. 1972.

Bru Brunnier has often been mistaken for a founding or charter member of SF Rotary, and in his recollection, he joined the club in 1908. Every indication, however, is that he did not join until 1909. His name is not among those listed in the morning-after article in *The Call* as attendees at the club's founding banquet (*The Call*, Nov. 13, 1908, 2). His name does not appear in the first club roster, dated January 15, 1909, but it is included in the next roster dated May 10. Moreover, his application to the club is dated April 27, 1909.

Bru is credited with originating the idea of Rotary districts in "Highpoints of District Development"; RI District 513 Governor's Monthly Newsletter, Dec. 1971; Program for District 513 Conference, 1965; "*The Golden Book of Rotary International District 513*"; and Mountin 125–26. However, the attribution has historically been challenged, with other sources indicating that it was Arch Klumph's (RI President 1916–17) idea, including Klumph himself, who took credit without mentioning Bru. No resolution to the challenge has yet been found in RI archives. At the very least, what seems likely is that Bru conceived the idea, and presented it to the International Association of Rotary Clubs. He was in fact the person who divided Rotary territory up into the initial district system.

Bru's founding of new clubs is seen in Bru Brunnier to Russell Bowell, President of SF Rotary Club, Aug. 6, 1958; SF Rotary Club officers to IA of RC, Jun. 17, 1918; and *Grindings*, Jul. 11, 1916, 5.

Chapter 4—Difficult Decades: Three Calls to Serve

World War I—The Dawn of International Service

Most of the story of SF Rotary during World War I is derived from *Grindings* during this period. Additional information is found in Mountin, 146–148, and Postel, 48–50. Marsh Blum recalled the story of his name in an interview by Adam Stevens, Mar. 24, 2000. Background information about the beginnings of Rotary's International Service is from Forward, 63, 159; RI, *Rotary: Fifty Years* (1955), 24, 38. SF Rotary reported its progress initiating the RI Aims and Objects Plan in reports to the district in 1929 and 1930.

The story of the Mallorcan Rotary Club presenting Father Junípero Serra's birthplace to San Francisco is from a collection of documents at the California Historical Society. The fascinating story was also told by SF Rotary Past President Ernest Ingold in his beautifully illustrated book, *The House in Mallorca* (San Francisco: Paul Elder & Company, 1950). After being illegally repossessed by Spain during the Franco regime, title to the property was subsequently restored to San Francisco. In the early 1980s, the city of San Francisco determined that it could not legally own property in a foreign country, and returned the property to Spain. The Rotary Club of Mallorca formed an organization that maintains and operates Father Serra's birthplace as a public museum. My thanks to SF Rotarian Eugene Lee for calling my attention to the story.

Boom and Bust—The 1920s and 1930s

SF Rotary's activities in support of Americanism were described regularly in *Grindings*. The same is true of the club's efforts during the Great Depression. The effects of the Depression on Rotary in general are from Jeffrey Charles, *Service Clubs in American Society*, 104–105. *Grindings* described the events of the Strike in 1934, as did Paul Rieger to Philip Lovejoy (RI), Jul. 24, 1934. For reporting on the 1939 Exposition and the runup to World War II, see *Grindings*.

World War II

Grindings reported on the war much earlier and more frequently than it had during World War I. RI published a one-page "Around the Rotary World in Wartime," in 1942 and 1945. SF Rotary President Herb Shuey described the club's efforts to assist servicemen during his year in a subsequent letter to Brad Swope, Jan. 11, 1971.

While SF Rotarian Charles Wheeler served as RI President (1943–44), his presidency was documented with newspaper clippings and other materials in a set of bound scrapbooks, now at the San Mateo County History Museum. Details of the "Work Pile" Project are primarily from this collection, as well as *Grindings*. See also "The Work Pile Driver," *The Rotarian*, Feb. 1944, 1; the *San Francisco Chronicle*, Jul. 3, 1943; and RI Convention Proceedings of 1943, 86. An explanation of Wheeler's meeting with the other service club heads and formulation of "The Specific Charter" is found in the *San Francisco Chronicle*, Dec. 7, 1943; and Charles Wheeler, in Herbert Shuey, Statement of Presidential Year (1943–44).

The Founding of the United Nations—A Point of Pride for Rotarians

Past RI President Charles Keller's speech at the Bohemian Club in San Francisco (June 23, 1995) can be seen in Sturgeon papers; and "Rotary Is World-Minded," *The Rotarian*, Dec. 1946, 10.

Rotary's part in the charter-signing conference was covered extensively in "Rotary at the Conference," *The Rotarian*, July 1945, 16; "Report from San Francisco," *The Rotarian*, July 1945, 8; and later in "Rotarians at the 1945 UN Chartering Conference," *The Rotarian*, March, 1995, 29. SF Rotary's hospitality work is described in Postel, 94; and *Grindings* before, during, and after the conference.

The 1955 tenth-anniversary conference was covered in "Appraisal at San Francisco," *The Rotarian*, Sep. 1955, 14–60. Past President Bill Koefoed described the fiftieth-anniversary celebration in 1995, in an interview by Theresa Whitener, July 19, 2005. See also Conference Program and Charles Keller address [Sturgeon papers]. The Model UN Session for high school students was described by Jim Bradley in letters to George Christopher, Jul. 14, 1995; Mike Kutsuris, Jun. 29, 1995; and Huey Ehsan, Jul. 14, 1995.

Chapter 5—The Service Club Matures: The Second Half Century

The Means to an End—The San Francisco Rotary Foundation

For the beginnings of the San Francisco Rotary Foundation, see Postel, 86–89, and *Grindings*, Apr. 7, 1959, 1; and Jan. 31, 1961, 1. Bru Brunnier is said to have left a $100,000 bequest, but the SF Rotary Foundation (SFRF) BdMin, Dec. 12, 1974 reported it at $81,000 (perhaps reduced by legal or other fees). The Foundation's growth and balance are reported through the years in the SFRF Board Minutes—see for example SFRF BdMin, Apr. 30, 1979; Jun. 11, 1985; Jan. 26, 1988; Jun. 11, 1996; and Feb. 27, 1997. Al Barnston and the Investment Committee were praised in many board meetings—see for example SFRF BdMin, Jun. 11, 1996; as well as *Grindings*, Jan. 21, 1997, 3. Other details about the Foundation and its workings are from interviews by Theresa Whitener with EVP Tessie Reyes, Dec. 6, 2007; and club Past Presidents Bill Sturgeon, Apr. 15, 2007; Jim Bradley, Nov. 16, 2006; and Curtis Burr, Jul. 31, 2006. See also SFRF BdMin, Sep. 27, 1983; and Jan. 28, 1997. Past President Bob Wilhelm's generosity was reported in *Grindings*, Mar. 20, 1979, 2; and Dec. 4, 1990, 2.

The establishment of the Homer Wood Fellow award was announced in SFR BdMin, May 2, 1995; and Jun. 29, 1995. Recipients of the award have been reported in the years since in Board Minutes and *Grindings*. Bill Koefoed described the Diamond Circle award in an interview by Theresa Whitener, Jul. 19, 2005. The establishment of the Bru Brunnier Fellow award was announced in Bill Ecker, memo to SFRF board [in SFRF BdMin, Jul. 15, 1980]; and subsequent changes in SFR BdMin, Apr. 2, 1996. The first three recipients were announced in *Grindings*, Feb 26, 1980, 2; and *Grindings* has reported each recipient since.

Club President Tom Paton's creation of the annual auction fund-raiser was described in BdMin, May 27, 1982. For the first auction/dinner-dance in 1983, see *Grindings* through March and April; and Jul. 12, 1983, 2. For subsequent years' auctions, see for example 1985 Auction Brochure [Auctions 1985–99 folder]; *Grindings*, Apr. 28, 1987, 2; Apr. 13, 1993, 2; (Tom Paton) "Club Two—1978 to 1988."; and SFR BdMin, May 11, 1993. Bill Koefoed discussed the change to a ball-park event in an interview by Theresa Whitener, Jul. 19, 2005. Past President Curtis Burr explained "Burr's Bogus Bucks" in an interview by Theresa Whitener, Jul. 31, 2006; and *Grindings* reports on its successor each week.

Community Service—The Club Broadens Its Good Works

For the club's ongoing work with handicapped children, see *Grindings*, Dec. 13, 1960, 1; Jul. 9, 1963, 1; Jan. 8, 1974, 2; Sep. 23, 1975; and Jan. 14, 1986, 2; SFR BdMin, Nov. 05, 1985; Postel, 77; and Marsh Blum, interview by Adam Stevens, Mar. 24, 2000.

A good deal of the information about work with the Boys & Girls Club was provided by Postel, 67–69; "San Francisco Boys & Girls Club Historical Background," Jan. 16, 1986; San Francisco Boys & Girls Club "Background Information" 1991; and interviews with Les Andersen, Feb. 20, 2002 and Jan. 23, 2007; and Rob Connolly, Apr. 12, 2007. Bill Ecker, interview by Theresa Whitener, Aug. 1, 2006; and Jim Patrick, interview by Theresa Whitener, Dec. 4, 2007 explained the building of the Camp Mendocino

Bridge of Friendship. Descriptions of other capital contributions are from SFR BdMin, Sep. 1, 1994; and Jun. 10, 1997; *Grindings*, May 2, 1995, 3; and Feb. 17, 2004, 2; Bill Koefoed, interview by Theresa Whitener, Jul. 19, 2005; and Tessie Reyes, notes, Dec. 6, 2007. The Internet Computer Lab was announced in "Internet Computer Lab" [in SFR BdMin, Aug. 20, 1996]. Several topics concerning fundraising for the club are from SFBC Newsletter Aug. 1981; *Grindings*, Sep. 17, 1985, 2; Jan. 4, 1983, 2; Sep. 18, 1984, 2; May 27, 1986, 2; and Aug. 12, 1980, 2. SF Rotary President John Hoch contributed information about the Centennial Mission Branch project in an interview by Theresa Whitener, Nov. 9, 2007.

Most information about Camp Enterprise is from interviews and discussions with Jim Patrick, Dec. 4, 2007; Jim Bradley, Nov. 16, 2006; Bill Sturgeon, Apr. 15, 2007; Jim Deitz, Dec. 20, 2007; Anita Stangl, Oct. 1, 2007; and Dana Gribben, Nov. 12, 2002. See also *Grindings*, (Special Issue), Sep. 15, 1984, 2; (Special Issue), Nov. 15, 1985, 1; and (Special Issue), Jan. 21, 1986, 2.

Most information about the Academic Decathlon came from discussions with Bill Koefoed, Oct. 27, 2006; Bill Sturgeon, Apr. 15, 2007; and Jim Bradley, Nov. 16, 2006. See also *San Francisco Business Times*, Feb. 8, 1988; *San Francisco Independent*, Feb. 15, 1989; "Academic Decathlon Awards Banquet brochure" Feb. 6, 1989 [Sturgeon papers]; 1999 Auction Brochure [Auctions folder 1985–99].

Career Day information is from interviews with Peter Lagarias, by Adam Stevens, Nov. 15, 2000; and Theresa Whitener, Jun. 21, 2006; as well as *Grindings*, Dec. 1, 1992, 2–3.

Jim Bradley, interview by Theresa Whitener, Nov. 16, 2006; and his memo to SF Rotary board, Apr. 7, 1998 were the sources for the Character/Counselor Project. Other recent Youth programs are described in the *Awards Books* for 1999–2000 and 2002–03; and by Allen Feder, interview by Theresa Whitener, Nov. 2, 2006.

For information about SF Rotary's various scholarships, see *Grindings*, May 11, 1976, 3; Oct. 28, 1980, 2–3; Jun. 27, 2000, 2; and Jul. 11, 2000, 2; as well as Letter SFR board to SFRF, July 1981; Bill Ecker to Libby Swope, Oct. 8, 1982 [Brad Swope Scholarship folder]; and EVP Tessie Reyes.

Historical examples of SF Rotary sponsoring good works by young people can be found in *Grindings*, Dec. 10, 1929, 3; Feb. 8, 1955, 1; Sep. 20, 1988, 3; and Apr. 23, 1991, 3. Background information about Interact is primarily from Forward, 174; and Wayne Hearn, e-mail to Theresa Whitener, Dec. 21, 2007. Most recent information about Interact is from Sharon Ghilardi-Udovich to Curtis Burr, Apr. 16, 1997 [in *1996–97 Awards Book*], Steve Talmadge, discussion with Theresa Whitener, Nov. 5, 2007; and Carol Christie, discussion with Theresa Whitener, Oct. 31, 2007. See also *Awards Book* for 2001–02 and 2004–05.

Early and background information about Rotaract is from RI, "*Rotary International: Rotaract.*" http://www.rotary.org/programs/rotaract/information/about.html; *Grindings*, Jul. 15, 1941, 1; Bob Lee, interview by Adam Stevens, Mar. 29, 2000; Forward, 175; and Wayne Hearn, e-mail Dec. 21, 2007. SF Rotary's early efforts to form Rotaract clubs are from SFR BdMin, Jul. 9, 1968; Aug. 8, 1978; *Grindings*, Dec. 16, 1990, 2; (Special Edition) Jun. 16, 1993; and Jun. 30, 1998, 3. The present-day Rotaract Club is described in *Rotaract Club of San Francisco, Annual Report*, Jun. 27, 2005; and *Annual Report*, 2006-07. Rotaractor Amanda Nguyen also contributed, in a discussion with Theresa Whitener, Nov. 9, 2007; as did Howard Waits, in an interview by Theresa Whitener, December 24, 2007.

Early considerations for an Immunization Project are from SFRF BdMin, Jun. 20, 1989; SFRF BdMin, Oct. 8, 1991; and SFRF BdMin, Mar. 10, 1992. Most information about the Immunization Project of 1994–95 is from discussions with Bill Koefoed, Aug. 31, 2007; and Zina Mirsky, Sep. 22, 2007. See also "Rotary in San Francisco," Supplement to *San Francisco Business Times*, Oct. 28–Nov. 4, 1994; and *Grindings,* Apr. 4, 1995, 2.

John Uth explained the Boeddeker Park Project in an interview by Theresa Whitener, Oct. 4, 2004. John also contributed many related documents among his president-year papers. Examples of the project's activities are in *Grindings,* Mar. 24, 1998, 2; May 26, 1998, 3; and Jul. 14, 1998, 2. "Boeddeker Buddies" are described in the *1999–2000 Awards Book.*

Service for San Francisco's senior citizens has been described in *Grindings,* May 28, 1918, 3; and more recently in Bill Ecker's interview by Theresa Whitener, Sep. 6, 2001. Examples of other community-service projects are from *Grindings*, Aug. 5, 1975, 2–3; Nov. 24, 1992, 3; and Apr. 1, 1997, 1; as well as Burt Berry's discussions with Theresa Whitener, May 1, 2006 and Nov. 5, 2007.

Examples of work for the homeless are in *Grindings,* Aug. 23, 1983, 3; (Special Edition), Jun. 16, 1993; Arch Monson Jr. to Robert Lee, Aug. 28, 1981. Work with the Salvation Army is from interviews with Cleo Donovan by Adam Stevens, May 5, 2000; Bill Ecker by Theresa Whitener, Sep. 6, 2001; John Hoch by Theresa Whitener, Nov. 9, 2007; Anita Stangl by Theresa Whitener, Oct. 1, 2007; and Greg Gutting, discussion with Theresa Whitener, Nov. 19, 2007. Kathy Beavers discussed Habitat for Humanity in an interview by Theresa Whitener, Apr. 17, 2004. John Hoch described a recent HFH project on Nov. 9, 2007.

For AIDS-related service, see *Grindings,* Feb. 9, 1993, 2; Jun. 29, 1993, 2; Jun. 22, 1999, 2; Jul. 27, 2004, 2; and May 6, 2003, 2. See also "Rotary's Many Projects," Supplement to *San Francisco Business Times*, week Oct. 28–Nov. 4, 1994; and Arlene Kaplan, memo to Bob Wilhelm [AIDS folder], as well as Jim Bradley, interview by Theresa Whitener, Nov. 16, 2006.

Dr. Howard Denbo described the Blood Donor Program, in a discussion with Theresa Whitener, Sep. 21, 2007. See also *Grindings*, Apr. 4, 1967, 1; and Mar. 30, 2004, 2. Description of the Organ Donor for Transplant Registration Program can be found in the *Awards Books* for 1999–2000, 2001–02, and 2004–05. Omar Valle added to this in a discussion with Theresa Whitener, Sep. 5, 2007.

Information about the Loma Prieta earthquake disaster relief is from SFRF BdMin, Dec. 5, 1989; *Grindings,* Jul. 10, 1990, 3; and a discussion with Bill Sturgeon, Oct. 24, 2007. Other cases of disaster relief are from *Grindings,* Apr. 22, 1986, 3; Nov. 5, 1991, 2; Letter, President Robert Wilhelm to membership, Jan. 20, 1994; and Anita Stangl, interview by Theresa Whitener, Oct. 1, 2007. Sept. 11, 2001, relief is described in *Grindings*, Oct. 2, 2001, 2; and Oct. 9, 2001, 2.

Chapter 6—Service Throughout the World: The International View Expands

Hands Across Borders—Goodwill Toward All

SF Rotary's practice of welcoming foreign visitors can be seen in *Grindings,* Jan. 16, 1973, 2; and Sep. 21, 1982, 3.

Background information about The Rotary Foundation is chiefly from RI, "History of The Rotary Foundation," http://www.rotary.org/foundation/about/history.html [Jan. 24, 2007]; and RGHF, "What Is a Paul Harris Fellow," http://www.rotaryfirst100.org/presidents/1992dochterman/phf.htm [Jan 26, 2007]. Specifics about SF Rotarians' contributions to Paul Harris Fellowships are in *Grindings*, Apr. 19, 1983, 2; Jan. 1, 1985, 2; Sep. 19, 1995, 2; Jan. 16, 2007; May 20, 1997, 2; SFR BdMin, Agenda Mar. 18, 1997; and Fred Marschner, discussion with Theresa Whitener, Dec. 19, 2007.

Background information about Ambassadorial Scholarships is from Forward, 116–117; and Wayne Hearn, e-mail Dec. 21, 2007. SF Rotary's participation in the scholarships is from *Grindings*, Jul. 3, 1962, 1; Mar. 28, 1995, 3; and Tessie Reyes, Dec. 6, 2007. Danielle Gordon's scholarship is from *Grindings*, Nov. 11, 2003, 2; Aug. 17, 2004, 2; and Jan. 10, 2006, 2; and Natasha Valentova from *Grindings*, Jun. 4, 2002, 2.

Information about Group Study Exchange is from Forward, 119–120; Wayne Hearn, e-mail Dec. 21, 2007; Postel, 95; and Roger Steiner, discussion with Theresa Whitener, Aug. 14, 2007. Specific groups is from *Grindings*, Mar. 21, 1995, 3; Apr. 4, 1995, 2; and Roger Steiner. Forward, 202–203. Roger Steiner, discussion with Theresa Whitener, Aug. 14, 2007, provided information about Rotary World Peace Fellows.

The history of SF Rotary welcoming local consuls is from Club Officers' Report to District, Mar. 2, 1929; *Grindings*, Dec. 2, 1930, 3; Jun. 28, 1966, 1; "American Solidarity—Pan-American Program," 1942; Herbert Shuey to Philip Lovejoy (RI Secretary), Sep. 29, 1942; and SFR BdMin, Oct. 17, 2000. The forerunners to World Wide Rotary Day are in *Grindings*, Mar. 28, 1961, 1; and "American Solidarity—Pan-American Program," 1942. Eugene Lee, discussion with Theresa Whitener, Jan. 8, 2007 explained World Wide Rotary Day. More about specific events is from Eugene Lee to Ambassador David Fischer, Jan. 31, 1998 [Eugene Lee materials]; the *1996–97 Awards Book*; and Letter to other Rotary Clubs Feb. 23, 1999 [Eugene Lee materials].

A few of the many sources about the 1951 luncheon program for Japanese visitors are J. E. Holbrook to Rotary Clubs of Japan, Sep. 13, 1951; Yukinori Hoshino, DG, to SFR Aug. 29, 1951; and "Greetings Program" Sep. 11, 1951.

Information about the PEP program for Russian visitors can be found in *Grindings*, Apr. 2, 2002, 2; May 21, 2002, 2; and Dec. 16, 2003, 2. Discussions with Cecile Chiquette, Sep. 25, 2007; and Eric Schmautz, Oct. 19, 2007, were also useful.

Help Across Borders—International Humanitarianism

Examples of SF Rotary's humanitarian response to disasters are in *Grindings*, Dec. 10, 1985, 3; Apr. 4, 1995, 3; and Aug. 9, 2005, 2; SFR BdMin, Jan. 16, 2001; President Jim Bradley to membership [in SFR BdMin, Feb. 18, 1999]; and Bill Koefoed, interview by Theresa Whitener, Jul. 19, 2005.

Forward, 121, 162–63, describes World Community Service. SF Rotary international-service projects are from *Grindings*, Sep. 5, 1972, 4; Jun. 24, 1986, 2; Nov. 15, 1988, 3; (Tom Paton) "Club Two—1978 to 1988"; Dick Rosen, interview by Theresa Whitener, Aug. 7, 2007; SFR BdMin, Aug.

4, 1994; and *2001–02 Awards Book*. The Nigerian and Indian projects were described in Boris Hesser, discussion with Theresa Whitener, Sep. 27, 2007; Boris Hesser, e-mail to Theresa Whitener, Sep. 28, 2007; John Hoch, interview by Theresa Whitener, Nov. 9, 2007; and Rosey Wong, discussions with Theresa Whitener, Nov. 9, 2007 and Dec. 14, 2007. Roots of Peace was described by John Hoch, Nov. 9, 2007; Jim Patrick, Dec. 10, 2007; and Heidi Kühn, Dec. 15, 2007.

PolioPlus background is from Forward, *Century of Service*, 232–233, 238–239, 240–242, 246; RI, "History of PolioPlus," http://www.rotary.org/foundation/polioplus/information/history.html; Global Polio Eradication Initiative, http://www.polioeradication.org/; Wayne Hearn, discussion with Theresa Whitener, Dec. 20, 2007; and Clem Renouf (RI President 1978–79) to Marvin Cardoza, May 1979. SF Rotary began support as described in *Grindings*, Sep. 17, 1985, 3; Dec. 2, 1986, 3; Jun. 9, 1987, 2; Oct. 6, 1987, 2; Nov. 17, 1987, 2; Jan. 19, 1988, 2; Feb. 9, 1988, 2; Jul. 12, 1988, 2; and discussion with Bill Sturgeon, Apr. 3, 2006. Later participation is from *Grindings*, Oct. 21, 1997, 3; Jul. 30, 2002, 2; *Award Book 1998*; Peter Lagarias, interview by Adam Stevens, Nov. 15, 2000; SFR BdMin, Aug. 20, 2002; and James Patrick, interview by Theresa Whitener, Dec. 6, 2001.

Rotaplast information is chiefly from Rotaplast International, "Rotaplast," http://www.rotaplast.org/about.html [2-29-2007]; *The Rotaplast Reporter* (Spring 1999), 1; World Community Service Award Application, 1993 [Lagarias papers]; *Twin Cities Times*, February 24–March 2, 1993; Pete Lagarias, discussion with Theresa Whitener, Nov. 3, 2007 and interview Jun. 21, 2006; Angelo Capozzi, interview by Theresa Whitener, Oct. 10, 2007; and discussion with Jennifer Swarr, Rotaplast International, Oct. 11, 2007.

Rotavision information is from Otis Paul, interview by Theresa Whitener, Sep. 19, 2007; August Reader, discussion with Theresa Whitener, Sep. 30, 2007; Jean Schore, discussion with Theresa Whitener, Sep. 20, 2007; *San Francisco Medicine*, Aug. 1998, 23, 26; and *1996–97 Awards Book*.

Alliance for Smiles information is from Anita Stangl, interview by Theresa Whitener, Oct. 1, 2007; and AFS, *Alliance Highlights*, July 2007.

Chapter 7—Always Taking Part: 100 Years of Women and Rotary

A Woman's Place

Early copies of the club's constitution and bylaws are found in club rosters "Constitution [as adopted November 12, 1908]—Article III Membership Qualifications, Section 1," in Roster #2 (1909). The Tri-City Club's first constitution of December 4, 1908, also omitted any mention of women. Constitution and bylaws, cited in *Rotarily Yours: A History of the Rotary Club of Oakland*, (Oakland: Rotary Club of Oakland, 1969); SF Rotary "Constitution [as amended May 12, 1914]—Article III Membership. Active Members. Section 1," cited in Roster (1916–17). The exact date of the change to male-only is unclear. The only available versions of SF Rotary's constitution (amended nine times) are in the club rosters that include the constitution, but it is clear that the amendment in question was April 22, 1913, or May 12, 1914.

Grindings advertisements directed to Rotarians' wives and mention of wives' attendance at club functions, conferences, and RI Conventions are well represented in Grindings during the club's first several decades. For attendance and attention to wives' needs at RI Conventions, see for example 1916 Convention Proceedings, 144; and 1921, 299; as well as "House of Friendship Committee report" 1947 [Massen papers]. SF Rotary functions for the ladies are exemplified in "Semi-Annual Report to the N. A. of R. C. of A.," March 1, 1911 [Sturgeon papers]; "Ladies' Night Jinks" menu, 1910. The first Ladies' Christmas Luncheon is mentioned in Grindings, Nov. 30, 1915, 3, 7. Although later accounts say the Christmas Ladies' Luncheon began in 1912, (Grindings, Dec. 16, 1930, 2; and Dec. 18, 1962, 1), there is no current record of one. The first year of Grindings (1913) mentions a Saturday May Ladies' Lunch as the big event of the year (Grindings, May 13, 1913, 7). The only Christmas festivity that year was a luncheon for the men. The year 1915 saw both a ladies' and men's' luncheons, in Grindings, Dec. 21, 1915, 2. A Mothers' Day event can be seen in Grindings, May 20, 1919, 3. Note: RI voted in 1922 not to adopt two resolutions that clubs should conduct "appropriate ceremonies in commemoration of the grand and noble service rendered by mothers of the nation," after receiving a telegram "from a man who wanted to propose observance of a 'Dad's Day,'" in 1922 Convention Proceedings 182–183.

Ladies' clubs in 1908 San Francisco are from San Francisco Chronicle, Nov. 7, 1908, 11. The story of the Duluth women's Rotary club is from The National Rotarian, Nov. 1911, 23, cited in Forward, 182; and The Rotarian, Sep. 1912, 11, cited in Forward, 182–183. The Belfast story is on "Origins," Rotary Club of Belfast, http://www.belfastrotary.org/ [9-15-04].

Rotarians' wives assisting in SF Rotary's community service is from Grindings, Dec. 17, 1918, 1; Dec. 14, 1920, 1; and Report of the Ways and Means Committee, 1920–21. The question of Ladies' Auxiliaries is in Grindings, Jan. 3, 1918, 2; Mar. 25, 1924, 1; and Chicago University, Social Science Survey Committee, Rotary? A University Group Looks at the Rotary Club of Chicago (Chicago: University of Chicago Press, 1934), 123. RI outlined its no-women policy in the "Manual of Procedure," 1922 Convention Proceedings, 436. See also 1931 Convention Proceedings, 16–17. For the Inner Wheel, see Forward, 185–186; and Carl Zapffe, Rotary! An Historical, Sociological and Philosophical Study Based upon the Half-Century Experience of One of the Larger Rotary Clubs (Baltimore: Rotary Club of Baltimore, 1963), 159–160.

Grindings used many different names for Rotarians' wives—see for example, Grindings, Feb. 27, 1917, 6; Dec. 18, 1917, 1; and Dec. 17, 1918, 1. Bru Brunnier's first-person story of "Rotary Ann" is from The Rotarian, Nov. 1951, 39. See Joseph A. Caulder, "The Joseph A. Caulder Collection, Album 1—Henry J. and Ann Brunnier," http://www.nlis.net/ ~ freedomi/rotary/caulder/BruandAnnFirstRotaryAnn.htm [10-2-05]; and Cliff Dochterman, The ABC's of Rotary, 21, for RI's changing position. SF Rotary's correspondence about women's auxiliaries is Paul Rieger to Chesley Perry, secretary RI, Apr. 13, 1923; and executive service secretary, RI, to Paul Rieger, Apr. 18, 1923.

Changing Times

For a woman's legal explanation of why club-membership discrimination was unfair to women, see RGHF, "Women in Rotary, Declaration of Katherine Fletcher," on http://www.rotaryfirst100 .org/women/issues-legal/seattle/ [4-2-2007]. SF Rotary's 1972 position against admitting women is from Norman J. Corlett to Charles Strope (DG) [in SFR BdMin Feb. 1, 1972]. Its position in favor is from (1980) SFR BdMin, Mar. 11, 1980; (1983) SFR BdMin Jan. 11, 1983; (1986) SFR BdMin, Sep. 10, 1985 and Bill Ecker to RI General Secretary Herbert Pigman, Dec. 5, 1985.

Duarte—"The Mouse That Roared"

The national press reported on Duarte, as in "Breaking Rotary Barrier: Matter of Survival for California Club," *New York Times*, May 8, 1987, A16; "High Court Says Rotary Can't Exclude Women: A Matter of Survival, Not Rights, Club Says," *Los Angeles Times*, May 5, 1987, 1-1; "The All-Male Club: Threatened on All Sides," *Business Week*, Aug. 11, 1980, 90. The court history of Duarte's case is recounted in RI's case to the U.S. Supreme Court—*Board of Directors of Rotary International, et al., v. Rotary Club of Duarte, et al.*, 481 U.S. 537 (1987).

For SF Rotary's deliberation as to whether to admit women in 1986, see board minutes through 1986; "Court Says States Can Force Jaycees to Admit Women," *New York Times*, Jul. 4, 1984, A1. Explanation of the club's decision to admit is from Peter Lagarias, interview by Theresa Whitener, Jun. 21, 2006. For more about the Seattle-ID club's intentions to admit women from the date of its founding in 1984, see RGHF, "Women in Rotary, Seattle International Rotary Club" http://www.rotaryfirst100.org/women/issues-legal/seattle/ [3-04-2007]. SF Rotary's agreement to join Seattle-ID in the *amicus curiae* brief is from Brian Stigglemeyer (Clerk U.S. Supreme Court), discussion with Theresa Whitener, Aug. 16, 2007.

For SF Rotary's events of October–November, 1986, see *Grindings*, Oct. 28, 1986, 2; Marsh Blum, interview by Adam Stevens, Mar. 24, 2000; "Foster City Rotary Staves Off Women," *San Francisco Chronicle*, Nov. 19, 1986, 8; *Grindings*, Oct. 28, 1986, 3; Nov. 4, 1986, 3. Peter Lagarias, interview by Theresa Whitener, Jun. 21, 2006; SFR BdMin, Oct. 14, 1986; SFR BdMin, Nov. 4, 1986; discussion with Bill Sturgeon, Jul. 27, 2007; *Grindings*, Dec. 9, 1986, 2; "S.F. Rotary Club Lets 4 Women Share the Chicken," *San Francisco Chronicle*, Nov. 26, 1986; Cleo Donovan, interview by Adam Stevens, May 5, 2000. Note: It is difficult to know where SF Rotary ranks among clubs admitting women. *San Francisco Chronicle*, November 26, 1986, reported that SF Rotary was the first club in Northern California, but *San Francisco Examiner*, November 26, 1987 reported that SF Rotary—with 540 members—was the largest club so far, but that the smaller Mid-County club in Santa Cruz had admitted women earlier in November.

After Duarte

For national press coverage of the U.S. Supreme Court decision, see, for example, "Catching Up with the Times," *Boston Globe*, May 6, 1987, 20; "A Court Ruling for Men Only," *Chicago Tribune*, May 8, 1987, 26; "Court to Rotary: Grow Up," *Washington Post*, May 5, 1987, A18; "Breaking the Barriers," *Los Angeles Times*, May 5, 1987, 2-4.

Examples of SF Rotary's subsequent attitude about women in the club are from Tom Paton, "Club Two—1978 to 1988"; and Allan Feder, interview by Theresa Whitener, Nov. 2, 2006. Kathy Beaver's club presidency is from Kathy Beavers, interview by Theresa Whitener, Apr. 17, 2004; SFR BdMin, Jan. 8, 1999. The story of Hong Kong's salute to SF Rotary is from *Grindings*, Feb 26, 1991, 3.

Chapter 8—Perspectives

Three Challenges

SF Rotary's membership numbers throughout the century are documented regularly in the club's board minutes, usually in July. Declining membership became a monthly topic of board discussion starting in 1989—see, for example, SFR BdMin, Nov. 7, 1989; SFR BdMin, May 7, 1991; and Membership Information [in SFR BdMin, Jun. 25, 1998]. Suggested reasons for the decline are from many sources, including *Grindings*, Jan. 27, 1981, 4; Nov. 25, 1997, 3; Summary of Club Plans and Objectives 1991–92, n.d; SFR BdMin, Mar. 2, 1993; Kathy Beavers, interview by Theresa Whitener, Apr. 17, 2004; Dick Rosen, interview by Theresa Whitener, Aug. 7, 2007. Efforts to slow the decline in the early 1990s include SFR BdMin, Nov. 3, 1992; Mar. 2, 1993; Sep. 2, 1993; Jan. 5, 1995; Jul. 11, 1995; *Grindings*, Sep. 13, 1994, 3; and Summary of Club Plans and Objectives [in SFR BdMin, Jul. 16, 1996]. Welcoming new members is from *Grindings*, Oct. 30, 1928, 2; Feb. 3, 1931, 2; Jim Bradley, interview by Theresa Whitener, Nov. 16, 2006. For the 49ers, see James Huckins, Statement of Presidential Year (1970-71); SFR BdMin, Jul. 7, 1992; Peter Lagarias, interview by Theresa Whitener, Jun. 21, 2006. For the Under-35 Club, Peter Lagarias, interview by Theresa Whitener, Jun. 21, 2006, and discussion, Nov. 4, 2007.

Examples of sources about the issue of public recognition are from *Grindings*, Feb. 17, 1914, 5; Feb. 2, 1966, 2; Jan. 29, 1991, 2; Jan. 22, 2002, 2; Pete Lagarias to *San Francisco Chronicle* and *San Francisco Examiner*, May 27, 1994 [in Rotaplast folder]; SFR BdMin, Sep. 1, 1994; John Hoch, interview by Theresa Whitener, Nov. 9, 2007.

The history of SF Rotary extension within San Francisco is from *Grindings*, Oct. 21, 1913, 5-6; Chicago University, *Rotary?*, 141; SFR BdMin, Feb. 10, 1970; Mar. 16, 1971; May 4, 1971; Feb. 1, 1972; Feb. 15, 1972; Jan. 2, 1979; May 27, 1982; Dec. 4, 1984; and "Our Chance to Share Rotary," to members from Tom Paton and Harold Gray Jr., Feb. 17, 1984 [Other Clubs folder]. The Outer Mission Club is in SFR BdMin, Sep. 6, 1988; (Tom Paton) "Club Two—1978 to 1988"; *Grindings*, Jun. 29, 1989, 2 and Aug, 1, 1989, 2; Frank Stryczek (RI) to William Ecker, Nov. 16, 1989 [Territory folder]. The Fisherman's Wharf club is in "Approval and Commitment for Organizing a Rotary Club" Apr. 17, 1990 [Other Rotary Clubs folder]. The Bayview club is in Pete Lagarias to RI Concerning Organization of a New Club" Aug. 20, 1999 [Other Rotary Clubs folder]; SFR BdMin, Mar. 21, 2000; and Peter Lagarias, discussion with Theresa Whitener, Nov. 4, 2007 (see same discussion for Golden Gate and Chinatown clubs).

Fellowship—A Bedrock Tradition

Throughout its lifetime, *Grindings* has reported each week on the luncheon, so few specifics are given here. Sources for the early "Assimilation" practice and first-names include *Grindings,* Nov. 28, 1916, 1–2; and Jan. 16, 1917, 3. A number of fellowship issues are from Jim Emerson, interview by Theresa Whitener, Nov. 20, 2007. Reports of the club's tradition of fines are from *Grindings,* Jul. 22, 1999, 2; Feb. 13, 1962, 1; Jul. 16, 1968, 1; Jun. 19, 1984, 3; Jul. 3, 1984, 3; Jul. 18, 1981, 2; Jul. 3, 1984, 3; and Jan. 30, 1979, 2. The prohibition of political and religious speech at luncheons can be seen in early *Grindings,* Aug. 25, 1914, 3; and Sep. 7, 1915, 3.

The first inter-club meeting was reported in the *San Francisco Chronicle,* Jan. 16, 1909. The Oakland club's "trial" of SF Rotary is from *Grindings,* Jan. 29, 2002, 2; and for the "charges" against SFR, see Jan. 8, 2002, 2. *Grindings,* Nov. 9, 1937, 1, gives the date of the first Los Angeles inter-city meeting.

Carroll Tornroth's experience with the ship-to-shore call is from Postel, 95. The trip to Clarence Wetmore's winery is from Mountin, 140. *Grindings,* Sep. 3, 1918, 3 and Aug. 31, 1920, 2, have typical descriptions of club outings.

SF Rotary's sports challenges with the Oakland club are mostly from Rotary Club of Oakland, *Rotarily Yours: A History of the Rotary Club of Oakland* (Oakland, CA: Rotary Club of Oakland, 1969). For the early history of the Sports Chapter, see *Grindings,* Jan. 20, 1920, 3; Sep. 28, 1920, 2; Sep. 14, 1965, 2; and Postel, 141. Recent sports descriptions are mostly from Steve Talmadge, discussion with Theresa Whitener, Nov. 5, 2007, as well as Harold Hoogasian, interview by Theresa Whitener, Dec. 31, 2007.

Presidents' efforts to increase fun in the club were described by Pete Taylor, interview by Theresa Whitener, Jun. 4, 2006; and Curtis Burr, interview by Theresa Whitener, Jul. 31, 2006. For the Rotary 2½ Club, see *Grindings,* May 20, 1982, 2; Jul. 24, 2001, 2; and Bill Sturgeon, discussion on Dec. 21, 2007. History of the club's early round table is from *Grindings,* Apr. 24, 1923, 1; Jul. 29, 1924, 1; Oct. 30, 1928, 2; Sep. 20, 1938, 1; and Mar. 14, 1939, 1. Jean Schore, discussion with Theresa Whitener, Sep. 17, 2007, described Rotafair (see also the *1996–97 Awards Book*) and Rotary Means Business.

A Club for San Francisco

The Rotary Meadow on Mount Sutro was described by Harold Hoogasian, interview by Theresa Whitener, Dec. 31, 2007 and John Hoch, interview by Theresa Whitener, Nov. 9, 2007 (see also the *2001–02 Awards Book*). Jim Bradley, interview by Theresa Whitener, Nov. 16, 2006 described Peaceful Streets. For the Four-Way Test plaque, see "Resolution No. 602–74"; *Grindings,* Mar. 18, 1975, 4; and Jun. 11, 2002, 2.

About the Chamber of Commerce, see SF Chamber of Commerce to Bru Brunnier, Jul. 22, 1914 [in *Grindings,* Aug. 4, 1914, 6].

Making It All Happen

For club Secretaries, see Mountin, 180; Postel, 123; *Grindings*, Jun. 9, 1964, Sep. 26, 1967, 1; May 23, 2000, 3; Jim Deitz, interview by Theresa Whitener, Oct. 29, 2002; Bill Ecker, interview by Theresa Whitener, Sep. 6, 2001; SFR BdMin, Jul. 11, 1995. Office Assistants are enumerated in *Grindings*, Jun. 16, 1931, 3; Jul. 18, 1939, 1; Sep. 19, 1967, 1; Sep. 29, 1992, 2; Postel, 131. Office technology was described in Scott Plakun, discussion with Theresa Whitener, Jan. 1, 2008.

Points of Pride

For the 1915 Convention, see *Grindings*, Sep. 29, 1914, 6; Jun. 16, 1914, 7; Sep. 15, 1914, 6; Sep. 29, 1914, 6; Jun. 15, 1915, 5. For the 1938 Convention, see *Grindings*, Feb. 1, 1938, 1; May 31, 1938, 1; Jun. 7, 1938, 1; Postel, 111. For 1947, *Grindings*, Jun. 10, 1947, 1. For 1977, Bob Lee in questionnaire [in ninetieth-anniversary folder]; *The Rotarian*, Aug. 1977, 24; and Postel, 115.

Anniversaries: 1948: *Grindings*, Nov. 2, 1948, 1; 1958: *The Rotarian*, Jan. 1959, 45; *Grindings*, Nov. 11, 1958, 1; 1983: SFR BdMin, Jul. 14, 1981; *Grindings*, Nov. 8, 1983, 1; Oct. 25, 1983; Aug. 23, 1983, 3; *S.F. Progress*, Nov. 9, 1983; *San Francisco Chronicle*, Nov. 2, 1983; (Tom Paton) "Club Two— 1978 to 1988"; President Harold W. Gray Jr. to Members Sep. 16, 1983 [in seventy-fifth-anniversary folder]; 1988: *Grindings*, Nov. 8, 1988, 2; Announcement for Monte Carlo Night, 1988 [in Casino Night folder]; 1998: Jim Bradley, interview by Theresa Whitener, Nov. 16, 2006; ninetieth-anniversary invitation [in ninetieth-anniversary folder].

Awards: Jesse Ellerton (RI) discussion with Theresa Whitener, Nov. 16, 2007; SFR BdMin, Jul. 11, 1990; *Grindings*, Aug. 9, 2003, 2; Lois Robertson, TRF, discussion with Theresa Whitener, Nov. 16, 2007; Anita Stangl, interview by Theresa Whitener, Oct. 1, 2007.

RI Presidents: *Grindings*, Apr. 5, 1932, 3; Oct. 21, 1930, 2; Aug. 11, 1981, 2; Jan. 5, 1982, 2; Feb. 17, 1981, 2; Dec. 7, 1982, 3; Apr. 16, 2002, 2; SFR BdMin, Jan. 4, 1972; Forward, 237.

Have We Made a Difference?

About the Boys & Girls Club, BGCSF, Video, http://www.bgcsf.org/video.html [Oct 14, 2007]; Rob Connolly, interview by Theresa Whitener, Apr 12, 2007. Rotaplast information is from a discussion with Jennifer Swarr, Rotaplast International, Oct 11, 2007. Rotavision information from 2007 SF Rotary District Report; and Otis Paul, interview by Theresa Whitener, Sep 19, 2007. Alliance for Smiles information from Anita Stangl, interview by Theresa Whitener, Oct 1, 2007; and AFS Description [Stangl papers].

INDEX